Politics in the Vernacular

Politics in the Vernacular: Nationalism, Multiculturalism and Citizenship

WILL KYMLICKA

OXFORD

UNIVERSITY PRESS

This book has been printed digitally and produced in a standard specification
in order to ensure its continuing availability

OXFORD
UNIVERSITY PRESS

Great Clarendon Street, Oxford OX2 6DP

Oxford University Press is a department of the University of Oxford.
It furthers the University's objective of excellence in research, scholarship,
and education by publishing worldwide in

Oxford New York

Auckland Bangkok Buenos Aires Cape Town Chennai
Dar es Salaam Delhi Hong Kong Istanbul Karachi Kolkata
Kuala Lumpur Madrid Melbourne Mexico City Mumbai Nairobi
São Paulo Shanghai Singapore Taipei Tokyo Toronto
with an associated company in Berlin

Oxford is a registered trade mark of Oxford University Press
in the UK and in certain other countries

Published in the United States
by Oxford University Press Inc., New York

ISBN 0-19-829665-7

ISBN 0-19-924098-1 (pbk)

Acknowledgements

These papers would not have been written were it not for the invitations from various journal editors, volume editors, and conference organizers: Wsevolod Isajiw, Christian Joppke (Chapter 1), Albert Musschenga (Chapter 2); Joseph Carens and Rainer Forst (Chapter 3), David Schneiderman (Chapter 4); Guy Laforest and Francisco Colom (Chapter 5), David Dyzenhaus (Chapter 6), Wendy Donner, Fen Hampson, and Judith Reppy (Chapter 7); Amy Gutmann (Chapter 8), Steven Lukes (Chapter 10), Mark Sacks (Chapter 11), Michael Walzer (Chapter 12), Pat Dutil (Chapter 13), John McGarry (Chapter 15), David McLaughlin and Mark Halstead (Chapter 16), Ian Shapiro (Chapter 17) and Anita Allen and Milton Regan (Chapter 18). Thanks to each for their interest, encouragement and comments.

I have also benefited from the extended comments of, or discussions with Rainer Baubock, Brian Barry, Rogers Brubaker, Raphael Cohen-Almagor, David Hollinger, Michael Oliver, Ellen Frankel Paul, Bhikhu Parekh, Jean-Robert Raviot, Denise Reaume, Nancy Rosenblum, Sawitri Saharso, Christine Sypnowich, Gijs van Oonen, Philippe Van Parijs, Daniel Weinstock, and Iris Young. Thanks also to the many, many people who have asked thoughtful questions at the various conferences, workshops, colloquiums, and courses where these ideas have been tried out.

I am grateful to the Social Sciences and Humanities Research Council of Canada for funding, and to the Rockefeller Foundation for inviting me to their idyllic study centre in Bellagio, Italy, where the final revisions to this book were made.

Special thanks to Dominic Byatt, my editor at OUP, for his boundless enthusiasm; to Christine Straehle, for permission to reprint Chapter 11, which we co-authored; to Magda Opalski, for introducing me to another world of ethnic diversity in Eastern Europe; to Idil Boran for excellent research assistance; to Wayne Norman, for his long-standing co-operation in various projects; and, above all, to Sue Donaldson, for everything.

W.K.

Queens University
Kingston, Ont.
March 2000

Contents

Introduction

The essays collected in this volume are part of an ongoing project to examine the rights and status of ethnocultural groups within Western democracies. In my 1995 book, *Multicultural Citizenship*, I attempted to provide the outlines of a liberal theory of minority rights. I offered some principles for distinguishing the claims of various sorts of minority groups, and for assessing their legitimacy within a liberal-democratic framework. The papers in this volume start from that basic theory, and seek to refine and extend it, and to address some tensions within it. The essays are connected by a number of common themes: I would like to mention three of them.

1. The first, and most fundamental, concerns what we could call the dialectic of nation-building and minority rights. As I try to show throughout this book, liberal-democratic states have historically been 'nation-building' states in the following specific sense: they have encouraged and sometimes forced all the citizens on the territory of the state to integrate into common public institutions operating in a common language. Western states have used various strategies to achieve this goal of linguistic and institutional integration: citizenship and naturalization laws, education laws, language laws, policies regarding public service employment, military service, national media, and so on. These are what I call the tools of state nation-building.

These policies are often targeted at ethnocultural minorities, who have only limited options when confronted with such a nation-building state. They can accept the state's expectation that they integrate into common national institutions and seek help in doing so, or they can try to build or maintain their own separate set of public institutions (e.g. their own schools, courts, media, legislatures), or they can opt simply to be left alone and live in a state of voluntary isolation. Each of these reflects a different strategy that minorities can adopt in the face of state nation-building. But to be successful, each of them requires certain accommodations from the state. These may take the form of multiculturalism policies, or self-government and language rights, or treaty rights and land claims, or legal exemptions. These are all forms of minority rights that serve to limit or modify the impact of state nation-building on minorities.

The crucial point here is that claims for minority rights must be seen in the context of, and as a response to, state nation-building. Minorities often feel threatened by state nation-building, and fear that it will create various burdens, barriers, or disadvantages for them. Minority rights, I believe, are best understood as mechanisms for protecting minorities from these possible injustices. Since different kinds of minorities face distinct threats from state nation-building, their corresponding minority rights claims will also differ. The injustices faced by indigenous peoples are not the same as those faced by immigrants, and this is reflected in the sorts of minority rights they claim.

This, in a nutshell, is the dialectic of state nation-building and minority rights. I try to flesh out this core idea, and give concrete examples, throughout the book. But it should be obvious, I hope, that viewing minority rights in this way—as a defensive response to state nation-building—requires revising our standard vocabulary for discussing these issues. In both scholarly analysis and everyday public debate, minority rights are often described as forms of 'special status' or 'privilege', and people wonder why all of these pushy and aggressive minorities are demanding concessions and advantages from the state. In reality, however, while minorities do make claims against the state, these must be understood as a response to the claims that the state makes against minorities. People talk about 'troublesome minorities', but behind every minority that is causing trouble for the state, we are likely to find a state that is putting pressure on minorities.

Many of these minority rights claims are, I believe, legitimate. That is, the minority rights being claimed really do serve to protect minorities from real or potential injustices that would otherwise arise as a result of state nation-building (Chapter 4). And indeed we can see a clear trend throughout the Western democracies towards accepting more of these claims. We see a shift towards a more 'multicultural' form of integration for immigrants, for example (Chapter 8).[1] We also see a greater acceptance of language rights and self-government claims for national minorities and indigenous peoples (see Chapters 5 and 6). There is growing recognition that such rights are needed to ensure justice in diverse societies.

If the presence of state nation-building helps to justify minority rights, one could also turn the equation around, and say that the adoption of minority rights has helped to justify state nation-building. After all, we cannot simply take for granted that it is legitimate for a liberal-democratic state to pressure minorities to integrate into institutions operating in the majority language. Liberal nationalists argue that there are certain valid purposes that are promoted by these nation-building policies, and I agree. But it is not legitimate to pursue these goals by assimilating, excluding, or disempowering minor-

---

[1] Here and elsewhere in the book I use the term immigrants to refer to those newcomers to a country who are legally admitted, and who have the right to gain citizenship. I distinguish them from guest-workers and illegal immigrants (and asylum seekers in certain countries) who do not have the right to become citizens, even though they may be permanent residents in the state. Following Michael Walzer, I call these latter groups 'metics'—the term used in Ancient Greece to refer to residents of Athens who were permanently excluded from citizenship.

ities, or by imposing costs and burdens on groups that are often already disadvantaged. Unless supplemented and constrained by minority rights, state nation-building is likely to be oppressive and unjust. On the other hand, where these minority rights are in place, then state nation-building can serve a number of legitimate and important functions (Chapters 10 and 11).

What we see, then, in the Western democracies, is a complex package of robust forms of nation-building combined and constrained by robust forms of minority rights. On my view, the two are interrelated, and must be understood and evaluated together. This is my first major theme.

2. The second major theme is that the particular package of nation-building and minority rights that we see emerging in Western democracies is in many respects working quite well. In particular, I focus on two broad patterns of minority rights that are increasingly common in the West: immigrant multiculturalism and multination federalism. My view is that these have both been a success, at least according to the various criteria that should matter to liberals, such as peace, democracy, individual freedom, economic prosperity, and inter-group equality. Partly as a result of adopting these minority rights, Western democracies have learned how to deal with ethnic diversity in a peaceful and democratic way, with an almost complete absence of militancy, terrorism, violence, or state repression. Ethnic conflict is now a matter of 'ballots not bullets' (Newman 1996). Moreover, this has been achieved within the framework of liberal constitutions, with firm respect for individual civil and political rights. It has also been achieved without jeopardizing the economic well-being of citizens—indeed, the countries which have adopted robust forms of immigrant multiculturalism and/or multination federalism are amongst the wealthiest in the world. And, last but not least, these minority rights have helped promote equality between majority and minority groups, reducing relations of ethnic hierarchy or domination/subordination. Minority rights have reduced the extent to which minorities are vulnerable to the economic, political, or cultural domination of majorities, and have helped to promote greater mutual respect between groups.

Of course, there are many difficult issues that remain to be resolved. There are many groups that are very far from achieving full equality: African-Americans in the United States, guest-workers in northern Europe, illegal immigrants in southern Europe, indigenous peoples in the Americas, Australasia, and Scandinavia. I discuss some of these cases in this volume (Chapters 6–9). Moreover, even where policies are working well there is always the danger that some of these advances will be reversed. And the fact that these policies are working well is often more a matter of good luck than foresight and careful planning. Still, I believe there are grounds for cautious optimism that Western democracies really have made important steps in learning how to deal with ethnocultural diversity in a way that respects and promotes liberal values of freedom, justice, and democracy. The particular package of state nation-building and minority rights that we see emerging in many Western democracies is better than our earlier approaches to ethnocultural diversity, and better than the apparent alternatives. This is my second main theme.

3. The third theme that recurs in the essays is the gap between the theory and practice of liberal-democracies. Liberal political theorists, until very recently, have had little or nothing to say about *either* state nation-building *or* minority rights, let alone the relationship between them. The existence of state nation-building and minority rights was ignored by liberal theorists, obscured by the myth of the ethnocultural neutrality of the state (Chapter 1). The major liberal theorists of the 1950s–1980s not only ignored these trends, but also employed a series of terms which implicitly denied or occluded these developments, such as civic nationalism, constitutional patriotism, common citizenship, non-discrimination, separation of state and ethnicity, colour-blind constitution, benign neglect, and so on. Or if discussed at all, these policies were considered of marginal importance to the basic structure of liberal theory. Prior to the 1990s, one would be hard-pressed to find a single sustained discussion of either the legitimate goals or tools of state nation-building, or the legitimate forms of minority rights. Even today, despite the recent explosion of interest in the topic of nationalism (see Chapter 10), we still lack a systematic account of what tools can legitimately be used by liberal states to pursue linguistic and institutional integration. (For example, is it legitimate to require immigrants to learn the official language before becoming citizens?). And despite the growing literature on minority rights, we still lack a systematic account of which sorts of minority claims are appropriate in which contexts for which groups—for example how the claims of indigenous people differ from those of other national groups (Chapter 6).

In short, there is a gulf between the real world of liberal democracies, which exhibit these complex combinations of state nation-building and minority rights, and the world of liberal political theory, which has largely ignored the way that liberal states are actively implicated in issues of nationhood and minority rights. My long-standing project, underlying both these essays and my earlier work, has been to close this gap between the theory and practice of liberal states, and to develop a theory that would help us to understand and evaluate these important real-world practices of nation-building and minority rights. Current practices in Western democracies have emerged in an *ad hoc* way without any clear models or explicit articulation of the underlying principles, and we need to develop tools that can help us to theorize these practices in relation to the deeper values of liberal democracy.

But do we need such a theory? After all, if the current package of state nation-building and minority rights is working reasonably well in practice, and if these successful approaches have emerged without the help or guidance of political theory, why do we need to develop a theory? Since I was trained as a political philosopher, it used to seem obvious to me that it was a problem to have such a large gap between theory and practice. But why is it a problem? For whom is it a problem? And for whom is a theory of minority rights helpful?

Indeed perhaps it was a good thing that there was no political theory to guide these recent developments. Current practices emerged in a theoretical vacuum, without any clear understanding of long-term goals or underlying principles. They have been adopted as *ad hoc* compromises to particular problems, often for reasons of stability rather than justice, without too much attention to their fit (or lack of fit) with basic liberal principles of freedom, equality, and democracy. They have been seen as discretionary policies, rather than as fundamental obligations or rights. But perhaps this pragmatic attitude was just what was needed. Perhaps excessive concern with underlying principles would only have served to harden the positions of both minorities and majorities, and thereby made compromise more difficult to achieve. Why think that developing a theory would make it easier to improve the actual practices on the ground?

A similar question about the relationship between theory and practice arises in reverse in other important areas of normative political theory. In the case of nation-building and minority rights, Western democracies have arguably worked out some successful practices despite the absence of normative theory. In other areas, we have some excellent theories but very poor practices. For example, there has been interesting and profound work done since the 1970s on developing a rigorous and systematic liberal theory of distributive justice. I believe that we have today a much more sophisticated understanding of principles of distributive justice than was available twenty-five or fifty years ago. Yet this has obviously done nothing to improve the level of distributive justice in our society, or in the world as a whole. Quite the contrary. One could argue that injustice in the distribution of economic resources has substantially increased over precisely the same period of time that our theories of distributive justice have improved.

Or consider the case of environmental ethics. It is generally agreed that there have been enormous strides made in this field in the last thirty years. Yet as Light and Katz note:

As environmental ethics approaches its third decade it is faced with a curious problem. On the one hand, the discipline has made significant progress in the analysis of the moral relationship between humanity and the non-human world. The field has produced a wide variety of positions and theories in an attempt to derive morally justifiable and adequate environmental policies. On the other hand, it is difficult to see what practical effect the field of environmental ethics has had on the formulation of environmental policy.[2]

---

[2] Light and Katz 1996: 1.

These examples do not provide much ground for optimism that developing better normative theories leads to better practices.

Of course no one supposes that developing a theory of distributive justice, environmental ethics, or minority rights will by itself change the world. If political theory can help improve the world, it will only do so in a more indirect way. But how does political theory help even indirectly? I recently participated in an interesting summer school organized by the Netherlands School for Practical Ethics called 'Theories of Justice: What's the Use?', which cast doubt on the practical usefulness of contemporary liberal theories of justice. One could ask the same question about theories of minority rights or environmental ethics. What's the use? Or more precisely, what kind of theory is helpful, under what conditions, to whom?

I find these questions unsettling. They raise deep questions about the nature and value of political theory as a discipline and vocation. I believe, however, at least in the area of ethnic relations, that there are several factors that might make the elaboration of a normative theory both relevant and useful.

There seems to be a clear shift in public opinion towards viewing minority rights not just as a matter of discretionary policies or pragmatic compromises, but rather as a matter of fundamental justice. Minority rights are increasingly seen precisely as 'rights', the violation of which can be an assault on basic dignity and respect. This is reflected in attempts to codify minority rights at the level of legislation or even the constitution. Policies that used to be seen as discretionary, experimental, and perhaps transitional are now seen as worthy of legislative enactments and constitutional protection.

This shift has two important implications. First, insofar as minority rights are seen as matters of fundamental rights and basic justice, there is pressure to *internationalize* them, and to make the treatment of minorities a matter, not only of domestic politics, but also of legitimate international concern and perhaps even international intervention. For example, the Organization on Security and Co-operation in Europe adopted principles regarding the rights of national minorities in 1991, and established a High Commissioner on National Minorities in 1993. The Council of Europe adopted a treaty on minority language rights in 1992 (the European Charter for Regional or Minority Languages), and a Framework Convention on the Rights of National Minorities in 1995. Indeed, various Western organizations have decided that respect for minority rights is a precondition for East European countries to join the club (e.g. NATO, EU), or to remain as members in good standing (e.g., Council of Europe, OSCE).[3] The General Secretary of the

[3] This will be the first serious test case for the feasibility and desirability of 'exporting' Western minority rights standards to the rest of the world, and so is worthy of careful consideration. It is the focus of my current research and next book (Kymlicka and Opalski 2001).

Council of Europe even went so far as to say that respect for minorities was the fundamental measure of our 'moral progress' (Burgess 1999).

This is part of a broader trend towards the codification of minority rights in international law. For example, the United Nations has been debating both a declaration on the Rights of Persons Belonging to National or Ethnic, Religious, and Linguistic Minorities and a Draft Declaration on the Rights of Indigenous Peoples (Chapter 6). If adopted, these will dramatically affect the way the treatment of minorities around the world is viewed. The Inter-American Commission on Human Rights is also playing a role in formulating regional standards of minority rights. Or consider the recent decision of the World Bank to include minority rights as one of the criteria for evaluating development projects around the world. There is even talk of trying to develop a 'universal declaration of minority rights', to supplement the 1948 universal declaration of human rights (see Chapter 4).

This widespread movement for the international codification and monitoring of minority rights only makes sense on the assumption that at least some minority rights have moved from the zone of discretion and pragmatic compromise to fundamental rights. But if we are to embark on this project of internationalizing minority rights, we need some theoretical tools that will enable us to isolate the underlying principles from the myriad local variations in the way these principles are institutionalized. We need to distinguish the fundamental principles from the contingent practices. Put another way, we need a theory that will help us identify standard threats which minorities face around the world, and which they need protection from, while leaving room for flexibility for countries to identify what sorts of remedies for these threats will work best in their own contexts.

A second implication of the shift in public opinion is that even within the West, people have become more conscious of, and sometimes more worried about, the 'logic' of minority rights and multiculturalism. When minority rights were perceived as ad hoc pragmatic compromises, they were not necessarily seen as setting a precedent or standard that could be appealed to in defence of other claims. But once minority rights are seen as matters of principle, then we are likely to get worries about the 'slippery slope'. Perhaps the same principle that underlies multicultural education for immigrants will also require us to condone illiberal practices within immigrant groups. Perhaps the same principle that underlies autonomy for national minorities will also require us to accept secession.

In short, the fear is that while existing minority rights may be innocuous or even beneficial, they are the first steps down a slippery slope towards a much more dangerous form of minority rights, involving separatism, ghettoization, or oppression. Once we view existing practices as matters of principle, then we need to think about the logical extension of these practices.

One way to put this is to say that most people have no clear sense of the *limits* of multiculturalism and minority rights. People are not averse to minority rights within limits, but they want to know that there are indeed limits. Perhaps current practices have worked up to this point in reconciling minority rights and nation-building, but only because the full 'logic' of minority rights has not yet been implemented. People who are willing to accept certain policies as a pragmatic compromise may reject the same policies if they are seen as endorsing a new principle with potentially far-reaching implications.

In other words, the stakes are now much higher for both defenders and critics of minority rights. We may come to regret this escalation in the significance attached to minority rights, both at home and abroad, but the horse is out of the barn. It is too late now to try to put minority rights back into the box of merely discretionary policies and pragmatic compromises. And once people have made this shift to viewing minority rights as a matter of fundamental principle and basic rights, there is no alternative but to try to articulate what these principles and rights are. Moreover, I personally believe that many issues of minority rights really *are* matters of justice and rights, and deserve proper legal protection and international codification (Chapter 4).

For these and other reasons, I think it is important to develop a theory of minority rights that explicitly examines how current practices relate to liberal-democratic principles, and that identifies both the grounds and the limitations of minority rights claims. This still leaves the question of what *kind* of normative theory is most helpful. The essays in this volume aim at what we could call 'mid-level' theory. I am not offering detailed prescriptions about particular policies in particular countries. For example, my chapter on citizenship education does not offer detailed proposals regarding multiculturalism in the education curriculum (Chapter 17), and the chapter on indigenous peoples and environmental protection doesn't offer a detailed proposal regarding land rights (Chapter 7). Nor, at the other end, am I addressing foundational philosophical questions regarding the nature of reason and personhood, and whether these concepts are universal or culturally relative. I flag these questions in a couple of places (Chapters 3, 4, and 7), but only to set them aside.

My aim, rather, is to examine critically some of the standard ways of discussing issues of nationhood and ethnocultural diversity in Western democracies. I try to identify biases, double-standards, conceptual blinders, and confusions in our everyday discourse on these issues—e.g. in the way we talk about such things as group rights, civic nationalism, citizenship, federalism, and cosmopolitanism. These terms are all normatively-laden, and while we often think we know what they mean, they are surprisingly ambiguous and vulnerable to misuse and inconsistent application. Moreover, as I try to show, these ambiguities and double-standards are not random or innocent mistakes, but work systematically to the disadvantage of minorities. My goal, therefore, is to make us more aware of the use and misuse of these terms, and to give us a clearer understanding of their links with the underlying values of a liberal democracy.

I hope that this sort of theorizing is helpful to people. I know that many philosophers will want a more high-level abstract theory that starts from first premises about the nature of reason, knowledge, and personhood. Some policy-makers will want lower-level practical applications and case studies. But I'm not qualified to do the latter, and have doubts about the usefulness of the former. So I have focused instead on a mid-level analysis of moral arguments and public discourse. I believe that's a worthwhile project, and can shed light, not only on issues of minority rights, but also on the nature of liberalism as a political tradition, particularly its notions of individualism, autonomy, equality, political community, and national identity.

The Structure of the Book

This is a collection of essays, not a monograph, and the essays cover a wide range of topics. They are linked by a common concern with the accommodation of ethnocultural diversity within liberal democracies, but they approach the topic from various angles. The book is divided into four parts. The first part, 'The Evolution of the Minority Rights Debate', summarizes 'the state of the debate' over the rights of ethnocultural minorities. Chapter 1 explains how the debate has evolved over the past fifteen years. Minority rights used to be seen as a subset of the old liberalism-vs-communitarianism debate, such that communitarians were assumed to support the rights of ethnocultural communities, and liberals were assumed to oppose them in the name of a rigorous individualism. However, it is increasingly recognized that debates over minority rights are debates *within* liberalism about how to fairly accommodate ethnocultural diversity within liberal institutions. In particular, liberals must address questions about the fair terms of integration for immigrants, and the appropriate forms and limits of 'nation-building' by majority groups or national minorities. Chapter 2 suggests that there may be a consensus emerging within the literature on what has been called 'liberal culturalism'—i.e. the view that liberal states should not only uphold the familiar set of individual civil and political rights which are protected in all democracies, but should also adopt various group-specific rights and policies which are intended to recognize and accommodate the distinctive identities and needs of ethnocultural groups. I suggest that the explanation for this emerging consensus is, in part, the lack of any credible alternatives. Chapter 3 gives a brief summary of my theory of minority rights as presented in

Multicultural Citizenship, and responds to two major objections—one about the distinction between 'nations' and immigrant 'ethnic groups', and one about the justification for relying on specifically *liberal* principles for a theory of multiculturalism. Together, these three chapters define the range of issues that are addressed in the rest of the volume, and lay out the basic terms and premises of my approach to them.

The second part is entitled 'Ethnocultural Justice'. The chapters in this part discuss the requirements of ethnocultural justice in a liberal democracy. Chapter 4 explains why the protection of individual human rights is insufficient to ensure justice between ethnocultural groups, and why minority rights must supplement human rights. It focuses in particular on three areas where minorities are vulnerable to injustice at the hands of the state even when their individual rights are respected: settlement policies, language policies, and decisions about the boundaries and powers of political subunits. Chapter 5 explores why some form of power-sharing is required to ensure justice for national minorities. It also outlines a form of 'multination federalism' (quite distinct from the American or German models of federalism) that might meet this need, and that is increasingly common around the world. Chapter 6, a review essay of James Anaya's *Indigenous Peoples in International Law*, explores the relationship between the rights of indigenous peoples and those of other stateless nations. International law has moved in the direction of recognizing indigenous peoples as requiring special rights, distinct from those of other national groups or peoples. I discuss the possible grounds for this distinction, and its implications for norms of self-determination. Chapter 7 examines one of the specific forms of injustice facing many indigenous peoples—namely, the impact of economic development and settlement policies on their traditional territories. Chapter 8 explores the requirements of fairness towards immigrant/ethnic groups, and in particular the fair terms of integration into the larger society. It offers a defence of recent moves by various Western countries in the direction of a more 'multicultural' model of immigrant integration, and challenges the perception that these policies are 'balkanizing' and/or a threat to individual rights. Chapter 9 considers whether this immigrant multicultural model can be extended to racial minorities in North America, or whether additional measures are required.

The third part is called 'Misunderstanding Nationalism'. The papers in this section explore some of the common misinterpretations and preconceptions that liberals have about nationalism, and defend the idea that there are genuinely liberal forms of both state nationalism and minority nationalism. Chapter 10 discusses the familiar (but potentially misleading) contrast between 'cosmopolitanism' and 'nationalism', and discusses why liberals have gradually moved away from an anti-nationalist form of cosmopolitanism towards a liberal (and hence partly cosmopolitan) form of nationalism. Chapter 11 (co-authored with Christine Straehle) surveys recent work on the idea of liberal nationalism. While broadly sympathetic to this literature, we identify some ambiguities and lacunae that need to be addressed. Liberal nationalists typically claim that liberal-democratic principles can best be achieved—and perhaps only achieved—within 'national' political units. But is this a defence of state nationalism, or minority nationalism, or both? And what are the implications of liberal nationalism for attempts to build transnational institutions? Chapter 12 discusses examples of how the long-standing liberal prejudice against minority nationalism continues to bias analyses of nationalism, particularly in the systematic misuse of the distinction between 'civic' and 'ethnic' nationalism. (Chapter 12 is a review essay on books on nationalism by Michael Ignatieff, William Pfaff, Liah Greenfeld, and Yael Tamir). Chapters 13 and 14 discuss examples of how these liberal prejudices not only impede our intellectual understanding of nationalism, but also render us unable to deal with urgent political issues around the world relating to the struggles of national minorities. Chapter 13, a review essay of Joseph Carens's *Is Quebec Nationalism Just?*, discusses the inability of liberals in Canada to respond to Quebec nationalism. Chapter 14, a discussion of David Hollinger's *Postethnic America*, argues that misunderstandings of minority nationalism have had pernicious consequences for American foreign policy. Chapter 15 attempts to test these claims about the liberal or illiberal nature of minority nationalism by examining the question of how national minorities deal with the increasing presence of immigrants in their traditional homelands. It explores the potential dilemmas that arise when the claims of minority nationalism conflict with those of immigrant multiculturalism.

The final section is called 'Democratic Citizenship in Multiethnic States'. The papers in this section explore how the practice of democratic citizenship can be sustained and enriched in our age of pluralism and diversity. Chapter 16 emphasizes the importance of education as a site of conflict between demands for the accommodation of ethnocultural diversity and demands for the promotion of the common virtues and loyalties required by democratic citizenship. Chapter 17, a commentary on David's Held work, explores the extent to which globalization requires us to think about citizenship in more global terms, or whether citizenship will remain tied to national institutions and political processes. Chapter 18, a critique of Michael Sandel's *Democracy's Discontent*, argues that liberal egalitarianism, rather than civic republicanism, offers the best hope for enhancing democratic citizenship in today's societies.

Earlier versions of these essays have been previously published. All have been lightly revised to update references, standardize terminology and reduce overlap. Chapters 5 and 8 are more substantially revised.

Chapter 1, 'The New Debate over Minority Rights', will appear in Wayne Norman and Ronald Beiner (eds.), *Canadian Political Philosophy: Contemporary Reflections* (Oxford University Press, Toronto, 2000). It draws upon 'An

Update from the Multiculturalism Wars: Commentary on Shachar and Spinner-Halev', in Christian Joppke and Steven Lukes (eds.), *Multicultural Questions* (Oxford University Press, 1999), 112–29.

Chapter 2, 'Liberal Culturalism: An Emerging Consensus?', was published as the introduction to a special issue of *Ethical Theory and Moral Practice* on 'Nationalism, Multiculturalism and Liberal Democracy', 1/2 (1998): 143–57.

Chapter 3, 'Do We Need a Liberal Theory of Minority Rights? Reply to Carens, Young, Parekh and Forst', was published in *Constellations*, 4/1 (1997): 72–87.

Chapter 4, 'Human Rights and Ethnocultural Justice', was presented as the Sixth J. C. Rees Memorial Lecture at the University of Wales, Swansea, and published in *Review of Constitutional Studies*, 4/2 (1998): 213–38.

Chapter 5, 'Minority Nationalism and Multination Federalism', is a substantially revised version of paper which was originally published in Spanish as 'Federalismo, Nacionalismo y Multiculturalismo', *Revista Internacional de Filosofia Politica*, 7 (1996): 20–54, and reprinted in English as 'Is Federalism an Alternative to Secession?', in Percy Lehning (ed.), *Theories of Secession* (Routledge, London, 1998), 111–50.

Chapter 6, 'Theorizing Indigenous Rights', appeared in *University of Toronto Law Journal*, 49 (1999): 281–93.

Chapter 7, 'Indigenous Rights and Environmental Justice', was originally published as 'Concepts of Community and Social Justice', in Fen Hampson and Judith Reppy (eds.), *Earthly Goods: Environmental Change and Social Justice* (Cornell University Press, Ithaca, NY, 1996), 30–51.

Chapter 8, 'The Theory and Practice of Immigrant Multiculturalism', is adapted from two separate papers: 'Ethnic Associations and Democratic Citizenship', in Amy Gutmann (ed.), *Freedom of Association* (Princeton University Press, Princeton, 1998), 177–213, and 'Teoria si Practica Multiculturalismului Canadian', *Altera* (Romania) 12 (1999): 48–67.

Chapter 9, 'A Crossroad in Race Relations', originally appeared as ch. 5 in my *Finding Our Way: Rethinking Ethnocultural Relations in Canada* (Oxford University Press, 1998).

Chapter 10, 'From Enlightenment Cosmopolitanism to Liberal Nationalism', was written for, and will appear in Steven Lukes (ed.), *The Enlightenment: Then and Now*, Verso. It has been translated into Romanian as 'De la cosmopolitismul luminilor la nationalismul liberal', *A Treia Europa*, 2 (1998): 439–451; in Catalan as 'Del Cosmopolitisme il.lustrat al nacionalisme liberal', in *Idees: Revista de temes contemporanis*, 2 (1999): 26–45; and in Dutch in *Ethiek en Maatschappij* 3/1 (2000): 3–20.

Chapter 11, 'Cosmopolitanism, Nation-States and Minority Nationalism: A Critical Review of Recent Literature', is a revised version of a paper which was published in *European Journal of Philosophy*, 7/1 (1999): 65–88 (co-authored with Christine Straehle).

Chapter 12. 'Misunderstanding Nationalism', originally appeared in *Dissent* (Winter 1995): 130–7. It has been reprinted in Ronald Beiner (ed.), *Theorizing Nationalism* (SUNY Press, New York, 1999), 131–40; and translated into Catalan as 'El nacionalisme mal entès', *El Contemporani*, 10 (1996): 39–45. It also draws upon 'Modernity and Minority Nationalism: Commentary on Thomas Franck', *Ethics and International Affairs*, 11 (1997): 171–6.

Chapter 13, 'The Paradox of Liberal Nationalism', was published in *Literary Review of Canada*, 4/10 (Nov. 1995): 13–15.

Chapter 14, 'American Multiculturalism in the International Arena', was originally published in *Dissent* (Fall 1998): 73–9. It is reprinted in German in Will Kymlicka, *Multikulturalismus und Demokratie: Uber Minderheiten in Staaten und Nationen* (Rotbuch Verlag, Hamburg, 1999), 84–102.

Chapter 15, 'Minority Nationalism and Immigrant Integration', was written for, and will appear in, John McGarry and Michael Keating (eds.), *Minority Nationalism, Globalization, and European Integration* (Oxford University Press, forthcoming).

Chapter 16, 'Education for Citizenship', was originally published in Mark Halstead and Terence McLaughlin (eds.), *Education in Morality* (Routledge, London, 1999), 79–102. It is reprinted in *The School Field* (Slovenia), 10/1 (1999), and translated into Spanish as 'Educación para la Ciudadanía', in Francisco Colom González (ed.), *La política del multiculturalismo* (Anthropos-Narino, Barcelona, 2000).

Chapter 17. 'Citizenship in an Era of Globalization: Commentary on Held', is a revised version of paper published in Ian Shapiro and Casiano Hacker-Cordon (eds.), *Democracy's Edges* (Cambridge University Press, 1999), 112–26. It also draws upon 'The Prospects for Citizenship: Domestic and Global', published in Thomas Courchene (ed.), *The Nation State in a Global/Information Era* (John Deutsch Institute for the Study of Economic Policy, Queen's University, 1997), 315–25.

Chapter 18. 'Liberal Egalitarianism and Civic Republicanism: Friends or Enemies?', was published in Anita Allen and Milton Regan (eds.), *Debating Democracy's Discontent: Essays on American Politics, Law, and Public Philosophy* (Oxford University Press, Oxford, 1998), 131–48.

PART I

The Evolution of the Minority Rights Debate

1

The New Debate over Minority Rights

The last ten years has seen a remarkable upsurge in interest amongst political philosophers in the rights of ethnocultural groups within Western democracies.[1] My aim in this chapter is to give a condensed overview of the philosophical debate so far, and to suggest some future directions that it might take.

As political philosophers, our interest is in the normative issues raised by such minority rights. What are the moral arguments for or against such rights? In particular, how do they relate to the underlying principles of liberal democracy, such as individual freedom, social equality, and democracy? The philosophical debate on these questions has changed dramatically, both in its scope and in its basic terminology. When I started working on these issues in the mid-1980s, there were very few other political philosophers or political theorists working in the area.[2] Indeed, for most of this century, issues of ethnicity have been seen as marginal by political philosophers. (Much the same can be said about many other academic disciplines, from sociology to geography to history.)

Today however, after decades of relative neglect, the question of minority rights has moved to the forefront of political theory. There are several reasons for this. Most obviously, the collapse of communism unleashed a wave of ethnic nationalisms in Eastern Europe that dramatically affected the democratization process. Optimistic assumptions that liberal democracy would emerge smoothly from the ashes of Communism were derailed by issues of ethnicity and nationalism. But there were many factors within long-established democracies which also pointed to the salience of ethnicity: the nativist backlash against immigrants and refugees in many Western

---

[1] I use the term 'rights of ethnocultural minorities' (or, for brevity's sake, 'minority rights') in a loose way, to refer to a wide range of public policies, legal rights and exemptions, and constitutional provisions from multiculturalism policies to language rights to constitutional protections of Aboriginal treaties. This is a heterogeneous category, but these measures have two important features in common: (*a*) they go beyond the familiar set of common civil and political rights of individual citizenship which are protected in all liberal democracies; (*b*) they are adopted with the intention of recognizing and accommodating the distinctive identities and needs of ethnocultural groups. For a helpful typology, see Levy 1997.

[2] The most important of whom was Vernon Van Dyke, who published a handful of essays on this topic in the 1970s and early 1980s (e.g. Van Dyke 1977; 1982; 1985). There were also a few legal theorists who discussed the role of minority rights in international law, and their connection to human rights principles of non-discrimination.

countries; the resurgence and political mobilization of indigenous peoples, resulting in the draft declaration of the rights of indigenous peoples at the United Nations; and the ongoing, even growing, threat of secession within several Western democracies, from Canada (Quebec) to Britain (Scotland), Belgium (Flanders), and Spain (Catalonia).

All of these factors, which came to a head at the beginning of the 1990s, made it clear that Western democracies had not resolved or overcome the tensions raised by ethnocultural diversity. It is not surprising, therefore, that political theorists have increasingly turned their attention to this topic. For example, the last few years have witnessed the first philosophical books in English on the normative issues involved in secession, nationalism, immigration, group representation, multiculturalism, and indigenous rights.[3]

But the debate has not only grown in size. The very terms of the debate have also dramatically changed, and this is what I would like to focus on. I will try to distinguish three distinct stages in the debate.

1. The First Stage: Minority Rights as Communitarianism

The first stage was the pre-1989 debate. Those few theorists who discussed the issue in the 1970s and 1980s assumed that the debate over minority rights was essentially equivalent to the debate between 'liberals' and 'communitarians' (or between 'individualists' and 'collectivists'). Confronted with an unexplored topic, it was natural that political theorists would look for analogies with other more familiar topics, and the liberal-communitarian debate seemed the most relevant.

The liberal-communitarian debate is an old and venerable one within political philosophy, going back several centuries, albeit in different forms, and I will not try to reproduce it in its entirety. But, in oversimplified terms, the debate essentially revolves around the priority of individual freedom. Liberals insist that individuals should be free to decide on their own conception of the good life, and applaud the liberation of individuals from any ascribed or inherited status. Liberal individualists argue that the individual is morally prior to the community: the community matters only because it contributes to the well-being of the individuals who compose it. If those individ-

---

[3] Baubock 1994; Buchanan 1991; Canovan 1996; Kymlicka 1995*a*; Miller 1995; Phillips 1995; Spinner 1994; Tamir 1993; Taylor 1992*a*; Tully 1995; Walzer 1997; Young 1990. I am not aware of full-length books written by philosophers in English on any of these topics predating 1990, with the exception of Plamenatz 1960. There have also been many edited collections of philosophical articles on these issues (Baker 1994; Kymlicka 1995*b*; Lehning 1998; Couture *et al.* 1998; Shapiro and Kymlicka 1997; Schwartz 1995; Raikka 1996). For a comprehensive bibliography, see Kymlicka and Norman 2000.

uals no longer find it worthwhile to maintain existing cultural practices, then the community has no independent interest in preserving those practices, and no right to prevent individuals from modifying or rejecting them.

Communitarians dispute this conception of the 'autonomous individual'. They view people as 'embedded' in particular social roles and relationships. Such embedded selves do not form and revise their own conception of the good life; instead, they inherit a way of life that defines their good for them. Rather than viewing group practices as the product of individual choices, communitarians view individuals as the product of social practices. Moreover, they often deny that the interests of communities can be reduced to the interests of their individual members. Privileging individual autonomy is therefore seen as destructive of communities. A healthy community maintains a balance between individual choice and protection of the communal way of life, and seeks to limit the extent to which the former can erode the latter.

In this first stage of the debate, the assumption was that one's position on minority rights was dependent on, and derivative of, one's position on the liberal-communitarian debate. If one is a liberal who cherishes individual autonomy, then one will oppose minority rights as an unnecessary and dangerous departure from the proper emphasis on the individual. Communitarians, by contrast, view minority rights as an appropriate way of protecting communities from the eroding effects of individual autonomy, and of affirming the value of community. Ethnocultural minorities in particular are worthy of such protection, partly because they are most at risk, but also because they still have a communal way of life to be protected. Unlike the majority, ethnocultural minorities have not yet succumbed to liberal individualism, and so have maintained a coherent collective way of life.

This debate over the relative priority and reducibility of individuals and groups dominated the early literature on minority rights.[4] Defenders of minority rights agreed that they were inconsistent with liberalism's commitment to moral individualism and individual autonomy, but argued that this just pointed out the inherent flaws of liberalism.

In short, defending minority rights involved endorsing the communitarian critique of liberalism, and viewing minority rights as defending cohesive and communally-minded minority groups against the encroachment of liberal individualism.

---

[4] For representatives of the 'individualist' camp, see Narveson 1991; Hartney 1991. For the 'communitarian' camp, see Garet 1983; Van Dyke 1977; 1982; Addis 1992; Johnston 1989; McDonald 1991a, 1991b; Svensson 1979; Karmis 1993.

2. The Second Stage: Minority Rights Within a Liberal Framework

It is increasingly recognized that this is an unhelpful way to conceptualize most minority rights claims in Western democracies. Assumptions about the 'striking parallel between the communitarian attack of philosophical liberalism and the notion of [minority] rights' have been increasingly questioned.[5]

In reality, most ethnocultural groups within Western democracies do not want to be protected from the forces of modernity in liberal societies. On the contrary, they want to be full and equal participants in modern liberal societies. This is true of most immigrant groups, which seek inclusion and full participation in the mainstream of liberal-democratic societies, with access to its education, technology, literacy, mass communications, etc. It is equally true of most non-immigrant national minorities, like the Québécois, Flemish, or Catalans.[6] Some of their members may wish to secede from a liberal democracy, but if they do, it is not to create an illiberal communitarian society, but rather to create their own modern liberal democratic society. The Québécois wish to create a 'distinct society', but it is a modern, liberal society—with an urbanized, secular, pluralistic, industrialized, bureaucratized, consumerist mass culture.

Indeed, far from opposing liberal principles, public opinion polls show there are often no statistical differences between national minorities and majorities in their adherence to liberal principles. And immigrants also quickly absorb the basic liberal-democratic consensus, even when they came from countries with little or no experience of liberal democracy.[7] The com-

---

[5] Galenkamp 1993: 20–5. The belief in such a 'striking parallel' is partly the result of a linguistic sleight of hand. Because minority rights are claimed by groups, and tend to be group-specific, they are often described as 'collective rights'. The fact that the majority seeks only 'individual' rights while the minority seeks 'collective' rights is then taken as evidence that the minority is somehow more 'collectivist' than the majority. This chain of reasoning contains several non sequiturs. Not all group-specific minority rights are 'collective' rights, and even those which are 'collective' rights in one or other sense of that term are not necessarily evidence of 'collectivism'. See Kymlicka 1995a; Ch. 3 and Ch. 4 below.

[6] By national minorities I mean groups that formed complete and functioning societies on their historic homeland prior to being incorporated into a larger state. The incorporation of such national minorities has typically been involuntary, due to colonization, conquest, or the ceding of territory from one imperial power to another, but may also arise voluntarily, as a result of federation. The category of national minorities includes both 'stateless nations' (like the Québécois, Puerto Ricans, Catalans, Scots) and 'indigenous peoples' (like the Indians, Innuit, Sami, Maori). For the similarities and differences between these two sorts of national minorities, see Ch. 6.

[7] On Canadian immigrants, see Frideres 1997; for American immigrants, see Harles 1993. On the convergence in political values between anglophones and francophones in Canada, see Ch. 13.

mitment to individual autonomy is deep and wide in modern societies, crossing ethnic, linguistic, and religious lines.

There are some important and visible exceptions to this rule. For example, there are a few ethnoreligious sects that voluntarily distance themselves from the larger world—the Hutterites, Amish, Hasidic Jews. And some of the more isolated or traditionalist indigenous communities fit this description as 'communitarian' groups. The question of how liberal states should respond to such non-liberal groups is an important one, which I discuss elsewhere.[8]

But the overwhelming majority of debates about minority rights are not debates between a liberal majority and communitarian minorities, but debates amongst liberals about the meaning of liberalism. They are debates between individuals and groups who endorse the basic liberal-democratic consensus, but who disagree about the interpretation of these principles in multiethnic societies—in particular, they disagree about the proper role of language, nationality, and ethnic identities within liberal-democratic societies and institutions. Groups claiming minority rights insist that at least certain forms of public recognition and support for their language, practices and identities are not only consistent with basic liberal-democratic principles, including the importance of individual autonomy, but may indeed be required by them.

This then has led to the second stage of the debate, in which the question becomes: what is the possible scope for minority rights *within* liberal theory? Framing the debate this way does not resolve the issues. On the contrary, the place of minority rights within liberal theory remains very controversial. But it changes the terms of the debate. The issue is no longer how to protect communitarian minorities from liberalism, but whether minorities that share basic liberal principles none the less need minority rights. If groups are indeed liberal, why do their members want minority rights? Why aren't they satisfied with the traditional common rights of citizenship?

This is the sort of question that Joseph Raz tries to answer in his recent work. Raz insists that the autonomy of individuals—their ability to make good choices amongst good lives—is intimately tied up with access to their culture, with the prosperity and flourishing of their culture, and with the respect accorded their culture by others. Minority rights help ensure this cultural flourishing and mutual respect.[9] Other liberal writers like David Miller, Yael Tamir, Jeff Spinner, and myself have made similar arguments about the importance of 'cultural membership' or 'national identity' to modern freedom-seeking citizens.[10] The details of the argument vary, but each of us, in our own way, argues that there are compelling interests related to culture and identity which are fully consistent with liberal principles of freedom and

---

[8] See Kymlicka 1995a: ch. 8, 1998a: ch. 4. I touch briefly on this in Ch. 16.

[9] Raz 1994; 1998; Margalit and Raz 1990.

[10] Tamir 1993; Miller 1995; Spinner 1994; Kymlicka 1989.

equality, and which justify granting special rights to minorities. We can call this the 'liberal culturalist' position.

Critics of liberal culturalism have raised many objections to this entire line of argument. Some deny that we can intelligibly distinguish or individuate 'cultures' or 'cultural groups'; others deny that we can make sense of the claim that individuals are 'members' of cultures; yet others say that even if can make sense of the claim that individuals are members of distinct cultures, we have no reason to assume that the well-being or freedom of the individual is tied in any way with the flourishing of the culture.[11] These are important objections, but I think they can be answered. In any event, they have not yet succeeded in dampening enthusiasm for liberal culturalism, which has quickly developed into the consensus position amongst liberals working in this field.[12]

However, even those sympathetic to liberal culturalism face an obvious problem. It is clear that some kinds of minority rights would undermine, rather then support, individual autonomy. A crucial task facing liberal defenders of minority rights, therefore, is to distinguish between the 'bad' minority rights that involve *restricting* individual rights, from the 'good' minority rights that can be seen as *supplementing* individual rights.

I have proposed distinguishing two kinds of rights that a minority group might claim. The first involves the right of a group against its own members, designed to protect the group from the destabilizing impact of *internal* dissent (e.g. the decision of individual members not to follow traditional practices or customs). The second kind involves the right of a group against the larger society, designed to protect the group from the impact of *external* pressures (e.g. the economic or political decisions of the larger society). I call the first 'internal restrictions', and the second 'external protections'. Given the commitment to individual autonomy, I argue that liberals should be sceptical of claims to internal restrictions. Liberal culturalism rejects the idea that groups can legitimately restrict the basic civil or political rights of their own members in the name of preserving the purity or authenticity of the group's culture and traditions. However, a liberal conception of multiculturalism can accord groups various rights against the larger society, in order to reduce the group's vulnerability to the economic or political power of the majority. Such 'external protections' are consistent with liberal principles, although they too become illegitimate if, rather than reducing a minority's vulnerability to the power of the larger society, they instead enable a minority to exercise economic or political dominance over some other group. To oversimplify, we can say that minority rights are consistent with liberal culturalism if (*a*) they

---

[11] For a pithy statement of these three objections, see Waldron 1995.

[12] It is an interesting question why this liberal culturalist view—which is a clear departure from the dominant liberal view for several decades—has become so popular. I address this in Ch. 2.

protect the freedom of individuals within the group; and (*b*) they promote relations of equality (non-dominance) between groups.[13] Other liberal culturalists, however, argue that some forms of internal restrictions can be accepted, so long as group members have an effective right of exit from the group.[14]

In the second stage of the debate, therefore, the question of minority rights is reformulated as a question within liberal theory, and the aim is to show that some (but not all) minority rights claims enhance liberal values. In my opinion, this second stage reflects genuine progress. We now have a more accurate description of the claims being made by ethnocultural groups, and a more accurate understanding of the normative issues they raise. We have gotten beyond the sterile and misleading debate about individualism and collectivism.

However, I think this second stage also needs to be challenged. While it has a better understanding of the nature of most ethnocultural groups, and the demands they place on the liberal state, it misinterprets the nature of the liberal state, and the demands it places on minorities.

3. The Third Stage: Minority Rights as a Response to Nation-Building

Let me explain. The assumption—generally shared by both defenders and critics of minority rights—is that the liberal state, in its normal operation, abides by a principle of ethnocultural neutrality. That is, the state is 'neutral' with respect to the ethnocultural identities of its citizens, and indifferent to the ability of ethnocultural groups to reproduce themselves over time. On this view, liberal states treat culture in the same way as religion—i.e. as something which people should be free to pursue in their private life, but which is not the concern of the state (so long as they respect the rights of others). Just as liberalism precludes the establishment of an official religion, so too there cannot be official cultures that have preferred status over other possible cultural allegiances.

For example, Michael Walzer argues that liberalism involves a 'sharp divorce of state and ethnicity'. The liberal state stands above all the various

---

[13] See Kymlicka 1995*a*: ch 3. I also argue that most of the minority rights sought by ethnocultural groups within Western democracies fall into the external protection category.

[14] This is likely to be the view of those who endorse a 'political' conception of liberalism, rooted in the value of tolerance, rather than a 'comprehensive' conception, rooted in the value of autonomy. See, for example, Galston 1995; Kukathas 1997. I discuss the differences between these approaches in Kymlicka 1995*a*: ch. 8. For a discussion of the complications in determining what constitutes an 'effective' right of exit, see Okin 1998.

ethnic and national groups in the country, 'refusing to endorse or support their ways of life or to take an active interest in their social reproduction'. Instead, the state is 'neutral with reference to language, history, literature, calendar' of these groups. He says the clearest example of such a neutral liberal state is the United States, whose ethnocultural neutrality is reflected in the fact that it has no constitutionally recognized official language.[15] For immigrants to become Americans, therefore, is simply a matter of affirming their allegiance to the principles of democracy and individual freedom defined in the US Constitution.

Indeed, some theorists argue that this is precisely what distinguishes liberal 'civic nations' from illiberal 'ethnic nations'.[16] Ethnic nations take the reproduction of a particular ethnonational culture and identity as one of their most important goals. Civic nations, by contrast, are 'neutral' with respect to the ethnocultural identities of their citizens, and define national membership purely in terms of adherence to certain principles of democracy and justice. For minorities to seek special rights, on this view, is a radical departure from the traditional operation of the liberal state. Therefore, the burden of proof lies on anyone who would wish to endorse such minority rights.

This is the burden of proof which liberal culturalists try to meet with their account of the role of cultural membership in securing freedom and self-respect. They try to show that minority rights supplement, rather than diminish, individual freedom and equality, and help to meet needs which would otherwise go unmet in a state that clung rigidly to ethnocultural neutrality.

The presumption in the second stage of the debate, therefore, has been that advocates of minority rights must demonstrate compelling reasons to depart from the norm of ethnocultural neutrality. I would argue, however, that this idea that liberal-democratic states (or 'civic nations') are ethnoculturally neutral is manifestly false. The religion model is altogether misleading as an account of the relationship between the liberal-democratic state and ethnocultural groups.

Consider the actual policies of the United States, which is the prototypically 'neutral' state. Historically, decisions about the boundaries of state governments, and the timing of their admission into the federation, were deliberately made to ensure that anglophones would be a majority within each of the fifty states of the American federation. This helped establish the dominance of English throughout the territory of the United States.[17] And the continuing dominance of English is ensured by several ongoing policies. For example, it is a legal requirement for children to learn the English language in schools; it is a legal requirement for immigrants (under the age of

---

[15] Walzer 1992d: 100–1. See also Walzer 1992b: 9.
[16] Pfaff 1993: 162; Ignatieff 1993.   [17] See Ch. 5.

50) to learn English to acquire American citizenship; and it is a *de facto* requirement for employment in or for government that the applicant speak English.

These decisions are not isolated exceptions to some norm of ethnocultural neutrality. On the contrary, they are tightly interrelated, and together they have shaped the very structure of the American state, and the way the state structures society. (Since governments account for 40–50 per cent of GNP in most countries, the language of government is not negligible).

These policies have all been pursued with the intention of promoting integration into what I call a 'societal culture'. By a societal culture, I mean a territorially-concentrated culture, centred on a shared language which is used in a wide range of societal institutions, in both public and private life (schools, media, law, economy, government, etc.). I call it a *societal* culture to emphasize that it involves a common language and social institutions, rather than common religious beliefs, family customs, or personal lifestyles. Societal cultures within a modern liberal democracy are inevitably pluralistic, containing Christians as well as Muslims, Jews, and atheists; heterosexuals as well as gays; urban professionals as well as rural farmers; conservatives as well as socialists. Such diversity is the inevitable result of the rights and freedoms guaranteed to liberal citizens, particularly when combined with an ethnically diverse population. This diversity, however, is balanced and constrained by linguistic and institutional cohesion; cohesion that has not emerged on its own, but rather is the result of deliberate state policies.

The American government has deliberately created such a societal culture, and promoted the integration of citizens into it. The government has encouraged citizens to view their life-chances as tied up with participation in common societal institutions that operate in the English language, and has nurtured a national identity defined in part by common membership in a societal culture. Nor is the Unites States unique in this respect. Promoting integration into a societal culture is part of a 'nation-building' project that all liberal democracies have adopted.

Obviously, the sense in which English-speaking Americans share a common 'culture' is a very thin one, since it does not preclude differences in religion, personal values, family relationships, or lifestyle choices.[18] While thin, it is far from trivial. On the contrary, as I discuss below, attempts to integrate

---

[18] Indeed, my use of the term 'societal culture' is in conflict with the way the term culture is used in most academic disciplines, where it is defined in a very thick, ethnographic sense, referring to the sharing of specific folk-customs, habits, and rituals. Citizens of a modern liberal state do not share a common culture in such a thick, ethnographic sense—indeed, the lack of a common thick ethnographic culture is part of the very definition of a liberal society. But it equally essential to modern liberal forms of governance that citizens share a common culture in a very different, and thinner, sense, focusing on a common language and societal institutions.

people into such a common societal culture have often been met with serious resistance. Although integration in this sense leaves a great deal of room for both the public and private expression of individual and collective differences, some groups have none the less vehemently rejected the idea that they should view their life-chances as tied up with the societal institutions conducted in the majority's language.

So we need to replace the idea of an 'ethnoculturally neutral' state with a new model of a liberal democratic state—what I call the 'nation-building' model. To say that states are nation-building is not to say that governments can only promote one societal culture. It is possible for government policies to encourage the sustaining of two or more societal cultures within a single country—indeed, as I discuss below, this is precisely what characterizes multination states like Canada, Switzerland, Belgium, or Spain.

However, historically, virtually all liberal democracies have, at one point or another, attempted to diffuse a single societal culture throughout all of its territory.[19] Nor should this be seen purely as a matter of cultural imperialism or ethnocentric prejudice. This sort of nation-building serves a number of important goals. For example, standardized public education in a common language has often been seen as essential if all citizens are to have equal opportunity to work in the modern economy. Indeed, equal opportunity is defined precisely in terms of equal access to mainstream institutions operating in dominant language. Also, participation in a common societal culture has often been seen as essential for generating the sort of solidarity required by a welfare state, since it promotes a sense of common identity and membership. Moreover, a common language has been seen as essential to democracy—how can 'the people' govern together if they cannot understand one another? In short, promoting integration into a common societal culture has been seen as essential to social equality and political cohesion in modern states.[20]

---

[19] For the ubiquity of the process, see Gellner 1983; Anderson 1983; Tilly 1975. To my knowledge, Switzerland is the only exception: it never made any serious attempt to pressure its French and Italian minorities to integrate into the German-speaking majority. All of the other Western multination states have at one time or another made a concerted effort to assimilate their minorities, and only reluctantly gave up this ideal.

[20] For defences of the importance and legitimacy of nation-building within liberal democracies, see Tamir 1993; Miller 1995, whose ideas I discuss in Chs. 10 and 11. Of course, this sort of nation-building can also be used to promote illiberal goals. As Margaret Canovan puts it, nationhood is like a 'battery' which makes states run—the existence of a common national identity motivates and mobilizes citizens to act for common political goals—and these goals can be liberal or illiberal (Canovan 1996: 80). Liberal reformers invoke the battery of nationhood to mobilize citizens behind projects of democratization, economic development and social justice; illiberal authoritarians invoke nationhood to mobilize citizens behind attacks on alleged enemies of the nation, be they foreign countries or internal dissidents. This is why nation-building is just as common in authoritarian regimes as in democracies (e.g. Spain under Franco, or Latin America under the military dictators). Authoritarian regimes also need a

So states have engaged in this process of 'nation-building'—that is, a process of promoting a common language, and a sense of common membership in, and equal access to, the social institutions based on that language. Decisions regarding official languages, core curriculum in education, and the requirements for acquiring citizenship, all have been made with the intention of diffusing a particular culture throughout society, and of promoting a particular national identity based on participation in that societal culture.

If I am right that this nation-building model provides a more accurate account of modern liberal democratic states, how does this affect the issue of minority rights? I believe it gives us a very different perspective on the debate. The question is no longer how to justify departure from a norm of neutrality, but rather do majority efforts at nation-building create injustices for minorities? And do minority rights help protect against these injustices?

This would be the third stage in the debate, which I am trying to explore in my own recent work. I cannot discuss all of its implications, but let me give two examples of how this new model may affect the debate over minority rights.

4. Two Examples

How does nation-building affect minorities? As Taylor notes, the process of nation-building inescapably privileges members of the majority culture:

If a modern society has an 'official' language, in the fullest sense of the term, that is, a state-sponsored , -inculcated, and -defined language and culture, in which both economy and state function, then it is obviously an immense advantage to people if this language and culture are theirs. Speakers of other languages are at a distinct disadvantage.[21]

This means that minority cultures face a choice. If all public institutions are being run in another language, minorities face the danger of being marginalized from the major economic, academic, and political institutions of the society. Faced with this dilemma, minorities have (to oversimplify) three basic options:

(a) they can accept integration into the majority culture, although perhaps attempt to renegotiate the terms of integration;

'battery' to help achieve public objectives in complex modern societies. What distinguishes liberal from illiberal states is not the presence or absence of nation-building, but rather the ends to which nation-building is put, and the means used to achieve them.

[21] Taylor 1997: 34.

(b) they can seek the sorts of rights and powers of self-government needed to maintain their own societal culture—i.e. to create their own economic, political and educational institutions in their own language. That is, they can engage in their own form of competing nation-building;

(c) they can accept permanent marginalization.

We can find some ethnocultural groups that fit each of these categories (and other groups that are caught between them, such as African-Americans).[22] For example, some immigrant ethnoreligious sects choose permanent marginalization. This would seem to be true, for example, of the Hutterites in Canada, or the Amish in the United States. But the option of accepting marginalization is only likely to be attractive to religious sects whose theology requires them to avoid all contact with the modern world. The Hutterites and Amish are unconcerned about their marginalization from universities or legislatures, since they view such 'worldly' institutions as corrupt.

Virtually all other ethnocultural minorities, however, seek to participate in the modern world, and to do so, they must either integrate or seek the self-government needed to create and sustain their own modern institutions. Faced with this choice, ethnocultural groups have responded in different ways.

(a) National Minorities

National minorities have typically responded to majority nation-building by fighting to maintain or rebuild their own societal culture, by engaging in their own competing nation-building. Indeed, they often use the same tools that the majority uses to promote this nation-building—e.g. control over the language and curriculum of schooling, the language of government employment, the requirements of immigration and naturalization, and the drawing of internal boundaries. We can see this clearly in the case of Québécois nationalism, which has largely been concerned with gaining and exercising these nation-building powers. But it is also increasingly true of the Aboriginal peoples in Canada, who have adopted the language of 'nationhood', and who are engaged in a major campaign of 'nation-building', which requires the exercise of much greater powers of self-government and the building of many new societal institutions.[23]

Intuitively, the adoption of such minority nation-building projects seems fair. If the majority can engage in legitimate nation-building, why not national minorities, particularly those which have been involuntarily incorporated into a larger state? To be sure, liberal principles set limits on *how*

---

[22] See Ch. 9 for a discussion of the complex demands of African-Americans.

[23] On the need (and justification for) Aboriginal 'nation-building', see RCAP 1996; Alfred 1995.

national groups go about nation-building. Liberal principles will preclude any attempts at ethnic cleansing, or stripping people of their citizenship, or the violation of human rights. These principles will also insist that any national group engaged in a project of nation-building must respect the right of other nations within its jurisdiction to protect and build their own national institutions. For example, the Québécois are entitled to assert national rights vis-à-vis the rest of Canada, but only if they respect the rights of Aboriginals within Quebec to assert national rights vis-à-vis the rest of Quebec.

These limits are important, but they still leave significant room, I believe, for legitimate forms of minority nationalism. Moreover, these limits are likely to be similar for both majority and minority nations. All else being equal, national minorities should have the same tools of nation-building available to them as the majority nation, subject to the same liberal limitations. What we need, in other words, is a consistent theory of permissible forms of nation-building within liberal democracies. I do not think that political theorists have yet developed such a theory. One of the many unfortunate side-effects of the dominance of the 'ethnocultural neutrality' model is that liberal theorists have never explicitly confronted this question.[24]

My aim here is not to promote any particular theory of permissible nation-building,[25] but simply to insist that this is the relevant question we need to address. The question is not, 'have national minorities given us a compelling reason to abandon the norm of ethnocultural neutrality?' but, rather, 'why should national minorities not have the same powers of nation-building as the majority?' This is the context within which minority nationalism must be evaluated—i.e. as a response to majority nation-building, using the same tools of nation-building. And the burden of proof surely rests on those who would deny national minorities the same powers of nation-building as those which the national majority takes for granted.

(b) Immigrants

Historically, nation-building has been neither desirable nor feasible for immigrant groups. Instead, they have traditionally accepted the expectation that they will integrate into the larger societal culture. Few immigrant

[24] As Norman notes, these questions about the morality of nation-building have been ignored even by philosophers working on nationalism. They tend to ask about the morality of nation-states, not about the morality of nation-building states. In other words, philosophers of nationalism typically take the existence of nation-states as a given, and ask whether it is a good thing to have a world of nation-states. They do not explore the processes by which such nation-states are created in the first place (i.e. what methods of nation-building are permissible). Norman 1999: 60.

[25] I made a preliminary attempt to develop criteria for distinguishing liberal from illiberal forms of nation-building in Kymlicka 1998b. An expanded attempt will appear in Kymlicka and Opalski 2001.

groups have objected to the requirement that they must learn an official language as a condition of citizenship, or that their children must learn the official language in school. They have accepted the assumption that their life-chances, and the life-chances of their children, will be bound up with participation in mainstream institutions operating in the majority language.

However, this is not to say that immigrants may not suffer injustices as a result of nation-building policies. After all, the state is clearly not neutral with respect to the language and culture of immigrants: it imposes a range of *de jure* and *de facto* requirements for immigrants to integrate in order to succeed. These requirements are often difficult and costly for immigrants to meet. Since immigrants cannot respond to this by adopting their own nation-building programmes, but rather must attempt to integrate as best they can, it is only fair that the state minimize the costs involved in this state-demanded integration.

Put another way, immigrants can demand fairer terms of integration. To my mind, this demand has two basic elements: (i) we need to recognize that integration does not occur overnight, but is a difficult and long-term process that operates inter-generationally. This means that special accommodations (e.g. mother-tongue services) are often required for immigrants on a transitional basis; (ii) we need to ensure that the common institutions into which immigrants are pressured to integrate provide the same degree of respect, recognition and accommodation of the identities and practices of immigrants as they traditionally have of the identities and practices of the majority group. This requires a systematic exploration of our social institutions to see whether their rules and symbols disadvantage immigrants. For example, we need to examine dress-codes, public holidays, even height and weight restrictions, to see whether they are biased against certain immigrant groups. We also need to examine the portrayal of minorities in school curricula or the media to see if they are stereotypical, or fail to recognize the contributions of immigrants to national history or world culture. These measures are needed to ensure that liberal states are offering immigrants fair terms of integration.

Others may disagree with the fairness of some of these policies. The requirements of fairness are not always obvious, particularly in the context of people who have chosen to enter a country, and political theorists have done little to date to illuminate the issue. My aim here is not to defend a particular theory of fair terms of integration (see Chapter 8), but rather to insist that this is the relevant question we need to address. The question is not whether immigrants have given us a compelling reason to diverge from the norm of ethnocultural neutrality, but rather how can we ensure that state policies aimed at pressuring immigrants to integrate are fair?

The focus of this third stage of the debate, therefore, is to show how particular minority rights claims are related to, and a response to, state nation-building policies. And the logical outcome of this stage of the debate will be to develop theories of permissible nation-building and fair terms of immigrant integration.[26]

Of course, this is just a general trend, not a universal law. In some countries, immigrant groups have not been allowed or encouraged to integrate (e.g. Turks in Germany). Even in the United States, the usual tendencies toward immigrant integration have sometimes been deflected, particularly if the newcomers were expected to return quickly to their country of origin (as with the original Cuban exiles in Miami); or if the immigrants were illegal, and so had no right to employment or citizenship (as with illegal Mexican migrants in California). These groups were exempted, or precluded, from the usual state-imposed pressure to integrate.

The extent to which national minorities have been able to maintain a separate societal culture also varies considerably. In some countries, national minorities have been almost completely integrated (e.g. Bretons in France). Even in the United States, the extent (and success) of nationalist mobilization varies. For example, compare the Chicanos in the South-West with the Puerto Ricans. The Chicanos were unable to preserve their own Spanish-speaking judicial, educational, or political institutions after being involuntarily incorporated into the United States in 1848, and they have not mobilized along nationalist lines to try to recreate these institutions. By contrast, Puerto Ricans mobilized very successfully to defend their Spanish-language institutions and self-government rights when they were involuntarily incorporated into the United States in 1898, and continue to exhibit a strong nationalist consciousness. The extent of nationalist mobilization also differs amongst the various Indian tribes in America. Moreover there are some groups which do not fit any of these categories—most obviously African-Americans—whose unique history has led to a very distinctive, and somewhat ambivalent, form of multiculturalism (see Chapter 9 below).

There are many such complicated cases that do not fit neatly into the 'ethnoreligious sect', 'immigrant' or 'national minority' patterns. I will return to some of these 'in-between' cases later on. But we can best understand the complexities and ambiguities of these cases if we first have a clear picture of the more standard cases, since the demands of in-between groups are often a complex hybrid of different (and sometimes contradictory) elements drawn from the more familiar models of ethnoreligious marginalization, immigrant integration, and separatist nationalism.

[26] I have discussed minority nationalism and immigrant multiculturalism in isolation from each other, but we also need to consider their interaction. Since both challenge the traditional model of a culturally homogeneous 'nation-state', they are often treated as complementary but separate processes of deconstructing the nation-state. In reality, however, immigration is not only a challenge to traditional models of the nation-state; it is also a challenge to the self-conceptions and political aspirations of those groups which see themselves as distinct and self-governing nations within a larger state. This raises a host of interesting questions about whether minority nationalisms themselves must become more 'multicultural'. See Ch. 15.

I believe that we could extend this method to look at other types of eth-nocultural groups which do not fit into the category of national minorities or immigrants, such as African-Americans, the Roma, guest-workers in Germany, or Russian settlers in the Baltics. In each case, I think it is possible— and indeed essential—to view their claims to minority rights as a response to perceived injustices that arise out of nation-building policies.[27] Each group's claims can be seen as specifying the injustices that majority nation-building has imposed on them, and as identifying the conditions under which major-ity nation-building would cease to be unjust.

The major task facing any liberal theory of minority rights is to better understand and articulate these conditions of ethnocultural justice. I expect that filling in these lacunae will form the main agenda for minority rights the-orists over the next decade.

5. A New Front in the Multiculturalism Wars?

So far, I have focused on the significant shifts in the recent minority rights debate. However, there has been an important assumption that is common to all three stages of the debate: namely, that the goal is to assess the *justice* of minority claims. This focus on justice reflects the fact that opposition to minority rights has traditionally been stated in the language of justice. Critics of minority rights had long argued that justice required state institutions to be 'colour-blind'. To ascribe rights on the basis of membership in ascriptive groups was seen as inherently morally arbitrary and discriminatory, neces-sarily creating first and second-class citizens.

The first task confronting any defender of minority rights, therefore, was to try to overcome this presumption, and to show that deviations from dif-ference-blind rules that are adopted in order to accommodate ethnocultural differences are not inherently unjust. As we have seen, this has been done in two main ways: (*a*) by identifying the many ways that mainstream institu-tions are not neutral, but rather are implicitly or explicitly tilted towards the interests and identities of the majority group. This bias creates a range of bur-dens, barriers, stigmatizations and exclusions for members of minority groups which can only or best be remedied by minority rights; and (b) by emphasizing the importance of certain interests which have typically been ignored by liberal theories of justice—e.g. interests in recognition, identity, language, and cultural membership. If these interests are ignored or trivial-ized by the state, then people will feel harmed—and indeed will be harmed— even if their civil, political and welfare rights are respected. If state institutions

---

[27] I discuss the claims of these other types of groups in Kymlicka and Opalski 2001.

fail to recognize and respect people's culture and identity, the result can be serious damage to people's self-respect and sense of agency.

If we accept either or both of these points, then we can see minority rights not as unfair privileges or invidious forms of discrimination, but as compensation for unfair disadvantages, and so as consistent with, and even required by, justice.

In my view, this debate over justice is drawing to a close. As I noted earlier, much work remains to be done in assessing the justice of particular forms of immigrant multiculturalism or minority nationalism. But in terms of the more general question of whether minority rights are *inherently* unjust, the debate is over, and the defenders of minority rights have won the day. I don't mean that defenders of minority rights have been successful in getting their claims implemented, although there is a clear trend throughout the Western democracies towards the greater recognition of minority rights, both in the form of immigrant multiculturalism and of-self-government for national minorities.[28] Rather I mean that defenders of minority rights have successfully redefined the terms of public debate in two profound ways: (*a*) few thoughtful people continue to think that justice can simply be *defined* in terms of difference-blind rules or institutions. Instead, it is now recognized that difference-blind rules can cause disadvantages for particular groups. Whether justice requires common rules for all, or differential rules for diverse groups, is something to be assessed case-by-case in particular contexts, not assumed in advance; (*b*) as a result, the burden of proof has shifted. The burden of proof no longer falls solely on defenders of minority rights to show that their proposed reforms would not create injustices; the burden of proof equally falls on defenders of difference-blind institutions to show that the status quo does not create injustices for minority groups.

So the original justice-based grounds for blanket opposition to minority rights have faded. This has not meant that opposition to minority rights has disappeared. But it now takes a new form. Or rather it takes two forms: the first questions the justice of specific multiculturalism policies in particular contexts, focusing on the way particular policies may entail an unjust

---

[28] There is also a trend towards codifying minority rights at the international level. It is now widely believed in the West that earlier attempts to suppress, coerce or exclude minority groups were unjust, as well as unworkable, and that some minimal set of minority rights is needed to ensure ethnocultural justice. Many scholars and NGOs are therefore trying to institutionalize at the international level emerging Western models of minority rights, in the same way that Western liberals after World War II were able to secure a Universal Declaration of Human Rights. Such an international charter of minority rights seems unlikely in the foreseeable future. The trend towards greater recognition of minority rights is strong within Western democracies, but in many parts of Asia and Africa minority rights are still anathema. It is interesting to note that whereas minority rights were opposed in the West on the ground that they violated Western individualism, in East Asia they are often opposed on the grounds that they violate Asian communitarianism! See He 1998.

distribution of the benefits and burdens associated with identity and culture; the second shifts the focus away from justice towards issues of citizenship, focusing not on the justice or injustice of particular policies, but rather on the way that the general trend towards multiculturalism threatens to erode the sorts of civic virtues and citizenship practices which sustain a healthy democracy. I will say a few words about each of these lines of argument.

(a) Justice in Context

Some critics accept that the justice of multicultural demands must be evaluated on a case-by-case basis, and so focus on the potential injustices of particular multicultural proposals in particular contexts, rather than making global claims about the inherent injustice of group-specific policies. These sorts of context-specific arguments are, I think, essential, and reflect real progress in the debate.

At the level of particular cases, the debate focuses, not on whether multiculturalism is right or wrong in principle, but rather on a range of more practical issues about the distribution of the benefits and burdens of specific policies—e.g. what exactly is the disadvantage which a minority faces within a particular institutional structure? Will the proposed multiculturalism reform actually remedy this disadvantage? Are the costs of a particular multiculturalism policy distributed fairly, or are some individuals or subgroups inside or outside the group being asked to shoulder an unfair share of the costs?[29] Are there alternative policies which would remedy the disadvantage in a more effective and less costly way?

A good example of this sort of debate is the recent work on affirmative action in America. Whereas older debates focused almost entirely on whether race-based preferences in admissions or hiring were morally wrong in principle, there is increasing recognition that this is too simple. It is widely accepted that African-Americans and other minorities face real disadvantages in certain institutional contexts, despite the professed colour-blind nature of these institutions, and that something needs to be done to remedy these disadvantages. The objection to affirmative action, therefore, is not that any deviation from colour-blind rules is unjust in principle, but rather that current affirmative action policies do not actually benefit the people who are

---

[29] As Shachar notes (1998; 1999), there is a tendency within some schemes of minority rights for women to bear disproportionate costs of minority protection. She calls this the 'paradox of multicultural vulnerability': i.e. some schemes for reducing the minority's vulnerability to the majority may increase minority women's vulnerability to discrimination within their own community. But, unlike Okin (1998), she does not view this as inherent in the very idea of minority rights, or as a blanket objection to the idea of minority rights, but rather as a crucial factor that needs to be kept in mind when examining the justice in context of particular policies.

most in need (i.e. they help middle-class Blacks, but not the inner-city poor), that the costs of affirmative action are borne disproportionately by one group (i.e. young white males, some of whom may themselves be disadvantaged), and that there are alternative policies which would be more effective (i.e. improved funding for inner-city schools). Others respond that affirmative action has been demonstrably successful, and that no alternative policy has been nearly as effective.[30]

This new debate on affirmative action in the US remains unresolved, to say the least, but at least it is the right *kind* of debate. It focuses, not on slogans about a colour-blind constitution, but on how particular educational or employment institutions do or do not disadvantage the members of particular groups, and on how proposed group-specific policies would or would not remedy that problem. And while the result of the debate may be to trim or amend existing affirmative action programs, it is unlikely that the result will be to eliminate all forms of race-conscious policies. On the contrary, it may well be that the alternatives which replace or supplement affirmative action will be equally group-specific in their focus—e.g. support for Black colleges, or state-sponsored mentoring programmes for promising Black students. That is, one form of multiculturalism policy will be replaced, or amended, or supplemented, with another form of multiculturalism policy (see Chapter 9).

Indeed, we can generalize this point. Since mainstream institutions privilege the majority's culture and identity is so many ways, and since people's interests in culture and identity are so important, the question we face is not whether to adopt multiculturalism, but rather which *kind* of multiculturalism to adopt. Once we jettison the idea that group-specific rights are wrong in principle, and instead get down to brass-tacks and examine particular institutions, then the question becomes which sort of multiculturalism is most fair and effective, and how best to combine group-specific multiculturalism policies with difference-blind common rights. It is in this sense, as Nathan Glazer put it recently, that 'we are all multiculturalists now' (Glazer 1997), even though we profoundly disagree over the merits of particular multiculturalism policies.

(b) Eroding Citizenship

Other commentators, however, still wish to make a more broad-ranging critique of minority rights and multiculturalism. Since it is no longer plausible to argue that all forms of multiculturalism are inherently unjust, critics have had to find another basis on which to condemn the very idea of minority rights. And the most common argument is one that focuses on stability

[30] Any plausible examination of this issue will show, I think, that affirmative action has worked well in some contexts, and less well in others. For an example of where it has been strikingly successful (the Army), see Moskos and Butler 1996.

rather than justice. Critics focus not on the justice or injustice of particular policies, but rather on the way that the general trend towards minority rights threatens to erode the sorts of civic virtues, identities and practices that sustain a healthy democracy.

This focus on civic virtue and political stability represents the opening of a second front in the 'multiculturalism wars'. Many critics claim that minority rights are misguided, not because they are unjust in themselves, but because they are corrosive of long-term political unity and social stability. Why are they seen as destabilizing? The underlying worry is that minority rights involve the 'politicization of ethnicity', and that any measures which heighten the salience of ethnicity in public life are divisive. Over time they create a spiral of competition, mistrust, and antagonism between ethnic groups. Policies that increase the salience of ethnic identities are said to act 'like a corrosive on metal, eating away at the ties of connectedness that bind us together as a nation'.[31]

This is a serious concern. As I discuss in Chapter 16, the health and stability of a democracy depends, not only on the justice of its basic institutions, but also on the qualities and attitudes of its citizens: e.g. their ability to tolerate and work together with others who are different from themselves; their desire to participate in the political process in order to promote the public good and hold political authorities accountable; their willingness to show self-restraint and exercise personal responsibility; and their sense of justice and commitment to a fair distribution of resources. There is growing fear that this sort of public-spiritedness may be in decline, and if group-based claims would further erode the sense of shared civic purpose and solidarity, then that would be a powerful reason not to adopt minority rights policies.

But is it true? There has been much armchair speculation on this question, but remarkably little evidence. Reliable evidence is needed here, because one could quite plausibly argue the reverse: namely, that it is the *absence* of minority rights which erodes the bonds of civic solidarity. After all, if we accept the two central claims made by defenders of minority rights—namely, that mainstream institutions are biased in favour of the majority, and that the effect of this bias is to harm important interests related to personal agency and identity—then we might expect minorities to feel excluded from 'difference-blind' mainstream institutions, and to feel alienated from, and distrustful of, the political process. We could predict, then, that recognizing minority rights would actually strengthen solidarity and promote political stability, by removing the barriers and exclusions which prevent minorities from wholeheartedly embracing political institutions. This hypothesis is surely at least as plausible as the contrary hypothesis that minority rights erode social unity.

---

[31] Ward 1991: 598.

We don't have the sort of systematic evidence needed to decisively confirm or refute these competing hypothesis. There is fragmentary evidence suggesting that minority rights often enhance, rather than erode, social unity. For example, the evidence from Canada and Australia—the two countries which first adopted official multiculturalism policies—strongly disputes the claim that immigrant multiculturalism promotes political apathy or instability, or the mutual hostility of ethnic groups. On the contrary, these two countries do a better job integrating immigrants into common civic and political institutions than any other country in the world. Moreover, both have witnessed dramatic reductions in the level of prejudice, and dramatic increases in the levels of interethnic friendships and intermarriage. There is no evidence that the pursuit of fairer terms of integration for immigrants has eroded democratic stability.[32]

The situation regarding the self-government claims of national minorities is more complicated, since these claims involve building separate institutions, and reinforcing a distinct national identity, and hence create the phenomenon of competing nationalisms within a single state. Learning how to manage this phenomenon is a profoundly difficult task for any state. However, even here there is significant evidence that recognizing self-government for national minorities assists, rather than threatens, political stability. Surveys of ethnic conflict around the world repeatedly confirm that 'early, generous devolution is far more likely to avert than to abet ethnic separatism'.[33] It is the refusal to grant autonomy to national minorities, or even worse, the decision to retract an already-existing autonomy (as in Kosovo), which leads to instability, not the recognizing of their minority rights.[34]

Much more work needs to be done concerning the impact of minority rights on social unity and political stability. This relationship will undoubtedly vary from case to case, and so requires fine-grained empirical investigation. It's not clear that philosophical speculation can contribute much here: we need to wait for more and better evidence.[35] But as with concerns about

---

[32] Kymlicka 1998a: ch. 2.   [33] Horowitz 1991: 224.

[34] Gurr 1993; Lapidoth 1996.

[35] Philosophers' claims about the relationship between minority rights and social unity are often doubly speculative: first we speculate about the sources of social unity (the 'ties that bind'), and then we speculate about how minority rights affect these ties. Neither sort of speculation is grounded in reliable evidence. For example, some political philosophers have suggested (a) that it is shared values which form the bonds of social unity in modern liberal states, and (b) that immigrant multiculturalism and/or multination federalism reduce the level of shared values. There is no good evidence for either of these speculations. I seriously doubt that minority rights have reduced shared values, but I equally doubt that it is shared values that hold societies together. (See Norman 1995). Other philosophers suggest that it is shared experiences, shared identities, shared history, shared projects or shared conversations that hold countries together. We have little evidence to support such claims about the source of social unity (and even less evidence about how minority rights affect these factors). We simply don't

justice, it is clear that concerns about citizenship cannot provide any grounds for rejecting minority rights *in general*: there is no reason to assume in advance that there is any inherent contradiction between minority rights and democratic stability.

6. Conclusion

I have tried to outline three stages in the ongoing philosophical debate about minority rights. The first stage viewed minority rights as a communitarian defence against the encroachment of liberalism. This has gradually given way to a more recent debate regarding the role of culture and identity within liberalism itself. In this second stage of the debate, the question is whether people's interests in their culture and identity are sufficient to justify departing from the norm of ethnocultural neutrality, by supplementing common individual rights with minority rights.

This second stage represents progress, I think, in that asks the right question, but it starts from the wrong baseline, since liberal democracies do not in fact abide by any norm of ethnocultural neutrality. And so the next stage of the debate, I propose, is to view minority rights, not as a deviation from ethnocultural neutrality, but as a response to majority nation-building. And I have suggested that this will affect the way we think of the demands of both national minorities and immigrant groups. In particular, it raises two important questions: 'What are permissible forms of nation-building', and 'What are fair terms of integration for immigrants?'

Looking back over the development of this debate, I am inclined to think that genuine progress has been made, although much remains to be done. It is progress, not in the sense of having come closer to resolving the disputes, but rather in the sense of getting clearer on the *questions*. The emerging debates about the role of language, culture, ethnicity, and nationality with liberal democracies are, I think, grappling in a fruitful way with the real issues facing ethnoculturally plural societies today. But getting clearer on the questions is no guarantee of getting clearer on the answers, and indeed I see no reason to expect that these debates will soon be resolved.

know what are the sources of social unity in multiethnic and multination states. To argue against minority rights on the grounds that they erode the bonds of social unity is therefore doubly conjectural.

2

Liberal Culturalism: An Emerging Consensus?

1. The Emerging Consensus

While the debate on multiculturalism and minority rights is relatively new, I think we can already detect an emerging consensus in the literature. First, there seems to be growing acceptance of the legitimacy of some or other form of *liberal nationalism*.[1] According to liberal nationalism, it is a legitimate function of the state to protect and promote the national cultures and languages of the nations within its borders. This can be done by creating public institutions which operate in these national languages; using national symbols in public life (e.g. flag, anthem, public holidays); and allowing self-government for national groups on issues that are crucial to the reproduction of their language and culture (e.g. schemes of federalism or consocialism to enable national minorities to exercise self-government).

These are familiar nationalist principles; what defines a *liberal* nationalism, however, is a set of constraints on these nationalist principles, such as:

• A liberal form of nationalism does not attempt to coercively impose a national identity on those who do not share it. Under a scheme of liberal nationalism, public institutions may be stamped with a particular national character (i.e. the institutions may adopt the language, holidays, and symbols of a particular national group). But individuals who do not belong to that national group are not prohibited from expressing and cherishing their own national identity. Individuals remain free to speak or publish in other languages, or to celebrate the holidays and symbols of other national groups. By contrast, illiberal forms of nationalism are likely to use coercion to promote a common national identity.
• Relatedly, whereas illiberal nationalisms often seek to prohibit forms of speech or political mobilization which challenge the privileging of a national

This chapter was written as an introductory paper to a Dutch–Israeli symposium on 'Nationalism, Multiculturalism and Liberal Democracy', published in *Ethical Theory and Moral Practice* vol. 1 (1998). The symposium contains articles by Yael Tamir, Albert Musschenga, Eerik Lagerspetz, Chaim Gans, Adrian Favell and Wibren van der Burg.

[1] For recent defences of liberal nationalism, see Tamir 1993; Margalit and Raz 1990; Miller 1995; Canovan 1996; Taylor 1992*a*, 1997; Walzer 1997; Spinner 1994.

identity, a liberal nationalism allows political activities aimed at giving public space a different national character. People are free to urge the adoption of a different official language, or even to seek the secession of a region to form a separate state. Advocating such changes is not necessarily seen as disloyalty, and even if it is seen as disloyal, this is not viewed as sufficient grounds for restricting democratic rights.

• Liberal nationalisms typically have a more open definition of the national community. Membership in the national group is not restricted to those of a particular race, ethnicity, or religion. Generally speaking, anyone can join the nation if they want to do so. In illiberal nationalisms, by contrast, non-nationals are often prevented from integrating into the national group even as they are prohibited from expressing their own national identity. Until recently, to be a 'true' Bulgarian, for example, one must have a Bulgarian surname, be descended from ethnic Bulgarians, belong to the Orthodox church, speak Bulgarian without an accent, and dress like a Bulgarian. Needless to say, it is very difficult for Turks living in Bulgaria ever to be accepted as members of the 'Bulgarian' nation, even if they wish to integrate.

• Partly as a result of this inclusiveness, liberal nations exhibit a much thinner conception of national identity. In order to make it possible for people from different ethnocultural backgrounds to become full and equal members of the nation, and in order to allow for the widest possible range of individual diversity and dissent, the terms of admission are relatively thin—e.g. learning the language, participating in common public institutions, and perhaps expressing a commitment to the long-term survival of the nation. Joining the nation does not require one to abandon one's surname, religion, customs, recreational practices, etc. This is reflected in the naturalization requirements adopted by most liberal states, which emphasize acquiring the language, learning something about the nation's history and institutions, and expressing allegiance to the long-term survival of the nation, but do not require adopting a particular religion or conception of the good life.[2]

• Liberal nationalism is non-aggressive, and does not seek to dismantle the self-governing institutions of other national groups within the same state or in other states. Liberal nationalism is therefore willing to accord public recognition to, and share public space with, those national minorities within a state which consistently and democratically insist upon their national distinctiveness. In particular, territorially-concentrated groups which were involuntar-

---

[2]   Insofar as liberal nation-building involves diffusing a common national culture throughout the territory of the state, it is a thin form of culture—what I have called a 'societal culture', centred on a shared language which is used in a wide range of societal institutions (schools, media, law, economy, government, etc.), rather than on common religious beliefs, family customs, or personal lifestyles (see Ch. 1). In non-liberal states, by contrast, acquiring a national identity typically requires a much thicker form of cultural integration, involving not only a common language and public institutions, but also elements of religion, ritual, and lifestyle.

ily incorporated into the state are not forced to adopt the majority's national identity. If groups like the Québécois, Catalans, Flemish, or Scots see themselves as distinct nations within the larger state, then their national distinctiveness will be recognized in public life and public symbols, through such things as official language status, self-government rights, and recognition of their distinct legal traditions. In accepting the legitimacy of these minority nationalisms, liberal nationalists reject the goal of a world of homogeneous nation-states, and accept the necessity and legitimacy of 'multination' states within which two or more self-governing nations are able to co-exist.

This is just a thumbnail sketch of liberal nationalism, and how it differs from illiberal forms of nationalism.[3] Theories of liberal nationalism provide us with a set of guidelines for how liberal democracies should accommodate those groups which see themselves as 'nations', and which seek rights of national recognition and self-government.

But in addition to these nations, there are also many types of non-national cultural groups which seek recognition and accommodation, such as immigrant and refugee groups, religious minorities, or even non-ethnic cultural groups like gays or the disabled. This leads us to the second area of possible convergence in the recent literature—namely, on ideas of *liberal multiculturalism*.[4] Liberal multiculturalism accepts that such groups have a valid claim, not only to tolerance and non-discrimination, but also to explicit accommodation, recognition, and representation within the institutions of the larger society. Multiculturalism may take the form of revising the education curriculum to include the history and culture of minority groups; creating advisory boards to consult with the members of minority groups; recognizing the holy days of minority religious groups; teaching police officers, social workers, and health-care professionals to be sensitive to cultural differences in

---

[3] Some commentators have attempted to summarize the differences between liberal and illiberal nationalism under the labels of 'civic' versus 'ethnic' nationalism (e.g. Ignatieff 1993). Civic nationalism, on this standard view, defines national membership purely in terms of adherence to democratic principles; whereas ethnic nationalism defines national membership in terms of a common language, culture, and ethnic descent. But this is potentially misleading. Even in the most liberal of democracies, nation-building goes beyond the diffusion of political principles. It also involves the diffusion of a common language and national culture. What distinguishes liberal nation-building from illiberal nationalism is not the absence of any concern with language, culture, and national identity, but rather the content, scope, and inclusiveness of this national culture, and the modes of incorporation into it. Moreover, there is not one distinction between liberal and illiberal nationalisms, but several. And each of these distinctions is a matter of degree. We cannot, therefore, divide real-world nationalist movements into two categories: 'liberal' and 'illiberal'. Rather, nationalist movements will turn out to be more liberal on some scales, and less liberal on others. For further discussion, see Kymlicka 1998*b*, and Ch. 12.

[4] For defenders of liberal multiculturalism, see Spinner 1994; Taylor 1992*a*; Baubock 1994; Raz 1994; Phillips 1995; Young 1990.

their work; developing regulations to ensure that minority groups are not ignored or stereotyped in the media; and so on.

Here again, we can specify a number of constraints that must be respected on a distinctly liberal conception of multiculturalism: membership of these groups must not be imposed by the state, but rather be a matter of self-identity; individual members must be free to question and reject any inherited or previously adopted identity, if they so choose, and have an effective right of exit from any identity group; these groups must not violate the basic civil or political rights of their members; and multicultural accommodations must seek to reduce inequalities in power between groups, rather than allowing one group to exercise dominance over other groups.

We can describe both liberal nationalism and liberal multiculturalism as forms of 'liberal culturalism'. Liberal culturalism is the view that liberal-democratic states should not only uphold the familiar set of common civil and political rights of citizenship which are protected in all liberal democracies; they must also adopt various group-specific rights or policies which are intended to recognize and accommodate the distinctive identities and needs of ethnocultural groups. Such policies range from multicultural education policies to language rights to guarantees of political representation to constitutional protections of treaties with indigenous peoples. For liberal culturalists, these various forms of group-specific measures are often required for ethnocultural justice, although to be consistent with liberal culturalism they must meet a number of conditions, like those listed above.[5] In particular, liberal culturalists support policies which make it possible for members of ethnic and national groups to express and promote their culture and identity, but reject any policies which impose a *duty* on people to do so.

Liberal culturalism has arguably become the dominant position in the literature today, and most debates are about how to develop and refine the liberal culturalist position, rather than whether to accept it in the first place.

2. What are the Alternatives to Liberal Culturalism?

How has this consensus been achieved so quickly, given that the claims being defended by liberal culturalists were ignored or decried by most liberals until very recently? One possible explanation is that the arguments provided by liberal culturalists have been so compelling and convincing that they have

---

[5] I summarize these constraints in the twin idea of 'freedom within groups' and 'equality between groups'. This requires accepting some forms of 'external protections' that reduce the vulnerability of minority groups to majority economic and political power, while rejecting 'internal restrictions' that involve attempts by groups to restrict the basic civil and political liberties of their own members. See Ch. 1.

persuaded everyone. As a defender of liberal culturalism, I wish this were true. But a more plausible explanation, I think, is that there is no clear alternative position. Liberal culturalism has won by default, as it were.

Of course, one can imagine alternatives to liberal culturalism, even if they have not yet been well developed in the literature. Two broad options come immediately to mind. One alternative would be to try to show that the earlier model of a unitary republican citizenship, in which all citizens share the identical set of common citizenship rights, can be updated to deal with issues of ethnocultural diversity, even though it was originally developed in the context of much more homogeneous political communities. One could argue that the interests we share in common are much more important than the identities that divide us, and that liberal culturalism is therefore distracting us from our more important common interests as fellow human beings. Moreover, one could argue that too great an emphasis on diversity threatens to undermine the very capacity for democratic deliberation about the common good.[6]

This position, however, faces the problem that its traditional pretensions to ethnocultural neutrality can no longer be sustained. Republicans used to argue that a regime of common citizenship rights was neutral amongst ethnocultural groups. By avoiding group-specific rights, the state treated ethnocultural identities as a matter of individual choice in the private realm, neither hindering nor helping any particular ethnocultural group.

However, this claim to neutrality has been effectively demolished by recent writers.[7] What appears on the surface to be a neutral system of common rights turns out, on inspection, to be a system that is heavily weighted in favour of the majority group. It is the majority's language that is used in public institutions; the majority's holidays that are recognized in the public calendar; the majority's history that is taught in schools; and so on. Moreover, these examples of the privileging of the majority's language and culture cannot be seen as minor or accidental deviations from the ideal of ethnocultural neutrality; they help define the very structure of the liberal state, which in turn shapes the structure of the larger society. Once the pretence of neutrality has been removed, the republican commitment to unitary citizenship becomes problematic. It avoids, rather than squarely addresses, the sorts of issues of ethnocultural justice which liberal culturalism seeks to address.

Republican concerns about protecting the possibility of civil dialogue and common public reason are valid, and so one area of recent work by liberal culturalists has focused on how to reconcile deliberative democracy and group-differentiated citizenship.[8] Whether republican concerns about civic

---

[6] This is arguably the position of van Gunsteren 1998; cf. Ward 1991.
[7] For critiques of this neutrality claim, see Tamir 1993; Spinner 1994.
[8] See e.g. M. Williams 1998; Phillips 1995; Young 1996; Spinner 1994. See also Ch. 16.

virtue can be fully accommodated within liberal culturalism remains to be seen. However, claims by neo-republicans that the unitary conception of citizenship can deal with issues of language, culture, and identity in a way that is fair to all ethnocultural groups remain little more than promissory notes.

A second alternative would be a more radical kind of pluralization of citizenship; one which rejects not only the republican commitment to a unitary citizenship, but also the liberal insistence that group-specific rights be constrained by liberal principles of individual freedom, social equality and political democracy. This sort of position draws on a variety of authors (William Connolly, Jacques Derrida, Julia Kristeva, Judith Butler, etc.), and can be given a variety of labels: postliberal, postmodernist, postcolonial. What all of these versions of a politics of difference share is that they do not seek to contain differences within the constraints of liberal justice. After all, they argue, liberal justice is itself just one amongst many cultural norms, none of which should be privileged, all of which must be politicized and contested in a multicultural society.[9]

One difficulty with this approach is that it operates at a more abstract or metatheoretical level than liberal culturalism, and so finding the exact points of debate is not always easy. It is sound advice that theorists in a multicultural society should not take 'our' liberal norms for granted, and should instead be willing to consider the objections and alternatives raised by non-liberal groups. But to say that we should consider such objections and alternatives is not yet to say that we should accept them. We should not exempt liberal culturalism from contestation, but nor should we rule out the possibility that it will emerge from the contest as the most promising approach to issues of ethnocultural justice. In any event, I do not think that postmodernists have provided any compelling reasons for ruling this out.

Indeed, insofar as the postmodernist approach attempts to offer a positive account of ethnocultural justice, it is not clear how it differs from liberal culturalism.[10] Postmodernists are often motivated by (a) a desire to avoid essentializing identities; (b) a desire to avoid Eurocentric cultural imperialism. How does this differ (except in rhetoric) from the liberal constraints I discussed above: i.e. (a) that individuals be free to question and reject ascribed identities; (b) that group-specific policies should aim to promote equality/ non-dominance between groups? How would the postmodernist concern with essentialism and ethnocentrism lead to a different theory of language rights, say, than the liberal culturalist approach? So far as I can tell, the postmodernist approach has simply not been developed in sufficient detail to

---

[9] For classic statements, see Connolly 1991, 1995.

[10] There is a long-standing dispute about whether postmodernists can endorse any substantive norms of justice without engaging in a 'performative contradiction'—i.e. without violating their own metatheoretical critiques of 'reason' and 'truth'. However, I will set that issue aside.

determine whether and how it differs on concrete issues from liberal culturalism.

So neither unitary republicanism nor postmodernism provide a clear alternative to liberal culturalism.[11] As a result, the liberal culturalist approach has become dominant by default. The old model of unitary citizenship has been exposed as a fraud; and the postmodern alternative is underdeveloped. This is arguably the greatest shortcoming in the debate. We need a broader range of approaches to issues of ethnocultural justice. It is impossible to evaluate properly the strengths and weaknesses of liberal culturalism until we have a clearer idea of what the alternatives are.

3. Unresolved Issues in Liberal Culturalism

While most authors in the literature are working within the broad camp of liberal culturalism, this doesn't mean that they are satisfied with the existing theories of liberal nationalism or of liberal multiculturalism. On the contrary, many questions have been raised about these theories. These questions can be organized under two broad headings: methodological and normative.

(a) Methodological Questions

Theories of liberal culturalism are often praised for having recognized and tackled issues of real-world importance which had previously been neglected. But they are also criticized for having misconceived the appropriate relationship between theory and practice.

For example, it has often been said that:

• Existing theories have been developed on a biased or selective sample of cases, and then wrongly generalized to all Western democracies. The worry here is not just that there may be complicating factors present in some countries (e.g. historical tensions between groups) which make it difficult to apply the theory, but also that the basic categories of liberal culturalism (e.g. 'multiculturalism', 'immigrants', 'minority rights') only make sense in some countries but not others.
• Existing theories neglect important developments in the study of ethnicity and culture by anthropologists, sociologists or political scientists. In particular, liberal culturalism underestimates the strategic uses of identity and group

---

[11] There are other possible approaches (e.g. religious fundamentalism; racialized forms of nationalism), but these are not likely to win many converts amongst Western political theorists.

membership; and overestimates the role of shared norms or beliefs in explaining the cohesion of cultural or political entities.

• Existing theories fail to adequately distinguish different levels of analysis. In particular, they fail to distinguish ideal theory (what an ideally just society would look like) from second-best prescription (what justice requires here and now) from empirical description (what are existing groups actually demanding). Or they conflate normative and explanatory statements. For example, the fact that certain group-specific rights may *in theory* be consistent with liberal-democratic values does not mean that the groups demanding these rights are *in practice* motivated by liberal-democratic values. Yet it is often difficult to determine which claim is being made by theorists of liberal culturalism. Are they defending the theoretical consistency of group-specific rights and liberal values, or offering a description and explanation of the motives of actual minority groups within liberal democracies?

• Existing theories lack the sort of institutional specificity that is needed to assess whether their proposals are attractive or even coherent. For example, what would it mean to ensure proportional representation of ethnocultural groups in the political process? How would we decide which groups are entitled to such guaranteed representation, and how would we decide who belongs to such groups? Without institutional specifics, it is difficult to evaluate principles of group representation.[12]

I think that these are all valid criticisms of at least some of the major writings on liberal culturalism (including my own). Yet it is unclear what exactly follows from them. After all, similar critiques could be made about virtually all of contemporary political philosophy, whether liberal, communitarian, republican, or postmodernist. These are the hazards of the profession, rather than the infirmities of any particular author or approach. It's not clear that these flaws are any worse in liberal culturalism than in other approaches, or that the central claims of liberal culturalism rest crucially on these flaws.[13]

In any event, it is worth recalling that this is still a relatively new field, and one has to expect a certain lack of sophistication at the early stages of any debate. Indeed it is impressive how much progress has been made in a relatively short period of time in correcting some of these methodological flaws. Theorists of liberal culturalism today are examining a much broader range of groups and countries, developing a broader range of arguments and principles, drawing on the expertise of a wider range of disciplines, and working

---

[12] These criticisms are discussed in Favell 1999.

[13] Indeed, I would argue that the traditional liberal hostility to group-specific rights rests on a series of selective cases and over-generalizations. For example, models of state–church relations have been wrongly generalized to other areas of ethnocultural diversity; and objections to segregated institutions for African-Americans have been wrongly generalized to all forms of 'separate but equal' treatment for ethnic groups.

at a much greater level of institutional specificity, than was evident just five or ten years ago.[14]

Moreover, my own reading is that the increasing methodological sophistication of the debate has tended to strengthen, not weaken, the central claims of liberal culturalism. The more cases we study, the stronger is the claim that ethnocultural justice cannot be secured by a regime of common rights.

(b) Normative Questions

Theories of liberal culturalism cover an enormous range of policy issues, from language rights to group representation to immigration policy to multicultural education. It would take a book to try to describe all of the proposals that liberal culturalists have made on these issues, or to evaluate all of the arguments that have been advanced for or against these proposals.

I would like, however, to mention a few more general questions which have been raised about the moral foundations of liberal culturalism. I noted earlier that liberal culturalism, in its more general formulation, is the view that liberal-democratic states should not only uphold the familiar set of common civil and political rights of citizenship, but should also adopt various group-specific rights or policies which are intended to recognize and accommodate the distinctive identities and needs of ethnocultural groups.

But why is it so important to recognize and accommodate ethnocultural identities and practices? Why does it matter whether society is multiculturalist? Why should we view membership in ethnocultural groups, or the potential loss of diverse cultures, as a matter of political importance, rather than simply private lifestyle choices? We can identify at least three distinct arguments within the liberal culturalist camp:

• Some theorists emphasize the importance of respect for *identity*. On this view, there is a deep human need to have one's identity recognized and respected by others. To have one's identity ignored or misrecognized by society is a profound harm to one's sense of self-respect. Minority rights satisfy the need for recognition.
• Some theorists provide a more instrumental argument for cultural rights, emphasizing the role that cultural membership plays in promoting individual *freedom* or autonomy. On this view, one's culture determines the boundaries of the imaginable, so that if the options available in one's culture diminish, so too does one's autonomy. Minority rights protect these cultural contexts of choice.

---

[14] To take one example, compare the discussions of group representation in Phillips 1995 and M. Williams 1998 to those in Young 1990 or Van Dyke 1977. I think any impartial reader would agree that enormous progress has been made in comprehensiveness, interdisciplinarity, and in institutional specificity.

• Finally, some people emphasize the intrinsic value of the *diverse cultures* present in a society. Different cultures are seen as the repository of unique forms of human creativity and accomplishment, and to let cultures die out is to lose something of intrinsic value. Minority rights preserve these intrinsically valuable cultures.

For example, in other papers presented at the Dutch–Israeli symposium, Yael Tamir discusses and defends the centrality of the identity argument in Isaiah Berlin's work; Eerik Lagerspetz relies heavily on the instrumental argument in his defence of language rights while avoiding reliance on the identity argument; Chaim Gans argues that the identity and freedom arguments are mutually interconnected, but need supplementing by other arguments; Albert Musschenga explores the intrinsic value argument, but concludes that it must be subordinate to the freedom and identity arguments; and Wibren van der Burg examines the identity argument, but concludes that it works better for some cases of recognition than for others.[15]

In short, while all these authors are working within a broadly liberal culturalist framework, there is no consensus amongst them concerning the normative foundations of this position. There is no agreement on the relative merits of these three justifications for liberal culturalism, or on what we should do when these justifications lead in different policy directions. Several other recent papers have also explored these disputes about the moral grounding of liberal culturalism.[16]

It is safe to say that liberal culturalism has struck an intuitive chord with many people. And this, combined with the lack of any well-developed alternatives, helps to explain why it has so quickly become the consensus position in the literature. But much work remains to be done in developing these intuitions into methodologically sophisticated and philosophically satisfying theories.

---

[15] These papers are now published in *Ethical Theory and Moral Practice*, 1/2 (1998).

[16] For other discussions of the moral foundations of liberal culturalism, attempting to identify and evaluate the sorts of interests people have in their language, culture, and national identity, see Waldron 1995; Margalit and Halbertal 1994; Tomasi 1995; Réaume 1995.

3

Do We Need a Liberal Theory of Minority Rights? Reply to Carens, Young, Pareth, and Forst

The theory of minority rights developed in my *Multicultural Citizenship* has been criticized from many directions. Some argue that it is insufficiently liberal, and too willing to compromise universal liberal principles to accommodate particularalistic and often non-liberal sentiments, identities and aspirations. Others argue, however, that it is too tied to universal liberal values, and insufficiently sensitive to contextual factors and to cultural differences. The commentators I am responding to in this chapter—Joseph Carens, Iris Young, Bhikhu Parekh, and Rainer Forst—all fall primarily into the latter category. My aim, therefore, is not to defend the need for minority rights (which these critics accept) but rather to explain how and why I have situated these rights within a liberal framework. I would like to begin by thanking my commentators for their thoughtful and fair comments on my work. They have interpreted my work fairly, understood the basic terms and arguments of my approach, and raised several important and difficult questions about it.

I am not sure how best to respond to their questions. The commentators have raised genuine problems. My approach requires us to make some hard choices, to try as best we can to draw clear lines in muddy waters, and sometimes to tolerate situations which we find objectionable while refusing requests with which we have some sympathy. The only way to defend my approach, therefore, is not to pretend that it gives everyone everything they want, but rather to show that alternative approaches have even greater costs in terms of our moral ideals.

To show this, however, would require comparing my approach to others across a range of issues, noting their respective strengths and weaknesses, and then deciding which is the most promising overall. This is an impossible task, not just because it would take an entire book to do, but more importantly, because we don't have enough alternatives on the table.

This chapter was originally prepared as a response to commentaries on my *Multicultural Citizenship* book from Joseph Carens, Iris Marion Young, and Bhikhu Parekh at an 'Author Meets Critics' panel during the 1996 American Political Science Association meeting in Chicago. The commentaries and reply were published, together with another commentary from Rainer Forst, in a symposium in *Constellations* 4/1 (1997).

Insofar as liberal theorists have discussed the status of ethnocultural groups, they have typically advanced a generalized principle of 'non-discrimination' as the key to justice in ethnocultural relations. They have assumed that the best approach is to adopt the same sort of strategy for ethnocultural groups which the liberal state has adopted towards religious groups. Ethnocultural groups, like religious groups, should be protected from discrimination, but the maintenance and reproduction of these groups should be left to the free choices of individuals in the private sphere, neither helped nor hindered by the state. Insofar as there is a well-established alternative approach to mine, this is it.

I argue that this orthodox liberal view is not only unfair to certain ethnocultural groups, but is in fact incoherent. The state cannot help but take an active role in the reproduction of cultures, for the reasons summarized in Carens' paper. And all of my commentators, it seems to me, agree with me on this point. My approach is not the only alternative to this orthodox liberal view, but as of yet, there are few well-developed alternatives available in the literature.[1] It is simply too early in the debate, therefore, to judge whether the objections raised by my commentators are fatal to my approach. They may turn out to be the sorts of hard choices and trade-offs which will accompany any worked-out theory, and which in fact are minimized by my approach. We need to get more theories on the table before we can judge the power of these objections. If nothing else, I hope that my book will encourage others to develop such alternative theories.

In the meantime, let me try at least to blunt the force of some of these objections. I will start by briefly restating the main motivation and methodology of the book, and then picking up a couple of the major points that are raised by the commentaries. My starting point, as Carens rightly notes, is the actual practices of liberal democracies towards ethnocultural groups. If we examine these practices, we will find that in virtually all liberal democracies, a sharp distinction is drawn between (legal/naturalized) immigrants[2] and national minorities.

---

[1] One important attempt to develop such a systematic account is Spinner 1994. However, I think his account is largely complementary to mine, in that it relies on some of the same basic distinctions (e.g. between immigrant ethnic groups and incorporated national minorities), and on some of the same interpretations of liberal principles (e.g. the role of autonomy). Other theorists have sketched some concepts or principles which they think should govern liberal approaches to ethnocultural demands (eg. Raz, Taylor, Habermas). But these are more outlines than systematic theories. It is impossible (for me at least) to tell what their abstract concepts imply for specific debates about the particular claims of particular groups

[2] I say 'legal and naturalized' to emphasize that I am talking about immigrants who enter the country legally with the right to become citizens, and indeed who are expected by the receiving government to take out citizenship. These sorts of immigrants are very different from illegal immigrants or guest-workers who are not expected to naturalize, and indeed have no right to do so, and who may not even have a right to work or to permanent residence. I discuss this below. In the rest of the chapter, I use the term 'immigrants' to refer to legally admitted immigrants with the right to naturalize, unless otherwise specified.

Immigrants are expected to integrate into the mainstream society, and this expectation is backed up with the force of laws and public policies. For example, immigrants must learn the dominant language of their new country, and the basic facts about its history and political institutions, to gain citizenship. Similarly, their children are legally required to learn the dominant language in school, and access to many government jobs, contracts, services and programs depends on fluency in the dominant language. They are encouraged, even pressured, into viewing their life-chances as bound up with participation in common educational, economic, political, and legal institutions which operate in the dominant language.

This sort of linguistic and institutional integration does not require complete cultural assimilation, and immigrants in many Western democracies are allowed and indeed encouraged to maintain some of their ethnocultural practices and identities. And they are increasingly given various rights and exemptions—what I called 'polyethnic' rights, but which might better be called 'accommodation rights'[3]—to enable the maintenance of these practices even as they integrate into common institutions.

National minorities are viewed in a different light in most Western democracies. They used to be subject to the same sort of pressure to accept linguistic and institutional integration as immigrants, particularly in the eighteenth and nineteenth centuries. But over the course of this century, a new pattern has emerged. Rather than pursuing integration, states have accorded national minorities various self-government powers, which enable them to live and work in their own educational, economic, and political institutions, operating in their own language.

This differential treatment of immigrants and national minorities is a striking fact about liberal democracies in this century. It is a well-established feature of liberal democracies, and one that is surprisingly uncontroversial in most countries. Yet it is undertheorized in normative liberal theory. It is difficult to think of a single major liberal theorist who has discussed this differential treatment, whether to defend it or to criticize it.

This is the starting-point of my investigation. We have here a long-standing feature of liberal democracies, but one that is more or less totally neglected in liberal political theory. The motivation for my book is to see whether we can close this gap between practice and theory—to see if we can

---

[3] I agree with Carens that the term 'polyethnic' rights is potentially biased (Carens, 1997: 37). Carens himself prefers the term 'recognition' rights. But that term too might have misleading implications. As Nancy Fraser has shown, much of the talk of the 'politics of recognition' has exaggerated the degree to which recognition is desired for its own sake, and neglected the extent to which 'recognition' really involves underlying issues of the redistribution of power and resources. I think that the term 'accommodation rights' helps emphasize that we are not just discussing a symbolic desire for recognition, but also substantive changes in the way institutions operate, so as to better meet the needs of a particular group. See Fraser 1995.

find an adequate justification within liberal theory for this differential treatment.

Some people believe that the historical treatment of ethnocultural groups—insofar as it diverges from the non-discrimination approach—simply reflects ethnocentric prejudice, and cannot be justified by liberal principles. The differential status of ethnocultural groups, on this view, simply reflects the nature or degree of majority prejudice against them. Others believe that the historical treatment of ethnocultural groups simply reflects power politics. If some ethnocultural groups have rights which other groups do not, it is simply because they have had more political power.

But neither of these explanations makes sense of the actual practices of liberal democracies. To be sure, the history of all liberal democracies has been scarred by ethnocentric prejudices, but this doesn't explain why immigrants and national minorities are treated differently. Majority cultures have typically been equally contemptuous of the ethnocultural identity and practices of homeland minorities and of immigrant groups—both have been seen as inferior to the superior culture of the dominant group. So why then have immigrants been pressured to integrate, while national minorities are viewed as separate and apart? Nor does power politics explain this differential treatment. After all, many immigrant groups have become extremely powerful, both economically and politically, while some national minorities have been effectively marginalized.

The reality, it seems to me, is that this differential treatment reflects different aspirations, and a different sense of legitimate expectations. Immigrants and national minorities have different beliefs about what is desirable, and about what they are rightfully entitled to, and some degree of differential treatment is widely accepted by both groups. This differential treatment has also come to be seen by the dominant group as acceptable to the basic norms and institutions of a liberal democracy. The historical development of ethnocultural relations in liberal democracies does not just reflect prejudice or power politics, but also a process of mutual accommodation in which each group's sense of rightful expectations has played a role in redefining the interpretation of liberal democratic norms and institutions. As Donald Horowitz has emphasized, the resolution of ethnic conflicts depends not just on numbers or power, but on conceptions of legitimacy.[4] And as I noted above, the result of this process—the differential treatment of immigrants and national minorities—is in fact widely accepted in most liberal democracies.

So it is worth contemplating the possibility that the patterns of ethnocultural relations which have emerged within constitutional liberal democracies reflect

---

[4] Horowitz 1985: 202, 139; cf. Belanger and Pinard's claim that 'ethnic competition leads to ethnic conflict movements if and only if the competition is perceived as unfair' (1991: 448). For an example of how ethnic conflicts are resolved not just by power or numbers but by perceptions of legitimacy, including historic claims of autonomy and territory, see Karklins 1994: 133.

the slow but steady working out of liberal principles. I believe that liberal democracies have in fact learned important lessons over the years about how to treat ethnocultural groups in a way that is consistent with constitutional guarantees of freedom and equality. These lessons have not yet been recognized by liberal theorists, or integrated into their statements of liberal principles. But insofar as these patterns have been worked out over decades by legislators and jurists within liberal democracies, and have become widely accepted by influential commentators and everyday citizens, then they provide useful clues about what a liberal theory of minority rights should look like.

How can liberal principles of freedom and equality justify such differential treatment? My basic argument can be summarized this way: modern states invariably develop and consolidate what I call a 'societal culture'—that is, a set of institutions, covering both public and private life, with a common language, which has historically developed over time on a given territory, which provides people with a wide range of choices about how to lead their lives. The emergence of a societal culture—which requires the standardization and diffusion of a common language, and the creation and diffusion of common educational, political, and legal institutions—is a feature of modernization, but is also actively supported by the state. Indeed, the state is the leading force behind linguistic standardization and institutional integration.[5]

These societal cultures are profoundly important to liberalism, I argue, because liberal values of freedom and equality must be defined and understood in relation to such societal cultures. Liberalism rests on the value of individual autonomy—that is, the importance of allowing individuals to make free and informed choices about how to lead their lives—but what enables this sort of autonomy is the fact that our societal culture makes various options available to us. Freedom, in the first instance, is the ability to explore and revise the ways of life which are made available by our societal culture.

Similarly, liberalism rests on a commitment to equality of opportunity—that is, equal access to educational and economic opportunities, as well to law courts, government services, and democratic forums—but what makes this sort of equality possible is the diffusion of a common language and institutions throughout society. Equality is, in the first instance, a matter of equal opportunity to participate in these common institutions. To ensure freedom and equality for all citizens involves, inter alia, ensuring that they have equal membership in, and access to, the opportunities made available by the societal culture.

Membership in a societal culture, then, is necessary for liberal freedom and equality. Put another way, liberals often say that they aspire to create a society of free and equal persons, but what is the relevant 'society'? I argue

[5] See the account of nation-building in Ch. 1.

that if we explore liberal notions of freedom and equality, the relevant 'society' turns out to be a societal culture.[6]

This link between societal cultures and liberal values provides one of the yardsticks for assessing the claims of ethnocultural groups. We need to take seriously the importance of membership in societal cultures, and any proposal that makes it impossible for people to have freedom and equality within viable societal cultures is inconsistent with liberal aspirations.

This explains, I believe, why it is appropriate to encourage and even pressure immigrants to integrate into the existing societal culture. One might think that liberalism should allow or encourage immigrants to establish their own society—with their own institutions operating in their own language—rather than pressuring them to integrate into institutions which operate in the dominant language. But for a variety of reasons discussed in my book, such a policy is not appropriate or workable for groups formed by individual and familial migration, who lack the sort of territorial concentration or historical institutions needed to sustain a vibrant societal culture (Kymlicka 1995a: 95–101). Immigrant groups would just have a shadowy existence at the margins of society, denied both equality in the mainstream, and the means to develop and maintain a flourishing societal culture alongside the mainstream. They would therefore be disadvantaged economically, educationally, and politically, and unable to support the autonomy of their members. The same would happen if the government simply took a hands-off approach to the linguistic integration of immigrants—neither encouraging nor assisting in the acquisition of the dominant language by immigrants or their children. This would simply result in the long-term marginalization of immigrant groups.

Freedom and equality for immigrants, therefore, requires freedom and equality within mainstream institutions. And this, I argue, is a twofold process: first, it involves promoting linguistic and institutional integration, so that immigrant groups have equal opportunity in the basic educational, political and economic institutions of society; and second, it involves reforming those common institutions so as to accommodate the distinctive ethnocultural practices of immigrants, so that linguistic and institutional integration does not require denial of their ethnocultural identities (see Chapter 8).

The situation is different, however, with national minorities (groups who formed functioning societies on their historical homelands prior to being incorporated into a larger state). These groups already possessed a societal culture—i.e. a full range of institutions operating in their own language—when they were incorporated into the larger state, and they have fought to maintain these institutions. They have demanded the sorts of language rights

---

[6] See Kymlicka 1995a: 82–93, where I show that the discussions of freedom in writers like Mill, Rawls, Dworkin, and Raz all presuppose membership in societal cultures. For further development of these ideas, see Chs. 10 and 11.

and regional autonomy needed to sustain these institutions, and these demands have increasingly been accepted by liberal democratic states (see Chapter 5).

Why is this not a violation of liberal principles? After all, does this not involve denying national minorities an equal opportunity in the larger society? Should not freedom and equality for national minorities, as for immigrants, be defined relative to participation in common institutions operating in the dominant language?

Not necessarily. Insofar as national minorities form a distinct society, then they can provide a satisfactory context for the autonomy of their members. Indeed, their societal culture provides a more satisfactory context than they would have if they were required to integrate into the mainstream society, since it is the culture they are familiar with, and identify with.[7] The process of integrating into another society is difficult and costly, and it is unfair and unreasonable to expect national minorities to pay this price. The integration of immigrants is the result of a voluntary choice to emigrate, and is the only viable path to achieve equality and freedom. By contrast, to expect the members of national minorities to integrate into the institutions of the dominant culture is neither necessary nor fair. Freedom for the members of national minorities involves the ability to live and work in their own societal culture.

Of course, some national minorities—like some majority nations—are illiberal, and so restrict the choice of their members. Some people argue that at least in this case liberals should try to assimilate their members to the liberal majority culture, rather than accept demands for self-government. But I argue that even in this case, our aim should be not to assimilate the minority culture, but rather to liberalize it, so that it can become the sort of 'society of free and equal citizens' which liberalism aims at.

In short, the aim of a liberal theory of minority rights is to define fair terms of integration for immigrants, and to enable national minorities to maintain themselves as distinct societies. This is just a thumbnail sketch of my argument. But it immediately raises two obvious objections, both of which are pressed by my commentators. One objection—pressed most strongly by

---

[7] Forst suggests that in the end, my argument for the rights of national minorities 'it is not primarily culture as a "context of choice" that is most important but culture as a "context of identity"' (1997: 66). But I view these as interdependent considerations. I admit that my argument here was unclear, but what I meant to argue was that considerations of identity provide a way of concretizing our autonomy-based interest in culture. In principle, either the minority's own culture or the dominant culture could satisfy people's autonomy-interest in culture, but considerations of identity provide powerful reasons for tying people's autonomy-interest to their own culture. Identity does not displace autonomy as a defence of cultural rights, but rather provides a basis for specifying which culture will provide the context for autonomy. For a helpful discussion of how identity concretizes our autonomy-interest in culture (and vice versa), see Chaim Gans, 'Freedom and Identity in Liberal Nationalism' (unpublished paper, Faculty of Law Tel Aviv University, 1996).

Joseph Carens and Iris Young—concerns intermediate cases. My approach focuses on two paradigmatic cases—voluntary immigrants and involuntarily incorporated national minorities—whose histories, current characteristics and future aspirations are very different. But in reality, is there not a range of groups with varying levels of cultural retention and institutional completeness? Even if we accept the general idea of developing a theory of minority rights based on the sorts of liberal principles I invoke, is the world not too complex to make the sorts of distinctions I want to draw? As Young puts it, my theory is 'too categorical', and we should instead think of ethnocultural groups as a fluid 'continuum' (Young, 1997: 50).

The second objection—pressed by Bhikhu Parekh and Rainer Forst—is more fundamental, and questions the very normative basis of the theory. Why should we presuppose that *liberal* values provide a satisfactory basis for justice in ethnocultural relations? After all, isn't liberalism itself just a cultural artefact, the historical development of one group's culture? How is imposing liberalism—particularly a form of liberalism which privileges autonomy— any different than imposing Christianity?

Let me take these two questions in order. First, it is true and important that there are many cases of ethnocultural groups that do not fit into the two categories of legal/naturalized immigrants and national minorities. For example, there are guest-workers and illegal immigrants, who are denied the right to gain citizenship, and prevented from integrating into the mainstream society. And what about the Roma (gypsies), whose homeland is everywhere, and nowhere? These cases are numerous and important for contemporary European politics.

Or consider African-Americans, whose current status and aspirations have been shaped by an almost unimaginable history of forced uprooting, enslavement, cultural suppression and physical segregation. Their demands have little in common with those of either immigrants or national minorities. Or one could mention the case of ethnic Russians in the Baltics—former colonizers, accustomed to the privileges of power, who have now become vulnerable minorities, fearing revenge from the peoples they used to rule. These ethnic Russians are demanding the sorts of rights which are typically demanded by national minorities—not just to citizenship, but also to separate schools and local autonomy. For the larger society, however, they are more like illegal immigrants, who had no right to enter in the first place, and who, at best, have the right to gain citizenship only after proving their loyalty and willingness to integrate. These last two (diametrically opposed) cases— the former slaves and the former colonizers—are at the heart of ethnic conflict in the United States and the former Soviet republics.

My theory, as yet, says little about these groups. I emphasized this limitation in the book, and deliberately left open the question of how the theory can be extended or applied to these hard cases or grey areas. This may seem like a devastating limitation of my theory, but there are good reasons, I think, for focusing on the two categories of immigrants and national minorities.

First, despite the many exceptions I've just mentioned, the fact remains that immigrants and national minorities form the most common types of ethnocultural pluralism in Western democracies. Making headway on these cases would surely be important and worthwhile.

Second, and equally importantly, these intermediary cases are all the result of, and permeated by, injustice. If we look at the cases that Young invokes, they are all cases where some group has been deemed to fall outside the scope of liberal norms of freedom and equality. In some cases, the group is still seen as outside these norms (e.g. illegal immigrants, Roma). In other cases, the legacy of an earlier period of exclusion is so great that the group is in danger of permanent marginalization (e.g. African-Americans). None of these cases provide models of *successful* ethnocultural accommodations; none of them present models that we can see as just or fair.

My project, by contrast, is to show how certain patterns of ethnocultural relations can be seen as instantiating norms of freedom and equality. I believe that the patterns developed for (legal/naturalized) immigrants and national minorities in many Western democracies provide two different but valid conceptions of how a culturally diverse society can be a society of 'free and equal citizens'. To be sure, many of these groups have also been subject to historical discrimination, but in many cases this has not proved an insuperable barrier to the gradual evolution of more legitimate arrangements.

There is no way to see the current status of guest-workers, gypsies, or African-Americans as morally legitimate. On the contrary, these are the sorts of situations that are more the product of prejudice and power politics than the gradual and consensual working out of liberal principles. Of course, the fact that these exceptional cases contain serious injustices means that it is perhaps more urgent to think about them than about the situation of immigrants and national minorities. Even if liberal theory has not yet incorporated the lessons we've learned about immigrants and national minorities, at least liberal practice is working tolerably well. Why not focus our attention on the cases that are not working at all well?

Part of the reason is that I really don't know how to reform these relationships to make them more successful. Some of these are genuinely hard cases—the injustices go so deep, and the political obstacles to real reform are so great, that it is difficult not to be discouraged.[8] In fact, my worry is that this sense of discouragement is becoming endemic in many societies, and is being generalized to all cases of ethnocultural relations. Discouraged by our apparent inability to improve the situation of gypsies or illegal immigrants or

[8] See Waldron (1999) for a thoughtful exploration of the 'stain of injustice', and why it defeats attempts at 'morally clean' solutions to situations of grave historic wrongs.

African-Americans, people are coming to think that conflict and inequality inherently characterize all ethnocultural relations.

To fight this sense of defeatism, I think it is important to emphasize the real and important successes. My hope is that focusing on these more successful cases will give us the confidence to tackle the more difficult cases. Moreover, I believe and hope that my theory *indirectly* helps identify solutions for these difficult cases, if only by clarifying what is distinctive about these cases. What is common to all these cases, I believe, is the fact that the groups are caught in a bind in terms of their access to a societal culture. They are denied equal access to the mainstream society (unlike immigrants), but lack the rights and resources needed to develop or maintain their own viable societal culture alongside the majority's (unlike national minorities). They are stuck at the margins of the majority's societal culture, and this indeed is one of the most pernicious consequences of the history of injustice they have faced. This, I think, provides us with a more helpful diagnosis of the plight of many of these groups than other familiar accounts.

It also raises the question whether, despite their differences, it is possible that the best way to improve the situation of these groups is to encourage them to adopt the 'immigrant' or 'national minority' model. Obviously, this will not always be possible. For example, I do not think that either model will work for African-Americans, although both have been tried historically. Some entirely new model will have to be worked out in this case, for reasons I discuss in Chapter 9. But insofar as secure membership in a viable societal culture is a precondition for the sort of freedom and equality that liberalism aspires to, then the immigrant/national minority models are worth considering, even if this would require both the majority and minority to rethink their self-identities. For example, it is possible in some countries to guide illegal immigrants and guest-workers into a more traditional 'immigrant' model of societal integration, through an amnesty and naturalization program. Similarly, the Baltic countries hope that the ethnic Russians will come to think of themselves as 'immigrants', even though they had a very different self-conception when they moved to the Baltics. Neither guest-workers nor Russian settlers saw themselves as immigrants, nor were they admitted by the host society as future citizens, but if both sides can rethink their attitudes, the immigrant model might work to achieve a society of free and equal citizens.[9]

And for the same reason, it is important to ensure that any *new* migration into democratic countries should take the form of legal/naturalized immigration. My theory may not work for some groups which were admitted or forced into the country in the past under different rules (e.g. as guest-

---

[9] I discuss this case and others from Eastern Europe in Kymlicka 1998*b*; Kymlicka and Opalski 2001.

workers, or slaves, or indentured labourers, or colonists). But it helps explain why these past rules were in fact illegitimate, and helps identify what a permissible immigration policy is for the future. I think any theory of ethnocultural relations should be forward-looking in this sense. It should not just say how to treat existing groups, but also specify the rules under which new groups may enter the society. And to my mind, any mode of admission that does not allow newcomers to follow the legal/naturalized immigrant model will almost certainly be unjust. Other approaches may be needed to deal with existing groups admitted under old rules, but these approaches would not provide a legitimate basis for future immigration decisions.

In short, I have focused on these two cases because they are the most common, the most successful, and the most relevant for future-oriented decisions. Finally, there is a more realpolitik reason for emphasizing the sharp distinction between immigrants and national minorities, rather than viewing them as simply two poles on a fluid and amorphous continuum. One of the most common objections to granting minority rights is that it would lead us down a 'slippery slope', in which more and more groups will demand more and more rights, leading to the eventual disintegration of society. This slippery slope concern presupposes that ethnocultural groups do not fall into identifiable types, with specific and finite needs and aspirations, but rather are totally amorphous, capable of radical changes in their demands from day to day. This fear has had a doubly pernicious effect on debates about minority rights. On the one hand, it is widely believed that if some groups (i.e. national minorities) are granted rights of self-government, then all other groups will also turn their back on integration, and seek separatism. Rather than risk such fragmentation, it is better, people think, to reject the self-government demands of national minorities. On the other hand, it is widely believed that if some groups (i.e. immigrant groups) are willing to accept integration into society, then surely all other ethnocultural groups can also be encouraged (or forced) to follow this model. Hence the constant assumption that our problems would be solved if Blacks/Indians/Puerto Ricans/Québécois just learned to act like immigrants. I believe that progress on the rights of minorities will only come about if we effectively tackle this 'slippery slope' view. And to do so, we need to show that ethnocultural groups do not form a fluid continuum, in which each group has infinitely flexible needs and aspirations, but rather that there are deep and relatively stable differences between various kinds of ethnocultural groups. Contrary to Young, I think it is important to insist that these groups differ in kind, not just in degree (Young, 1997: 51).

The second major objection to my approach concerns its reliance on liberal principles. This reliance on liberalism sets limits on the sorts of rights that groups can claim, limits that many groups may not agree with. Since liberalism (as I understand it) is grounded on respect for individual autonomy, a liberal conception of minority right will insist that the members of ethnocultural groups have the right to question and revise traditional cultural practices. It will therefore deny the legitimacy of 'internal restrictions'—i.e. of claims by a group to limit the civil or political rights of its members in the name of preserving 'tradition' or 'cultural purity'.

As Parekh and Forst rightly note, not all ethnocultural groups share this conception of autonomy and culture. Some groups view their culture, not as providing a set of options from which individuals have a right to choose, but rather as embodying a sacred trust which members have a duty to maintain and uphold. Or they may simply value norms of authority and deference over autonomy and rational reflection. Mainstream Western societies may have exalted autonomy, but this is hardly a universal value. Is it not then incongruous to base a theory of multicultural citizenship on a value which is itself part of the heritage of just one cultural tradition? As Parekh puts it, this is 'a paradoxical and incoherent enterprise' (Parekh, 1997: 59).

There is a real issue here, but I think that many people exaggerate it, and misidentify it. First, it is simply untrue that most conflicts between ethnocultural groups in the West are over the legitimacy of liberal principles. On the contrary, most members of most groups accept liberal democratic norms, whether they are immigrants or national minorities. Consider minority nationalisms in Europe—e.g. the Catalans, Scots, or Flemish. There is no evidence that they differ from the majority in their basic political values. Or consider the groups for whom the first policies in the world that used the name of 'multiculturalism' were adopted—namely, immigrant groups in Canada and Australia in the 1970s. These groups were already well integrated into the political system, and fully subscribed to its basic liberal democratic orientation. The evidence from these countries—as from other countries where immigrants have a right to naturalize—is that within a remarkably short period of time, immigrants become virtually indistinguishable from native-born citizens in their level of commitment to democracy and individual rights. Or consider African-Americans, who are often considered the most important proponents of multiculturalism in the United States. Here again there is no significant difference in their commitment to democracy, the US Constitution and its Bill of Rights. Parekh's claim that minority groups in the West are 'generally' non-liberal seems to me to be demonstrably false (Parekh, 1997: 57).

Parekh implies that if ethnocultural groups share liberal values, then there would be no need for a theory of multiculturalism. But this is false. There is no evidence that the convergence on liberal values between majorities and minorities has diminished in any way the level or intensity of conflicts over the accommodation of ethnocultural differences. These groups may agree on liberal-democratic principles, but they disagree on the implications of these principles for concrete questions about the distribution of power between federal and regional governments, or about the legitimacy of affirmative action, or about naturalization rules, or about the designation of public holidays, or about the scope of minority language rights. Nor is it surprising that these disputes should arise, since theorists in the liberal tradition have had virtually nothing to say about these topics, and what little they have said is manifestly inadequate.[10] The overwhelming majority of the day-to-day disputes between ethnocultural groups in the West are of this variety, where both sides appeal to shared liberal democratic principles, but disagree over their interpretation and application.

Philosophers who address issues of multiculturalism face a professional hazard. As philosophers, we have a natural tendency to jump to the cases where there is a deep difference of principle, since these are the most philosophically interesting. Disputes about the division of power in a federal system, or about bilingual education, are not very interesting philosophically—they depend on a complicated mixture of murky facts about historical arrangements, current needs, and future aspirations, none of which can be deduced or understood by simply examining philosophical principles. By contrast, it is much more interesting and exciting if we can present multiculturalism as a 'clash of civilizations', in which the majority seeks to impose its Western liberal democratic traditions on minorities who resist in the name of some other world-historic culture with its distinctive political traditions. It is tempting for philosophers to present multiculturalism this way, but it is false. For better or worse, the heart of multiculturalism in the West is about how to interpret liberal democratic principles, not about whether those principles are legitimate.

Of course, there are some groups who really do challenge the legitimacy of liberal norms. There are, for example, the Hasidic Jews and the Amish in the United States. These groups are ritually invoked in philosophical discussions of multiculturalism, even though they are tiny, and have had no significant impact on real-world policies of multiculturalism (and indeed their claims were addressed long before, and independently of, any 'multiculturalism' policy).

Some people try to typecast Muslim immigrants as the modern-day equivalent of the turn-of-the-century Hasidic Jews—i.e. as a group which rejects the norms of liberal democracy, and so retreats into a self-contained world where these norms are rejected. But this is a fantasy. The overwhelming majority of Muslims in Western democracies want to participate in the larger

---

[10] We have inherited a set of assumptions about what liberal principles require, but these assumptions first emerged in 18th-cent. United States, or 19th-cent. England, where there was very little ethnocultural heterogeneity. Virtually all citizens shared the same language, ethnic descent, national identity, and Christian faith. It is increasingly clear that we cannot simply rely on the interpretation of liberalism developed in those earlier times and places. We need to judge for ourselves what liberalism requires under our own conditions of ethnocultural pluralism.

societal culture, and accept its constitutional principles. The majority of their demands are simply requests that their religious beliefs be given the same kind of accommodation that liberal democracies have historically given to Christian beliefs.[11]

Parekh is misled here, I think, because he exaggerates the extent to which my approach rejects or precludes the idea that cultures can have intrinsic value, or form a 'sacred trust' (Parekh, 1997: 59). There is nothing in my approach that prevents individuals from adopting such an attitude towards their culture. This is one of many attitudes towards one's culture that is fully permissible within a liberal society. What is true, of course, is that my theory does not rest upon such an attitude. It is the instrumental, not the intrinsic, value of culture that grounds claims for political powers and resources in my liberal theory. As a result, while individuals are free to adopt such an attitude for themselves, and to try to persuade others to do so, it doesn't allow the group to restrict the basic civil liberties of its members in the name of the 'sacredness' of a particular cultural tradition or practice. It is up to the individuals themselves to decide how sacred they view the particular traditions and practices of their culture.

To be sure, as Parekh says, this is just one way of conceiving the role of culture in political theory. There are political theories that would see the sacredness of culture, not just as a permissible attitude, but as an obligation the state should impose. But this could not be a liberal theory. If we accepted the idea that the state should view cultural practices are sacred, then liberalism would never have arisen. In every society where liberalism has emerged, it has emerged precisely by defeating the claims of cultural conservatives that existing practices and traditions are sacrosanct. And it is this liberal attitude that is now shared amongst virtually all ethnocultural groups in the West, whether racial, immigrant, or national minorities.

But let us assume that some particular group really is disputing these liberal principles. My commentators worry that I am, in a potentially ethnocentric way, imposing 'our' liberal values on other groups. But here too the objection is overstated. After all, I emphasized myself that liberals cannot simply presuppose that they are entitled to impose liberal norms on non-liberal groups. And I argued that any enduring solution will require dialogue (Kymlicka 1995a: 163–70).[12]

I am not sure, therefore, what the real dispute is between us. The main difference, it seems to me, is that I take it as profoundly important for such a dialogue that 'we'—the liberal majority—have a clear idea about what our own

---

[11] Insofar as the Muslim scarf affair in France can be seen as a conflict between liberalism and illiberalism, it was the French officials who were illiberal.

[12] Hence Forst is wrong when he says I argue 'that only "liberal" cultural groups can be tolerated by the larger liberal society' (Forst, 1997: 68). I explicitly reject this view, as he himself admits later in his paper (70).

liberal principles entail on questions of minority rights. We can't assume that we are entitled to impose our views on others, but it is essential that we accurately *identify* our views. This will then help us identify the real points of disagreement with other non-liberal groups in society, and thereby have a meaningful dialogue.

At the moment, by contrast, the public debate is seriously distorted because most liberals misapply their own principles. Liberals object to proposals that are not in fact objectionable from the point of view of liberal principles, and condone proposals that in fact perpetuate injustices that violate liberal principles. The majority then labels the minority as illiberal, and reinterprets the debate over multiculturalism as a debate over how to accommodate illiberal groups. The resulting 'dialogue' is generally pointless, if not actually counterproductive, since it is based on an initial misunderstanding. It preempts the search for shared understandings, and ignores the minority's powerful sense that the majority is applying its principles in an unfair and selective manner. It exaggerates the actual distance between the majority and minority, entrenches an 'us versus them' mentality, and replaces a real dialogue about the accommodation of conflicting needs and identities with a pseudo-dialogue about 'the clash of civilizations'.

As I noted earlier, one motivation for my book is my belief that liberal theorists have either ignored or misidentified the implications of their principles for issues of minority rights. So far as I can tell, none of my commentators disagree with this claim. Yet they seem to think that it is unnecessary—even inappropriate—for liberals to correct these mistakes and come up with a more accurate liberal theory of minority rights. They seem to think that the project of developing a liberal theory of minority rights is misguided. But how can it be inappropriate for liberals to clear up their own thinking about minority rights? How can this be harmful to a dialogue with other groups? How can it be preferable for liberals to enter such a dialogue with vast misconceptions about the gulf between the liberal majority and ethnocultural minorities? I really don't understand this objection.

Perhaps Parekh thinks that developing a coherent liberal theory of minority rights is only a first, and relatively easy and trivial, step in the process of resolving disputes between ethnocultural groups. All of the real action, he implies, comes in thinking about how then to negotiate conflicts between these liberal principles and the demands of nonliberal groups. But as I have already suggested, this is a serious mistake. Developing a coherent liberal theory is a not trivial step, since the overwhelming majority of real-world political disputes between ethnocultural groups in the West are precisely over the application of liberal principles. This is where the real action is. Moreover, this is not an easy step, since the liberal tradition has badly mishandled the issues, and it is by no means clear or self-evident what liberal principles entail.

To be sure, articulating such a theory will still leave us with difficult questions about how to accommodate non-liberal groups. I don't have all the answers to this question, just as I don't have all the answers to the question of how to deal fairly with exceptional cases. The commentators suggest that, since my theory is grounded in liberal values, I will be biased in favour of imposing liberal principles on non-liberal groups. I agree that this is a danger, and I tried to tackle it head-on in the book. I emphasized repeatedly that liberals cannot assume that they are entitled to impose their principles, and I gave some examples of why some illiberal groups should be tolerated, as well as some suggestions about the kinds of extreme circumstances where state intervention is justified (Kymlicka 1995a: 165–70). So far as I can tell, my commentators do not really dispute these suggestions, or offer any concrete alternative criteria. So the claim that my theory justifies the excessive imposition of liberal values seems, as yet, undefended.

In any event, this is a problem that any theory is going to face. There is no single conception of autonomy, or culture, or justice, or moral justification, which every group will accept. For example, I do not see that it would help to adopt Forst's proposal that we should abandon the liberal focus on personal autonomy for the Kantian focus on 'moral autonomy'. This is similar to Rawls's suggestion that we shift to a more 'political' conception of liberalism, and it is subject to the same problems, which I discuss in my book (Kymlicka 1995a: 158–63). Forst gives no evidence that people who reject the ideal of personal autonomy are likely to accept the ideal of moral autonomy, and there is every reason to think that they won't.[13] Moral autonomy is just as much (or as little) disputed in the West as personal autonomy, and for just the same reasons. To base a theory of multicultural citizenship on moral autonomy creates the same problem as a theory based on personal autonomy—i.e. it rests on a value which is part of the heritage of one cultural tradition, and which is now widely shared, but is not universally accepted. Are we entitled to impose 'our' conception of moral autonomy on other groups that reject it?

Forst tries to get around this by defining morality in terms of the giving of reasonable justifications to morally autonomous people. If we accept this definition or morality, which is adapted from Scanlon's theory of contractarian morality, then anyone who rejects moral autonomy is not just rejecting our conception of autonomy, but also rejecting morality tout court. So long as ethnocultural groups make moral claims on us, then we can legitimately

---

[13] Forst argues that people who reject personal autonomy 'could still accept' the norm of moral autonomy (68). Of course it is true that people could do so. Anything is possible. But the question is whether such people are *likely* to accept the norm of moral autonomy. Is there anything within their belief system that requires them to do so? It seems to me that Forst's argument here just reduces to the tautology that insofar as people accept moral autonomy, then they accept moral autonomy.

assume that they accept the value of moral autonomy, since moral autonomy is implicit in the very act of making moral claims. As Forst puts it, 'to deny this form of [moral] autonomy in a normative context is *by definition* unjustifiable' (1997: 70, my emphasis).

But of course this is just a stipulative definition of morality, which is widely disputed by many other cultures, and indeed by many people within our own culture. There are many other equally reasonable ways of defining morality. In fact, I myself think that Scanlon's contractualist definition of morality is clearly wrong. For one thing, it cannot make any sense of our moral obligations to beings incapable of moral autonomy, such as children, the demented or non-human animals. We can make recognizably moral claims by appealing to notions of equal consideration for individuals' interests, or to notions of Divine Will or natural law, without accepting that society should be organized around the promotion of moral autonomy.[14] To be sure, any conception of morality that does not emphasize respect for moral autonomy will be paternalistic—it will allow some people to define the rights and responsibilities of others. But many (most?) moral systems around the world are paternalistic in this way. Just because we in the West have rejected this sort of moral paternalism, we cannot assume that all ethnocultural groups have done so. Indeed, moral paternalism is likely to be rejected only by those groups who reject paternalism more generally—i.e. by those groups who share a belief in the value of personal autonomy. As I noted earlier, Forst gives no evidence that groups that reject personal autonomy are likely to adopt a definition of morality that privileges moral autonomy. If they accept paternalism generally, why would they not continue to accept a definition of morality that allows for moral paternalism?

So I do not see that there is any gain in shifting from personal autonomy to moral autonomy. But even if there is, it will not eliminate the question of intervening in groups that reject the underlying value. Even if fewer groups reject moral autonomy than reject personal autonomy, there will still be some groups that reject it. And so we will still face difficult issues about intervening in groups on the basis of a theory which the group itself rejects. Presumably Forst does not think that the state should coercively intervene in any group which disputes his conception of moral autonomy. Presumably this dispute too must be addressed peacefully, by dialogue, except under extreme circumstances. So Forst's approach redescribes the problem, but does not solve it—he is left with the same problem I face. And so far as I can tell, his answer to this question—about when to intervene—may be the same as mine.

This is not an objection to Forst's approach—and I look forward to seeing how he or others develop it. It is not an objection to his account of multiculturalism that some ethnocultural groups reject its underlying premiss of

---

[14] See Kymlicka 1990*b*.

moral autonomy. This will be true of any theory. But for just that reason, it is no objection to my theory that some groups reject it.

In short, I agree that a liberal theory of culture will contradict some other conceptions of the nature and role of culture, and so some groups will not accept its conception of minority rights. This will be true of any attempt to develop a theory of minority rights. It follows that no single theory can provide all the answers to all the questions which ethnocultural pluralism raises. But developing a more coherent and defensible theory is the first step towards resolving these questions. And in our society, developing a coherent *liberal* theory of minority rights is the first priority.[15]

---

[15] There are several other issues raised by the commentators raise which I wish I could respond to. In particular, let me pick up on one other point Both Young and Carens question whether we should continue to use the term 'nation' for the sorts of groups which I have called 'national minorities'. I agree that the term 'nation' has some unfortunate connotations, particularly in a world where it is seen as 'normal' that nations posses their own states. However, I do not believe that there is any viable alternative to the language of nationhood. This terminology serves many valuable functions for national minorities, and to attempt to discourage or deny this self-identity would be counter-productive. Or so I argue in Kymlicka 1998a: ch. 10.

PART II

Ethnocultural Justice

4

Human Rights and Ethnocultural Justice

1. Introduction

It is an honour for me to dedicate this chapter to the memory of John Rees, whose influential book on John Stuart Mill helped to clarify my understanding of liberalism and liberal democracy.[1] Liberal democracy rests on principles of freedom and equality, but as Rees noted, it is not easy to define these principles. He suggested, however, that these principles are perhaps best illustrated or reflected in the doctrine of human rights—i.e. the doctrine that each person has an intrinsic moral worth; that each person's interests must be taken into consideration by the state; and that each person should receive certain inviolable protections against mistreatment, abuse, and oppression.[2]

The articulation and diffusion of the doctrine of human rights is indeed one of the great achievements of post-war liberalism. This year represents the 50th anniversary of the Universal Declaration of Human Rights, and it is impressive how far we have come in those fifty years in ensuring the protection of human dignity and human rights. Yet amidst the anniversary celebrations there are an increasing number of sceptics and critics who attack the doctrine of human rights for neglecting the realities of ethnocultural diversity, and for being unable to deal with the conflicts which arise from this diversity, either within a society or between societies.

This is an issue that Rees did not foresee, and perhaps could not have foreseen. But it is an urgent issue for anyone who wishes to defend and promote the liberal project into the next century. But what exactly is the challenge which ethnocultural diversity raises for human rights? We can distinguish two separate challenges. The first is foundational. Some critics argue that the conception of human personhood and human needs underlying the doctrine of human rights is culturally biased. More specifically, it is 'Eurocentric', and exhibits a European commitment to individualism, whereas non-Western cultures have a more collectivist or communitarian conception of human identity. On this view, given the depth of cultural differences around the world, the very idea of developing a single set of universal human rights is

Presented as the Sixth Annual J. C. Rees Memorial Lecture at the University of Wales, Swansea, 23 February 1998.

[1] Rees 1985. [2] Rees 1971: p. x.

inherently ethnocentric, and involves imposing one culture's view of human personality and human identity on other cultures.

The second challenge is more modest. Some critics say that the idea of universal human rights is acceptable in principle, but that the current list of human rights is radically incomplete. In particular, it fails to protect minority cultures from various forms of injustice, and so needs to be supplemented with an additional set of what are sometimes called 'collective rights' (or 'group rights', 'minority rights', or 'cultural rights').

Most discussions of cultural diversity and human rights have focused on the first, foundational, challenge. In this chapter, however, I will focus on the second, since it is less explored. Many commentators tend to confuse and conflate the two challenges; they assume that any group which is demanding 'collective rights' must be doing so because they are 'collectivist' in their cultural outlook and attitudes, and so are, implicitly at least, raising the foundationalist challenge to the very idea of universal human rights. If we conflate the two debates in this way, it will seem that we need to revisit the foundationalist issue every time an ethnocultural group demands collective rights.

This tendency to conflate the two debates is, I think, profoundly unhelpful. It is a source not only of philosophical misunderstanding, but also of political confusion that has prevented liberals from understanding and effectively responding to ethnocultural conflicts around the world. So my aim in this Lecture is to discuss the second issue on its own terms. I will try to show why current conceptions of human rights leave serious issues of ethnocultural injustice unaddressed, and why these issues of injustice are not reducible or dependent on the foundationalist challenge to human rights. I hope to show that these claims of injustice are relevant and urgent even for those of us who reject the foundationalist critique of human rights. Indeed, I think that we will only be in a position to address effectively the foundationalist critique of human rights if we have first made sure that our conception of human rights deals satisfactorily with these issues of ethnocultural injustice.

The Lecture is divided into two main sections. In the first I discuss why human rights are insufficient for ethnocultural justice, and may even exacerbate certain injustices; and hence why human rights standards must be supplemented with various minority rights. In the second I ask whether, if human rights are supplemented with minority rights, we can expect to get greater agreement on the transnational application of human rights. I argue that we can indeed hope for greater agreement on the *principles* of human rights, but that there will still be difficult issues remaining about appropriate institutions for the *enforcement* of these rights. I conclude with some broader reflections on the relationship between cultural diversity and human rights.

2. Individual Rights and Group Rights

According to many commentators, human rights are paradigmatically individual rights, as befits the individualism of Western societies, whereas non-European societies are more interested in 'group' or 'collective' rights, as befits their communalist traditions.

I think this way of framing the debate is misleading. For one thing, individual rights have typically been defended within the Western tradition precisely on the grounds that they enable various group-oriented activities. Consider the paradigmatic liberal right—namely, freedom of religion—which Rawls argues is the origin and foundation for all other liberal rights. The point of endowing individuals with rights to freedom of conscience and freedom of worship is to enable religious groups to form and maintain themselves, and to recruit new members. And indeed according individuals rights to religious freedom has proven very successful in enabling a wide range of religious groups—including many non-Western religions—to survive and flourish in Western societies.

Based partly on this example of religious tolerance, many commentators have argued that individual rights provide a firm foundation for justice for all groups, including ethnocultural minorities. Indeed, this was explicitly the argument given after World War II for replacing the League of Nations' 'minorities protection' scheme—which accorded collective rights to specific groups—with the UN's regime of universal human rights. Rather than protecting vulnerable groups directly, through special rights for the members of designated groups, cultural minorities would be protected indirectly, by guaranteeing basic civil and political rights to all individuals regardless of group membership. Basic human rights such as freedom of speech, association, and conscience, while attributed to individuals, are typically exercised in community with others, and so provide protection for group life. Where these individual rights are firmly protected, liberals assumed, no further rights needed to be attributed to the members of specific ethnic or national minorities:

the general tendency of the postwar movements for the promotion of human rights has been to subsume the problem of national minorities under the broader problem of ensuring basic individual rights to all human beings, without reference to membership in ethnic groups. The leading assumption has been that members of national minorities do not need, are not entitled to, or cannot be granted rights of a special character. The doctrine of human rights has been put forward as a substitute for the concept of minority rights, with the strong implication that minorities whose members enjoy individual equality of treatment cannot legitimately demand facilities for the maintenance of their ethnic particularism.[3]

---

[3] Claude 1955: 211. For a restatement of the claim that respecting individual civil and political rights is sufficient for ethnocultural justice, see Donnelly 1990: 46.

Guided by this philosophy, the United Nations deleted all references to the rights of ethnic and national minorities in its Universal Declaration of Human Rights.

There is much truth in this claim that individual rights protect group life. Freedom of association, religion, speech, mobility, and political organization enable individuals to form and maintain the various groups and associations which constitute civil society, to adapt these groups to changing circumstances, and to promote their views and interests to the wider population. The protection afforded by these common rights of citizenship is sufficient for many of the legitimate forms of group diversity in society.

However, it is increasingly clear that the list of common individual rights guaranteed in Western democratic constitutions, or in the UN Declaration, is not sufficient to ensure ethnocultural justice,[4] particularly in states with national minorities. By national minorities, I mean groups that formed functioning societies, with their own institutions, culture, and language, concentrated in a particular territory, prior to being incorporated into a larger state. The incorporation of such national minorities is usually involuntary, as a result of colonization, conquest, or the ceding of territory from one imperial power to another, but may also occur voluntarily, through some treaty or other federative agreement. Examples of national minorities within Western democracies include the indigenous peoples, Puerto Ricans, and Québécois in North America, the Catalans and Basques in Spain, the Flemish in Belgium, the Sami in Norway, and so on. Most countries around the world contain such national minorities, and most of these national minorities were involuntarily incorporated into their current state—a testament to the role of imperialism and violence in the formation of the current system of 'nation-states'.

Very few national minorities are satisfied merely with respect for their individual human rights, and it is easy to see why. I will discuss three examples where individual rights do not adequately protect their interests: decisions

---

[4] There are now several attempts to define a theory of ethnocultural justice in the literature (e.g. Minow 1990a; Young 1990; Kymlicka 1995a). It would take a separate paper to explain or defend any particular one. But for the purposes of this paper we can use a minimalist definition of ethnocultural justice as the absence of relations of oppression and humiliation between different ethnocultural groups. A more robust conception of ethnocultural justice could be developed by asking what terms of coexistence would be freely consented to by the members of different ethnocultural groups in a Habermasian/Rawlsian setting where inequalities in bargaining power have been neutralized. For example, a Rawlsian approach to ethnocultural justice would ask what terms of coexistence would be agreed to by people behind a 'veil of ignorance', who didn't know whether they were going to be born into a majority or minority ethnocultural group. Such a Rawlsian approach is likely to produce a more demanding conception of ethnocultural justice than the mere absence of oppression and humiliation, but the main claim of this paper is that human rights are insufficient even to ensure this minimal component of ethnocultural justice.

about internal migration/settlement policies, decisions about the boundaries and powers of internal political units, and decisions about official languages.

In each of these examples, and throughout the chapter, I will be using the term 'human rights' in an imprecise way. I am not referring to any particular canonical statement or declaration of international human rights, but rather to the constellation of individual civil and political rights which are formulated in Western democratic constitutions, and which many advocates of human rights would like to see entrenched and enforced as transnational standards of human rights. Some of these rights are included in the original Declaration, others in subsequent conventions (e.g. the 1966 Covenant on Civil and Political Rights), others are still being debated. In short, I am referring more to a particular public and political discourse of 'human rights', than to the actual list of human rights in any particular document.

(a) Internal Migration/Settlement Policies

National governments have often encouraged people from one part of the country (or new immigrants) to move into the historical territory of the national minority. Such large-scale settlement policies are often deliberately used as a weapon against the national minority, both to break open access to their territory's natural resources, and to disempower them politically, by turning them into a minority even within their own traditional territory.[5]

This process is occurring around the world, in Bangladesh, Israel, Tibet, Indonesia, Brazil, etc.[6] It has also happened in North America. The nineteenth-century Canadian Prime Minister, Sir John A. MacDonald, said of the Métis that 'these impulsive half-breeds . . . must be kept down by a strong hand until they are swamped by the influx of settlers'.[7] And the same process occurred in the American South-West, where immigration was used to disempower the indigenous peoples and Chicano populations who were living on that territory when it was incorporated into the United States in 1848.

This is not only a source of grave injustice, but is also the most common source of violent conflict in the world. Indigenous peoples and other homeland minorities typically resist such massive settlement policies, even with force, if necessary.[8] One would hope, therefore, that human rights doctrines would provide us with the tools to challenge such policies.

Unfortunately, there is nothing in human rights doctrine that precludes such settlement policies (so long as individual members of the minority are not deprived of their civil and political rights). Other elements of international law might be of some help in exceptional circumstances. For

---

[5] See McGarry 1998.   [6] See Penz 1992, 1993. I discuss these cases in Ch. 7.
[7] MacDonald, quoted in Stanley 1961: 95.   [8] Gurr 1993.

example, UN Resolution #2189, adopted in December 1967, condemns attempts by colonial powers to promote systematically the influx of immigrants into their colonized possessions. But this only applies to overseas colonies or newly-conquered territories, not to already-incorporated national minorities and indigenous peoples. So it is of no help to the Métis or Tibetans.

Human rights doctrines are not only silent on this question, but in fact may exacerbate the injustice, since the UN Charter guarantees the right to free mobility within the territory of a state. Indeed, ethnic Russians in the Baltics defended their settlement policies precisely on the grounds that they had a *human right* to move freely throughout the territory of the former Soviet Union. It is important to remember that most countries recognized the boundaries of the Soviet Union, and so the UN Charter does indeed imply that ethnic Russians had a basic right to settle freely in any the Soviet republics, even to the point where the indigenous inhabitants were becoming a minority in their own homeland. Similarly, human rights doctrines, far from prohibiting ethnic Han settlement in Tibet, imply that Chinese citizens have a basic human right to settle there.

To protect against these unjust settlement policies, national minorities need and demand a variety of measures. For example, they may make certain land claims—insisting that certain lands be reserved for their exclusive use and benefit. Or they may demand that certain disincentives be placed on immigration. For example, migrants may need to pass lengthy residency requirements before they can vote in local or regional elections. Or they may not be able to bring their language rights with them—that is, they may be required to attend schools in the local language, rather than having publicly-funded education in their own language. Similarly, the courts and public services may be conducted in the local language. These measures are all intended to reduce the number of migrants into the homeland of the national minority, and to ensure that those who do come are willing to integrate into the local culture.

These are often cited as examples of the sort of 'group rights' which conflict with Western individualism. They are said to reflect the minority's 'communal' attachment to their land and culture. But in fact these demands have little if anything to do with the contrast between 'individualist' and 'communalist' societies. Western 'individualist' societies also seek protections against immigration. Take any Western democracy. While the majority believes in maximizing their individual mobility throughout the country, they do not support the right of individuals outside the country to enter and settle. On the contrary, Western democracies are typically very restrictive about accepting new immigrants. None has accepted the idea that transnational mobility is a basic human right. And those few immigrants who are allowed in are pressured to integrate into the majority culture. For example, learning the majority language is a condition of gaining citizenship, and publicly-funded education is typically provided only in the majority's language.

Western democracies impose these restrictions on immigration into their country for precisely the same reason that national minorities seek to restrict immigration into their territory—namely, massive settlement would threaten their society and culture. The majority, like the minority, has no desire to be overrun and outnumbered by settlers from another culture.

To say that the desire of national minorities to limit immigration reflects some sort of illiberal communalism is therefore quite hypocritical. When the majority says that mobility within a country is a basic human right, but that mobility across borders is not, they are not preferring individual mobility over collective security. They are simply saying that *their* collective security will be protected (by limits on immigration), but that once their collective security is protected, then individual mobility will be maximized, regardless of the consequences for the collective security of minorities. This is obviously hypocritical and unjust, but it is an injustice which human rights doctrines do not prevent, and may even exacerbate.[9]

(b) The Boundaries and Powers of Internal Political Subunits

In states with territorially concentrated national minorities, the boundaries of internal political subunits raise fundamental issues of justice. Since national minorities are often territorially concentrated, boundaries can be drawn in such a way as to empower them—i.e. to create political subunits within which the national minority forms a local majority, and which can therefore be used as a vehicle for autonomy and self-government.

In many countries, however, boundaries have been drawn so as to *disempower* national minorities. For example, a minority's territory may be broken up into several units, so as to make cohesive political action impossible (e.g. the division of France into eighty-three 'departments' after the Revolution, which intentionally subdivided the historical regions of the Basques, Bretons, and other linguistic minorities; or the division of nineteenth-century

---

[9] It would not be hypocritical to criticize minority demands to limit immigration if one *also* criticized state policies to limit immigration—i.e. if one defended a policy of open-borders. But such a policy has virtually no public support, and is certainly not endorsed by most of the people who criticize minority demands. However, this raises an important limitation on my argument. I am discussing what justice requires for minorities in the world as we know it— i.e. a world of nation-states which retain significant control over issues of migration, internal political structures and language policies. One could (with difficulty) imagine a very different world—a world without states, or with just one world government. The rights of minorities would clearly be different in such a hypothetical world, since the power of majorities would be dramatically reduced, including their ability to impose relations of oppression and humiliation. My focus, however, is on what ethnocultural justice requires in our world. See also n. 20.

Catalonia); conversely, a minority's territory may be absorbed into a larger political subunit, so as to ensure that they are outnumbered within the subunit as a whole (e.g. Hispanics in nineteenth-century Florida).[10]

Even where the boundaries coincide more or less with the territory of a national minority, the degree of meaningful autonomy may be undermined if the central government usurps most or all of the subunit's powers, and eliminates the group's traditional mechanisms of self-government. And indeed, we can find many such instances in which a minority nominally controls a political subunit, but has no substantive power, since the central government has (i) removed the traditional institutions and procedures of group self-government; and (ii) arrogated all important powers, even those affecting the very cultural survival of the group—e.g. jurisdiction over economic development, education, language. (Consider the plenary power of the American Congress over Indian tribes in the United States.)

This usurpation of power is, I believe, a clear injustice, particularly when it involves seizing powers or undermining institutions which were guaranteed to the minority in treaties or federating agreements. Yet here again, it seems that human rights doctrines are inadequate to prevent such injustice. So long as individual members maintain the right to vote and run for office, then human rights principles pose no obstacle to the majority's efforts to gerrymander the boundaries or powers of internal political subunits in such a way as to disempower the national minority.[11] This is true even if the arrogation of power violates an earlier treaty or federative agreement, since such internal treaties are not considered 'international' agreements (i.e. the minority which signed the treaty is not seen under international law as a sovereign state, and so its treaties with the majority are seen as matters of domestic politics, not international law).

Not only do human rights doctrines not help prevent this injustice, but they may exacerbate it. Historically, the majority's decisions to ignore the traditional leadership of minority communities, and to destroy their traditional

[10] Cf. Ch. 5. In cases where national minorities are not territorially concentrated different mechanisms of disempowerment are often invoked. During the period of devolved rule in Northern Ireland (1920–72), for example, the Catholics were disempowered not so much by the gerrymandering of boundaries (although this occurred), but by the adoption of an electoral system (with single-member constituencies and plurality rules) designed to ensure unity within the Protestant majority while ensuring an ineffective Catholic opposition. This is another example of how a rhetorical commitment to democracy and human rights can coexist alongside the oppression of a national minority.

[11] Various attempts have been made to show that existing human rights principles implicitly prohibit this sort of disempowering of minorities (see Wheatley 1997; Lewis-Anthony 1998). These interpretations have not, however, been widely accepted. One encouraging development is that the recent Framework Convention on the Rights of National Minorities explicitly precludes altering electoral boundaries so as to dilute minority representation. However, this only concerns electoral boundaries, not the division of powers: it does not prevent central governments from eliminating or gutting forms of territorial autonomy.

political institutions, have been justified on the grounds that these traditional leaders and institutions were not 'democratic'—i.e. they did not involve the same process of periodic elections as majority political institutions. The traditional mechanisms of group consultation, consensus, and decision-making may well have provided every member of the minority community with meaningful rights to political participation and influence. However, they were swept away by the majority in the name of 'democracy'—that is, the right to vote in an electoral process within which minorities had no real influence, conducted in a foreign language and in foreign institutions, and within which they were destined to become a permanent minority. Thus the rhetoric of human rights has provided an excuse and smokescreen for the subjugation of a previously self-governing minority.[12]

To avoid this sort of injustice, national minorities need guaranteed rights to such things as self-government, group-based political representation, veto rights over issues that directly affect their cultural survival, and so on. Again, these demands are often seen as conflicting with Western individualism, and as proof of the minority's 'collectivism'. But in reality, these demands simply help to redress clear political inequalities. After all, the majority would equally reject any attempt by foreign powers unilaterally to change its boundaries, institutions, or self-government powers. So why should not national minorities also seek guarantees of their boundaries, institutions, and powers?

In a recent paper, Avigail Eisenberg details how the debate over Aboriginal political rights in the Canadian north has been distorted by the focus on Western 'individualism' versus Aboriginal 'collectivism'. This way of framing the debate misses the real issues, which are the ongoing effects of colonization—i.e. the political subordination of one people to another, through the majority's unilateral efforts to undermine the minority's institutions and powers of self-government.[13]

[12] A related example is the law which existed in Canada prior to 1960 which granted Indians the vote only if they renounced their Indian status, and so abandoned any claim to Aboriginal political or cultural rights. In order to gain a vote in the Canadian political process (a process they had no real hope of influencing), they had to relinquish any claims to participate in longstanding Aboriginal processes of self-government. This transparent attempt to undermine Aboriginal political institutions was justified in the name of promoting 'democracy'. And after citizenship was finally granted to all Indians in 1960, the Canadian government then challenged attempts by Indians to use UN forums for indigenous peoples on the grounds that Indians are Canadian citizens (Boldt 1993: 48, 83).

[13] Eisenberg 1998. Similarly, Tibor Varady argues that debates over individualism and collectivism are confusing and unhelpful in the Serbian context, and obscure the real issue, which concerns power relations between the majority and minority (Varady 1997: 28, 39–42).

(c) Official Language Policy

In most democratic states, governments have typically adopted the majority's language as the one 'official language'—i.e. as the language of government, bureaucracy, courts, schools, and so on. All citizens are then forced to learn this language in school, and fluency in it is required to work for, or deal with, government. While this policy is often defended in the name of 'efficiency', it is also adopted to ensure the eventual assimilation of the national minority into the majority group. There is strong evidence that languages cannot survive for long in the modern world unless they are used in public life, and so government decisions about official languages are, in effect, decisions about which languages will thrive, and which will die out.[14]

Just as the traditional political institutions of minorities have been shut down by the majority, so too have the pre-existing educational institutions. For example, Spanish schools in the American South-West were closed after 1848, and replaced with English-language schools. Similarly, French-language schools in western Canada were closed once English-speakers achieved political dominance.

This can be an obvious source of injustice. Yet here again, principles of human rights do not prevent this injustice (even when, as in the South-West, there were treaties guaranteeing Hispanics the right to their own Spanish-language schools). Human rights doctrines do preclude any attempt by the state to suppress the use of a minority language in private, and may even require state toleration of privately funded schools that operate in the minority language. But human rights doctrines say nothing about rights to the use of one's language in government.[15] On some interpretations of more recent international conventions that include minority rights, public funding for mother-tongue classes at elementary level may under some circumstances be seen as a 'human right'. But this remains a controversial development.[16] Moreover, mother-tongue education at the elementary level is clearly insufficient if all jobs in a modern economy require education at higher levels conducted in the majority language. Indeed, the requirement that education at senior levels be in the majority language creates a disincentive for minority parents to enrol their children in minority-language elementary schools in the first place.[17]

[14] On the necessity of extensive language rights for the survival and flourishing of linguistic minorities, see Kymlicka 1995a: ch. 6.

[15] The view that language rights are not part of human rights was explicitly affirmed by the Canadian Supreme Court in MacDonald v City of Montreal [1986] 1 S.C.R. 460; Société des acadiens du Nouveau-Brunswick v Minority Language School Board no. 50 [1986] 1 S.C.R. 549.

[16] For a comprehensive review of the current status of language rights in international human rights law, see de Varennes 1996.

[17] Low enrolment is then often (perversely) cited by majority politicians as evidence that most members of the minority are not interested in preserving their language and culture, and that it is only a few extremists in the minority group who are the cause of ethnic conflict.

To redress the injustice created by majority attempts to impose linguistic homogeneity, national minorities may need broad-ranging language policies. There is evidence that language communities can only survive intergenerationally if they are numerically dominant within a particular territory, and if their language is the language of opportunity in that territory. But it is difficult to sustain such a predominant status for a minority language, particularly if newcomers to the minority's territory are able to become educated and employed in the majority language (e.g. if newcomers to Quebec are able to learn and work in English). It may not be enough, therefore, for the minority simply to have the right to use its language in public. It may also be necessary that the minority language be the *only* official language in their territory.[18] If immigrants, or migrants from the majority group, are able to use the majority language in public life, this may eventually undermine the predominant status, and hence viability, of the minority's language.[19] In other words, minorities may need not personal bilingualism (in which individuals carry their language rights with them throughout the entire country), but rather territorial bilingualism (in which people who choose to move to the minority's territory accept that the minority's language will be the only official language in that territory). Yet this sort of territorial bilingualism—which denies official language status to the majority language on the minority's territory—is often seen as discriminatory by the majority, and indeed as a violation of their 'human rights'.

These demands for language rights and territorial bilingualism are often taken as evidence of the minority's 'collectivism'. But here again the minority is just seeking the same opportunity to live and work in their own language that the majority takes for granted. There is no evidence that the majority attaches any less weight to their ability to use their language in public life.[20]

---

[18] This is called the 'territorial imperative', and the trend towards territorial concentration of language groups is a widely-noted phenomenon in multilingual Western countries. I discuss this further in Ch. 10.

[19] This is the rationale given for requiring immigrants to Quebec to send their children to French-language schools. See Ch. 15.

[20] Here again, it would not be hypocritical to criticize minority demands regarding self-government rights and language rights if one applied the same standard to majorities. For example, one could imagine letting the United Nations determine the boundaries and language policies of each state. Imagine that the UN, in a free and democratic vote, decided to merge all countries in the Americas (North, South, and Central) into a single Spanish-speaking state. If the anglophone majority in Canada or the United States would accept such a decision—i.e. if they were willing to abandon their own self-government powers and language rights—then it would not be hypocritical to criticize the demands of Francophone, Hispanic, or Aboriginal minorities in North America. But I don't know any English-speaking Canadians or Americans who would agree to amalgamate into a single Spanish-speaking state, even if this merger was supported by most countries in the Americas (and/or by most people living in the Americas). In reality, the anglophone majorities in both the United States and Canada

One could mention other issues where human rights are insufficient for ensuring ethnocultural justice (e.g. public holidays, school curriculum, national symbols, dress-codes, etc). But enough has been said, I hope, to make the general point. Moreover, it is important to note that the three issues I have examined—migration, internal political subunits, and language policy—are all connected. These are all key components in the 'nation-building' programmes that every Western state has engaged in.[21] Every democratic state has, at one time or another, attempted to create a single 'national identity' amongst its citizens, and so has tried to undermine any competing national identities, of the sort which national minorities often possess. Policies designed to settle minority homelands, undermine their political and educational institutions, and impose a single common language have been important tools in these nation-building efforts. There is no evidence that states intended to relinquish these tools when they accepted human rights conventions, and indeed no evidence that states would have accepted a conception of human rights that would preclude such nation-building programmes.

Of course, human rights standards do set limits on this process of nation-building. States cannot kill or expel minorities, or strip them of citizenship, or deny them the vote. But human rights standards do not preclude less extreme forms of nation-building. And if these nation-building measures are successful, then it is not necessary to restrict the individual civil and political rights of the minority. Where nation-building programmes have succeeded in turning the incorporated group into a minority even within its own homeland, and stripping it of its self-governing institutions and language rights, then the group will not pose any serious threat to the power or interests of the majority. At this point, there is no need to strip minority members of their individual rights. This is not necessary in order to gain and maintain effective political control over them.

In short, human rights standards are insufficient to prevent ethnocultural injustice, and may actually makes things worse. The majority can invoke human rights principles to demand access to the minority's homeland, to scrap traditional political mechanisms of consultation and accommodation, and to reject linguistic policies that try to protect the territorial viability of minority communities.

In these and other ways, human rights have indirectly served as an instrument of colonization, as various critics have argued. However, I would not agree with those critics who view this solely as a problem of 'Western impe-

zealously guard their right to live in a state where they form a majority, and their right to have English recognized as a language of public life. This defence of the boundaries and linguistic policies of existing nation-states is as 'collectivist' as the demands of minorities for protection of their self-government and language rights.

[21] See the discussion of nation-building in Ch. 1.

rialism' against non-European peoples. After all, these processes of unjust subjugation have occurred *between* European groups (e.g. the treatment of national minorities by the majority in France, Spain, Russia), and *between* African or Asian groups (e.g. the treatment of the Yao minority by the Chewa majority in Malawi; the treatment of the Tibetan minority by the Han majority in China), as well as in the context of Western colonization of non-Western peoples. These processes have occurred in virtually every state with national minorities, and to ascribe it to Western individualism is to seriously underestimate the scope of the problem.

If human rights are not to be an instrument of unjust subjugation, then they must be supplemented with various minority rights—language rights, self-government rights, representation rights, federalism and so on. Moreover, these minority rights should not, I think, be seen as secondary to traditional human rights. Even those who are sympathetic to the need for minority rights often say that we should at least *begin* with human rights. That is, we should first secure respect for individual human rights, and then, having secured the conditions for a free and democratic debate, move on to questions of minority rights. When national minorities oppose this assumption, they are often labelled as illiberal or antidemocratic. But as I've tried to show, we cannot assume that human rights will have their desired consequences without attending to the larger context within which they operate. Unless supplemented by minority rights, majoritarian democracy and individual mobility rights may simply lead to minority oppression. As we've seen, various forms of oppression can occur while still respecting the individual rights of minorities. As a result, the longer we defer discussing minority rights, the more likely it is that the minority will become increasingly weakened and outnumbered. Indeed, it may over time become so weakened that it will become unable even to demand or exercise meaningful minority rights (i.e. it may lose the local predominance or territorial concentration needed to sustain its language, or to exercise local self-government). It is no accident, therefore, that members of the majority are often loudest in their support for giving priority to democracy and human rights over issues of minority rights. They know that the longer issues of minority rights are deferred, the more time it provides for the majority to disempower and dispossess the minority of its land, schools, and political institutions to the point where the minority is in no position to sustain itself as a thriving culture or to exercise meaningful self-government.[22]

This is why human rights and minority rights must be treated together, as equally important components of a just society. Of course, it would be an equally serious mistake to privilege minority rights over human rights. In questioning the priority of traditional human rights over minority rights, I

[22] We can see this in Eastern Europe, as I discuss in Ch. 14.

am not disputing the potential for serious rights-violations within many minority groups, or the need to have some institutional checks on the power of local or minority political leaders. On the contrary, *all* political authorities should be held accountable for respecting the basic rights of the people they govern, and this applies as much to the exercise of self-government powers by national minorities as to the actions of the larger state. The individual members of national minorities can be just as badly mistreated and oppressed by the leaders of their own group as by the majority government, and so any system of minority self-government should include some institutional provisions for enforcing traditional human rights within the minority community.

It is not a question of choosing between minority rights and human rights, or of giving priority to one over the other, but rather of treating them together as equally important components of justice in ethnoculturally plural countries. We need a conception of justice that integrates fairness between different ethnocultural groups (via minority rights) with the protection of individual rights within majority and minority political communities (via traditional human rights).[23]

3. The Enforcement of Human Rights

Assuming that we can come up with some new theory that combines human rights and minority rights, would the existing level of opposition to transnational human rights standards diminish? Would we then get consensus on the enforcement of international standards of human rights?

We can expect, I think, that the elites of some groups will continue to say human rights principles contradict their cultural 'traditions'. I will return to this possibility in my conclusion. But my guess is that much of the current opposition to human rights would fade away. As I noted earlier, human rights are not inherently 'individualistic', and do not preclude group life. They simply ensure that traditions are voluntarily maintained, and that dissent is not forcibly suppressed. To be sure, self-serving political elites who want to suppress challenges to their authority from within the community will continue to denounce human rights as a violation of their 'traditions'. This explains recent criticisms of human rights doctrines by the Indonesian and Chinese governments. But my guess is that if human rights doctrines are no longer seen as a tool for subordinating one people to another, but rather as a tool for protecting vulnerable individuals from abuse by their political leaders, then

---

[23] See the analysis in de Sousa Santos 1996. He argues that attention to the claims of indigenous peoples and ethnic minorities can help develop a new 'non-hegemonic' conception of human rights which would retain its commitment to protecting the weak and vulnerable without serving as an instrument of Western colonialism (e.g. 353).

such opposition to human rights will increasingly be seen simply as a self-serving defence of elite power and privilege.[24]

So I would hope that we could gain greater international consensus on the *principles* of human rights. But this is not to say that we are likely to get consensus on the appropriate *enforcement mechanisms* of human rights/minority rights, either at the international level or even in the domestic setting. There are at least two major difficulties here. First, it is difficult to see how minority rights can be codified at the international level. Minorities come in many different shapes and sizes. There are 'national' minorities, indigenous peoples, immigrants, refugees, guestworkers, colonizing settlers, descendants of slaves or indentured labourers, Roma, religious groups, and so on. All of these groups have different needs, aspirations, and institutional capacities. Territorial autonomy will not work for widely dispersed groups, and even territorially concentrated groups differ dramatically in the sort of self-government they aspire to, or are capable of. Similarly, language rights (beyond the right to private speech) will not be the same in India or Malaysia (which contain hundreds of indigenous languages) as in France or Britain.

This is why international declarations of minority rights tend to waver between trivialities like the 'right to maintain one's culture' (which could simply mean respect for freedom of expression and association, and hence add nothing to existing declarations of human rights), and vague generalities like the 'right to self-determination' (which could mean anything from token representation to full-blown secession).[25] Minorities are not going to accept the lowest common denominator, which even the smallest or most dispersed group seeks, but majorities are not going to give all groups the maximal rights demanded by the largest and most mobilized groups (which may include secession).

I see no easy way to overcome this problem. While minority rights are indeed essential, the solution is not necessarily to add a detailed list of minority rights to human rights declarations in international law. Instead, we must accept that traditional human rights are insufficient to ensure ethnocultural

[24] As a general rule, we should be wary about the claims of elite members of a group to speak authoritatively about the group's 'traditions'. Some individuals may claim to speak for the group as a whole, and may say that the group is united against the imposition of 'alien' ideas of human rights. But in reality, these people may simply be protecting their privileged position from *internal* challenges to their interpretation of the group's culture and traditions. In other words, debates over the legitimacy of human rights should not necessarily be seen as debates over whether to subordinate local cultural traditions to transnational human rights standards, although this is how conservative members of the group may put it. Instead, debates over human rights are often debates over who within the community should have the authority to influence or determine the interpretation of the community's traditions and culture. When individual members of the group demand their 'human rights', they often do so in order to be able to participate in the community's process of interpreting its traditions.

[25] For an acute criticism of existing minority rights declarations, see Horowitz 1997.

justice, and then recognize the need to supplement them *within each country* with the specific minority rights that are appropriate for that country. As I will discuss later, international bodies can play a useful role in adjudicating minority rights conflicts, but this role is unlikely to take the form of adjudicating or enforcing a single codified international list of minority rights.

This then leads to the second problem. If human rights and minority rights must be integrated at the domestic level, rather than through a single international code, can we find an impartial body to adjudicate and enforce these rights at the domestic level? Many people will naturally assume that these rights should be listed in a single national constitution that is then adjudicated and enforced by a single supreme court. Certainly most liberals have assumed that the supreme court in each country should have final jurisdiction regarding both human rights and minority rights.

But in fact we find strong resistance to this idea amongst some minority groups, even if they share the principles underlying the set of human rights and minority rights listed in the national constitution. Consider the situation of Indian tribes in the United States. American constitutional law protects both certain minority rights for Indian tribes (they are recognized as 'domestic dependent nations' with treaty-based rights of self-government), and also a general set of individual human rights (in the Bill of Rights). This could be seen as at least the beginnings of an attempt to integrate fairly minority rights and human rights at the domestic level.[26]

But who should have the power to enforce these constitutional provisions regarding individual and minority rights? American liberals typically assume that the federal Supreme Court should have this power. But many American Indians oppose this idea. They do not want the Supreme Court to be able to review their internal decisions to assess whether they comply with the Bill of Rights.[27] And they would prefer to have some international body monitor the extent to which the American government respects their treaty-based minority rights. So they do not want the federal Supreme Court to be the ultimate protector either of the individual rights of their members, or of their minority rights.

---

[26] It is, at best, an imperfect beginning, in large part due to the Plenary Power which Congress arbitrarily asserts over Indian tribes. See Kronowitz *et al.* 1987; O'Brien 1989.

[27] Indeed, tribal councils in the United States have historically been exempted from having to comply with the federal Bill of Rights, and their internal decisions have not been not subject to Supreme Court review. Various efforts have been made by federal legislators to change this, most recently the 1968 Indian Civil Rights Act, which was passed by Congress despite vociferous opposition from most Indian groups. American Indian groups remain strongly opposed to the 1968 Act, just as First Nations in Canada have argued that their self-governing band councils should not be subject to judicial review by the Canadian Supreme Court under the Canadian Charter of Rights and Freedoms. They do not want their members to be able to challenge band decisions in the courts of the mainstream society.

Needless to say, Indian demands to reduce the authority of the federal Supreme Court have met with resistance. The American government has shown no desire to accept international monitoring of the extent to which the treaty rights of Indians are respected. Indeed, the American government has jealously guarded its sovereignty in these matters, and so refused to give any international body jurisdiction to review and overturn the way it respects the treaty rights, land claims, or self-government rights of indigenous peoples.

And the demand to have internal tribal decisions exempted from scrutiny under the Bill of Rights is widely opposed by liberals, since it raises the concern in many people's minds that individuals or subgroups (e.g. women) within American Indian communities could be oppressed in the name of group solidarity or cultural purity. They argue that any acceptable package of individual rights and minority rights must include judicial review of tribal decisions by the American Supreme Court to ensure their compliance with the Bill of Rights.

Before jumping to this conclusion, however, we should consider the reasons why certain groups are distrustful of federal judicial review. In the case of American Indians, these reasons are, I think, obvious. After all, the federal Supreme Court has historically legitimized the acts of colonization and conquest that dispossessed Indians of their property and political power. It has historically denied both the individual rights and treaty rights of Indians on the basis of racist and ethnocentric assumptions. Moreover, Indians have had no representation on the Supreme Court, and there is reason to fear that white judges on the Supreme Court may interpret certain rights in culturally biased ways (e.g. democratic rights). Why should Indians agree to have their internal decisions reviewed by a body which is, in effect, the court of their conquerors? And why should they trust this Court to act impartially in considering their minority and treaty rights?

For all these reasons, to assume that supreme courts at the national level should have the ultimately authority over all issues of individual and minority rights within a country may be inappropriate in the case of indigenous peoples and other incorporated national minorities.[28] There are good reasons why American Indians do not trust federal courts either to uphold the minority rights needed for ethnocultural justice between majority and minority, or to determine fairly whether the minority is respecting human rights internally.

---

[28] See also the analysis in Schneiderman 1998. There has been considerable discussion in some Eastern Europe countries about the development of such regional or international forums for protecting minority rights. In Moldova, for example, there have been recommendations that a special organ be created or adapted to monitor the special status of Transdniestria, such as the Court of Conciliation and Arbitration of the OSCE. See ECMI 1998: 28.

It is quite understandable, therefore, that many Indian leaders seek to reduce the role of federal judicial review. But at the same time they affirm their commitment to the basic package of human rights and minority rights which is contained in the US constitution. They endorse the principles, but object to the particular institutions and procedures that the larger society has established to enforce these principles. As Joseph Carens puts it, 'people are supposed to experience the realisation of principles of justice through various concrete institutions, but they may actually experience a lot of the institution and very little of the principle'.[29] This is exactly how many indigenous peoples perceive the Supreme Court in both Canada and the United States. What they experience is not the principles of human dignity and equality, but rather a social institution that has historically justified their conquest and dispossession.

What we need to do, therefore, is to find impartial bodies to monitor compliance with both human rights and minority rights. We need to think creatively about new mechanisms for enforcing human rights and minority rights that will avoid the legitimate objections which indigenous peoples and national minorities have to federal courts.

What would these alternative mechanisms look like? To begin with, many Indian tribes have sought to create or maintain their own procedures for protecting human rights within their community, specified in tribal constitutions, some of which are based on the provisions of international protocols on human rights. It is important to distinguish Indian tribes, who have their own internal constitution and courts which prevent the arbitrary exercise of political power, from ethnocultural groups which have no formal constitutions or courts, and which therefore provide no effective check on the exercise of arbitrary power by powerful individuals or traditional elites. We should take these internal checks on the misuse of power seriously. Indeed, to assume that the federal courts should replace or supersede the institutions which Indians have themselves evolved to prevent injustice is evidence of an ethnocentric bias—an implicit belief that 'our' institutions are superior to theirs.[30]

Indian tribes have also sought to create new transnational or international procedures to help monitor the protection of their minority rights. The international community can play an important role, not so much by formulating

[29] Carens 2000: 190.

[30] To be sure, some Indian tribal constitutions are not fully liberal or democratic, and so are inadequate from a human rights point of view, but they are forms of constitutional government, and so should not be equated with mob rule or despotism. As Graham Walker notes, it is a mistake to conflate the ideas of liberalism and constitutionalism. There is a genuine category of non-liberal constitutionalism, which provides meaningful checks on political authority and preserves the basic elements of natural justice, and which thereby helps ensure that governments maintain their legitimacy in the eyes of their subjects. See Walker 1997.

a single list of minority rights that applies to all countries (for that may be impossible), but rather by providing an impartial adjudicator to monitor the extent to which domestic provisions regarding minority rights are fairly negotiated and implemented.

From the point of view of ethnocultural justice, these proposals might be preferable to the current reliance on the federal Supreme Court. But it would be even better, I think, to establish international mechanisms that would monitor *both* the individual rights and minority rights of Indian peoples. While the internal courts and constitutions of tribal governments are worthy of respect, they—like the courts and constitutions of nation-states—are imperfect in their protection of human rights. So it would be preferable if all governments—majority and minority—are subject to some form of international scrutiny.

Many Indian leaders have expressed a willingness to accept some form of international monitoring of their internal human rights record. They are willing to abide by international declarations of human rights, and to answer to international tribunals for complaints of rights violations within their communities. But they would only accept this if and when it is accompanied by international monitoring of how well the larger state respects their treaty rights. They accept the idea that their tribal governments, like all governments, should be accountable to international human rights norms (so long as this isn't in the court of their conquerors). But they want this sort of external monitoring to examine how well their minority rights are upheld by the larger society, not just to focus on the extent to which their own decisions respect individual human rights. This seems like a reasonable demand to me.

These international mechanisms could arise at the regional as well as global level. European countries have agreed to establish their own multilateral human rights tribunals. Perhaps North American governments and Indian tribes could agree to establish a similar multilateral tribunal, on which both sides are fairly represented.

My aim here is not to defend any particular proposal for a new impartial body to monitor the protection of individual rights and minority rights. My aim, rather, is to stress again the necessity of treating individual rights and minority rights together when thinking about appropriate enforcement mechanisms. On the one hand, we need to think about effective mechanisms that can hold minority governments accountable for the way individual members are treated. I see no justification for exempting minority self-government from the principles of human rights—I believe that any exercise of political power should be subject to these principles. But we need to simultaneously think about effective mechanisms for holding the larger society accountable for respecting the minority rights of these groups. As I argued in section 2, minority rights are equally important as individual human rights in ensuring ethnocultural justice, and so should be subject to equal scrutiny.

Moreover, focusing exclusively on the latter while neglecting the former is counter-productive and hypocritical. Minority groups will not agree to greater external scrutiny of their internal decisions unless they achieve greater protection of their minority rights. And since existing institutional mechanisms are typically unable to meet this twin test of accountability, we need to think creatively about new mechanisms that can deal impartially with both individual human rights and minority rights.

I should emphasize again that in questioning the role of federal courts in reviewing the internal decisions of tribal governments, I am not trying to diminish the significance of human rights. On the contrary, my goal is to find fairer and more effective ways to promote human rights, by separating them from the historical and cultural baggage that makes federal courts suspect in the eyes of incorporated peoples. History has shown the value of holding governments accountable for respecting human rights, and this applies equally to Indian tribal governments. But the appropriate forums for reviewing the actions of self-governing indigenous peoples may skip the federal level, as it were. Many indigenous groups would endorse a system in which their self-governing decisions are reviewed in the first instance by their own courts, and then by an international court, which would also monitor respect for minority rights. Federal courts, dominated by the majority, would not be the ultimate adjudicator of either the individual or minority rights of Indian peoples.

The human rights movement has always set itself against the idea of unlimited sovereignty, and pushed for limitations on the power of governments to mistreat their citizens. But we need to do this in an even-handed manner. We should hold the minority accountable for respecting the human rights of its members, but we need also to hold the majority accountable for respecting minority rights, and we need to find impartial enforcement mechanisms which can do both of these together.

4. Conclusion

I have argued that our aims should be twofold: (*a*) to supplement individual human rights with minority rights, recognizing that the specific combination will vary from country to country; and (*b*) to find new domestic, regional or transnational mechanisms which will hold governments accountable for respecting both human rights and minority rights.

If we manage to solve these two (enormous) tasks, then I believe that the commitment to universal human rights need not be culturally biased. Indeed, if we resolve these issues satisfactorily, then the idea of human rights can become what it was always intended to be—namely, a shield for the weak against the abuse of political power, not a weapon of the majority in subjugating minorities.

If the arguments in this chapter are at all valid, then it suggests a number of new avenues for future research—avenues that would depart dramatically from the existing patterns of research and debate. At the moment, wherever there is a conflict between 'local practices' and 'transnational human rights standards', commentators tend to locate the source of the conflict in the 'culture' or 'traditions' of the group, and then look for ways in which this culture differs from 'Western' culture. This tendency is exacerbated by the rhetoric of a 'politics of difference', which encourages groups to press their demands in the language of respect for cultural 'difference'.

My suggestion, however, is that we should not jump to the conclusion that cultural differences are the real source of the problem. Rather, in each case where a group is objecting to the domestic or transnational enforcement of human rights, we should ask the following questions:

• Has the majority society failed to recognize legitimate minority rights? If so, has this created a situation in which the implementation of human rights standards contributes to the unjust disempowerment of the minority? I have discussed three contexts or issues where human rights standards can exacerbate ethnocultural injustice if they are unaccompanied by minority rights, but it would be interesting to come up with a more systematic list of such issues.

• Is there any reason to think that the existing or proposed judicial mechanisms for adjudicating or enforcing human rights are biased against the minority group? Have these judicial mechanisms treated minorities fairly historically? Is the minority group fairly represented on the judicial bodies? Were these judicial mechanisms consensually accepted by the minority when it was incorporated into the country, or is the imposition of these judicial mechanisms a denial of historical agreements or treaties which protected the autonomy of the group's own judicial institutions?

My guess is that in many cases where minority groups object to transnational human rights standards, it will be for one of these reasons, rather any inherent conflict between their traditional practices and human rights standards. Where these problems are addressed, I expect that many minority groups will be more than willing to subscribe to human rights standards.

I don't mean to deny the existence of illiberal or antidemocratic practices within minority communities or non-Western societies. But it is important to note that at least in some cases the existence of such practices is itself the consequence of some prior ethnocultural injustice. That is, many minorities feel compelled to restrict the liberties of their own members because the larger society has denied their legitimate minority rights. As Denise Réaume has noted, part of the 'demonization' of other cultures is the assumption that these groups are naturally inclined to use coercion against their members. But insofar as some groups seem regrettably willing to use coercion to preserve group practices, this may be due, not to any innate illiberalism, but to the fact that the larger society has failed to respect their minority rights. Unable to get justice from the larger society, in terms of protection for its lands and institutions, the minority turns its attention to the only people it does have some control over, namely, its own members.[31]

This tendency does not justify the violation of the human rights of group members, but it suggests that before we condemn a minority for imposing such restrictions on its members, we should first make sure we are respecting all of its legitimate minority rights. In short, the current conflict between local practices and transnational standards may not be the result of a deep attachment to some long-standing 'tradition' in the local community, but rather the (regretted) result of some new vulnerability which has arisen from the denial of their minority rights.

To be sure, there will be some cases where members of a group really do object to the very content of the human rights standard on the grounds that it is inconsistent with their cultural traditions. Even if we solve the problem of minority rights and enforcement mechanisms, we will still find some people rejecting 'Western' notions of human rights. They will say that restricting the liberty of women or suppressing political dissent is part of their 'tradition', and that human rights theories reflect a biased eurocentric or 'individualistic' standard.[32] These claims may come from minority groups or from powerful majority groups or governments, as in Indonesia or China.

I do not want to enter into that debate, and the issues of cultural relativism that it raises. We are all familiar with that debate, and I have little to add to it. My aim, rather, is to insist that this is not the only debate we need to have. On the contrary, we may find that such conflicts are fewer once we have properly dealt with the issues of ethnocultural justice.

---

[31] Réaume 1995.

[32] As I said earlier, I do not think that the substantive interests protected by human rights doctrines are either individualistic or Eurocentric. However, it may well be that to talk of these interests in terms of 'rights' is a specifically European invention which does not fit comfortably with the discourse or self-understandings of many cultures. I don't think we should get hung up on 'rights talk'. What matters, morally speaking, is that people's substantive interests in life and liberty are protected, but we should be open-minded about what institutional mechanisms best provide this protection. There is no reason to assume that the best way to reliably protect people's basic interests will always take the form of a judicially enforceable constitutional list of 'rights'. For a critique of the language of rights as Eurocentric, see Turpel 1989–90. On ways to protect the substantive human interests underlying human rights without using the language of 'rights', see Pogge 1995.

5

Minority Nationalism and Multination Federalism

Around the world, multination states are in trouble. Many have proven unable to create or sustain any strong sense of solidarity across ethnonational lines. The members of one national group are indifferent to the rights and interests of the members of other groups, and are unwilling to make sacrifices for them. Moreover, they have no trust that any sacrifice they might make will be reciprocated. Recent events in Eastern Europe and the former Soviet Union show that where this sort of solidarity and trust is lacking, demands for secession are likely to arise.

Some commentators have argued that secession is indeed the most appropriate response to the crisis of multination states. On this view, the desire of national minorities to form a separate state is often morally legitimate, and it is unjust to force them to remain within a larger state against their will. International law should therefore define the conditions under which a group has the right of secession, and the procedures by which that right can be exercised.[1]

Critics of this approach argue that recognizing a right of secession, either at the level of normative political theory or international law, would encourage more secessionist movements, and thereby increase the risk of political instability and violence around the world. On this view, secession often leads to civil war, and may start a chain reaction in which minorities within the seceding unit seek to secede in turn. Moreover, even if actual secession never occurs, the very threat of secession is destabilizing, enabling groups to engage in a politics of threats and blackmail.[2]

I will not directly address the question of whether national groups have a moral or legal right to secede. Focusing exclusively on this question may blind us to the really significant fact of our current situation—namely, that so many people *want* to secede, or are at least prepared to consider it. It is a striking fact that the members of so many national groups in the world today feel that their interests cannot be satisfied except by forming a state of their own.

Nor is this problem confined to the Second and Third Worlds. Various multination democracies in the West whose long-term stability used to be taken for granted now seem rather more precarious. Consider recent events

---

[1] See e.g. Philpott 1995; Buchanan 1991; Walzer 1992c.   [2] See Horowitz 1997.

in Belgium or Canada. Even though they live in prosperous liberal states, with firm guarantees of their basic civil and political rights, the Flemish, Scots and Québécois all have strong independence movements. The threat of secession has arisen in both capitalist and Communist countries, in both democracies and military dictatorships, in both prosperous and impoverished countries.

The prevalence of secessionist movements suggests that contemporary states have not developed effective means for accommodating national minorities. Whether or not we recognize a right to secede, the fact is that secession will remain an ever-present threat in many countries unless we learn to accommodate this sort of ethnocultural diversity. As long as national minorities feel that their interests cannot be accommodated within existing states, they will contemplate secession.

In this chapter, I want to focus on one of the most commonly cited mechanisms for accommodating national minorities—namely, federalism. Many commentators argue that federalism provides a viable alternative to secession, since it is uniquely able to accommodate the aspirations of national minorities. Federalism, it is said, respects the desire of national groups to remain autonomous, and to retain their cultural distinctiveness, while none the less acknowledging the fact that these groups are not self-contained and isolated, but rather are increasingly and inextricably bound to each other in relations of economic and political interdependence. Moreover, since federalism is a notoriously flexible system, it can accommodate the fact that different groups desire different levels or forms of self-government.[3]

I think there is much truth in this picture of the value of federalism in accommodating national minorities. On any reasonable criteria, democratic federations (as opposed to Communist federations) have been surprisingly successful in accommodating minority nationalisms. Both historic multination federations, like Switzerland and Canada, and more recent multination federations, like Belgium and Spain, have not only managed the conflicts arising from their competing national identities in a peaceful and democratic way, but have also secured a high degree of economic prosperity and individual freedom for their citizens. This is truly remarkable when one considers the immense power of nationalism in this century. Nationalism has torn apart colonial empires and Communist dictatorships, and redefined boundaries all over the world. Yet democratic multination federations have succeeded in taming the force of nationalism. Democratic federalism has domesticated and pacified nationalism, while respecting individual rights and

---

[3] As Burgess puts it, 'the genius of federation lies in its infinite capacity to accommodate and reconcile the competing and sometimes conflicting diversities having political salience within a state. Toleration, respect, compromise, bargaining and mutual recognition and its watchwords and "union" combined with "autonomy" its hallmark' (Burgess 1993: 7; cf. Elazar 1987a; 1994).

freedoms. It is difficult to imagine any other political system that can make the same claim.

Of course, many federal systems were not designed as a response to ethnocultural pluralism—e.g. the United States or Australia. In these federal systems, the federal units do not correspond in any way with distinct ethnocultural groups who desire to retain their self-government and cultural distinctiveness. I will discuss the American model of federalism in section 2, but my focus in this chapter is on countries that have adopted federalism in order to accommodate national minorities.

While democratic multination federations have been quite successful to date, federalism is no panacea for ethnonational conflicts, and my aim in this paper is to explore some of the difficulties in using federalism to accommodate minority nationalism. The success of federalism depends on many factors, but I will focus in particular on how the boundaries of federal subunits are drawn, and how powers are distributed between different levels of government. These are pivotal issues for the fair accommodation of minority nationalisms, yet it is extremely difficult to get consensus on them, and they are (and will remain) the subject of intense and interminable controversy (sections 2 and 3).

Moreover, even where federalism has been designed in such a way as to accommodate fairly national minorities, it does not guarantee the removal of any threat of secession (section 4). One might have expected that if a federation is successful in accommodating minority nationalism—successful in the sense of fairly managing these conflicts in a peaceful and democratic way, while protecting individual rights and prosperity—then secessionist movements would lose all of their political legitimacy and popular support. But there is no evidence that this is occurring. The 'success' of federalism has not eliminated, or even substantially reduced, support for secession amongst national minorities in the West. Support for secession in Quebec, Flanders, Scotland, Puerto Rico, or Catalonia varies from poll to poll, but there is no evidence for any general downward trend in support. Successful multination federations often contain secessionist movements with substantial levels of popular support. Active and popular secessionist movements are an everyday and accepted part of life in democratic multination federations.

This will strike many people as a paradox. How can one say that a country is 'successful' in managing its ethnonational conflicts if there is a significant number of people who wish to break up the country? Many people will agree with John Rawls that the citizens of a just society should view themselves as members of 'one cooperative scheme in perpetuity'.[4] On most traditional

---

[4] In developing his well-known contractarian theory of distributive justice, John Rawls argued that the parties to the social contrast should view themselves as members of 'one cooperative scheme in perpetuity'. This might be a reasonable assumption in the case of unitary states or territorial federations. But it is not a plausible assumption, either sociologically or morally, in the case of multination federations.

conceptions of political community, such a commitment to perpetual togetherness is necessary for the polity to be successful or 'well-ordered'. I will
argue, however, that this is an inappropriate yardstick to apply to multination
federations. Federalism can help to keep certain multination countries
together, but the best we can hope for in such circumstances is a looser and
more provisional form of 'togetherness' which coexists with ongoing questioning of the value of maintaining the federation. The nature of this looser
form of togetherness is somewhat mysterious—certainly there is very little in
contemporary political theory which sheds light on it—but I will argue that
it is both real and surprisingly resilient (section 6).

1. Federalism and the Accommodation of Ethnocultural Groups

There is no universally accepted definition of 'federalism'. For the purposes
of this paper, I take federalism to refer to a political system which includes a
constitutionally entrenched division of powers between a central government and two or more subunits (provinces/lander/states/cantons), defined
on a territorial basis, such that each level of government has sovereign
authority over certain issues. This distinguishes federalism from both (*a*)
administrative decentralization, where a central government establishes
basic policy in all areas, but then devolves the power to administer these policies to lower levels of government, typically regional or municipal governments; and (*b*) confederation, where two or more sovereign countries agree
to co-ordinate economic or military policy, and so each devolves the power
to administer these policies to a supranational body composed of delegates
of each country.[5]

It is possible to combine elements from these different models, and some
political systems may be difficult to categorize. All of these systems involve
power-sharing, but the path by which these powers come to be shared differs.
In both administrative decentralization and confederation, the central government within each country is assumed to possess complete decision-
making authority over all areas of policy; it then chooses to devolve some of

[5] Other characteristic features of federalism include the existence of a bicameral legislature
at the federal level, with the second chamber intended to ensure effective representation for
the federal subunits in the central government. Thus, each federal subunit is guaranteed representation in the second chamber, and smaller subunits tend to be overrepresented.
Moreover, each subunit has a right to be involved in the process of amending the federal
constitution, but can unilaterally amend its own constitution. In defining federalism in this
manner, I am following Wheare's classic account (Wheare 1964: chs. 1–2; Lemco 1991: ch. 1).
For a typology of various 'federal-type' arrangements—which distinguishes federations from
confederations, consociations, federacies, legislative unions, associated states, and condo-
miniums—see Elazar 1987*a*: ch. 2.

this authority upwards or downwards on the basis of its perceived national interest. But this devolution is voluntary and revocable—it retains ultimate sovereignty over these areas of policy, and so it retains the right to unilaterally reclaim the powers it has devolved. By contrast, in a federal system, both levels of government have certain sovereign powers as a matter of legal right, not simply on a delegated and revocable basis. Both the central government and the federal subunits posses sovereign authority over certain policy areas, and it is unconstitutional for one level of government to intrude on the jurisdiction of the other. The central government cannot 'reclaim' the powers possessed by the federal subunits, because those powers never belonged to the central government. Conversely, the subunits cannot reclaim the powers possessed by the central government, because those powers never belonged to the subunits. In short, unlike administrative decentralization and confederation, both levels of government in a federal system have a constitutionally protected existence, and do not just exist on the sufferance of some other body.

Is this an appropriate mechanism for accommodating national minorities? In most multination states, the component nations are inclined to demand some form of political autonomy or territorial jurisdiction, so as to ensure the full and free development of their cultures, and to promote the interests of their people. They demand certain powers of self-government that they say were not relinquished by their (often involuntary) incorporation into a larger state. At the extreme, nations may wish to secede, if they think self-government is impossible within the larger state.

One possible mechanism for recognizing claims to self-government is federalism. Where national minorities are regionally concentrated, the boundaries of federal subunits can be drawn so that the national minority forms a majority in one of the subunits. Under these circumstances, federalism can provide extensive self-government for a national minority, guaranteeing its ability to make decisions in certain areas without being outvoted by the larger society.

For example, under the federal division of powers in Canada, the province of Quebec (which is 80 per cent francophone) has extensive jurisdiction over issues that are crucial to the survival of the francophone society, including control over education, language, culture, as well as significant input into immigration policy. The other nine provinces also have these powers, but the major impetus behind the existing division of powers, and indeed behind the entire federal system, is the need to accommodate the Québécois. At the time when Canada was created in 1867, most English-speaking Canadian leaders were in favour of a unitary state, like England, and agreed to a federal system primarily to accommodate French Canadians. Had Quebec not been guaranteed these substantial powers—and hence protected from the possibility of being outvoted on key issues by the larger anglophone population—

it is certain that Quebec either would not have joined Canada in 1867, or would have seceded sometime thereafter.

Historically, the most prominent examples of federalism being used in this way to accommodate national minorities are Canada and Switzerland. The apparent stability and prosperity of these countries has led other multination countries to adopt federal systems in the post-war period (e.g. Yugoslavia), or upon decolonization (e.g. India, Malaysia, Nigeria). Even though many of these federations are facing serious difficulties, we are currently witnessing yet another burst of interest in federalism in multination countries, with some countries in the process of adopting federal arrangements (Belgium, Spain, Russia), and others debating whether it would provide a solution to their ethnic conflicts (e.g. South Africa).[6]

This widespread interest in federalism reflects a welcome, if belated, acknowledgement that the desire of national minorities to retain their distinct cultures should be accommodated, not suppressed. For too long, academic theorists and political elites assumed that modernization would inevitably involve the assimilation of minority nationalities, and the withering away of their national identity. Central governments around the world have tried to dissolve the sense amongst national minorities that they constitute distinct peoples or nations, by eliminating their previously self-governing political and educational institutions, and/or by insisting that the majority language be used in all public forums. However, it is increasingly recognized that these efforts were both unjust and ineffective, and that the desire of national minorities to maintain themselves as culturally distinct and political autonomous societies must be accommodated.[7]

Federalism is one of the few mechanisms available for this purpose. Indeed, it is quite natural that multination countries should adopt federal systems—one would expect countries that are formed through a federation of peoples to adopt some form of political federation. But while the desire to satisfy the aspirations of national minorities is welcome, we should be aware of the pitfalls involved. Federalism is no panacea for the stresses and conflicts of multination states. In the rest of the paper, I will discuss a number of qualifications regarding the potential value of federalism in multination states.

I will separate my concerns into three areas. First, the mere fact of federalism is not sufficient for accommodating national minorities—it all depends on how federal boundaries are drawn, and how powers are shared. Indeed, federalism can and has been used by majority groups as a tool for disempowering national minorities, by rigging federal units so as to *reduce* the power of national minorities. We need therefore to distinguish genuinely multination federations which seek to accommodate national minorities

---

[6] See the discussion of the 'federalist revolution' in Elazar 1987a: ch. 1.

[7] For a discussion of why national identity has been so enduring, and why national minorities differ in this respect from immigrants, see Kymlicka 1995a: chs. 5–6.

from merely territorial federations which do not (section 2). Second, federalism is not as flexible as its proponents often claim. Where the subunits of a federal system vary in their territory, population, and their desire for autonomy, as is often the case, developing an 'asymmetric' form of federalism has proven to be very complicated (section 3). Finally, even where federalism is successfully working to accommodate the aspirations of national minorities, its very success may legitimate, rather than erode, secessionist sentiments (section 4).

2. Multination vs. Territorial Federalism

While federalism is increasingly being considered as a solution to the problems of multination states, it is important to note that many federal systems arose for reasons unrelated to ethnonational diversity.[8] In fact, the most famous and widely studied federation—the American system—makes no effort to respond to the aspiration of national minorities for self-government.

Anglo-Saxon settlers dominated all of the original thirteen colonies that formed the United States. As John Jay put it in the Federalist Papers, 'Providence has been pleased to give this one connected country to one united people—a people descended from the same ancestors, speaking the same language, professing the same religion, attached to the same principles of government, very similar in their manners and customs.' Jay was exaggerating the ethnocultural homogeneity of the colonial population—most obviously in ignoring Blacks[9]—but it was true that none of the thirteen colonies were controlled by a national minority, and that the original division of powers within the federal system was not defined with a view to the accommodation of ethnocultural divisions.

The status of national minorities became more of an issue as the American government began its territorial expansion to the south and west, and eventually into the Pacific. At each step of this expansion, the American government was incorporating the homelands of already settled, ethnoculturally distinct peoples—including American Indian tribes, Chicanos, Alaskan Eskimos, native Hawaiians, Puerto Ricans, and the Chamoros of Guam. And at each step, the question arose whether the American system of federalism should be used to accommodate the desire of these groups for self-government.

---

[8] For the rest of the chapter I will use the term 'ethnonational' in the context of national minorities in a multination state, as distinct from the more general term 'ethnocultural', which encompasses both national minorities and immigrant groups.

[9] Hamilton, Madison, and Jay 1982. Jay not only ignores the sizeable black population, but also pockets of non-English immigrants (particularly Germans), and the remnants of Indian tribes who had been dispossessed of their lands.

It would have been quite possible in the nineteenth century to create states dominated by the Navaho, for example, or by Chicanos, Puerto Ricans, and native Hawaiians. At the time these groups were incorporated into the United States, they formed majorities in their homelands. However, a deliberate decision was made *not* to use federalism to accommodate the self-government rights of national minorities. Instead, it was decided that no territory would be accepted as a state unless these national groups were outnumbered within that state. In some cases, this was achieved by drawing boundaries so that Indian tribes or Hispanic groups were outnumbered (Florida). In other cases, it was achieved by delaying statehood until anglophone settlers swamped the older inhabitants (e.g. Hawaii; the South-West).[10] As a result, none of the fifty states can be seen as ensuring self-government for a national minority, the way that Quebec ensures self-government for the Québécois.

Indeed, far from helping national minorities, there is reason to believe that American federalism has made them worse off. Throughout most of American history, Chicanos, American Indian tribes, and native Hawaiians have received better treatment from the federal government than from state governments. State governments, controlled by colonizing settlers, have often seen national minorities as an obstacle to greater settlement and resource development, and so have pushed to strip minorities of their traditional political institutions, undermine their treaty rights, and dispossess them of their historic homelands. While the federal government has of course been complicit in much of the mistreatment, it has often at least attempted to prevent the most severe abuses. We can see the same dynamic in Brazil, where the federal government is fighting to protect the rights of Indians in Amazonia against the predations of local state governments (see Chapter 7).[11]

In short, American-style territorial federalism, far from serving to accommodate national minorities, has made things worse. This should be no surprise, since the people who devised American federalism had no interest in accommodating these groups. In deciding how to arrange their federal system—from the drawing of boundaries, to the division of powers and the role of the judiciary—their aim was to consolidate and then expand a new coun-

---

[10] Hence Nathan Glazer is wrong when he says that the division of the United States into federal units preceded its ethnic diversity (Glazer 1983: 276–7). This is true of the original thirteen colonies, but decisions about the admission and boundaries of new states were made after the incorporation of national minorities, and these decisions were deliberately made so as to avoid creating states dominated by national minorities.

[11] Similarly, Aboriginals in Australia fought for many decades to have jurisdiction over Aboriginal issues taken away from state governments, which were notoriously oppressive, and given to the federal government instead. This transfer of jurisdiction occurred in 1967. See Peterson and Sanders 1998: 11–19.

try, and to protect the equal rights of individuals within a common national community, not to recognize the rights of national minorities to self-government.[12] As I discuss below, insofar as national minorities in the US have achieved self-government, it has been outside—and to some extent, in spite of—the federal system, through non-federal units such as the 'commonwealth' of Puerto Rico, the 'protectorate' of Guam, or the 'domestic dependent nations' status of American Indian tribes.

Since American federalism was not intended to accommodate ethnocultural groups, why then was it adopted? There are several reasons why the original colonists, who shared a common language and ethnicity, none the less adopted federalism—reasons which are famously explored in The Federalist Papers. Above all, federalism was seen as a way to prevent a liberal democracy from degenerating into tyranny. As Madison put it, federalism helped to prevent 'factions'—particularly an economic class or business interest—from imposing its will through legislation to the detriment of 'the rights of other citizens, or to the permanent and aggregate interests of the community'. Federalism makes it more difficult for those who 'have a common motive to invade the rights of other citizens' to 'act in unison with each other'. The 'influence of factious leaders may kindle a flame within their particular States, but will be unable to spread a general conflagration through the other States'.[13] Conversely, the existence of strong, independent state governments provided a bulwark for individual liberties against any possible encroachment by a federal government that is captured by sinister factions.

Federalism was just one of several mechanisms for reducing the chance of tyranny. An equal emphasis was placed on ensuring a separation of powers *within* each level of government—e.g. separating the executive, judicial, and legislative powers at both the state and federal levels. This too helped minimize the amount of power that any particular faction could command, as did the later adoption of a Bill of Rights. The adoption of federalism in the United States should be seen in the context of this pervasive belief that the power of government must be limited and divided so as to minimize the threat to individual rights.

It is important to note that Madison was not thinking of ethnocultural groups when talking about 'factions'. Rather, he was concerned with the sorts of conflicts of interest which arise amongst 'a people descended from

[12] See Thomas-Woolley and Keller 1994: 416–17. Despite emphasizing this difference between the American experience and the situation of most multination federations, Thomas-Woolley and Keller do not fully consider its implications for the relevance of the American model to other countries.

[13] Madison, in Hamilton *et al.* 1982: #10, pp. 54, 61. The belief that federalism helps prevent tyranny was one reason why the Allies imposed federalism on Germany after World War II. It was supposed to help prevent the re-emergence of nationalist or authoritarian movements. For a critique of the claim that federalism is inherently more protective of individual liberty, see Minow 1990b; Neumann 1962.

the same ancestors, speaking the same language'. These include, above all else, economic divisions between rich and poor, or between agricultural, mercantile, and industrial interests. Madison's preoccupations are reflected in his list of the 'improper or wicked projects' which federalism will help prevent—namely, 'A rage for paper money, for an abolition of debts, for an equal division of property'.[14]

The subsequent history of the United States suggests that federalism offers other, more positive, benefits. For example, it has helped provide room for policy experimentation and innovation. Faced with new issues and problems, each state adopted differing policies, and those policies that proved most successful were then adopted more widely. Moreover, as the United States expanded westward and incorporated vast expanses of territory with very different natural resources and forms of economic development, it became increasingly difficult to conceive how a single, centralized unitary government would be workable. Some form of territorial devolution was clearly necessary, and the system of federalism adopted by the original thirteen colonies on the Atlantic coast served this purpose very well.

So there are many reasons, unrelated to ethnocultural diversity, why a country would adopt federalism. Indeed, any liberal democracy that contains a large and diverse territory will surely be pushed in the direction of adopting some form of federalism, regardless of its ethnocultural composition. The virtues of federalism for large-scale democracies are manifested, not only in the United States, but also in Australia, Brazil, and Germany. In each of these cases, federalism is firmly entrenched, and widely endorsed, even though none of the federal units are intended to enable ethnocultural groups to be self-governing.

In some countries, then, federalism is adopted, not because it accommodates the desire of national minorities for self-government, but rather because it provides a means by which a single national community can divide and diffuse power. Following Philip Resnick, I will call this 'territorial federalism', as distinct from 'multination federalism'.[15]

My concern in this chapter is with multination federations. Most scholarly discussions of federalism, however, have focused on territorial federalism. This is partly due to the historical influence of American federalism. Perhaps because it was the first truly democratic federation, American federalism has become the model, not just of territorial federalism, but of federalism *tout court*, or at least of 'mature' or 'classic' federalism. Similarly, the Federalist Papers are often taken to be the paradigm expression of 'the federalist principle'. Other federal systems are then categorized on the basis of how closely

---

[14] As he put it, 'the most common and durable source of factions has been the various and unequal distribution of property'. A lesser concern was the periodic schisms within the Protestant churches, which often gave rise to upsurges of religious conflict.

[15] P. Resnick 1994: 71.

they conform to the basic attributes of the American system.[16] Thus, for example, Australia is typically seen as a more truly federal system than Canada or India, since the latter deviate significantly from the American model.

Yet if our concern is with multination federalism, then we cannot use the United States as our model. The American federal system, and the Federalist Papers, offers us no guidance on how to accommodate ethnocultural groups. On the contrary, as I noted earlier, federal subunits were deliberately manipulated to ensure that national minorities could not achieve self-government through federalism. More generally, territorial federalism, in and of itself, is no guarantee that ethnocultural groups will be accommodated. Whether the allocation of powers to territorial subunits promotes the interests of national minorities depends on how the boundaries of those subunits are drawn, and on which powers are allocated to which level of government. If these decisions about boundaries and powers are not made with the conscious intention of empowering national minorities, then federalism may well serve to worsen the position of national minorities, as has occurred in the United States, Brazil, Australia, and other territorial federalisms.

3. How Flexible is Multination Federalism?

For a federal system to qualify as genuinely multination, decisions about boundaries and powers must consciously reflect the needs and aspirations of minority groups.[17] But to what extent can the boundaries and powers of federal units be defined so as to accommodate these groups? As I noted earlier, many theorists argue that federalism is appropriate precisely because it has great flexibility in answering these questions. Even a cursory survey of

[16] See e.g. Verney 1995, who argues that the US is the only true 'federal federation', whereas other countries, like Canada and India, are quasi-federations which mimic certain federal institutions but lack any federalist theory or principles.

[17] If the United States is the paradigm of territorial federalism, what is the prototype of multination federalism? Elazar argues that Switzerland is 'the first modern federation built upon indigenous ethnic and linguistic differences that were considered permanent and worth accommodating' (Elazar 1987b: 20). Yet, as Murray Forsyth notes, the old Swiss confederation, which existed for almost 500 years, was composed entirely of Germanic cantons, in terms of ethnic origin and language. While French and Italian-speaking cantons were added in 1815, the decision to adopt a federal structure was not primarily taken to accommodate these ethnolinguistic differences. According to Forsyth, the Canadian federation of 1867 was the first case where a federal structure was adopted to accommodate ethnocultural differences. This is reflected in the fact that the 1867 Constitution not only united a number of separate provinces into one country, it also divided the largest province into two separate political units—English-speaking Ontario and French-speaking Quebec—to accommodate ethnocultural divisions (see Forsyth 1989: 3–4).

federal systems shows that there is a great variety in how boundaries are drawn, and powers distributed. There seem to be few if any a priori rules regarding the size, shape, or powers of federal subunits.

I believe, however, that federalism is less flexible than many people suppose. There are significant limitations on how powers can be divided, and on how boundaries can be drawn. I will discuss these two problems in turn.

(a) Dividing Powers in a Multination Federation

Let us assume that boundaries can be drawn in such a way that national minorities form a majority in their federal subunit, as with Quebec or Catalonia. This provides a starting-point for self-government, but whether the resulting federal system is satisfactory to national minorities will depend on how powers are distributed between the federal and provincial levels. The historical record suggests that this issue may lead to intractable conflicts, because different units may seek different powers, and it is difficult for federalism to accommodate these divergent aspirations.

This is particularly true if only one or two of the federal units are vehicles for self-governing national minorities, while the rest are simply regional divisions within the majority national group. This is the case in Canada, for example, where the province of Quebec secures self-government for the Québécois, but the nine remaining provinces reflect regional divisions within English-Canada. A similar situation exists in Spain, where the Autonomous Communities of Catalonia, the Basque Country, and Galicia secure self-government for national minorities, while most of the other fourteen Autonomous Communities, such as La Mancha or Extremadura, reflect regional divisions within the majority Spanish national group.[18]

In both countries, then, some units embody the desire of national minorities to remain as culturally distinct and politically self-governing societies (what I will call 'nationality-based units'), while others reflect the decision of a single national community to diffuse powers on a regional basis (what I will call 'regional-based units').

It is likely that nationality-based units will seek different and more extensive powers than regional-based units. As a general rule, we can expect nationality-based units to seek greater powers, while regional-based units are less likely do so, and may indeed accept a gradual weakening of their powers. This is reflected in the way the American and Canadian federal systems have

---

[18] Some of the remaining fourteen Communities are not simply regional divisions, but form culturally distinct societies, even if they are not self-identified as distinct 'nations'. This is true, for example, of the Balearic Islands, Valencia, and Asturias, where distinct languages or dialects are spoken. But many of the Autonomous Communities do not reflect distinct ethnocultural or linguistic groups. For a discussion of Spain's Autonomous Communities, and their varying levels of ethnocultural distinctiveness, see Brassloff 1989.

developed. It has often been pointed out that the United States, which began as a strongly decentralized federation, with all residual powers attributed to the states, has gradually become one of the most centralized; whereas Canada, which began as a strongly centralized federation, with all residual powers attributed to the federal government, has gradually become one of the most decentralized. This is often said to be paradoxical, but is understandable when we remember that the United States is a territorial federation, composed entirely of regional-based units. Because none of the fifty states in the US are nationality-based, centralization has not been seen as a threat to anyone's national identity. While many Americans object to centralization as inefficient or undemocratic, it is not seen as a threat to the very survival of anyone's national group. By contrast, centralization in Canada is often seen as a threat to the very survival of the Québécois nation, insofar as it makes French-Canadians more vulnerable to being outvoted by anglophones on issues central to the reproduction of their culture, such as education, language, telecommunications, and immigration policy.

This difference has had a profound effect on how the US and Canada have responded to the pressures for centralization in this century. In both countries, there have been many occasions—most notably the Depression and the two world wars—when there were great pressures to strengthen the federal government, at least temporarily. In Canada, these pressures were counterbalanced by the unyielding insistence of French-Canadians that the self-governing powers of Quebec be protected, so that any temporary centralization would ultimately be reversed. In the United States, however, there was no similar countervailing pressure, and the various forces for greater centralization have gradually and cumulatively won out.

The fact that regional-based and nationality-based units typically desire different levels of power is also reflected within both Canada and the United States. For example, while most Québécois want an even more decentralized division of powers, most English-speaking Canadians favour retaining a strong central government.[19] Indeed, were it not for Quebec, there is good reason to believe that Canadian federalism would have succumbed to the same forces of centralization which won out in the United States. And while the regional-based American states have gradually lost power, we find a very different story if we look at the quasi-federal units used to accommodate national minorities—e.g. the Commonwealth of Puerto Rico, Indian tribes, or the Protectorate of Guam. In these cases of nationality-based units, we see a clear trend toward greater powers of self-government, in order to sustain their cultural distinct societies.[20]

[19] See Citizen's Forum on Canada's Future 1991: fig. 2, p. 158. See also Resnick 1994: 73, and the references in n. 22 below.

[20] For recent overviews of the rights and status of national minorities in the United States, see (on Puerto Rico): Aleinikoff 1994; Martinez 1997; Portillo 1997; Rubinstein 1993; Barreto

We find the same pattern throughout Europe as well. For example, Catalonia and the Basque Country have expressed a desire for greater autonomy than is sought by other regional-based units in Spain. Corsica seeks greater autonomy than other regional-based units in France. And in the new Russian federation, adopted after the collapse of the Soviet Union, there is considerable asymmetry between the thirty-two nationality-based units (e.g. Tatarstan, North Ossetia) and the other fifty-six federal units which simply reflect regional divisions within the majority Russian national group. The nationality-based units have demanded (and received) not only explicit constitutional recognition as 'nations', but also greater powers than the regional-based units.[21]

While many European countries are engaging in forms of regional decentralization, particularly if they had previously been highly centralized states, this process is going much farther in countries where the resulting units are nationality-based (e.g. Belgium) than regional-based (e.g. Italy). And of course the most extreme assertion of self-government—namely, secession—has only been made by nationality-based units, whether it be in the former Czechoslovakia, Yugoslavia or the Soviet Union.

In a federal system which contains both regional-based and nationality-based units, therefore, it seems likely that demands will arise for some form of *asymmetrical federalism*—i.e. for a system in which some federal units have greater self-governing powers than others. Unfortunately, it has proven extraordinarily difficult to negotiate such an asymmetrical model. There seems to be great resistance, particularly on the part of majority groups, to accepting the idea that federal units can differ in their rights and powers. As a result, national minorities have found it very difficult to secure the rights and recognition that they seek.

The difficulty in negotiating asymmetry is, in one sense, quite puzzling. If most English-speaking Canadians want a strong federal government, and most Québécois want a strong provincial government, asymmetry would seem to give both groups what they want. It seems perverse to insist that all subunits have the same powers, if it means that English-speaking Canadians

1998. On American Indians, see O'Brien 1989; Prucha 1994; J. Resnik 1989. On Guam, see Statham 1998. For a more general survey, see O'Brien 1987.

[21] G. Smith 1996: 392, 395. It is interesting to note that Russia contemplated adopting an American-style model of symmetrical/territorial federalism, but national minorities were 'outraged at [the plan] to deny special status and to acknowledge their cultural difference' (395), and Russia quickly adopted instead an explicitly multination/asymmetrical model of federalism. It's also worth noting that one of these thirty-two nationality-based units—Chechyna—has since declared its independence. For further discussion of asymmetric Russian federalism, see Ilishev 1998; Teague 1994; Khasanov 1999; Hughes 1999. It's also worth noting that upon independence, India contemplated adopting a purely territorial model of federalism, unrelated to the claims of ethnolinguistic minorities, but ended up adopting an explicitly asymmetric/multination model (see Patil 1998; Banerji 1992).

have to accept a more decentralized federation than they want, while French-Canadians have to accept a more centralized federation than they want.

Yet most English-speaking Canadians overwhelmingly reject the idea of 'special status' for Quebec. To grant special rights to one province on the grounds that it is nationality-based, they argue, is somehow to denigrate the other provinces, and to create two classes of citizens.[22] Similar sentiments have been expressed in Spain about the demand for asymmetrical status by the Basques and Catalans.[23] Some commentators—such as Charles Taylor—argue that this simply reflects confused moral thinking.[24] Liberal democracies are deeply committed to the principle of the moral equality of persons, and equal concern and respect for their interests. But equality for individual citizens does not require equal powers for federal units. On the contrary, special status for nationality-based units can be seen as promoting this underlying moral equality, since it ensures that the national identity of minorities receives the same concern and respect as the majority nation. Insofar as English-speaking Canadians view the federal government as their 'national' government, respecting their national identity requires upholding a strong federal government; insofar as Québécois view Quebec as their national government, respecting their national identity requires upholding a strong provincial government. Accommodating these differing identities through asymmetrical federalism does not involve any disrespect or invidious discrimination.[25]

It is difficult to avoid the conclusion that much of the opposition to asymmetry amongst the majority national group is rooted in a latent ethnocentrism—i.e. a refusal to recognize that the minority has a distinct national identity that is worthy of respect. This fits into the long history of neglecting or denigrating the desire of national minorities to remain culturally distinct societies, which I discussed earlier.

Another factor underlying the opposition to asymmetry is the profound influence of the American model of federalism. As I noted earlier, many people have supposed that American federalism is the model of federalism *tout court*, and that all federalisms should aim to be purely territorial. On this view, any special accommodations for nationality-based units are seen as

---

[22] On English-Canadian opposition to special status, see Cairns 1991; Milne 1991; Stark 1992; Resnick 1994; and Dion 1994, who cites a poll showing 83 per cent opposition to special status. A certain amount of *de facto* asymmetry in powers has been a long-standing aspect of Canadian federalism, but as these authors discuss, most English-Canadians have been unwilling to formally recognize or entrench this in the constitution, let alone to extend it.

[23] Brassloff 1989: 44.   [24] Taylor 1991; Webber 1994: 232–51.

[25] English-Canadians often say to Quebecers, 'Why can't we all be Canadians first, and members of provinces second?', without realizing that this involves asking the Québécois to subordinate their national identity, whereas for English-Canadians it simply involves strengthening their national identity *vis-à-vis* their regional identity.

merely transient measures that are not appropriate in a 'mature' territorial federalism.

The problem is not simply that regional and nationality-based units happen to desire different powers. These variations in desired powers reflect an even deeper difference in the very conception of the nature and aims of political federation. For national minorities, federalism is, first and foremost, a federation of *peoples*, and decisions regarding the powers of federal subunits should recognize and affirm the equal status of the founding peoples. On this view, to grant equal powers to regional-based units and nationality-based units is in fact to deny equality to the minority nation, by reducing its status to that of a regional division within the majority nation. By contrast, for members of the national majority, federalism is, first and foremost, a federation of *territorial units*, and decisions regarding the division of powers should affirm and reflect the equality of the constituent units. On this view, to grant unequal powers to nationality-based units is to treat some of the federated units as less important than others.

This difference in the conception of federalism can lead to conflicts even when there is little variation in the actual powers demanded by regional-based and nationality-based units. For example, some people have proposed a radical across-the-board decentralization in Canada, so that all provinces would have the same powers currently demanded by Quebec. This is intended to avoid the need to grant 'special status' to Quebec. The response by many Quebec nationalists, however, was that this missed the point. The demand for special status was a demand, not just for this or that power, but also for *national recognition*. As Resnick puts it, 'They want to see Quebec recognized as a nation, not a mere province; this very symbolic demand cannot be finessed through some decentralizing formula applied to all provinces.'[26] Quebec nationalists want asymmetry, not just to gain this or that additional power, but also for its own sake, as a symbolic recognition that Quebec alone is a nationality-based unit within Canada.[27]

This may seem like a petty concern with symbols rather than the substance of political power. But we find the same response in other multination federations. For example, prior to the break-up of Czechoslovakia, some people proposed a decentralized federation composed of three units with equal powers—Slovakia and two Czech regions (Moravia and Bohemia). This would enable Slovak national self-government, while also accommodating Moravia's historical status as a distinct region within the Czech nation. However, Slovak nationalists dismissed this proposal, since 'it would have

---

[26]   Resnick 1994: 77.
[27]   As I note below (n. 32), changes to the boundaries of the North-West Territories have created a new nationality-based unit, controlled by the Innuit, known as 'Nunavut'.

meant equivalence between the Slovak nation and Moravian cultural and historical specificity, thus lessening the relevance of Slovak nationhood'.[28]

Or consider the response of Catalan and Basque nationalists to the proposal to make the same maximal level of autonomy exercised by their nationality-based units available to all federal units in Spain, including the regional-based units (i.e. to 'generalize' autonomy):

the 1978 Constitution assumed the principle of autonomy because it was absolutely essential to resolve the claims to self-government made by Catalonia and the Basque country if indeed a democratic system was to be installed which aimed not just at the freedom and rights of citizens but also of peoples. When the attack began via what has been called the generalization of autonomies, the politicians tried to forget what was originally intended.[29]

We can now see why disputes about the division of powers within a multination federation are so difficult to resolve. The problem is not simply that units differ in their preferences regarding the extent of autonomy. Reasonable people of good will can often resolve that problem. And indeed many English-speaking Canadians are willing to accept a more decentralized federation than they would ideally like in order to accommodate Quebec; while many Québécois are willing to accept a less decentralized federation than they would ideally like in order to accommodate English-speaking Canada. Reasonable people are willing to compromise, within limits, on the precise powers they seek for their federal units.

Unfortunately, the problem goes deeper than this. While the majority may be willing to compromise on the precise degree of decentralization, they are unwilling to compromise on what they take to be a basic principle of federalism—namely, that all federal units should be equal in their rights and powers. Conversely, while the national minority may be willing to compromise on its demands for autonomy, it is not willing to compromise on what it takes to be a basic principle of federalism—namely, that its status as one of the founding peoples must be symbolically recognized through some form of asymmetry between nationality-based and region-based units. As a result, even if both regional-based and nationality-based units happen to desire a roughly similar set of powers, serious conflicts are likely to remain. For each side rejects on principle what the other side views as part of the very nature and purpose of federalism. For the majority nation, federalism is a compact between equal territorial units, which therefore precludes asymmetry; for the national minority, federalism is a compact between peoples, which therefore requires asymmetry between nationality-based units and regional-based units.

This helps explain why asymmetry has been so difficult to negotiate within multination federations. But there are other problems that further reduce the

[28] Pithard 1994: 164.   [29] M. Fernandez, quoted in Brassloff 1989: 35.

flexibility of federalism in adopting asymmetry. Let's assume that the conflicts I have just been discussing are somehow solved, and there is a widespread acceptance of the need for some form of asymmetry for nationality-based units. There remain some practical problems to be solved, particularly regarding the representation of the nationality-based unit in the federal government. These problems are, I believe, formidable, and we have very few models around the world of how to resolve them.

Let us imagine, then, that an asymmetrical transfer of powers from the federal government to Quebec occurs, so that the federal government would be passing laws that would apply to all provinces except Quebec. Under these circumstances, it seems only fair that Quebecers not have a vote on such legislation (particularly if they could cast the deciding vote). For example, it would seem unfair for Quebec's elected representatives at the federal level to vote on federal legislation regarding immigration if the legislation does not apply to Quebec. In short, insofar as the jurisdiction of the federal government over a national minority is reduced, compared to other regional-based units, this seems to entail that the minority group should have reduced influence (at least on certain issues) at the federal level.

Some national minorities do have this sort of reduced influence at the federal level. For example, because residents of Puerto Rico have special self-governing powers that exempt them from certain federal legislation, they have reduced representation in Washington. They help select presidential candidates in party primaries, but do not vote in presidential elections. And they have only one representative in Congress, a 'commissioner' who has a voice but no vote, except in committees. This reduced representation is seen by some as evidence that Puerto Rico is 'colonized' by the United States. But while the details of the existing arrangement are subject to criticism, the existence of reduced representation can be seen as a corollary of Puerto Rican self-government, not just its colonial subjugation. The less that a group is governed by the federal government, the less right it has to representation in that government. An asymmetry in powers entails an asymmetry in representation.

But how exactly should an asymmetry in the powers of subunits be reflected in terms of representation at the federal level? If a particular subunit has greater powers, one would expect its representatives to be fewer in number, and/or restricted in their voting power. Both of these apply to Puerto Rico. But the Puerto Rican model has obvious weaknesses. While Puerto Rico has very limited federal representation, it is still very much subject to Congressional authority in some areas. It would seem preferable, therefore, to reduce their influence in a more issue-specific way—for example, by allowing their Congressional representative to have a full vote on legislation which applies to Puerto Rico, but no vote on legislation from which Puerto Rico is exempt. Unfortunately, this is easier said than done. Many pieces of legislation deal with areas of jurisdiction that Puerto Rico is partly exempt from, and partly subject to. There is no way to divide up the business of government into such clear-cut groupings. Moreover, this leaves unanswered the question of how many representatives a nationality-based unit should have at the federal unit. A strong asymmetry in powers for federal subunits suggests that there should be a compensating reduction in the number of representatives, but what is a fair trade-off here?

This has been a serious stumbling-block in developing a workable model of asymmetrical federalism in Canada. It is increasingly accepted that a strongly asymmetrical status for Quebec will require reducing the influence of Quebec's elected representatives in the federal legislature. However, there is no available model that tells us how to do this.[30] And of course this problem links up with the previous problem of differing conceptions of federalism. Since members of the majority are already inclined to view any form of asymmetry as an unfair privileging of the minority, they will be keenly sensitive to any evidence that the minority is exercising undue power at the federal level (e.g. by voting on legislation from which they are themselves exempt).

Yet we can expect the national minority to resist any serious reduction of their representation at the federal level. After all, they are already, by definition, a minority at the federal level, and to reduce their influence even further will just make the federal government seen more remote, and indeed more of a threat. It will seem increasingly like an 'alien' government. The more Quebec's influence is reduced at the federal level, the more tempting it will be for Quebecers to decide to simply go it alone, and seek secession. Why stay within the federation if their influence on federal policy is gradually eroding?

So there are many reasons why federal systems have difficulty adopting asymmetrical arrangements. Indeed, these problems are so severe that some people have claimed that a federal system cannot survive for long if it adopts asymmetry. This is an overstatement, but there are greater limits on the flexibility of federalism than many proponents of federalism admit.[31]

The inability of federalism to accommodate asymmetry is exacerbated by the fact that the procedure for amending the constitution in a federal system is so cumbersome. For example, to amend the constitution in the United States requires the consent of thirty-five states, and two-thirds of the members of Congress. In Canada, depending on the nature of the proposed change, a constitutional amendment requires the consent of both federal houses, plus either seven provinces containing 50 per cent of population, or

---

[30] For an attempt to develop a workable model of asymmetrical federal representation, see Resnick 1994.

[31] For a survey of various forms of asymmetrical federalism, see Elazar 1987a: 54–7; and Dion 1994.

all ten provinces. Recent experience with the Equal Rights Amendment in US, or the Meech Lake and Charlottetown Accords in Canada, suggests that achieving this level of agreement is very difficult. If implementing asymmetrical federalism requires amending the powers of federal subunits, or the system of federal representation, the obstacles are enormous. Whereas a unitary state can typically amend its constitution by a single majority or super-majority vote, federalism requires the consent of concurrent majorities—i.e. majorities in the country as a whole, plus in all of its constituent units. This sets the threshold so high that even a widely supported proposal for asymmetry may fall short.

Drawing Boundaries in a Multination Federation

One limitation on federalism's ability to accommodate national minorities, then, is that it may be difficult to achieve the desired division of powers. But in addition to dividing powers, we must also draw boundaries, and this raises another limit on the flexibility of multination federalism. For federalism to serve as a mechanism for self-government, it must be possible to draw federal subunits in such a way that the national minority forms a majority within a particular subunit, as the Québécois do in Quebec. This is simply not possible for some national minorities, including most indigenous peoples in the United States or Canada, who are fewer in number, and who have been dispossessed of much of their historic territory, so that their communities are often dispersed, even across state/provincial lines. With few exceptions, indigenous peoples currently form a small minority within existing federal units, and no redrawing of the boundaries of these federal subunits would create a state, province, or territory with an indigenous majority.[32] It would have been possible to create a state or province dominated by an Indian tribe in the nineteenth century, but given the massive influx of settlers since then, it is now virtually inconceivable.

For most indigenous peoples in the US or Canada, therefore, self-government can only be achieved outside the federal system. Self-government has been primarily tied to the system of reserved lands (known as tribal 'reservations' in the United States, and band 'reserves' in Canada). Substantial powers are exercised by the tribal/band councils that govern each reserve. Indian tribes/bands have been acquiring increasing control over health, education, family law, policing, criminal justice and resource development. (Or, more accurately, they have been reacquiring these powers, since of course they governed themselves in all these areas before their involuntary incorporation into the larger Canadian or American polity.) They are becoming, in effect, a

---

[32] Two exceptions would be the Navaho in the American South-West, and the Innuit in the Canadian North-West. And indeed the boundaries of the North-West Territories in Canada have just been redrawn (in 1999) so as to create an Inuit-majority unit within the federation.

kind of 'federacy', to use Daniel Elazar's term, with a collection of powers that is carved out of both federal and state/provincial jurisdictions.[33]

One could, in principle, define each of these reserved lands as a new state or province within the federal system. But that is impractical, given that there are so many separate tribes/bands in the United States and Canada (over 600 in Canada alone), and that many of these groups are very small both in population and territory, and that they are located within existing federal subunits. Moreover, Indian peoples do not want to be treated as federal subunits, since the sort of self-government they seek involves a very different set of powers from that exercised by provinces. They would only accept the status of a federal subunit if this was a strongly asymmetrical status, which included powers typically exercised by both the federal and provincial levels. Furthermore, Indian tribes/bands differ enormously amongst themselves in the sorts of powers they desire. They seek not only asymmetry, but varying degrees of asymmetry. Yet, for the reasons I've just discussed, it is extremely difficult to achieve that sort of flexibility within a federal system. Hence Indians have pursued self-government through a sort of 'federacy' relationship that exists outside the normal federal system.

As the term suggests, a 'federacy' has important analogies with federalism—for example, both involve a territorial division of powers. But because most Indian tribes now form a minority even within their historic homelands, and so are territorially located within existing states or provinces, their self-government occurs outside of, and to some extent in opposition to, the federal system. Rather than possessing the standard rights and powers held by federal subunits, and governing under the same rules which apply to federal subunits, they instead possess a set of group-specific powers and exemptions which partially removes them from the federal process, by reducing the jurisdiction of both the federal and state/provincial governments over them. As I noted earlier, federalism in the United States and Canada, far from empowering Indian peoples, has in fact simply increased their vulnerability, by making their self-governance subject to encroachment from both federal and state/provincial governments. The achievement of Aboriginal self-government through 'federacy', therefore, involves protection against the federal system.

The fact that Indians in the United States do not control state governments has tended to make them more vulnerable, since their self-government powers do not have the same constitutional protection as states' rights. They are therefore more subject to the 'plenary power' of Congress, which has often been exercised to suit the needs and prejudices of the dominant society, not of the national minority. However, the fact that they lie outside the federal

---

[33] Elazar 1987a: 229. For the relation of Indian self-government to federalism, see Cassidy and Bish 1989; J. Resnik 1989; Elkins 1992; Long 1991; Henderson 1994.

structure has compensating advantages. In particular, it has provided much greater flexibility in redefining those powers to suit the needs and interests of the minority. Whereas there is pressure within federal systems to make all subunits equal in their powers and federal representation, 'federacy' arrangements allow for greater variations. Moreover, it is much easier to negotiate new self-government provisions for the Navaho than to amend the powers of individual states.

The same applies to other national minorities in the United States. For example, because Puerto Rico is a 'Commonwealth' not a state, it has been easier to amend its self-governing powers, and to negotiate an asymmetrical status in terms of both powers and federal representation. This might have proved impossible had Puerto Rico been granted statehood when it was incorporated by the United States in 1898.[34]

For a variety of reasons, then, federalism may lack the flexibility needed to accommodate national minorities. It may be impossible for a small national minority to form a majority in one of the federal subunits. For such groups, self-government can only be achieved outside the federal system, through some special non-federal or quasi-federal political status. And even if the boundaries can be drawn in such a way that the national minority forms a majority within a federal subunit, it may be impossible to negotiate a satisfactory division of powers, particularly if the federation includes both nationality-based and regional-based subunits.

Therefore, in many cases, the aspirations of national minorities may best be achieved through political institutions which operate outside the federal system—as 'commonwealths', 'federacies', 'protectorates', or 'associated states'—rather than by controlling a standard federal subunit. Standard models of federalism, with their implicit assumptions of equal powers and regional-based units, and their complex amendment procedures, may not be capable of responding to the distinctive interests and desires of nationality-based units.

4. Federalism, Secession, and Social Unity

So far, I have been discussing limits on the ability of federalism to accommodate the needs of national minorities. Let's imagine, however, that these problems have been overcome. Let's assume that national minorities are satisfied with the boundaries of their subunit, that they possess sufficient self-governing powers to maintain themselves as culturally distinct societies, and that

[34] On Puerto Rico's status, and the limits of potential statehood, see Rubinstein 1993; Aleinikoff 1994.

some form of asymmetry has either been accepted or proven unnecessary. In short, let's assume that federalism is working as its proponents envisage to combine shared rule with respect for ethnocultural differences. There is one further problem that is worth considering. The very success of federalism in accommodating self-government may simply encourage national minorities to seek secession. The more that federalism succeeds in meeting the desire for self-government, the more it recognizes and affirms the sense of national identity amongst the minority group, and strengthens their political confidence. Where national minorities become politically mobilized in this way, secession becomes more conceivable, and a more salient option, even with the best-designed federal institutions.

One way to describe the problem is to say that there is a disjunction between the legal form of multination federalism and its underlying political foundations. *Legally speaking*, as I noted earlier, federalism views both levels of government as possessing inherent sovereign authority. This distinguishes it from a confederation, where sovereign states delegate certain powers to a supranational body, powers that they can reclaim. In a federal system, however, the general government has inherent, not just delegated, power to govern its citizens. Just as the province of Quebec has the inherent authority to govern all Quebecers—an authority which the federal government did not delegate and cannot unilaterally revoke—so the federal government of Canada has the inherent authority to govern all Canadians (including Quebecers), an authority which the provincial governments did not delegate, and cannot unilaterally revoke.

This is the legal form of federalism. But *political perceptions* of it are likely to be rather different. National minorities often view multination federations as if they were closer to confederations. National minorities typically view themselves as distinct 'peoples', whose existence predates that of the country they currently belong to. As separate 'peoples', they possess inherent rights of self-government.[35] While they are currently part of a larger country, this is not seen as a renunciation of their original right of self-government. Rather it is seen as a matter of transferring some aspects of their powers of self-government to the larger polity, on the condition that other powers remain in their own hands. In countries that are formed from the federation of two or more national groups, the (morally legitimate) authority of the central

---

[35] The right of national groups to self-determination is affirmed in international law. According to the United Nations' Charter, for example, 'all peoples have the right to self-determination'. However, the UN has not defined 'peoples', and it has generally applied the principle of self-determination only to overseas colonies, not internal national minorities, even when the latter were subject to the same sort of colonization and conquest as the former. This limitation on self-determination to overseas colonies (known as the 'salt-water thesis') is widely seen as arbitrary, and many national minorities insist that they too are 'peoples' or 'nations', and, as such, have the right of self-determination.

government is limited to the powers that each constituent nation agreed to transfer to it. And these national groups often see themselves as having the (moral) right to take back these powers, and withdraw from the federation, if they feel threatened by the larger community.[36]

Legally speaking, nationality-based federal units do not have the right to reclaim the powers exercised by the federal government. Legally, these powers are inherently vested in the federal government, and the subunits cannot 'reclaim' what was never theirs. But the political perceptions of national minorities may not match these legal niceties. For them, the larger country feels more like a confederation than a federation, in the sense that the larger country's existence is seen as morally dependent on the revocable consent of the constituent national units. As a result, the larger political community has a more conditional existence than a unitary state, or a territorial federalism.

In short, the basic claim made by national minorities is not simply that the political community is culturally diverse (as immigrants, for example, typically claim).[37] Instead, the claim is that there is more than one political community, and that the authority of the larger state cannot be assumed to take precedence over the authority of the constituent national communities. If democracy is the rule of 'the people', national minorities claim that there is more than one people, each with the right to rule themselves. Multination federalism divides the people into separate 'peoples', each with its own historic rights, territories, and powers of self-government; and each, therefore with its own political community. They may view their own political com-

---

[36] I should emphasize that I am speaking of political perceptions, not historical facts. A rigorous historical examination may show that the existence of the national minority as a separate people did not predate that of the larger country. In some cases, the sense of national distinctiveness arose concurrently with the development of the larger federation, rather than preceding it, so that the original formation of the larger country was not, historically speaking, a 'federation of peoples'. While nationalist leaders often imply that their nation has existed since time immemorial, historians have shown that the sense of national distinctiveness is often quite recent, and indeed deliberately invented (see Anderson 1983; Gellner 1983). What matters, however, is not historical reality, but present-day perceptions. If a minority group today has a strong sense of national identity, and a strong belief in its right of self-government, then it will tend to view the federation as having only derivative authority, whatever the historical facts.

[37] As I discuss in Ch. 8, immigrants are increasingly demanding special political recognition in the form of certain 'polyethnic' rights or multicultural accommodations. But this is rarely a threat to political stability, since in making these demands, immigrants generally take the authority of the larger political community for granted. They assume, as John Rawls puts it, that citizens are members of 'one cooperative scheme in perpetuity'. Immigrants assume that they will work within the economic and political institutions of the larger society, demanding only that these institutions be adapted to reflect the increasing cultural diversity of the population they serve. National minorities, by contrast, may question the legitimacy and permanence of the larger country.

munity as primary, and the value and authority of the larger federation as derivative.[38]

The reason why multination federalisms are likely to be contested should now be obvious. The more a federal system is genuinely multinational—that is, the more it recognizes and affirms the demand for self-government—the more it will strengthen the perception amongst national minorities that the federal system is *de facto* a confederal system. That is, the more successful a multination federal system is in accommodating national minorities, the more it will strengthen the sense that these minorities are separate peoples with inherent rights of self-government, whose participation in the larger country is conditional and revocable. And if the attachment of national minorities to the larger state is conditional, then one would expect at any given time that at least some members of the minority will ask whether circumstances have changed in such a way that staying within the federation is no longer beneficial. The members of the minority are likely to disagree about this, and many of them may conclude that the federation remains the best option. But it will always be a salient question, and a source of lively debate within the national minority.

Federalism also provides national minorities with the experience of self-government, so that they will feel more confident of their ability to go it alone, and with an already recognized territory over which they are assumed to have some prima facie historical claim.[39]

Moreover, if the secession itself can be achieved peacefully, then the costs of going it alone as a small state have dramatically fallen. In the past, national minorities needed to join larger countries in order gain access to economic markets, and/or to ensure military security. But these benefits of federalism can now be achieved through confederal arrangements (like the European Union, or the North American Free Trade Agreement), and through the gradual strengthening of international law. If Quebec or Catalonia seceded, they would still be able to participate in continental or international free trade and security arrangements.[40]

---

[38] To reduce this danger, federal governments have encouraged national minorities to identify with, and feel loyalty towards, the federal government. This new identification, it is hoped, would then compete, and possible even supersede, their original national identity. However, the historical record suggests that these efforts have limited success. See, on this, Wheare 1962; Howse and Knop 1993; Norman 1994; and Kymlicka 1995a: ch. 9.

[39] This is only a prima facie claim, since the territory encompassed by the federal subunit may include the homeland of other national groups. This is a serious issue in Quebec, where the northern part of the province is the historic homeland of various indigenous peoples. These indigenous groups argue that their right of self-determination is as strong as that of the Québécois, and that if Quebecers vote to secede, they may decide to stay in Canada, so that an independent Quebec would only include the southern part of the province. See Turpel 1992.

[40] On the importance of external threats in the formation and maintenance of federations, see Lemco 1991: ch. 8. This is particularly important for understanding the Swiss

In any event, the option of secession will always be present. Indeed, in a sense, it may become the default position, or the baseline against which participation in the federation is measured. Amongst national minorities, the starting point may not be, 'Why should we seek greater autonomy?' but rather, 'Why should we continue to accept these limits on our inherent self-government?' After all, there seems to be no natural stopping point to the demands for increasing self-government. If limited autonomy is granted, this may simply fuel the ambitions of nationalist leaders who will be satisfied with nothing short of their own nation-state. Any restrictions on self-government—anything short of an independent state—will need justification.

For all these reasons, it seems likely that multination federalism will contain secessionist movements pushing for confederation or simply break up.

5. The Surprising Resilience of Multination Federations

And yet, despite all these tendencies towards secession, the remarkable fact is that no multination federation in the West has yet fallen apart. While secessionist parties have been competing freely and actively in several Western democracies for decades, they have never received a democratic mandate for secession, and no referendum on secession has succeeded. Paradoxically, multination federations appear to be combine a weak sort of unity with a surprising degree of resilience.

In thinking about social unity, therefore, we must be modest in our aims. The sort of unity that we can achieve is very different from that which uni-national states often possess. We cannot expect the Québécois to express unconditional allegiance to Canada, or to put 'Canada first'. The only sort of unity we can achieve is one which allows national minorities to give equal standing, or even primacy, to their national identity, and to give conditional allegiance to Canada. The only sort of unity we can hope to achieve, therefore, is one which coexists with the firm belief amongst national minorities that they have the right to secede, and with ongoing debate about the conditions under which it would be appropriate to exercise that right.

Yet if we lower our sights in this way, there are grounds for cautious optimism. There is no reason to take the ever-present possibility of secession as proof that multination federations will fail, and that secession must occur. On

federation. Switzerland is often cited as an example of a stable multination federation, with a strong sense of shared loyalty. But what made the development of a Swiss patriotism possible was the shared experience, over some 500 years, of having common enemies, and having to rely on each other's military support. Insofar as international bodies reduce the threat of war, the result, paradoxically, may be to undermine one of the few factors that supported the development of stable multination federations.

the contrary, the experience to date in the West suggests that democratic multination federations are remarkably resilient. This suggests that weak bonds of social unity may nonetheless be enduring bonds, and that conditional allegiances may nonetheless be powerful allegiances.

What then can keep a multination federation together? Since the main instrumental arguments for federation (economic markets and military security) have lost much of their force, it seems that we need to focus more on the intrinsic benefits of belonging to a federation—that is, the value of belonging to a country which contains national diversity. In some circumstances, I think this can be a very powerful argument. For example, Petr Pithart, the former Prime Minister of Czechoslovakia, reflecting on its dissolution, stated that:

In the last 55 years, the Czechs have lost—as co-tenants in their common house—Germans, Jews, Ruthenians, Hungarians and Slovaks. They are now, in effect, an ethnically cleansed country, even if it was not by their own will. It is a great intellectual, cultural, and spiritual loss. This is particularly true if we consider central Europe, which is a kind of mosaic. We are still living touristically from the glory of Prague, which was a Czech–German–Jewish city and a light that reached to the stars. But you cannot win elections with that kind of argument.[41]

It seems to me that there often is a 'great intellectual, cultural and spiritual loss' when multination states dissolve. And, contrary to Pithard, I think you can sometimes win elections with those kinds of arguments. As I noted earlier, no referendum on secession from a democratic multination federation has succeeded in the West.[42] It may not be easy to explain the benefits of living in a multination state, or to articulate the losses when it dissolves, which would in any event vary tremendously from country to country, depending on its history and demography. But average citizens are capable of seeing the benefits of living in a multination federation, and of comparing it with the alternatives, most (all?) of which have a much worse track record in dealing with ethnonational diversity.[43]

[41] Pithard 1994: 198.

[42] It's worth noting that even in the case of Czechoslovakia there was no referendum in Slovakia on secession, and many observers argue that had a referendum been held, it would not have passed. Meciar avoided a referendum precisely because he worried that secessionists would lose to the federalists in a free and fair referendum.

[43] Also, in Western multination federations, we see the phenomenon of what David Miller calls 'nested nationalities', in which some members of the national minority may have dual national identities. When asked their national identity, they might say that both Quebec and Canada are their nation (or both Scottish/British, Catalan/Spanish), even if one of these primary. This is quite unlike non-democratic multination states that are only held together by force: few Kosovar Albanians would say that they feel Serbian in any sense (Miller 1998).

6. Conclusion

In this paper I have explored the conditions under which federalism provides a mechanism for the fair accommodation of national minorities, and hence a viable alternative to secession in multination states. The legitimacy of federalism depends on the ways that boundaries are drawn in a federal system, and on the ways that powers are distributed. It is often difficult to make these decisions in a way that truly satisfies the aspirations of national minorities, and ongoing frustration on these issues will encourage some members to consider secession. Moreover, even when federalism is working well to satisfy these aspirations, it may simply reinforce the belief amongst some people that the group is able and rightfully entitled to secede and exercise full sovereignty. This indeed is the paradox of multination federalism: while it provides national minorities with a workable alternative to secession, it also helps to make secession a more realistic alternative to federalism.

So it would be a mistake to think that implementing federalism will remove the issue of secession from the political agenda. Federalism does not provide a magic formula for the resolution of national differences. It provides at best a framework for negotiating these differences, and to make it work requires an enormous degree of ingenuity, goodwill and indeed good luck. And even with all the good fortune in the world, multination federations will face secessionist movements.

Some people take this ongoing presence of secessionist movements as a reason for rejecting multination federalism. As I noted in Chapter 1, political theorists are increasingly concerned, not only with justice, but also with social unity, and with ensuring that any new institutions would secure the loyalty and allegiance of citizens. Before adopting federal arrangements, therefore, we should think issues of loyalty and allegiance. This is a legitimate concern, but too often we have adopted the wrong standard for measuring unity and allegiance. We have defined unity and loyalty as the elimination of the very idea of secession. This is not a reasonable or realistic standard for any multination state. We shouldn't expect citizens of a multination federation to view themselves as members of 'one cooperative scheme in perpetuity', as Rawls puts it. To demand that sort of unconditional allegiance is to set a standard that multination federations are unlikely to meet.

Rather than trying to make secession impossible or unthinkable, we should instead focus on identifying the benefits which people gain from living in a multination federation. A well-designed federal system can give national minorities good reasons to reject secession, perhaps indefinitely. As we've seen, federalism is often the only option available for accommodating conflicting national identities within a multination state, and has proven surprisingly resilient.[44] But we can only see the success of multination federalism if we rid ourselves of the traditional assumption that a 'successful' political community is one in which questions of secession do not arise.

[44] And even if a federal system eventually dissolves, it may bequeath important lessons regarding the nature and value of democratic tolerance. For example, even if Canadian federalism eventually fails, it would not have been a moral failure. On the contrary, I would argue that it has been a success, whatever happens with Quebec, since it has enabled Canadians to achieve prosperity and freedom with an almost complete absence of violence. Moreover, federalism has made possible the development of strong liberal and democratic traditions within both English and French Canada. As a result, should Canadian federalism fail, the result would almost surely be two peaceful and prosperous liberal democracies where there used to be one. Multination federalism in Canada may prove to be simply a transitional phase between British colonization and the birth of two independent liberal-democratic states, but if so, it will have been a good midwife.

6

Theorizing Indigenous Rights

In my previous work, I have tended to treat indigenous peoples as a subset of the broader category of national minorities, along with 'stateless nations' like the Catalans, Scots, Québécois, Flemish, or Puerto Ricans. While having certain unique characteristics, it seems to me that indigenous peoples typically share the tendency of these other national minorities to resist state nation-building policies, and to fight instead for some form of territorial self-government. Moreover, they offer similar justifications for doing so, appealing to their unjust incorporation into the state, and/or historic agreements guaranteeing their self-government, and/or the central importance of their land, language and culture to their identity and autonomy. In this respect, indigenous peoples raise many of the same issues as stateless nations, and it seems to me that whatever principles inform our response to the former should also inform our response to the latter (and vice-versa).

Many people argue, however, that indigenous peoples cannot be subsumed under the heading of national minorities, and must be seen as an entirely distinct category, with sui generis rights. And this seems to be the tendency of recent international law, which has sharply divorced questions of indigenous rights from the rights of other national minorities. James Anaya's book *Indigenous Peoples in International Law* provides perhaps the most sustained account of this development in international law. It also offers an intriguing explanation of how the rights of indigenous peoples are both related to, but also distinct from, that of other peoples or nations. In this review, I explore some tensions in Anaya's theory, and suggest that more work remains to be done in exploring the relationship between indigenous peoples and other national groups.

James Anaya's book provides a clear and systematic overview of the status of indigenous peoples in international law. There have been dramatic developments in international law regarding indigenous peoples in the last two decades, and Anaya provides a very helpful guide through this changing legal landscape.

The most striking development is perhaps the Draft UN Declaration on the Rights of Indigenous Peoples, which is working its way through the labyrinthine structure of the United Nations, and which Anaya discusses in

A review of S. James Anaya, *Indigenous Peoples in International Law* (Oxford University Press, New York, 1996).

depth.[1] But he also pays attention to other international bodies, such as the Inter-American Commission on Human Rights, and suggests that these regional bodies deserve more attention, since they may prove to be of pivotal importance in the implementation of international norms.

Throughout the book, Anaya discusses not only the official legal texts that relate to indigenous peoples, but also the preparatory documents and background debates. Indeed, it is in the analysis of these background debates and documents where the real dynamics of international law are exposed. When the push for new international norms began in earnest in the 1970s, these debates often revealed the crass self-interest and hypocrisy of many nation-states, combined with certain genuine fears and misunderstandings. And even now, with a growing consensus on certain norms of indigenous rights, there remains the interminable search to find the exact terms and definitions which can satisfy, or at least paper over, the different expectations of the various parties. Behind every phrase of the new Draft Declaration lies years of endless negotiations, compromises, misunderstandings and conflicting interests.

Anaya's book will undoubtedly serve as the standard reference on this topic for years to come. But Anaya wishes to do more than simply catalogue these developments. He also wishes to provide a theory of indigenous rights: he wants to show that new international norms of indigenous rights are not just an *ad hoc* compromise between contending groups, but embody a coherent and defensible set of moral principles.

Since I come to this topic as a political theorist, rather than an international lawyer, it is Anaya's theoretical claims, laid out in chapters 3 and 4, which are of most interest to me.[2] But they are also the most frustrating part of his book. In many cases, they seem to simply rephrase, rather than actually resolve, the theoretical puzzles surrounding the issue of indigenous rights.

To explain my worries, I need to fill in a bit of the context. The emergence of new international norms regarding indigenous peoples is part of a broader shift regarding the rights of 'national' minorities. By national minorities, I

[1] It was drafted by a UN Working Group on Indigenous Populations between 1985 and 1993, and approved by the UN Subcommission on the Protection of Minorities in 1994 (an independent body of experts), but has several barriers to overcome before ratification by the General Assembly.

[2] Chapters 1 and 2 lay out the history of indigenous peoples in international law; chapters 5 and 6 describe implementation issues. The first two chapters will be of general interest to people interested in indigenous rights, since the history of international law tells us much about the changing attitudes and assumptions underlying the treatment of indigenous peoples. The final chapters, by contrast, are likely to be of interest only to specialists in international law: they are full of rather arcane details about the reporting mechanisms associated with the many councils, subcommissions, commissions, agencies, etc., which oversee international norms.

mean groups which have been settled for centuries on a territory which they view as their homeland; groups which typically see themselves as distinct 'nations' or 'peoples', but which have been incorporated (often involuntarily) into a larger state. The category of national minorities (or what others call 'homeland minorities') includes indigenous peoples, like the Innuit in Canada or Sami in Scandanavia, but also includes other incorporated national groups, like the Catalans in Spain, Scots in Britain, or Québécois in Canada. These latter groups are sometimes called 'stateless nations' or 'ethnonational groups', to distinguish them from indigenous peoples.

There are no universally agreed criteria for distinguishing indigenous peoples from stateless nations, but one criterion concerns the role these groups played in the process of state-formation. As a rule, stateless nations were contenders but losers in the process of European state-formation, whereas indigenous peoples were entirely isolated from that process until very recently, and so retained a pre-modern way of life until well into this century. Stateless nations would have liked to form their own states, but lost in the struggle for political power, whereas indigenous peoples existed outside this system of European states. The Catalans, Puerto Ricans, Flemish, Scots, and Québécois, then, are stateless nations, whereas the Sami, Innuit, Maori, and American Indians are indigenous peoples.

The last decade has witnessed a remarkable shift in international norms regarding stateless nations, as well as indigenous peoples. Various recent international documents deal with stateless nations. For example, the Organization on Security and Cooperation in Europe adopted a declaration on the Rights of National Minorities in 1991, and established a High Commissioner on National Minorities in 1993. The United Nations has been debating a Declaration on the Rights of Persons Belonging to National or Ethnic, Religious and Linguistic Minorities (1993); and the Council of Europe adopted a declaration on minority language rights in 1992 (the European Charter for Regional or Minority Languages), and a Framework Convention on the Rights of National Minorities in 1995.

In short, there is a common trend to codify and strengthen the rights of national minorities, although this has taken the form of two parallel developments: one set of conventions and declarations concerning indigenous peoples, and another set of conventions and declarations concerning stateless nations.[3]

This recent preoccupation with the rights of national minorities is a dramatic shift from the post-war approach. After the failure of the minority protection scheme of the League of Nations, the claims of national minorities largely disappeared from the post-war international law context, replaced

---

[3] There have also been important recent developments in international law regarding migrant groups, but in this review I will focus on national/homeland minorities.

with a new focus on 'human rights'. National minorities who wanted something more than, or other than, the protection of their individual civil and political rights received little support from international law for their claims. In effect, international law provided only two unsatisfactory options for such minorities: they could appeal to article 1 of the United Nations Charter, which says that all 'peoples' have a right to 'self-determination'; or they could appeal to article 27 of the International Covenant on Civil and Political Rights, which says that 'members of minorities' have the right to 'enjoy their own culture . . . in community with other members of their group'.

We can see why new norms were required by considering why these two older options are unsatisfactory. To oversimplify, for most national minorities, be they stateless nations or indigenous peoples, article 1 (as traditionally understood) is too strong, and article 27 (as traditionally understood) is too weak. Most national minorities need something in-between, and recent developments in international law regarding minority rights are precisely an attempt to codify certain standards in-between articles 1 and 27.

The right to 'self-determination' in article 1 is too strong, for it has traditionally been interpreted to include the right to form one's own state. Precisely for this reason, its scope has been drastically restricted in international law. In effect, it has been limited by what is called the 'salt-water thesis': peoples who are subject to colonization from overseas have the right to independence, but national minorities within a (territorially contiguous) state do not have a right to independence. Hence internal minorities are not defined as separate 'peoples' with their own right of self-determination, even if they have been subject to similar processes of territorial conquest and colonization as overseas colonies. So the indigenous peoples of Vanuatu in the Pacific Ocean have a right of self-determination, since they were colonized from overseas, whereas the indigenous peoples of Scandinavia do not have a right of self-determination, according to the salt-water thesis, since their colonizers came by land not by sea.

For those national minorities denied recognition as 'peoples' under article 1, the only other option was to appeal to article 27 of the International Covenant on Civil and Political Rights. But this is too weak, for 'the right to enjoy one's culture' has traditionally been understood to include only negative rights of non-interference, rather than positive rights to assistance, funding, autonomy, or public recognition. In effect, it simply reaffirms that members of national minorities must be free to exercise their standard rights of freedom of speech, freedom of association, freedom of assembly, and freedom of conscience.

Needless to say, there is a vast space between article 1 rights to an independent state and article 27 rights to freedom of cultural expression and association. Indeed, almost all of the real-world debates about national minorities are precisely about this middle area: e.g. the right to use a minority language in courts or local administration; the funding of minority schools; the extent of local or regional autonomy; the guaranteeing of political representation for minorities; the protection of minority homelands from economic development or settlement, and so on. These sorts of debates are frequent sources of ethnic conflict and political instability around the world, yet international law, until recently, has had virtually nothing to say about any of them.

As a result, national minorities have been vulnerable to serious injustice. Article 27 has helped protect certain civil rights relating to cultural expression. But it has not stopped states from rescinding funding for minority-language schools, or abolishing traditional forms of local autonomy, or encouraging settlers to swamp minority homelands. None of these policies, which can be catastrophic for national minorities, violate the rights to cultural expression and association protected in article 27.[4] To protect against these injustices, national minorities require certain guarantees regarding their lands, cultural institutions, and political self-government. One way to state this is to say that national minorities need rights to 'self-determination', as declared in article 1. Unfortunately, article 1 invokes too narrow a conception of the possible forms of self-determination. Many national minorities do not need, and do not want, their own independent state. They want some form of autonomy within a larger state, rather than seeking secession. Moreover, article 1 has an arbitrary account of which groups can claim self-determination. The salt-water thesis, which restricts self-determination rights to overseas colonies, is unjustified. Internal national minorities can be just as oppressed, and just as in need of self-determination, as overseas colonies.

For these and other reasons, we need a new conception of the rights of national minorities which accords internal minorities substantive rights of autonomy and self-determination (unlike article 27), but which works within the framework of larger states (unlike article 1). This is precisely what the various declarations and conventions listed above have sought to do.

I think these developments are of great importance, and reflect genuine progress in our understanding of the needs and aspirations of national minorities. But they also raise some deep theoretical puzzles that Anaya addresses without really resolving.

One question concerns the distinction between indigenous peoples and stateless nations. As we've seen, there have been important developments in international law regarding both stateless nations and indigenous peoples. But to date, they have been dealt with under separate instruments, and accorded quite different rights. To oversimplify, I would say that recent

---

[4] For a more detailed elaboration of the way that traditional human rights principles fail to protect national minorities from grave injustice, see Ch. 4.

developments regarding indigenous peoples accept that they are entitled to self-determination, and seek to modify existing notions of self-determination to accommodate the fact that they do not seek their own state. Put another way, the UN draft declaration can be seen as an expanded but more modest version of article 1: it extends self-determination to include indigenous peoples, but provides a more modest account of what self-determination means, focusing on internal autonomy rather than independent statehood.

By contrast, the Council of Europe framework convention for stateless nations can be seen as a strengthened version of Article 27, extended to include a few more rights (e.g. to publicly funded minority-language schools). But it shies away from any clear commitment to notions of self-determination or political autonomy for stateless nations.

What explains this distinction? On what basis can we say that indigenous peoples have a stronger claim to self-determination than other national minorities? Why should the Sami have a right to self-determination under international law and not the Catalans? Why the Innuit and not the Québécois? Why the hill tribes in India and not the Kashmiris or Sikhs? Why indeed do we need to single out indigenous peoples at all under international law? Why not simply include indigenous peoples under a broader category of national minorities, and assert that all national minorities have rights of self-determination?

There are two familiar justifications for according indigenous peoples stronger rights of self-determination than stateless nations. The first claims that indigenous peoples exercised historical sovereignty that was wrongfully taken from them, and so self-determination is simply restoring their inherent sovereignty. Indigenous claims to self-determination, on this view, are analagous to the claim of the previously-independent Baltic countries to secede from the Soviet Union: it simply restores their historic status as sovereign polities. By contrast, while stateless nations may have had various levels of autonomy over the centuries, and may have been passed involuntarily from one empire to another several times, they rarely formed their own sovereign states.

Anaya rejects this 'historic sovereignty' line of argument, both because it is unlikely to be accepted by the international community, and because it 'ignores the multiple, overlapping spheres of community, authority and interdependency that actually exist in the human experience' (p. 78). It is questionable whether pre-contact indigenous communities had (or desired) the sort of 'sovereignty' which Western states jealously claimed. In any event, claims based on historic sovereignty would only be appropriate if the aim was to establish independent states (like the Baltic states). If the aim instead is to 'rearrange the terms of integration' within existing states (p. 79), then we need a conception of self-determination which sets limits on state sovereignty, rather than a conception of self-determination which simply relocates state sovereignty.[5]

A second familiar line of argument says that indigenous peoples need self-determination to preserve their pre-modern way of life. On this view, state-less nations typically share a common civilization with the majority, and so do not need self-determination in the same way as indigenous peoples, whose way of life is incompatible with modern state structures.

Anaya also implicitly rejects this argument. One problem with this line of argument is that it implies that once indigenous peoples participate in the modern world, then they lose their claim to self-determination.[6] Yet for Anaya, the whole point of self-determination is not to preserve cultural isolation or a static way of life, but rather to ensure fair terms of interaction, and to enable indigenous peoples to decide for themselves when and how to borrow from other cultures (183).

But if Anaya rejects these two arguments, on what basis does he say that indigenous peoples have a stronger right to self-determination than other national groups? The short answer is that he doesn't make this claim. On the contrary, he accepts that all national groups have the same right of self-determination. Or, more accurately, he says that all national groups have the same *substantive* rights of self-determination. These substantive rights have two dimensions: (*a*) 'constitutive self-determination', which means that political structures should be created by processes that are guided by the will of the peoples governed by them; and (*b*) 'ongoing self-determination', which means that governing institutions, however they were initially created, should be such that people living under them can live and develop freely on a continuous basis (80–1).

According to Anaya, all national groups—all 'peoples'—can claim these rights of substantive self-determination. What this requires in practice, he says, will vary from context to context. In determining the practical meaning of self-determination, he suggests that we can specify self-determination in terms of five discrete subordinate norms: non-discrimination; cultural integrity; control over land and resources; social welfare and development; and self-government. According to Anaya, all national groups have claims to substantive self-determination with respect to these five dimensions of social and political life.

---

[5] In effect, to defend indigenous self-determination on the basis of historic sovereignty challenges the arbitrary assumption that article 1 only applies to 'saltwater' colonies, but it does not challenge the assumption that article 1 self-determination involves or entails sovereignty. Hence it is not useful for developing new forms of self-determination within larger states.

[6] This is indeed is what Brazil used to argue: that Indians in the Amazon aren't 'real' Indians anymore, since they wear Western clothes, and enter into agreements with multinational companies, and so don't need any special rights. See Ch. 7.

Does this mean that there is no basis for singling out indigenous peoples under international law? Not necessarily. According to Anaya, what distinguishes indigenous peoples is the *remedial* aspect of self-determination. Indigenous peoples have special claims because their substantive rights to self-determination have been violated more systematically than other national groups, and continue to be more vulnerable to violation. Special remedies are required for indigenous peoples that are not required for other national groups.

Anaya's theory is an intriguing one, which I personally find quite attractive, particularly if it is offered as a normative theory of how international law ought to be structured. But Anaya does not offer this as a normative theory; he offers it as an interpretation of 'actually existing' international law. He argues that these substantive and remedial norms of self-determination are already present in international law, and that he is just bringing out their internal logic or rationale.

And here I have some difficulties. Viewed as an interpretation of current international law, rather than as a proposal for reforming international law, I think Anaya's account suffers from some serious problems. First, I see no evidence that the international community accepts a right of self-determination for non-indigenous national minorities. As I noted earlier, there have been important developments regarding the rights of stateless nations, particularly in Europe, but they have explicitly avoided any reference to territorial autonomy or political self-determination.[7]

This may simply reflect power politics: according self-determination to indigenous peoples, who tend to be small in number and geographically isolated, threatens the state to a far lesser degree than according self-determination to large minorities who are potentially capable of secession and independent statehood. Perhaps a morally consistent position would accord self-determination to both indigenous peoples and stateless nations. But so far as I can tell, the international community has not (yet) accepted any general principle of self-determination for national groups, and, a fortiori, such a general principle cannot be what underlies recent developments in the international law regarding indigenous peoples.

Second, even if certain groups need distinctive remedial rights in light of historic violations of self-determination, does this require or justify having separate conventions for indigenous peoples and stateless nations? It seems to me that, if we examine the ways in which self-determination has been denied to national minorities, the difference between indigenous peoples and stateless nations is often a matter of degree, not of kind. In many countries, both kinds of groups have systematically been denied their claims to language, self-government, and control over land and resources.

[7] For example, Eastern European countries are very reluctant to accept territorial autonomy for their national minorities. See Kymlicka and Opalski 2001.

To be sure, this process has often been worse for indigenous peoples. But there have been many national minorities who have suffered terribly. Consider the Crimean Tatars, who were deported en masse from Crimea, deprived of all their land and property, and who have returned to find that all evidence of their earlier habitation has been systematically obliterated (e.g. all the street and city names have been changed, libraries and mosques closed, etc.). It seems to me that the violation of their rights to self-determination by the Soviets is quite comparable to the violations suffered by the indigenous peoples in the Soviet Far North.[8]

In any event, even if we can point to important differences in the forms or extent of historical rights-violations, won't the relevance of this difference diminish over time? Remedial rights are, in most cases, temporary or transitional (consider affirmative action). They are needed to overcome the effects of a historic injustice, but if successful, they will help restore a group to its rightful status and strength. At that point, remedial rights are no longer required. By contrast, substantive rights are more permanent—they are, if you like, 'inherent' rights of self-determination.

This suggests that even if indigenous peoples have certain distinctive remedial rights of self-determination, this wouldn't justify establishing any permanent system of differential rights between indigenous peoples and stateless nations. It would only make sense to establish a permanent distinction between indigenous peoples and stateless nations if they had different *inherent* rights of self-determination. Yet that is what Anaya seems to deny.

In short, I doubt whether Anaya's ingenious account really captures or explains the emerging norms of international law. I don't think that the distinction between the 'substantive' and 'remedial' aspects of self-determination can do the work Anaya requires of it. On the one hand, his claim that all nations enjoy the same 'substantive' self-determination is far stronger than international law has yet accepted; on the other hand, if the distinctive rights of indigenous peoples are purely remedial, rather than inherent, then it is not clear why we need a separate charter which establishes permanent distinctions between indigenous peoples and stateless nations.

This suggests that there must be some other reason why the international community is (slowly) converging on new norms regarding indigenous peoples. A desire to remedy past wrongs is surely part of the explanation, but I suspect that another, more important, reason is the belief that the cultural differences between majorities and indigenous peoples are much greater than with stateless nations. Indigenous peoples do not just constitute distinct

---

[8] As it happens, the Crimean Tatars actually describe themselves as 'indigenous peoples'. However, this reflects the old Soviet terminology according to which groups that lack a kin-state are 'indigenous', whereas groups with a kin-state are 'national minorities'. This is obviously an idiosyncratic definition, since the Catalans, Scots, Welsh, Corsicans, and Basques would all count as indigenous on this definition.

cultures, but they form entirely distinct forms of culture, distinct 'civilizations', rooted in a premodern way of life that needs protecting from the forces of modernization, secularization, urbanization, 'Westernization', etc.

In other words, the basis for international protection of indigenous peoples is not so much the scale of mistreatment in the past, but rather the scale of cultural difference. It is important to realize that these are, in principle, quite different grounds for rights. There can be horrible mistreatment between groups that share a common 'civilization': consider the violence between Catholics and Protestants in Ireland; or between Serbs and Croats in Yugoslavia. In both cases, most commentators argued that the two groups are almost indistinguishable in their basic ways of life, yet this has done nothing to ensure peaceful coexistence or mutual respect.[9] Or consider Franco's attempt to eliminate all traces of the Catalan language in Spain; or France's attempt to eliminate all traces of the Basque and Breton languages.

Conversely, there can be enormous cultural difference, without any history of mistreatment. In parts of Asia, rulers have often been much more ruthless towards 'communal contenders' (i.e. groups which can mount an effective challenge for state power, and which often share a common civilization with the rulers) than towards indigenous peoples, who may be radically 'Other' in terms of culture, but who pose no threat to the ruling powers (Kingsbury 1999).

I suspect that, for many people, the basis for singling out indigenous peoples is not their history of mistreatment, but their cultural 'Otherness'—in particular, their isolation from, and repudiation of, modern ways of life.

Anaya is strangely silent on this question. He neither affirms nor denies the widespread belief that indigenous peoples adhere to a radically different and 'incommensurable' form of life. He simply sets this question to the side, as if it was not relevant to the international law regarding indigenous rights.

However, I think this issue cannot be avoided. I understand why Anaya wishes to avoid relying on any claims about radical cultural difference. As I noted earlier, this line of argument would put severe constraints on the direction of indigenous self-determination. It would imply that as soon as indigenous peoples start driving cars, going to university, working in modern corporations, and adopting other aspects of modern Western lifestyles, then they lose their claim to self-determination. They could only maintain distinctive rights to self-determination if they maintain a traditional way of life.

Moreover, this line of argument has often been accompanied by a certain kind of paternalism. It implies that indigenous peoples not only have a different way of life, but also that they cannot safely be exposed to other ways

---

[9] Indeed, Ignatieff argues that groups become *more* likely to persecute others the more similar they become (Ignatieff 1993). I don't think this is true as a general statement, but he is surely right that the reduction in cultural difference does not, it itself, reduce the danger of persecution.

of life: they are incapable of making an informed judgement about whether or when to borrow influences from other cultures. It leads to cultural and political isolation, rather than cultural and political self-determination.

By contrast, Anaya repeatedly emphasizes that indigenous peoples are already active participants in larger social and political structures, and they need a form of self-determination that enables them to negotiate on fair terms with the larger world, rather than remaining isolated from it. This implies that cultural differences between indigenous peoples and the larger society may diminish over time, as each side learns from, and adapts to, the other.

Given his commitment to an interactionist, rather than an isolationist, conception of indigenous self-determination, one would have expected Anaya to tackle head on the popular argument that indigenous rights are grounded in radical cultural difference. Yet as I noted earlier, he simply avoids addressing this claim, perhaps because he realizes that he might alienate many supporters of indigenous rights.

By setting aside the issue of radical cultural difference, Anaya also sidesteps another major controversy concerning indigenous rights—namely, whether standard human rights norms apply to indigenous self-government, or whether it is a form of cultural imperialism to expect indigenous communities to abide by 'Eurocentric' principles of individual civil and political rights.

Since Anaya defends indigenous rights on the basis of a universal right to self-determination, he has no reason to say that familiar human rights principles don't apply as much to indigenous peoples as to stateless nations or other self-determining national groups. And indeed he emphasizes that indigenous self-determination is integrally connected to and derivative of traditional norms of human rights, rather than in conflict with these norms (55). It follows, for example, that indigenous governments should be democratic, and indeed Anaya explicitly says this (109–10).

Yet some defenders of indigenous rights, in Canada and elsewhere, argue that individual civil and political rights are grounded in 'western individualism', and have no place in indigenous cultures. This is reflected in the demand of some indigenous communities that their internal governments be exempted from the Bill of Rights in the United States, or the Charter of Rights in Canada. To be sure, as I discussed in Chapter 4, there are many reasons why indigenous groups might seek such an exemption without rejecting the underlying norms of human rights. However, the role of individual civil and political rights is controversial in many indigenous communities, and it is surprising that Anaya simply takes for granted the application of traditional human rights norms.

This is particularly surprising in his discussion of the principle of 'cultural integrity', which he defines as one of the five major elements of self-determination (98–104). Some indigenous spokespersons would say that expecting indigenous governments to be democratic violates the 'integrity' of indigenous cultures, which may have centuries-old traditions of non-democratic governance. Similarly, norms of sexual equality might conflict with deeply-rooted traditions. Does the norm of 'cultural integrity' provide indigenous peoples with a right to ignore or set aside human rights principles that conflict with their traditions? Or does the norm of cultural integrity only apply to cultural practices that are consistent with human rights norms?

Anaya does not address this question. He does not discuss cases where illiberal or undemocratic traditions violate existing human rights norms, and does not tell us what the norm of cultural integrity implies or entails in such cases. Instead, he focuses solely on benign examples of claims to 'cultural integrity'—e.g. using indigenous languages in court, or the protection of sacred sites. Few people would disagree with a principle of 'cultural integrity' if it were limited to such benign cases. But at least in popular debates, the norm is applied more widely, as a basis for perpetuating traditions which violate people's individual civil and political rights. People's attitudes towards the norm of 'cultural integrity' will depend a great deal on whether it does or doesn't provide a justification for maintaining oppressive traditions.

This is a particular problem for those who wish to defend indigenous rights on the grounds of radical cultural difference. It would be strange to defend indigenous self-determination on the grounds that indigenous cultures are radically incommensurable with Western ways of life, and then insist that 'cultural integrity' only applies to cultural traditions which conform with Western norms of human rights. Since Anaya avoids any appeal to radical cultural difference, it might be easier for him, in principle, to say that indigenous governments must abide by traditional human rights norms. But I think he needs to address the question more explicitly, since it is surely one of the major sources of controversy regarding indigenous self-government.

Conclusion

Anaya presents an innovative account of the theoretical basis for indigenous rights. One of the ways in which it is innovative is in downplaying the intrinsic distinctiveness of indigenous peoples and cultures. On Anaya's account, the focus is on the contingent history of rights-violations, rather than intrinsic cultural difference. He emphasizes that indigenous peoples share the same substantive rights of self-determination as other national groups, differing only in their remedial rights.

This account is interesting, but I think it faces a number of objections: it is in considerable tension with the realities of international law (which has not accepted a general principle of self-determination for national groups); it conflicts with the self-understandings of many defenders of indigenous rights (who place more emphasis on intrinsic cultural difference); and it seems to justify only transitional, rather than permanent, differences in the rights of indigenous peoples and stateless nations.

I am not suggesting that Anaya cannot persuasively respond to these objections. Indeed, I personally find his account quite attractive, and I suspect that much more could be said on its behalf. What is puzzling is that Anaya himself tends to avoid these objections, rather than confront them head on. He does not try to show that international law has accepted or will accept a more general principle of national self-determination; he does not challenge those who rely on claims of radical cultural difference; and he does not explain why differences in remedial rights require or justify permanent differences under international law. In these ways, Anaya's account is both frustrating and intriguing.[10]

[10] I should emphasize again that I have focused on Anaya's theoretical claims in the middle section of the book. I have not said anything about the final part, which provides a clear and comprehensive overview of issues relating to the implementation of international norms. This part of his book is beyond my area of expertise, but I am none the less inclined to question Anaya's optimistic tone regarding the prospects for implementing these new international norms. For example, Anaya cites the case of the Lubicon Cree Indians in Canada to show that international law now supports indigenous peoples in their struggles, since the United Nations Human Rights Committee declared in 1990 that their rights are being violated by the Canadian government (*Omniyak, Chief of the Lubicon Lake Band v. Canada*, 1990). But as Anaya himself notes, the UN judgement did not specify any remedy for this rights-violation, and very little has in fact improved for the Lubicon. (Insofar as the Lubicon have gained anything in recent years, it is arguably due, not to international law, but to an international boycott of the lumber company exploiting their lands). Moreover, and more importantly, the UN affirmed that it is up to the Canadian government to decide how to deal with the problem, with no threat of penalties or sanctions. In this sense, one can read *Omniyak* as giving the Lubicon Cree a moral victory, but as giving the Canadian government the real power. This seems to me true of most of the other cases which Anaya cites. He provides very few examples where international law has provided concrete benefit to indigenous peoples. Despite his optimistic tone in chapters 5 and 6, it seems to me that the prospects for effective enforcement of international norms of indigenous self-determination are very low. Indigenous peoples may get moral victories from international law, but the real power remains vested in the hands of sovereign states, who can (and do) ignore international norms with impunity. Anaya may be right that 'international law, although once an instrument of colonialism, has developed and continues to develop, however grudgingly and imperfectly, to support indigenous peoples' demands' (4). But I would emphasize how 'imperfect' this support really is.

7

Indigenous Rights and Environmental Justice

1. Introduction

If we are to tackle effectively global environmental issues we will need a theory of distributive justice in international relations.[1] The development of such a theory involves a break with the Western political theory tradition, which has generally viewed international relations as a Hobbesian 'state of nature'. Norms of justice are seen as inapplicable in such a state, because there is no mechanism or institution (such as a sovereign authority) to ensure that moral actions are reciprocated. However, several commentators have shown that this position cannot be sustained without invoking a more global moral scepticism that would equally apply to domestic justice.[2]

Any plausible conception of international justice will have to include a number of different elements. For example, it will have to reconcile the sometimes competing demands of economic development and environmental preservation. On the one hand, countries in the Third World claim a right of development, including the transfer of resources and technology to enable them to industrialize and thereby bring their standard of living closer to those in the First World.[3] On the other hand, if development in the Third World continues along its current path, it will lead to the destruction of the global environment. If the Third World ever reaches levels of production matching the First World—with its corresponding use of fossil fuels, CFCs, water, forests etc.—the world as a whole will become uninhabitable.[4] A theory of international justice must recognize the legitimate demands for economic development, as well as the need for environmental protection, but combining both into a single theory is going to be complicated.[5]

---

[1] Goodin 1990.

[2] See e.g. Beitz 1979, Part 1; Cohen 1985. It may be true that certain norms of justice require the sort of international coordinating mechanisms that do not yet exist. However, the absence of such mechanisms is not a reason to ignore justice—rather, it gives rise to a duty to create the necessary institutions (Shue 1988).

[3] For a survey of issues raised by the right to development, see Dupuy 1980.

[4] Dobson 1991: 64–70.

[5] These issues are comprehensively discussed in Shue 1992; 1993.

In this paper, I want to talk about a further complication that a theory of distributive justice must address—namely, that justice between states does not guarantee justice for sub-state communities, such as indigenous peoples. I don't just mean the obvious point that elites in Third World countries may impose development/preservation policies in a discriminatory or corrupt way. My concern, rather, is that even if there is a good-faith effort to distribute the costs and benefits fairly, this may still have devastating effects on indigenous peoples, effects that may lead us to question our existing understanding of justice.

The situation of indigenous peoples raises a number of important questions about the presuppositions of both domestic and international justice—e.g. the relationship between the claims of individuals, communities and states; the nature of sovereignty; and the accommodation of cultural differences. I want to look at these questions, and how they affect discussions of social justice and environmental protection.

2. Distributive Justice and Indigenous Peoples

Consider the following cases.[6] The government of Bangladesh has encouraged urban poor from the overpopulated heartland to settle and develop the Chittagong Hill Tracts, traditionally occupied by various Tibeto-Burman tribes.[7] Similarly, the government of Indonesia has encouraged some of its Javanese citizens to develop and settle western New Guinea, the traditional homeland of indigenous Papuans. In both cases, the state has sponsored the settlement of less populated frontier lands held by indigenous peoples, as a response to poverty and landlessness in the heartland.

In both cases, the indigenous peoples are slowly being overrun by settlers—becoming a minority in their own homeland. This has led to resistance movements by the indigenous inhabitants, who claim a right to control their traditional homelands and to exclude others from that land. A similar policy was started by the government of Brazil, now partly retracted under international pressure,[8] to encourage landless people to settle in Amazonia. In each case, the government justified the settlement policy on the grounds that the lands held by indigenous peoples belonged to the country as a whole, and should be used for the benefit of all the people, both indigenous and non-indigenous, particularly the poorest people. A more intensive population and cultivation of frontier land would promote a more equitable distribution of resources, and ensure a better life for more people.

---

[6] My description of these cases, and of the issues they raise, is heavily indebted to Peter Penz's excellent article on development policy and indigenous peoples. See Penz 1992.

[7] For a detailed discussion of this policy, see Ahmed 1993.   [8] Hurrell 1992.

In some cases, the reason why these homelands are relatively less populated is that the indigenous population has been decimated by deliberate killing, and/or by diseases brought by settlers.[9] Obviously, no plausible conception of justice would allow settlers to decimate the local population, and then justify their settlement by the fact that there are few indigenous inhabitants left. But the extent of depopulation varies from case to case, as does the culpability of those who are now being encouraged to settle in indigenous homelands. In at least some cases, desperately poor people from the heartland, who may themselves be migrants from other areas, cannot be said to be responsible for, or the beneficiaries of, acts of genocide committed against indigenous peoples.

For those of us who believe both in resource egalitarianism and in the rights of indigenous peoples, this justice-based argument for settling indigenous lands creates an awkward dilemma.[10] Resource egalitarianism insists that there are some limits on the size of the resources that any group can claim— limits to the size of the benefits they can demand or withhold from others. Are the rights demanded by indigenous peoples therefore inconsistent with an egalitarian view of social justice?

There are many reasons to be sceptical of this justification for settlement. Most indigenous groups are not resource-rich—on the contrary, they have already been dispossessed of their most valuable land, and settlement policies take advantage of their vulnerability to appropriate what little is left. Moreover, insofar as indigenous groups do seem better off than the urban poor, this is probably because the poor have outstanding claims of justice against the elites in their own society, or against the First World. Indeed, the policy of promoting settlement in the Amazon is used by Brazilian elites precisely to deflect efforts at reforming one of the most unequal systems of land ownership in the world.[11] If these obligations of justice towards the urban poor were met, it seems likely that indigenous peoples would no longer have more per capita resources than people in the heartland. Indeed, it may turn out that resource egalitarianism would require redistribution from the heartland to indigenous peoples. It seems reasonable that the obligations of heartland elites and First World countries should be met first, before looking to indigenous resources, if only because there is a much lower level of contact and interdependence between indigenous peoples and the heartland poor, and so the former are less implicated in the latter's condition. So the likelihood that settling indigenous lands would promote resource egalitarianism in the real world is small.

[9] Hemming 1987. It is estimated that two to five million Indians lived in Brazil when European colonizers first arrived. They now number only around 200,000.

[10] By 'resource egalitarianism', I mean the view that justice requires some sort of equality in the distribution of resources. I describe and defend one version of equality of resources in Kymlicka 1990a: ch. 2.

[11] Engel 1988: 252–3.

Moreover, experience has taught us that when elites justify settlement policies on the ground that these policies aid the heartland poor, this is often a dishonest rationalization for their own enrichment, and they make sure that they acquire title to the most valuable land or mineral resources.[12] To be sure, this varies from country to country. According to Norman Myers, subsistence farmers (what he calls the 'shifted cultivator') account for about half of the deforestation world-wide, with the other half resulting from a combination of commercial logging, ranching, mining, or infrastructure development (roads, dams, etc). So the pressure for settlement is at least in part a demand of the poor, not just a scheme of the elites, and their needs must be addressed if the pressure is to be lessened.[13]

But even when well-intentioned, these forms of settlement are almost always unsustainable. Turning rainforest into farms just doesn't work—land clearance leads to soil damage, erosion, and pollution, with soil exhaustion after one or two harvests, which leads to abandonment of the land and further deforestation.[14] Perhaps the only sustainable forms of use are those already practised by the indigenous peoples, which is not surprising since they know most about the possibilities and limits of their environment.

Settlement plans are almost always flawed in one or more of these three ways—that is, they serve the rich rather than the poor; and/or they lead to environmental destruction rather than sustainable development; and/or they target indigenous groups which are in fact resource-poor rather than resource-rich.

Indeed, this may be all that needs to be said for real-world policy debates; but I think it is worth pursuing this issue, for two reasons. First, people in the Third World may see First World dismissal of settlement policies as hypocritical.[15] After all, much of our wealth came precisely from the settlement of frontier lands that were the traditional homelands of indigenous peoples. This is true of Canada, the United States, Australia, New Zealand, and other developed countries. And it was sustainable development. Even if our current agricultural and mining practices are not sustainable, the fact is that settling and cultivating our frontier has improved the standard of living of millions of people for over one hundred years. And some of the people who benefited from this settlement were the urban, landless poor. Indeed, this is the very essence of our national mythologies—people with little to their name could 'go West', and start a new life. This may be partly a myth—and

[12] For the extensive role of commercial interests in tropical deforestation, see Swaney and Olson 1992.

[13] Myers 1992: 432, 447; cf. Wallace 1996.

[14] See de Onis (1992). de Onis himself argues that a sustainable form of settlement and development is possible, if a suitable system of land use zoning is established, including preservation of large areas of intact rainforest and Indian lands.

[15] Hurrell 1992: 406–8; McCleary 1991: 692.

certainly the elites also gained from opening up the West—but it is a powerful myth.

Moreover, we do not act as if this settlement of the frontier was inherently unjust. Of course, there are many aspects of the settlement we now see as unjust—too much coercion and violence was used, too many treaties were broken, and too little land was left for the original indigenous inhabitants. Most people favour some form of compensation for these historical injustices. But this compensation does not take the form of restoring all of the original homeland to the tribe. That is, we act as if the manner of settlement was unjust, but settlement was not necessarily unjust—it was not inherently wrong to expect the indigenous populations in western North America to share at least some of their land with the expanding population in the east.[16]

So people in the First World should be cautious in telling governments in the Third World that settling frontier lands is not a viable or just route to development. Of course, the Prairies are not the Rainforest. And, as I noted earlier, the evidence suggests that few if any settlement policies are enacted out of a sincere commitment to justice. But we should be sensitive to the perception amongst Third World leaders that we are imposing a double-standard in this area; we should explain our opposition to these policies carefully, rather than dismissing them out of hand. The charge of hypocrisy will be raised, and rightly so, whenever our attitude towards conservation in the Third World appears to be merely self-serving, and so we must address the issue of justice head on.

Another reason for pursuing this issue is that there are important philosophical questions here. While resource egalitarians and indigenous rights advocates both oppose settlement policies, they seem to have different and perhaps conflicting reasons for their opposition. Many indigenous groups claim that they have an inherent or morally fundamental right to their traditional homelands, including rights to the mineral resources in them, no matter how large these resources are. Brazilian Indians, for example, constitute 0.16 per cent (1/600th) of the population, but have rights to 8.5 per cent (1/12th) of the land.[17] This seems to conflict with resource egalitarianism, which insists that there are limits on the size of the resources that any group can claim—limits to the size of the benefits they can demand or withhold from others. Resource egalitarianism may support indigenous land claims, but only in a more qualified and conditional form, not as inherent rights.

Moreover, the claim by indigenous peoples that they have inherent rights over their land underlies their stance, not only on settlement policies, but also on a wide range of other issues, such as self-government rights, treaty rights, hunting and fishing rights, and exemptions from some forms of taxation. There is a growing international movement towards the international

---

[16] For a discussion of these issues, see Waldron 1992.   [17] da Cunha 1992: 282.

recognition and protection of these rights, through a separate charter of indigenous rights.[18] The idea that indigenous peoples have a morally fundamental claim to these rights is widely seen as inconsistent with liberal egalitarianism, which insists on equality not only in resources, but also in political rights and legal status. There seems to be an underlying tension between liberal egalitarianism and indigenous rights that is worth examining, since it arises in many areas.

In particular, this apparent conflict raises the question whether resource egalitarianism, and liberal justice more generally, is missing something. Many people will feel uneasy with the idea that justice could, even in principle, endorse settlement policies that encroach on the homelands of indigenous peoples. This suggests that liberal justice is unable to take proper account of the legitimate values and claims of communities and cultures. Is there a more community- or culture-sensitive way to interpret or apply principles of justice?

3. The Environment and Social Justice

It would take a book to sort through all these issues. What I would like to do is simply to flag some of the more important concerns that can and have been raised about liberal egalitarianism, and that should be kept in mind when thinking about global distributive justice.

There are a variety of objections one could raise to resource egalitarianism. One environmentalist objection says that the whole framework of distributive justice is inappropriate when discussing land and the natural environment generally. According to some environmentalists, the language of distributive justice promotes a view of the natural world as a 'resource' to be used for human consumption. As Robyn Eckersley puts it, to circumscribe the problem in terms of distributive justice can 'serve to reinforce rather than challenge the prevailing view that the environment is simply a human resource (albeit a resource to be utilized more efficiently and equitably)'.[19]

The language of justice, on this view, reflects and promotes consumerism, or the 'politics of getting'. We need to shift from this focus on consuming resources to a perspective which distinguishes true needs from false wants, and which emphasizes stewardship rather than possession of the environment.[20]

---

[18] Anaya 1996; Kingsbury 1995; Daes 1993. See Ch. 6.   [19] Eckersley 1992: 9.

[20] *Ibid*, p. 18; Dobson 1990: 91–2. More generally, some people see a conflict between the values of social justice and ecology, each of which must be compromised in the name of the other. To insist on perfect equality or absolute social justice, they say, would amount to demanding 'fair shares in extinction' (Sandy Irvine and Alec Ponton, quoted in *ibid*. 173).

There are two ways of interpreting this objection. One interpretation sees the language of justice as inherently instrumentalist and consumerist, and hence as playing no legitimate role in decisions about the environment; the other sees the language of justice as serving a valid but limited function, which needs to be supplemented and constrained by other 'ecocentric' considerations. The first says that the language of justice is not appropriate for describing the claims and interests of humans with respect to the environment, the second says that the claims of humans are not the only ones that need to be considered.

Regarding the first interpretation, I do not believe that the language of justice is intrinsically linked to a conception of human relationships as instrumental or consumerist.[21] But even if we drop the language of justice for another language that emphasizes our connectedness with nature and with each other, this will not solve the problem at hand. For the question facing us is precisely which groups of people should be 'connected' with which tracts of land. The task of assigning territory to people remains, whether we ask it in the language of 'rights to resources' or in the language of 'responsibilities over the natural environment'. And a plausible principle to guide such decisions is the resource egalitarian one—i.e. that decisions about territory should be made in such a way that everyone has the same opportunity to benefit.

Many real-world settlement policies reflect greed and consumerism. But if these policies are genuinely motivated by equality, then their aim is to help meet the basic needs of the poor rather than merely enriching the elites.[22] In such cases, we cannot avoid the question of fairly allocating people and land.

The second interpretation says that while the language of justice is appropriate for adjudicating the claims of human beings, other living beings or ecosystems also have moral standing and moral claims which must be weighed against the claims of human justice. We must adopt a non-anthropocentric moral theory that recognizes not only the rights of humans (e.g. to a fair share of resources), but also the rights of animals or nature. And once we do this, our obligations to nature will preclude any settlement policy, even if justice to humans otherwise required this.

For example, Katz and Oechsli argue that if we remain within the language of justice, then Brazil should be free to develop the Amazon. It is unjust to preserve the Amazon for the benefit of a few Indians, or for the benefit of the developed world, when it can dramatically improve the well-being of many poor Brazilians. As they put it, 'The demand for anthropocentric justice

---

[21] See Kymlicka 1989: 122–6; 1990a: 164–9.
[22] It is important to note that two-thirds of Brazil's population is living at the subsistence level (McCleary 1991: 700).

dooms the preservation of the natural environment.'[23] But, they go on to say, the pre-eminence of justice in the debate reflects the fact that 'the policy discussion has been limited to a consideration of human interests'.[24] If we shift to a non-anthropocentric world-view, then issues of justice become secondary. They suggest that the debate about who should control the rainforest is like a debate between two criminals over how to distribute fairly the gains from robbing and murdering an innocent bystander. Since the bystander has rights to his or her person and property, neither criminal has any right to those gains. Similarly, no one has any right to the benefits from a settlement policy that violates the inherent rights of the rainforest. As they put it,

questions of the trade-off and comparisons of human benefits and questions of justice for specific human populations do not dominate the discussion . . . The competing claims become insignificant in light of the obligations owed to [the rainforest] . . . the obligation to the rain forest makes many of the issues about trade-offs of human goods irrelevant.[25]

While there may seem to be a dilemma if we focus solely on fairness between groups of humans, 'Once we move beyond the confines of human-based instrumental goods, the environmentalist position is thereby justified, and no policy dilemma is created.[26]

I will call this the 'ecocentric' argument against settlement. I can't evaluate it in depth, since it raises questions of the intrinsic value of the environment, and how these non-human claims are to be weighed against the claims of people to the satisfaction of their basic needs.[27] I will just make two comments. First, even if we think that certain parts of the Third World should be preserved from development for non-anthropocentric reasons, this does not render issues of justice 'irrelevant'. It would still be essential to ensure that the costs of environmental preservation were distributed fairly, and did not fall disproportionately on the Third World poor.

Second, it would be misleading to view this as a defence of the claims of indigenous peoples. For one thing, we can't assume that the lands held by indigenous peoples are always the most valuable in terms of the claims of non-human animals or ecosystems. The traditional homelands of indigenous peoples are often seen as 'wilderness' areas.[28] And wilderness areas generally

---

[23] Katz and Oechsli 1993: 56. They mention the possibility that Brazil could be compensated by the First World for the benefits it forgoes by preserving Amazonia, but think this unlikely, and so are looking for an argument for preserving the Amazon that would 'trump' considerations of human justice.

[24] *Ibid.* 56.   [25] *Ibid.* 57–8.   [26] *Ibid.* 58.

[27] These issues are discussed in Donner 1996.

[28] As Eckersley notes, there is an element of ethnocentrism in many everyday references to 'wilderness', since they ignore the fact that indigenous peoples have often practised ecological management of these 'wilderness' areas (e.g. by fire-lighting) (Eckersley 1992: 40). However,

contain a great wealth of non-human life that would be harmed by settlement. But we cannot assume that the land identified by an ecocentric theory as particularly valuable is going to be identical to the land identified by indigenous peoples as their own. It's important to note that more intensive development of the heartland also harms animals and ecosystems, and so an ecocentric theory may find that that option also violates the claims of non-human life.[29]

More importantly, the ecocentric argument against settlement policies would also argue against attempts by the indigenous peoples themselves to develop their resources. If the basis for preserving indigenous land from settlement is that it is wilderness—and if, as Daly and Cobb argue, the only pattern of human habitation and use compatible with it remaining wilderness is hunting and gathering[30]—then the ecocentric argument would preclude indigenous people from shifting towards a more agricultural or urbanized lifestyle. It would preclude any attempt at modernization (unless they choose to move from their traditional homelands to the heartland).

Paradoxically, then, the ecocentric argument would reinforce the efforts of the Brazilian government to deny the rights of Indians. As da Cunha notes, the Brazilian government has tried to reinterpret Indian land rights so that they only apply to 'real Indians'—i.e. those who have maintained their 'traditional culture'. The intended result is that 'Ultimately, there would be virtually no holders of Indian rights and coveted lands would become available.'[31] As da Cunha notes, this misunderstands the nature of ethnic identity, which is dynamic not static. The ecocentric argument would have the same result of limiting Indian claims to groups whose cultural practices and ethnic identity have become frozen in time.

Many indigenous peoples have chosen not to adopt a more modern way of life. They do not want modernization forced upon them. But nor do they want to be prevented from modifying their traditional lifestyles. They demand the right to decide for themselves what aspects of the outside world they will incorporate into their cultures, and many indigenous groups have in fact moved some way toward a more urban and agricultural lifestyle. And they demand the right to use their traditional resources in that process. The ecocentric argument, therefore, is not really compatible with the claims of many indigenous peoples.[32]

while these areas cannot be seen as 'pristine' wilderness, they have not been subject to the radical transformations entailed by either urbanization or agricultural use.

[29] Indeed, one of the reasons why Brazil objects to the international preoccupation with the Amazon is that it ignores other environmental problems in Brazil, particularly the enormous environmental degradation around Brazil's urban centres (Hurrell 1992: 421).

[30] Daly and Cobb 1989: 253.   [31] da Cunha 1992: 284.

[32] As da Cunha notes, many environmentalist discussions of Brazil have seen indigenous peoples as 'part of the natural scenery'. There has been a 'naturalization' of indigenous groups,

4. Community and Social Justice

Another set of objections to resource egalitarianism focuses on its alleged 'individualism', and the need to adopt a more 'communitarian' approach to justice. But what does it mean to incorporate community in a theory of justice? It is a central tenet of Green theorists that we must situate individuals as members of communities. The basic unit of political theory, they say, should be the 'individual-in-community', not the atomistic individual of liberalism, which abstracts the individual from social relationships.[33]

There is some truth to the claim that resource egalitarianism neglects the way people are situated in communities. There are many versions of this claim, each of which has different implications for social justice. When Green theorists talk about the 'individual-in-community', the sort of community they usually have in mind is some form of sub-national, geographically-defined community. This may be an existing territorial sub-unit, such as a province or county, or a new environmentally-defined unit, such as a 'bioregion'.[34] Decisions made at the community level are seen as more environmentally responsible than decisions made at a society-wide level, since people are more aware of their local environment, and are tied to each other in bonds of both economic and ecological interdependence. A substantial part of recent Green theorizing has focused on how to decentralize power to such communities, and how to promote people's sense of identity with them. Proposals range from a more decentralized form of federalism, to greater democratization at the local level, to the communal ownership of some or all land. I will call this the 'decentralist' argument.[35]

There is much to be said in favour of these proposals. Certain kinds of community, and collective action, are only possible in smaller groups. Membership in these groups can give a sense of belonging and participation. For that reason, we should protect these smaller groups from being undermined by economic or political pressure from the larger society—e.g. by reducing the constant pressure in a capitalist society for people to migrate from one region to another for economic reasons, thereby undermining the sense of local community.

who are not seen as 'agents with their own specific projects' (*ibid.* 286–7). A similar conflict arose in Canada, where an alliance between environmentalists and Aboriginals regarding the James Bay hydro development collapsed when Aboriginals began to emphasize, not only environmental preservation, but also their rights to self-government including the right to control development in their own interests (see Feit 1980).

[33] Daly and Cobb 1989: 159–75; Eckersley 1992: 53–5.

[34] e.g. Dobson 1990: 117–22; 1991: 73–83; Eckersley 1992: 160–76.

[35] For discussions of decentralization as a strategy for empowering citizens and protecting the environment, see Kothari 1996; Camilleri 1996.

It is important not to exaggerate the point. There are many aspects of economic, social, and environmental policy that can only be effectively dealt with at the federal level. Too much decentralization of power may result, not in the empowering of smaller communities, but simply in leaving everyone powerless in the face of global economic and political trends.

In any event, this decentralist argument does not necessarily help us reconcile justice and the claims of indigenous peoples. It may justify a general devolution of power from larger to smaller jurisdictions or communities. It may also justify defining some environmentally sensitive land and resources as communal property rather than individual property. But it can't explain why these powers and resources are distributed differentially amongst smaller communities, as is implicit in the claims of indigenous peoples. Nor can it explain why these local communities should be defined on the basis of ethnic criteria.

For example, the decentralist argument might justify devolving powers from the federal to the state level in Brazil, or to the bioregion of Amazonia. But this wouldn't help the indigenous peoples, since settlers constitute the overwhelming majority both at the state level and in Amazonia as a whole. And indeed the governors of the states in Brazil which include the Amazonian Indians are in favour of greater settlement and development, and have bitterly opposed the plans of the federal government to create large native reserves.[36]

This has created a paradox in government policy towards the Amazon. The federal government has enacted policies to protect the environment and indigenous communities. However, the closer one gets to the proposed development site within Brazil, the more likely it is that the majority of the local population opposes these policies and favours development. Conversely, the greatest support for these policies often comes from outside Brazil, from the international community which pressures the Brazilian government to adopt them. This 'democratic deficit' has made it virtually impossible for the federal government to actually enforce its policies.[37] Decentralization would make it even more difficult to ensure respect for indigenous rights.

What indigenous peoples demand is not a general decentralization, but rather that political boundaries be redrawn, based on ethnic criteria, to give them a self-governing enclave. That is, they want a specifically 'multination' conception of federalism or decentralization.[38] The idea of protecting local communities cannot by itself explain this aspect of indigenous rights.

Moreover, the decentralist argument doesn't tell us why per capita resources should differ between communities, be they states, counties, or

---

[36] de Onis 1992: 227.   [37] See Daudelin 1993.
[38] See Ch. 5 for a more detailed description of the theory and practice of multination federalism.

bioregions. Even if we accept that some resources should be distributed in the form of communal property, we still need to know why indigenous communities should have more property on a per-capita basis than non-indigenous villages.

What the decentralist argument seems to be missing is the importance of certain culturally defined groupings. Certain cultural groups—including indigenous cultures, and many other ethnocultural groups as well—claim that they have special rights to both powers and resources. If we are to assess this claim, it is important to see people not only as 'individuals-in-community', but also as 'individuals-in-cultures'.

Why does it matter that indigenous peoples are distinct cultures? There are at least three answers, which I call the 'cultural relativism', 'minority disadvantage', and 'national self-determination' arguments.

(a) Cultural Relativism

Cultural relativism is the view that each culture has its own standards of justice and morality which must be accepted as valid for it, since there are no rational grounds on which to prefer one culture's views to another. Hence we should not interfere with another culture on the basis of some allegedly universal theory of justice.

This is a common theme in recent communitarian critiques of liberalism. Many communitarians claim that liberals misinterpret justice as an ahistorical and external criterion for criticizing the ways of life of every society. Utilitarians, liberal egalitarians, and libertarians may disagree about the content of justice, but they all seem to think that their preferred theory provides a standard that every society should live up to. They do not see it as a decisive objection that their theory may be in conflict with local beliefs.

Michael Walzer argues that this quest for a universal theory of justice is misguided. There is no such thing as a perspective external to the community, no way to step outside our history and culture. The only way to identify the requirements of justice, he claims, is to see how each particular community understands the value of social goods. A society is just if it acts in accordance with the shared understandings of its members, as embodied in its characteristic practices and institutions. Hence identifying principles of justice is more a matter of cultural interpretation than of philosophical argument.[39]

Walzer's theory is, of course, a form of cultural relativism, and it is beyond the scope of this paper to discuss that age-old philosophical debate. But it is worth noting two common objections to communitarian attempts to define justice in terms of a community's shared understandings. First, and paradox-

[39] Walzer 1983.

ically, Walzer's theory violates one of our deepest shared understandings. According to Walzer, slavery is wrong if our society disapproves of it. But that isn't how most people understand claims of justice. They put the causal arrow the other way around—i.e. we disapprove of slavery because it is wrong. Its wrongness is a reason for, not the product of, our shared understanding. Second, there may not be many shared understandings about justice, especially if we attend not only to the voices of the vocal and powerful, but also to the weak and marginalized. In order to resolve these disagreements, we need to assess competing understandings in the light of a more general conception of justice. So even if we start with local understandings, as Walzer suggests, we are driven by the existence of disagreement, and our own critical reflection, towards a more general and less parochial standpoint.[40]

However, even if these objections can be answered, cultural relativism is unhelpful in this context. For one thing, it is not true that endorsing cultural relativism leads to the principle of non-interference. What cultural relativism says is that each culture rightly acts on the basis of its own moral code. So if the indigenous people see the Amazon as their homeland and birthright, then they can rightfully defend their lands. But if Brazilians see the Amazon as their frontier and the source of their future riches, then they can rightfully settle their frontier. This is part of their national identity and mythology, just as settling the frontier is part of the American national mythology.

Cultural relativism does not help us decide which side is in the right, since both are acting in accordance with their own culture's understanding of the meaning of the Amazon. Cultural relativism says that both cultures can act on their own morality, which cannot be judged from the outside. So it would protect indigenous peoples from the demands of universalist theories of justice, but not from the demands of the particularist theories held by surrounding cultures.

Also, while cultural relativism might protect indigenous peoples from the redistributive demands of universalist justice, it would equally insulate the First World from any obligation to redistribute resources to the Third World (including to poor indigenous groups in the Third World). If a Western country sees itself as rightfully owning all of its wealth, then we cannot criticize it for refusing to share it with the developing world.

More generally, cultural relativism reduces intercultural relations to issues of mutual advantage, rather than issues of justice. But that is precisely what we are trying to get away from when discussing social justice and global environmental change.

---

[40] I discuss this in Kymlicka 1989: 67–9, 231–3. See also Gutmann 1993.

(b) Minority Disadvantage

If we wish to respect cultural difference without falling into the trap of relativism, we need to find some more specific feature of indigenous cultures that might justify special rights. One obvious possibility is that the indigenous peoples are a *minority* culture, and as such have certain disadvantages and vulnerabilities that require special resources.

According to this argument, special rights are needed to ensure that all citizens are treated with genuine equality. On this view, 'the accommodation of differences is the essence of true equality', and special rights are needed to accommodate our differences.[41] Many liberal individualist critics reject this argument. They argue that a system of universal individual rights already accommodates cultural differences, by allowing each person the freedom to associate with others in the pursuit of shared religious or ethnic practices. Freedom of association enables people from different backgrounds to pursue their distinctive ways of life without interference. Every individual is free to create or join various associations, and to seek new adherents for them, in the 'cultural marketplace'. On this view, giving political recognition or support to particular cultural practices or associations is unnecessary and unfair. It is unnecessary, because a valuable way of life will have no difficulty attracting adherents. And it is unfair, because it subsidizes some people's choices at the expense of others.[42]

An equality-based argument for special rights, therefore, must show that some groups are unfairly disadvantaged in this cultural marketplace, and that political recognition and support rectifies this disadvantage. I believe this can be shown. What the liberal individualist view ignores is that the cultural marketplace may be unfairly biased against certain groups. Minority cultures are often vulnerable to economic, political, and cultural pressure from the larger society. The viability of their communities may be undermined by economic and political decisions made by the majority. They could be outbid or outvoted on resources and policies that are crucial to the survival of their communities. The members of the majority culture do not face this problem. Moreover, state policies regarding language, education, citizenship, and government employment systematically privilege the majority's language and culture, and disadvantage the minority's. Minority rights, such as land claims, veto powers, language rights, guaranteed representation, and local autonomy, can help rectify this disadvantage by alleviating the vulnerability of minority cultures to majority decisions and state policies. The exact nature of these rights will vary with each culture. Indigenous peoples are often the

---

[41] As stated by the Supreme Court of Canada, in explaining the meaning of the equality guarantees in the Charter of Rights and Freedoms. See *Andrews v. Law Society of British Columbia* (1989) 10 C.H.R.R. D/5729 (S.C.C.).

[42] See e.g. Knopff 1979.

most vulnerable because of their size, and the great distance between their cultures and European cultures, and their susceptibility to disease. As a result they often require considerable protection, in the form of reserved lands and self-governing powers.

Hence special rights compensate for unequal circumstances which put the members of minority cultures at a systemic disadvantage in the cultural marketplace. I will call this the 'equality argument', and have defended it at length elsewhere.[43] This is similar to the debate over another group-specific policy: affirmative action for women or people with disabilities. Like special rights for minority cultures, affirmative action programmes differentially distribute rights or opportunities on the basis of group membership. Proponents argue that they are required for genuine equality. Critics respond that the economic marketplace (like the cultural marketplace) already respects equality, by treating job applicants without regard for their group membership. However, an equality-based argument for group-specific affirmative action can be made if the actual operation of the economic marketplace works to the disadvantage of certain groups. As with special rights for minority cultures, the equality argument for affirmative action seeks to show how the structure of universal individual rights is intended to treat all people equally, but in fact works to the disadvantage of the members of a particular collectivity. Many group-specific claims can be seen in this way—i.e. as compensating for the disadvantages and vulnerabilities of certain groups within the structure of universal individual rights. Of course, affirmative action for women or people with disabilities differs in many ways from rights for minority cultures, since they are compensating for very different kinds of injustices. The former is intended to help disadvantaged groups integrate into society, by breaking down unjust barriers to full integration. The latter is intended to help cultural communities maintain their distinctiveness, by protecting against external pressures to assimilate. This means that the former are (in theory) temporary, whereas the latter are permanent, barring dramatic shifts in population.

This equality argument for special rights and resources is not unlimited. At some point, additional resources assigned to indigenous peoples would not be necessary to protect against vulnerabilities, but rather would simply provide unequal opportunities to them. In these circumstances—which may not exist anywhere on the globe—indigenous peoples would have an obligation to redistribute some of their wealth to other peoples. Even in these circumstances, the exact form of redistribution is important. Given the dependence of indigenous peoples on their land, a radical redistribution could have devastating effects on the sustainability of the culture. Indigenous peoples should be given the time to 'progressively economize' on their use of resources, and thereby adapt their cultures to the requirements of justice.[44]

---

[43] Kymlicka 1995a: ch. 6; 1989: chs. 7–10.   [44] Penz 1992: 122.

Some proponents of indigenous rights object to the idea that their land claims should be viewed as 'special protection rights' that protect a vulnerable minority culture from the majority. They worry that this will promote the view that indigenous peoples should be treated paternalistically as wards, or that land rights should only be granted to indigenous communities that maintain their 'traditional' culture. To avoid these dangers, indigenous lands claims should be seen as ordinary, historical property rights based on prior occupancy.[45] From a strategic point of view, this may be the best way to defend indigenous rights in particular circumstances. However, as I discuss below, from the point of view of egalitarian justice, claims of prior occupancy are very weak. Indeed, the whole point of resource egalitarianism is that 'first-come, first-serve' is not a valid theory of justice.

(c) National Self-Determination

Indigenous peoples are not just minority cultures, they are also 'colonized' minorities. What I mean is that they are distinct cultural communities which were previously self-governing, but whose homeland has now been included in a larger state against their will. They occupied and governed their lands before the state was even in existence.

I think this is very important. The point isn't that indigenous peoples 'were here first', and so have property rights as the initial appropriators of the land. On the contrary, the essence of resource egalitarianism is that 'First come, first serve' is not a plausible theory of justice. There are several reasons why 'we were here first' is not enough to justify indigenous land claims. For one thing, it is not clear that the initial appropriation by indigenous peoples was devoid of force or fraud, as is required by theories of justice in initial acquisition. There is strong evidence of conflict between different groups of indigenous peoples, even before European settlement, and the land occupied by a tribe today may well have been acquired by force or fraud from another tribe. If such force against earlier indigenous tribes gives rise to legitimate title, then why can't European settler groups use force against the current indigenous owners? More importantly, the underlying theory of property is untenable. People should only be able to insist on exclusive use of parts of the natural world if they leave 'enough and as good' for others. While that condition may have applied when indigenous peoples originally occupied their homelands, it is no longer true today. Since there is no unclaimed land left for the heartland poor to appropriate for themselves, any claims to property must be judged against a standard of equality. Moreover, accepting this theory of property would have the same unintended effect as endorsing cultural relativism: while it may insulate indigenous peoples from redistributive

---

[45] da Cunha 1992: 284–5.

demands, it would also insulate wealthy countries from any obligation to redistribute resources to the Third World (including indigenous groups in the Third World).

So the point is not simply that indigenous peoples were the initial appropriators of the land. The point, rather, is to question the boundaries of the political community. This highlights a problematic underlying assumption of the equality argument. The equality argument assumes that the state must treat its citizens with equal respect. But there is the prior question of determining which citizens should be governed by which states. For example, should the Brazilian government have the authority to govern the Yanonami Indians, or are they self-governing? Should the government of Bangladesh have legitimate authority to govern the indigenous peoples in the Chittagong Hill Tracts, or are they rightfully self-governing? After all, the indigenous peoples were originally self-governing, and had the balance of power been different, they could have maintained their independence. They only lost their self-government as a result of coercion and colonization. They view this, rightly I think, as a violation of their inherent right to self-government. (For this reason, it is appropriate that settlement policies are often described by the government as 'colonization' policies).

Under international law, all 'peoples' are entitled to self-determination—i.e. an independent state. This principle has been applied to grant independence to overseas colonized peoples who were forcibly included in European empires. However, it has not been applied to internal colonized peoples, such as indigenous peoples, who were forcibly included in larger contiguous states.

There is no principled reason for this differential treatment of internal and overseas colonized peoples. Indigenous groups in Brazil, as in Africa, are peoples—that is, previously self-governing, territorially concentrated, culturally distinct societies. The process of colonization was just as coercive in Brazil as in Africa, and its effects have been just as devastating.

I don't mean that indigenous peoples should all demand or be granted an independent state. This is not a viable or desirable option for all such groups. However, their incorporation into a larger state is only legitimate if it is a voluntary act of federation. Agreeing to enter a federation with other cultures is one way in which a people can exercise their right of self-determination. And if we ask what are the terms under which two or more peoples would voluntarily federate, it seems clear that indigenous peoples would only choose to enter such a federation if it recognized their inherent rights of self-government over their traditional homelands.[46] If not independence, they would at least demand self-government and recognition as a distinct people. These demands are at the heart of the recent proposal for an international charter of indigenous rights.

---

[46] Kymlicka 1995a: ch. 6.

The fact that indigenous peoples can be seen as peoples with inherent rights of self-determination does not absolve them from redistributive obligations.[47] After all, we do not want to absolve the citizens of First World countries of their redistributive obligations to the Third World just because they are independent peoples with rights of national self-determination. However, this does mean that if an indigenous community has an obligation progressively to economize on the use of resources, this should *not* take the form of an involuntary appropriation of their lands.

Instead, it should probably take the form of a resource tax.[48] It would be up to the indigenous peoples themselves to decide how to manage their resources to pay for this tax. Some communities may decide to sell some of their land, or lease it, or develop some of their mineral wealth, or invite outside people to develop the wealth for them. These are the options facing First World countries in deciding how to fulfil obligations of justice, and this sort of decision is rightly decided by self-governing peoples.

So there are two ways in which principles of justice should be adapted to accommodate the special status of indigenous peoples—extra resources may be required to rectify the disadvantages they face as minority cultures; and indigenous peoples, as colonized peoples with inherent rights of self-government, should be free to decide for themselves how to manage their traditional homelands in accordance with principles of justice.

These two arguments also apply, with lesser force, to non-indigenous national minorities. They too may face disadvantages in virtue of their minority status, and may have rights of self-government which were lost when they were forcibly incorporated into a larger federation. If so, then resource egalitarianism may need to be adapted to provide special rights and resources for some non-indigenous minority cultures as well.[49]

5. Conclusion

I have just touched on some of the issues about community and culture that need to be addressed in a global theory of distributive justice. There are many other issues, such as how to measure the sorts of disadvantages faced by

[47] Nor does it absolve them from the obligation to respect the human rights of their own individual members. A community's right to self-determination *vis-à-vis* other communities does not include or entail the right to oppress people within the community. I discuss the relationship between 'internal' (intra-group) and 'external' (inter-group) aspects of the right of self-determination in Kymlicka 1995a: chs. 3 and 8.

[48] Penz 1992: 121.

[49] For more on the similarities and differences between indigenous peoples and other national minorities, see Ch. 6.

minority cultures; and how various forms of federalism, decentralization, and secession can accommodate the special needs of minority cultures. We also need to think carefully about how to maintain social unity and stability in a society that recognizes and institutionalizes these sorts of cultural differences. Many countries have resisted the idea that indigenous peoples are 'nations' on the ground that this might promote secessionism.[50] Even where the national minority is not secessionist, the fact that citizens see themselves as belonging to distinct nations may affect the functioning of a democratic society. Many people worry that citizens divided by rival national identities may not be willing to make the sort of sacrifices for each other which are needed for a stable and just democratic society.[51]

There are also important questions about how to make use of the special ecological wisdom held by indigenous peoples; and whether sacred sites should be exempted from theories of distributive justice. And there are questions about how these sub-state communities can be adequately represented in international debates about global justice. Given the special claims of justice that indigenous peoples have to their lands, it is clearly essential that they be properly represented at such debates. To date, this has not happened.[52]

The answers to these questions are often elusive. What is clear is that we must develop an approach to justice that is sensitive to community. Neither mainstream conceptions of social justice nor the more recent environmentalist theories have tackled the many dilemmas raised in this area. We need a theory which requires the First World to help Third World countries develop, but which does so in a way that does not undermine either the environment or indigenous cultures. In short, we need a theory that combines a commitment to international (and intercultural) redistribution, environmental protection, and respect for cultural difference.

[50] da Cunha 1992: 282.

[51] See e.g. Cairns 1993. I try to respond to these concerns in Kymlicka 1995a: ch. 9; 1998a: ch. 13.

[52] For a discussion of the political and epistemological obstacles to the representation of such groups, and to the recognition of their knowledge and authority, see Kothari 1996; Jasanoff 1996; Reuts-Smith 1996.

8

The Theory and Practice of Immigrant Multiculturalism

The major immigrant countries in the West—the United States, Australia, Canada—pride themselves on their historical record in integrating immigrants. These countries now have over 150 years of experience with large-scale immigration, and have managed to integrate large numbers of immigrants from all over the world without any serious threat to unity, stability, or prosperity. There are few (if any) examples of immigrant groups mobilizing behind secessionist movements, or nationalist political parties, or supporting revolutionary movements to overthrow elected governments. Instead, they have integrated into the existing political system, just as they have integrated economically and socially, and have contributed enormously to the economic, political, and cultural life of the larger society. This must be seen as an impressive achievement.

Today, however, many people worry that this historic pattern of successful integration is in jeopardy. There is widespread fear that today's immigrants will remain 'ghettoized', and that as a result society will become increasingly 'balkanized'. This is sometimes blamed on the immigrants themselves, who are said to be less able or willing to integrate than earlier waves of immigrants. But more often it is blamed, not on the immigrants themselves, but on changes in government policies towards immigrants. In particular, the recent adoption of various 'multiculturalism' policies is said to be discouraging immigrants from integrating. On this view, while multiculturalism policies may have noble and sincere intentions—to create a more inclusive and just society—they have had dire consequences in practice, encouraging 'ethnic separatism'.

Others argue that the 'logic' of multiculturalism requires accepting cultural practices that are incompatible with liberal-democratic values. If multiculturalism entails accommodation of ethnocultural diversity, must we then accept the practice of female clitoridectomy, for example, or proposals for the legal recognition of compulsorily arranged marriages? Must we accept the legal enforcement of traditional Muslim family law, or allow husbands to cite 'culture' as a defence when charged with beating their wives? Will multiculturalism be the 'trojan horse' (Schmidt 1997) which undermines our most cherished values and principles of freedom and equality?

In this chapter, I will evaluate these fears. There have indeed been dramatic changes in the way Western democracies treat immigrants in the last thirty years, changes that are often described as a shift from 'assimilation' to 'multiculturalism'. However, I will argue that (most of) these policies are justified in principle, and successful in practice. In order to see this, however, we need to understand how multiculturalism fits into a larger set of government policies regarding ethnocultural relations. It is precisely this larger context which is typically ignored in debates about multiculturalism. I will try to show how multiculturalism works within, and is limited by, the larger context of common public institutions (sections 2–3); and how multiculturalism works within, and is limited by, the larger context of basic liberal-democratic principles (section 4). I hope to show that these limits, while often implicit, are neither arbitrary nor ad hoc, but form a coherent and defensible conception of immigrant integration.

One terminological note. By 'immigrants', I mean people who arrive under an immigration policy which gives them the right to become citizens after a relatively short period of time—say, 3–5 years—subject only to minimal conditions (e.g. learning the official language, and knowing something about the country's history and political institutions). This has been the traditional policy governing immigration in the major countries of immigration, and multiculturalism in this context is seen as a supplement to, not a substitute for, citizenship. I am not discussing the case of illegal immigrants or guest-workers or other migrants who are not admitted with the right or expectation of becoming citizens. Michael Walzer calls such groups 'metics', the term used in Ancient Greece for people who were permanently resident in Athens but denied citizenship (Walzer 1983). Where multiculturalism is adopted for metics (e.g. for Turks in Germany), it often has a very different flavour, and is sometimes employed as a rationalization for exclusion, rather than a means for improved integration. I return to this point in section 4 below.

1. From Anglo-Conformity to Multiculturalism

Until the 1960s, all three of the major immigrant countries adopted an 'Anglo-conformity' model of immigration. That is, immigrants were expected to assimilate to existing cultural norms, and, over time, become indistinguishable from native-born citizens in their speech, dress, leisure activities, cuisine, family size, identities, and so on. This strongly assimilationist policy was seen as necessary to ensure that immigrants become loyal and productive members of society, and was further rationalized through ethnocentric denigration of other cultures. Indeed, some groups were denied entry if they were seen as unassimilable (e.g. restrictions on Chinese immigrants in Canada and the United States; the 'whites-only' immigration policy in Australia).

However, beginning in the 1970s, under pressure from immigrant groups, all three countries rejected the assimilationist model and adopted more tolerant and pluralistic policies that allow and indeed support immigrants to maintain various aspects of their ethnic heritage. This is no longer seen as unpatriotic or 'unAmerican'. Moreover, public institutions are being instructed to modify their rules, practices, and symbols to accommodate the beliefs and practices of immigrant groups.

The first country to officially adopt such a 'multiculturalism' policy at the national level was Canada in 1971. But it has since been adopted in many other countries, from Australia and New Zealand to Sweden, Britain, and the Netherlands. And while the United States does not have an official multiculturalism policy at the federal level, it too has implicitly adopted such an approach. One can find multiculturalism policies at virtually all levels of American government and in virtually all public institutions, from school boards and hospitals to the police and army. As Nathan Glazer puts it, 'we are all multiculturalists now'.[1]

Because this approach is still relatively new, many people are fearful of immigrant multiculturalism. Critics worry that it involves repudiating not only Anglo-Conformity, but the entire idea of integration. According to Schlesinger, multiculturalism in the United States is encouraging the 'fragmentation of the national community into a quarrelsome spatter of enclaves, ghettoes, tribes . . . encouraging and exalting cultural and linguistic apartheid' (Schlesinger 1992: 137–8). Similarly, Neil Bissoondath says that multiculturalism in Canada is encouraging the idea that immigrants should form 'self-contained' ghettos 'alienated from the mainstream'. This 'undeniable ghettoization' is 'not an extreme of multiculturalism but its ideal: a way of life transported whole, a little outpost of exoticism preserved and protected'. He concurs with Schlesinger's claim that multiculturalism rests upon a 'cult of ethnicity' which 'exaggerates differences, intensifies resentments and antagonisms, drives even deeper the awful wedges between races and nationalities. The endgame is self-pity and self-ghettoization'.[2]

On this view the immigrant demand for multiculturalism reflects a rejection of the historical tendency towards integration, and the quest for something closer to the rights and powers of national minorities, in which each immigrant group would seek to form and maintain its own distinct societal culture.

---

[1] Glazer 1997. Amongst the Western democracies with sizeable numbers of immigrants, France is perhaps the only country that remains wedded to the assimilationist model.

[2] The passages quoted in this paragraph are from Bissoondath 1994: 111, 110, 98 and 111. The citation is from Schlesinger 1992: 138. For similar views, see Gwyn 1995.

I think these claims are seriously mistaken, in part because they view multiculturalism in isolation, as if it were the only government policy affecting the integration of immigrants. This is a very misleading picture. Multiculturalism is not the only—or even the primary—government policy that affects the place of immigrant ethnic groups in Western democracies. It is just one modest component in a larger package. Many aspects of public policy affect these groups, including policies relating to naturalization, education, job training and professional accreditation, human rights and anti-discrimination law, civil service employment, health and safety, even national defence. It is these other policies which are the major engines of integration. They all encourage, pressure, even legally force immigrants to take steps towards integrating into society.

For example, it is a legal requirement for gaining citizenship that the immigrant know the national language (unless they are elderly), as well as some basic information about the nation's history and institutions. Similarly, it is a legal requirement that the children of immigrants learn the official language, and learn a common core curriculum. Moreover, immigrants must know the official language to gain access to government-funded job training programmes. Immigrants must know the official language in order to receive professional accreditation, or to have their foreign training recognized. The most highly skilled pharmacist won't be granted a professional license to practise pharmacy in the United States or Canada if she can only speak Portuguese. And of course knowledge of the official language is a precondition for working in the bureaucracy, or to gain government contract work.

These citizenship, education, and employment policies have always been the major pillars of government-sponsored integration in Western democracies, and they remain fully in place today. They are part of the 'nation-building' policies I described in Chapter 1. Moreover, if we examine the amount of money spent on these policies, it vastly eclipses the money spent on multiculturalism in Western democracies.

In a variety of ways, then, the government actively encourages and pressures immigrants to integrate into common educational, economic, and political institutions operating in the national language. And ethnocultural minorities have only a limited range of options when confronted with these sort of nation-building policies. Demands for 'multiculturalism' reflect one particular sort of response to nation-building, and the best way to understand the nature and consequences of this response is to compare it with other possible responses.

2. Comparing Immigrant Multiculturalism and Minority Nationalism

Nation-building policies have historically been targeted not only at immigrants, but also at national minorities. National minorities have also been subject to pressures to integrate into the majority's public institutions. While subject to similar pressures, immigrants and national minorities have historically responded in quite different ways. National minorities have resisted integration and fought to maintain or rebuild their own societal culture, while immigrants have accepted the expectation that they will integrate into the dominant societal culture.

Is there any reason to think that demands for 'multiculturalism' are changing this pattern? To answer this question, we need to consider what would be required for an ethnocultural minority to consolidate its own societal culture within a larger state. In this section, therefore, I want to look at how national minorities have resisted state nation-building policies. The thought that multiculturalism could enable immigrants groups to form and sustain their own societal cultures rests on a failure to recognize what is actually involved in such a project. The fact is that to maintain a separate societal culture in a modern state is a very ambitious and arduous project.

We can get a sense of what this involves by thinking about what the Québécois have had to do to maintain their societal culture within Canada. Obviously, the first demand was that their children be able to attend French-language schools. This is a pivotal step in reproducing a societal culture, since it guarantees the passing on of the language and its associated traditions and conventions to the next generation. But this by itself did nothing to create or sustain French-language public institutions. It ensured that children learned the language, but it didn't ensure that they had opportunity to speak it in public life. It is very difficult for languages to survive in modern industrialized societies unless they are used in public life—e.g. in political, economic, and academic institutions. Given the high demands for literacy in work, and widespread interaction with government agencies, any language which is not a public language becomes so marginalized that it is likely to survive only amongst a small elite or in isolated rural communities, or in a ritualized form, not as a living and developing language underlying a flourishing culture.

The Québécois also, therefore, fought for various substantial positive rights to use their language when interacting with government institutions—i.e. in courts, legislatures, welfare agencies, health services, etc. But this is not sufficient either, since people only interact with the state on an episodic basis. The real key to the reproduction of a societal culture is the ability to use one's language in one's day-to-day employment.

Hence the Québécois sought the right to use their language within government employment. It is important to remember that the government is a very large employer. In modern states, public expenditures often account for 50 per cent of the economy. To survive, therefore, minority groups must have a fair share of government employment and government contracts. For example, consider the army. In many countries, the army is a major employer, and military service is often compulsory. If all units in the army operate in the majority language, military service becomes a crucial tool for integrating minorities. This is true, for example, in Israel, where military service has been the single most important institution for integrating immigrants into a Hebrew-speaking society. It was also a pivotal institution for integration in France. A classic study has shown that the spread of the French language—which was largely restricted to Paris at the time of the French Revolution—was primarily the result of the fact that conscripts had to learn French. The army was key in 'turning peasants into Frenchmen' (Weber 1976).

A minority that is content to accept marginalization can avoid integration by simply seeking exemption from military service. This is true of the Amish and Hutterites. But if a minority seeks to maintain a modern national society, then they will instead demand that some army units operate in their own language. Hence the Québécois have fought for the right for French-language military training and French-language military units.

The same applies to other areas of government employment—from food inspectors to tax accountants. In all of these cases, some part of the public service must be conducted in the minority's language. It is not enough that one can interact with the state in one's language—given the role of the state as the single largest employer, minorities must also be able to work within the state in their own language. But the state is not the only large employer, and so considerable efforts have been made to ensure that French is the language of the workplace even in private firms. This is an important—and largely successful—feature of Quebec's language laws. And in order to train the doctors, scientists, and skilled workers who will staff these public institutions and private workplaces, the minority must create its own higher education system— not simply at the elementary and secondary school levels, but up to university and professional schools. Hence the insistence on forming several French-language universities and colleges.

The requirements for sustaining a national culture go even further. For example, decisions regarding immigration and naturalization also affect the viability of societal cultures. Immigration can strengthen a culture, so long as the numbers are regulated and immigrants are encouraged (or required) to learn the nation's language and history. But if immigrants into Canada integrate into the majority anglophone culture, then the Québécois will be increasingly outnumbered and so increasingly powerless in political life, both federally and within Quebec. A minority that seeks to sustain a distinct societal culture must, therefore, have some control over immigration policies. And control over immigration has been one of the key features of modern Quebec nationalism. They have sought (and gained) the right to define their own immigration criteria (which favour French-speakers), to set their own target levels (based on their calculations regarding the absorption capacity of their society), and indeed to send their own immigration officers overseas.[3]

So the historical experience of the Québécois suggests that a minority can only sustain its societal culture if it has substantial powers regarding language, education, government employment, and immigration. If the minority can be outvoted on any of these issues, their hope of sustaining their societal culture would be seriously jeopardized. But they can only exercise these powers if they have some forum of collective decision-making. That is, there must be some political body or political unit that they substantially control. This is reflected in the Québécois commitment to federalism—i.e. to a system which decentralizes power to federal subunits, and whose boundaries are drawn so that the Québécois form a majority within one of these subunits. And to ensure that they are not deprived of their self-government, the Québécois have insisted that the boundaries of their province, and the powers it exercises, themselves be constitutionally guaranteed, so that the majority cannot unilaterally reduce their self-governing powers.[4]

This is just a brief sketch of the measures that the Québécois have found necessary to sustain their societal culture in the face of the anglophone majority in Canada. One could list many other factors, from bilingual product labels to bilingual currency. But most commentators would agree that *la survivance* in Quebec has depended on a number of these very basic conditions: French-language education, not only in childhood, but through to higher education; the right to use one's language, not only when interacting with government, but also in one's day-to-day job, whether in the public service or private employment; the right not only to exempt francophone immigrants from the requirement to learn English to gain citizenship, but also the right to select, integrate, and naturalize immigrants; the right not only to a fair share of political power at the federal level, but also the right to self-government, as embodied in a federal subunit which has the power to make decisions with respect to education, employment and immigration.

A similar story could be told about the conditions that have proved necessary to sustain a distinct societal culture in Puerto Rico, Flanders, or Catalonia. For example, Puerto Rico has not only demanded Spanish-language schools, up to and including the university level, but also that Spanish be the language of government employment, and that immigrants

---

[3] For more on the way national minorities deal with issues of immigration, see Ch. 15.
[4] On the role of federalism in accommodating national minorities, see Ch. 5.

be able to naturalize in Spanish rather than English. (Puerto Rico is the only place within the United States where immigrants are exempt from the requirement to know English to gain citizenship).

It is important to reflect on how onerous these efforts at cultural reproduction have been. Sustaining a societal culture in the modern world is not a matter of having yearly ethnic festivals, or having a few classes taught in one's mother-tongue as a child. It is a matter of creating and sustaining a set of public institutions which enables a minority group to participate in the modern world through the use of its own language.

Put another way, it is not enough for a minority to simply resist the majority's efforts at diffusing a single common language. The minority must also engage in its own competing form of state-sponsored nation-building. Nationalists in Quebec or Puerto Rico realize that to sustain their national culture, they too must seek to diffuse a common culture and language throughout their society so as to promote equality of opportunity and political solidarity. And they must use the same tools that the majority nation uses in its program of nation-building—i.e. standardized public education, official languages, including language requirements for citizenship and government employment, etc. The historical evidence is that the capacity and motivation to undertake such an ambitious nation-building project is only found in national minorities, rather than immigrant groups. As I discuss in the next section, there is no basis for thinking that this is changing.

3. Is Immigrant Multiculturalism Separatist?

It should be obvious, I hope, that immigrant multiculturalism has little in common with the sort of nation-building pursued by national minorities. Consider any of the sorts of policies commonly associated with immigrant multiculturalism, whether it is curriculum reform in schools (e.g. revising the history and literature curriculum within public schools to give greater recognition to the historical and cultural contributions of ethnocultural minorities; bilingual education programmes for the children of immigrants at the primary school level), or institutional adaptation (e.g. revising work schedules or dress-codes so as to accommodate the religious holidays and practices of immigrant groups; adopting workplace harassment codes prohibiting racist comments; regulatory guidelines about ethnic stereotypes in the media), or public education programmes (e.g. anti-racism educational campaigns; cultural diversity training for the police, social workers or health-care professionals), or cultural development programmes (e.g. funding of ethnic festivals and ethnic studies programmes; providing mother-tongue literacy courses for adult immigrants), or affirmative action (e.g.

preferential treatment of visible minorities in access to education, training, or employment).

Each of these policies raises its own unique issues, and so it is misleading to talk about 'the impact of multiculturalism' in general, as if all of these policies have the same motivations and consequences. Having said that, however, it is important to note that *none* of them—either by themselves or taken together—involves anything close to a programme of nation-building. For example, none of these policies involve creating Spanish-language army units, or Vietnamese-language universities. And none of them involve creating new political units that would enable Ukrainians or Somalis to exercise self-governing powers over government employment or immigration. Nor have immigrant groups demanded any of these types of measures.

One might think that existing multiculturalism policies are first steps down the road towards a proto-nationalist project of maintaining a separate societal culture, and away from integration. As I argue below, I think that is an implausible interpretation of these demands. On the contrary, most of them actually promote the societal integration of immigrants. However, let's imagine, for the sake of argument, that an immigrant group within the United States or Canada—say, the Chinese—really did want to form and maintain their own societal culture. It is worth emphasizing how much farther such a group would need to go, in terms of its institutional capacities and political powers.

It is certainly possible *in theory* for Chinese to become a national minority, if they settle together and acquire self-governing powers. After all, this is what happened with English colonists throughout the British Empire, Spanish colonists in Puerto Rico, and French colonists in Quebec. These colonists did not see themselves as 'immigrants', since they had no expectation of integrating into another culture, but rather aimed to reproduce their original society in a new land. It is a defining feature of colonization, as distinct from individual emigration, that it aims to create an institutionally complete society, rather than to integrate into an existing one. It would, in principle, be possible to encourage Chinese immigrants today to view themselves as colonists.

But think about what this would require. As we have seen, reproducing a societal culture requires not only that children be taught Chinese in public schools, but also that there be Chinese-language universities; it requires not only that there be Chinese-language ballots or welfare forms, but also that Chinese be the working language of the government workplace, including Chinese-language army units or hospitals; it requires not only that Chinese not be underrepresented in parliament, but also that there be a political body within which Chinese form a majority; it requires not only that Chinese need not learn English to acquire citizenship, but also that the Chinese community can maintain itself over time by selecting and naturalizing future immigrants on the basis of their integration into the Chinese-speaking community.

The simple fact is that existing multiculturalism policies have not created *any* of the public institutions needed to create and sustain a separate societal culture for Chinese or any other immigrant group. None of the academic, political, or economic institutions that would enable an immigrant group to participate in modern life through their mother-tongue have been created. If Chinese-Americans want to access the opportunities made available by modern society, they must do so within the economic, academic and political institutions of the anglophone societal culture.

This should not be surprising, because multiculturalism has not replaced any of the broader panoply of government policies and structures that sponsor societal integration. For example, it is still the case that immigrants must learn to speak English to gain citizenship, or to graduate from high-school, or to get government employment, or to gain professional accreditation. As I discussed earlier, these are the basic pillars of government-supported integration within liberal democracies, and none of them have in any way been eroded by multiculturalism policies. Nor was multiculturalism intended to erode these.

This leaves open the possibility that some leaders of ethnic groups hope that multiculturalism policies will provide a springboard to a more comprehensively separatist policy. If so, it is a vain hope that massively underestimates the sort of support needed to create and sustain a separate societal culture. But it makes more sense, I believe, to simply accept the obvious: there is no rational basis for the fear that multiculturalism policies will be used to enable immigrant groups to sustain their own societal cultures. It is a red herring, without any basis in reality. There is simply no evidence from any of the major Western immigration countries that immigrants are seeking to form themselves into national minorities, or to adopt a nationalist political agenda.

Once we let go of this red herring, we can look more objectively at the actual intentions and implications of immigrant multiculturalism policies. As I noted in Chapter 1, if a nationalist movement for self-government is either undesired or unfeasible, then minorities have two choices. One option is to accept permanent marginalization—i.e. become isolated enclaves that do not participate in the larger society, and which lack the public institutions needed to form their own societal cultures. The other option is to integrate into the existing societal culture while seeking better or fairer terms of integration.

The fundamental question regarding immigrant multiculturalism policies, I believe, is whether we view them as accepting marginalization or seeking better terms of integration. There are some examples of groups accepting permanent marginalization—e.g. the Amish. But these groups are unique in wishing to avoid the modern world, which they view as sinful and corrupt. They do not want to become police officers, doctors, engineers, or legislators. Therefore, they have no interest in controlling their own political units or universities. These groups are the exception that proves the rule that participating in modernity requires integration into a societal culture.

Do multiculturalism policies encourage immigrants today to become marginalized like the Amish? Or are they instead seeking to improve the terms of integration, encouraging immigrants to integrate into the dominant societal culture while still maintaining pride in their ethnic and religious identities, and thereby enriching and pluralizing the larger societal culture? Do these policies promote what Jeff Spinner calls 'partial citizenship' (Spinner 1994: 98)—i.e. passive isolationism and withdrawal from mainstream society and political life? Or do they promote active civic participation and effective integration amongst immigrants?

4. Multiculturalism as Fair Terms of Integration

I believe that the vast bulk of the multiculturalism policies demanded by immigrants and adopted by Western countries of immigration involve improving the terms of integration, to make them fairer. The underlying premiss can be put this way: if Western democracies are going to pressure immigrants to integrate into common institutions operating in the national language, then we need to ensure that the terms of integration are fair. To my mind, this has two basic elements: (*a*) we need to recognize that integration does not occur overnight, but rather is a difficult and long-term process which operates inter-generationally. Hence special accommodations are often required for immigrants on a transitional basis. For example, certain services should be available in the immigrants' mother tongue, and support should be provided for those groups and organizations within immigrant communities which assist in the settlement/integration process; (*b*) we need to ensure that the common institutions into which immigrants are pressured to integrate provide the same degrees of respect and accommodation of the identities of ethnocultural minorities that have traditionally been accorded to the majority group's identity. Otherwise, the insistence that immigrants integrate into majority-language institutions is tantamount to privileging the interests and lifestyles of the descendants of the original inhabitants or settlers.

Fairness therefore requires an ongoing, systematic exploration of our common institutions to see whether their rules, structures and symbols disadvantage immigrants. Where necessary, these institutions must be reformed to eliminate or mitigate these barriers. Such measures are needed to ensure that we are offering immigrants fair terms of integration. The idea of multiculturalism can be seen as precisely an attempt to negotiate such terms. And in my view, the vast majority of what is done under the heading of multiculturalism policy in Canada, Australia, and the United States, not only at the federal level, but also at state and municipal levels, and indeed within school boards and private companies, can be defended as promoting fairer terms of integration.

Consider the following list of twelve reforms that are often advanced under the rubric of 'multiculturalism':

1. Adopting affirmative action programmes which seek to increase the representation of immigrant groups (or women and the disabled) in major educational and economic institutions.
2. Reserving a certain number of seats in the legislature, or government advisory bodies, for immigrant groups (or women and the disabled).
3. Revising the history and literature curriculum within public schools to give greater recognition to the historical and cultural contributions of immigrant groups.
4. Revising work schedules so as to accommodate the religious holidays of immigrant groups. For example, some schools schedule Professional Development days on major Jewish or Muslim holidays. Also, Jewish and Muslim businesses are exempted from Sunday closing legislation.
5. Revising dress-codes so as to accommodate the religious beliefs of immigrant groups. For example, revising the army dress code so that Orthodox Jews can wear their skullcaps, or exempting Sikhs from mandatory motorcycle helmet laws or construction-site hardhat laws.
6. Adopting anti-racism educational programmes.
7. Adopting workplace or school harassment codes which seek to prevent colleagues/students from making racial (or sexist/homophobic) statements.
8. Mandating cultural diversity training for the police or health care professionals, so that they can recognize individual needs and conflicts within immigrant families.
9. Adopting government regulatory guidelines about ethnic stereotypes in the media.
10. Providing government funding of ethnic cultural festivals and ethnic studies programmes.
11. Providing certain services to adult immigrants in their mother-tongue, rather than requiring them to learn English as a precondition for accessing public services.
12. Providing bilingual education programmes for the children of immigrants, so that their earliest years of education are conducted partly in their mother-tongue, as a transitional phase to secondary and post-secondary education in English.

This is not a comprehensive list, but it gives a fairly accurate reflection, I think, of the sorts of issues which are raised in the public debate over immigrant multiculturalism, and which have been adopted or at least seriously proposed by Western governments. I have also chosen these policies because they seem particularly relevant for assessing the question of 'balkanization' versus 'integration'.[5]

I will start with the first ten policies, since they are examples of accommodating diversity within common institutions, and then examine the final two policies, which are more complicated, since they involve a degree of institutional separateness.

I do not have the space to discuss all of these policies in detail, only to examine the list briefly. Affirmative action policies and guarantees of group representation in the political process are clearly integrationist in their aim. They are intended precisely to increase the numbers of immigrants who participate within mainstream institutions, by guaranteeing them a certain share of the positions in various academic, economic, or political institutions. They bring members of different groups together, require them to co-operate in common tasks and common decision-making, and then require them to abide by these common decisions. They are, therefore, the very opposite of policies designed to promote ethnic separatism. (Whether they are fair means of promoting integration is a complicated question, which I will address in Chapter 9, since it is inextricably linked with issues of race relations in both Canada and the United States.)

Affirmative action and group representation, then, are intended to help immigrants enter mainstream societal institutions. The next seven multiculturalism policies are intended to make immigrant groups feel more comfortable within these institutions once they are there. This is true, for example, of demands that the curriculum in public schools be revised so as to provide greater recognition for the historical contributions of immigrant groups; or of demands that public institutions recognize the religious holidays of immigrant groups (e.g. recognizing Muslim and Jewish as well as Christian holidays); or of demands that official dress-codes for schools, workplaces, and police forces be amended so that Sikh men can wear turbans, or Jewish men can wear skullcaps, or Muslim women can wear the hijab; or of demands that schools and workplaces provide a welcoming environment for people of all races and religions by prohibiting hate speech; or of demands that the media avoid ethnic stereotyping, and give visible representation to

---

[5] Other proposals raise the question of the relationship between multiculturalism and individual rights—e.g. regarding the practice of female clitoridectomy, or compulsorily arranged marriages. Although these practices are sometimes debated under the label of 'multiculturalism', no Western government has accepted them. They have been rejected, not because they would directly affect the societal integration of immigrant groups, in terms of their participation in mainstream economic, academic, and political institutions, but rather because they involve a denial of individual liberties and equality rights. I return to these issues in section 5 below.

society's diversity in their programming; or of demands that professionals in the police, social work, or health care be familiar with the distinctive cultural needs and practices of the people in their care.

None of these policies involve encouraging immigrant groups to view themselves as separate and self-governing nations with their own public institutions. On the contrary, they are intended precisely to make it easier for the members of immigrant groups to participate within the mainstream institutions of the existing society. Immigrant groups are demanding increased recognition and visibility. within the mainstream society. In short, these multiculturalism policies involve a revision in the terms of integration, not a rejection of integration *per se*. They are rejecting Anglo-conformity, but not integration.

Critics of these policies typically focus entirely on the fact that they involve public affirmation and recognition of immigrants' ethnic identity—a process that is said to be inherently separatist. But they ignore the fact that this affirmation and recognition occurs *within common institutions*. There is no sense in which any of these policies encourage either an Amish-like withdrawal from the institutions of mainstream society, or a Québécois-like nationalist struggle to create and maintain separate public institutions. On the contrary, these policies are flatly in contradiction with both ethnic marginalization and minority nationalism, since they encourage integration into mainstream institutions. They encourage more immigrants to participate within existing academic, economic, and political institutions, and modify these institutions to make immigrants more welcome within them.

Of course, these policies may cause a backlash amongst non-immigrant groups. For example, the demand by Sikh men to be exempted from the requirement to wear the ceremonial headgear of the national police force was seen by many Canadians as a sign of disrespect for one of Canada's 'national symbols'. But from the immigrants' point of view, such accommodations are integrative. The fact that Sikh men wanted to be part of Canada's national police force is ample evidence of their desire to participate in and contribute to the larger society, and the exemption they were requesting should be seen as promoting, not discouraging, their integration.

Indeed, it is the failure to adopt such policies that creates the serious risk of marginalization. For example, without the accommodation of their religious beliefs in school holidays and dress-codes, immigrant groups might feel compelled to leave the public school system and set up their own separate schools. These policies can only realistically be seen as helping to fight the potential sources of marginalization.

The situation gets more complicated when some form of institutional separateness is involved. Consider, for example, the issue of mother-tongue education for adult newcomers, such as recent programmes to teach illiterate newcomers how to read and write in their mother-tongue. Such experimental programmes reflect a significant departure from the traditional assumption that adult immigrants must learn English first as a precondition for accessing any further education or government services.

The idea of separate classes for people of a particular ethnic group is very worrisome to some people, as is the idea that immigrants should be encouraged to use and develop their mother-tongue. Are these policies the first steps towards either marginalization or nationalism, rather than integration? It should be obvious by now, I hope, that these policies are not guided by any ideal of nation-building. The assumption that immigrants who want to learn basic literacy in their mother-tongue will subsequently demand mother-tongue universities or army units is deeply implausible. But are these policies marginalizing? That depends, I believe, on their long-term consequences. Critics assume mother-tongue programmes prevent or discourage immigrants from learning English. This is a serious concern, because the evidence is clear that fluency in English is pivotal to the economic prospects of most immigrants, and indeed to their more general ability to participate in social and political life.

But does teaching literacy in the immigrant's mother-tongue in fact diminish the likelihood that they will successfully learn English? There is little evidence for this assumption. On the contrary, the evidence suggests that many people have great difficulty learning literacy in English until they acquire literacy in their mother-tongue (Burnaby 1992). Under existing policies, they are effectively permanently marginalized from the larger society. Providing literacy classes in a newcomer's mother-tongue, therefore, may be the first step towards enabling literacy in English.

In other cases, people may be psychologically unprepared for learning a new language upon arrival in their new country. This is particularly true if they are refugees fleeing violence and family tragedy. But it may also be true of other immigrants who have to cope with the trauma of struggling to survive in a strange new country, and to make a home for oneself and one's family, without any of the social supports that one is accustomed to.

For newcomers who are likely to take many years to acquire English, the goal of integration might best be served if they have access to various services or classes in their mother-tongue in the early years after their arrival. For example, they could learn more about their new country through mother-tongue classes, such as the nature of the legal system and job market. Or they could upgrade some of their job skills by taking classes in their mother-tongue.

The issue is not whether immigrants should be encouraged to learn English. As I noted earlier, failure to acquire literacy in English is likely to lead to serious marginalization. Moreover, this disadvantage often gets passed down to the next generation, if neither parent is able to communicate with their children in English. The issue is much more practical—what sort of policy actually works best to enable various types of immigrants to learn English? The current expectation that all immigrants should try to learn English as soon as they arrive is simply not working for certain groups of immigrants. It condemns to perpetual marginalization anyone who cannot learn English quickly when they arrive (Donaldson 1995).

It may seem logical to say that people will integrate best if they are encouraged to participate in fully integrated institutions as quickly as possible. But how immigrants learn English best is not a question of logic. It is a complicated empirical question of pedagogy and socio-linguistics. The same holds true for the related case of bilingual education for immigrant children. To try to decide these questions without reference to the facts is unhelpful, and potentially counter-productive.

In short, none of these multiculturalism policies for immigrant groups necessarily promotes either minority nationalism or marginalization. The first ten policies are, I believe, clearly integrationist, and, while the latter two involve short-term forms of institutional separateness, they can be seen as promoting long-term institutional integration. If we examine genuine cases of marginalization—such as the educational and military exemptions accorded ethnoreligious sects that enable them to live apart from the mainstream society—we find that they predate the multiculturalism policy. Many of the criticisms that are wrongly levelled at recent multiculturalism policies are much more plausibly levelled at the policies adopted early in the twentieth century towards Amish and Hutterites. Indeed, one could argue that there is an element of racism in the way that many Americans and Canadians accept the historical accommodations made for these white Christian sects—accommodations which are genuinely separatist and marginalizing—while bitterly opposing the accommodations made for more recent non-white, non-Christian immigrant groups, even though these accommodations are integrationist.

The fact that immigrants have accepted this sort of *institutional* integration does not necessarily mean that they have 'integrated' in a more purely psychological sense. That is, immigrants who accept the need to participate in English-language institutions in the United States may have little sense of being 'American'. They may show little interest in learning about the rest of the country, and may wish to focus as much as possible on the glories of the Old World, rather than embracing the opportunities available in the New World.

The idea that multiculturalism is promoting an apartheid-like system of institutional separatism is, I think, wholly misplaced. But is it promoting a kind of *mental* separatism, encouraging immigrants to dwell on the life they left behind, rather than the opportunities available in their new country? This is a more plausible worry. However institutional integration is likely to generate over time a sense of psychological identification.[6] The fact that

---

[6] This is one of the central insights of the new literature on 'associational life', and its role in promoting democratic virtues (e.g. Putman 1993). I discuss this in Ch. 16.

common institutions bring together the members of different ethnic groups has important ramifications both personally and politically. At the personal level, it means that people meet (and indeed often fall in love with) members of other ethnic groups, promoting inter-ethnic friendships and marriages. These relationships are intimately tied up with one's new life here, not with the Old World. Politically, it means that people must learn how to negotiate with the members of other ethnic groups. An immigrant group might want to incorporate material about their homeland into the school curriculum, but since these are common institutions, they will have to persuade the members of other groups about the value of this material. The inevitable result is that groups must focus on how to contribute to the new life here, rather than simply dwelling on the society left behind. In short, institutional integration makes possible the kind of civic engagement that supports democratic citizenship.[7]

We can call this form of multiculturalism 'pluralizing' or 'hybridic'.[8] It is 'pluralizing' in two distinct senses. Unlike isolationist or nationalist multiculturalism, its aim is not to separate the minority group from the larger society, but rather to participate in the larger society, and thereby pluralize it. But it also promotes pluralism within immigrant groups themselves. When liberal societies promote integration in civil society, and encourage people to interact in a non-discriminatory manner with members of other ethnic groups, they not only protect immigrant groups, they also limit their ability to maintain their cultural distinctiveness. Non-discrimination in civil society means that cultural boundaries tend to break down. Members of one ethnic group will meet and befriend members of other groups, and adopt new identities and practices. Conversely, members of the larger society will adopt practices previously associated with one particular group. Over time, liberal citizenship results in 'pluralistic integration'.[9] This does not involve the preservation of distinct cultures (since ethnic identities weaken and incorporate aspects of

---

[7] There is no reason to leave this sort of psychological integration completely to chance, and it is worth examining specific policies to see if they can be improved on this score. In assessing policies regarding the funding of ethnic studies programmes or ethnic presses, for example, I think it is right and proper that the government be encouraging immigrant groups to focus primarily (though not exclusively) on their contribution to their new country, rather than the accomplishments of the society they have left behind. Similarly, government-funded bilingual education programmes for children, or mother-tongue literacy programmes for adults, should be used primarily as a vehicle for teaching immigrants about their new country, not about the history of the Old World.

[8] It should not be confused, however, with what David Hollinger calls 'pluralist multiculturalism', which he equates with ethnoseparatism and minority nationalism. It is much closer to what he calls 'cosmopolitan multiculturalism'. I explore his account of multiculturalism in Ch. 14, and explain why I think his terminology is unhelpful.

[9] See Spinner 1994: 73 for a useful discussion of what he calls 'pluralistic integration'. See also Ch. 16 below.

the larger culture), but nor is it assimilation (since ethnic groups change the larger society as they integrate).

Of course, even if immigrant multiculturalism policies are integrationist from the point of view of immigrants, they may create ethnic tensions, and so inhibit integration, if they lead to a backlash on the part of native-born citizens. But this problem is not new. Much of the fear which native-born citizens express today regarding the integration of Muslims, for example, is virtually identical to the rhetoric expressed 100 years ago regarding the integration of Catholics. Catholics were perceived as undemocratic and unpatriotic, since their allegiance was to the Pope, and as separatist, since they demanded their own schools. Every new wave of immigration brings its own stresses, conflicts, and misunderstandings that take time to overcome. In any event, if the real problem is not with the willingness of immigrants to integrate, but rather the backlash against immigrant multiculturalism amongst native-born citizens, then the problem we need to address is the attitudes of the majority, not the legitimate demands of the immigrants.

In short, the logic of multiculturalism involves accepting the principle of state-prescribed integration, but renegotiating the terms of integration. And immigrant groups fully recognize and accept this. They accept the expectation that they will integrate into the larger society, as they have always done. Few immigrant groups have objected to the requirement that they must learn an official language as a condition of citizenship, or that their children must learn an official language in school. On the contrary, immigrant groups in Western democracies have consistently affirmed their support for these principles. And they have accepted the assumption that their life-chances, and even more so the life-chances of their children, will be bound up with participation in mainstream institutions operating in the national language. Indeed, one of their most common demands is for greater language-training assistance precisely so that they can integrate into these institutions.

So immigrants accept the principle of integration into common institutions: they are simply seeking fairer terms of integration. If the state is going to pressure immigrants to integrate into common institutions operating in the national language, then immigrant groups understandably want to ensure that the terms of integration are fair. This demand is not only justified, but long overdue.

The picture I have presented so far of immigrant multiculturalism is very different from the picture painted by its critics. Whereas critics see it as promoting balkanization and separatism, I have argued that its goal is to promote better and fairer terms of integration. But how is it working in practice? Since this sort of multiculturalism is relatively new, it may be too early to assess the actual implications of these policies. However, evidence is gradually accumulating. The first country to adopt an official multiculturalism policy was Canada in 1971, followed shortly thereafter by Australia, so we now have almost thirty years of experience to assess. And the evidence, so far, is very positive. For example, on every major indicator of integration, immigrants integrate more quickly in Canada today than they did before the adoption of the multiculturalism policy in 1971. They are more likely to naturalize, to vote, to learn an official language, to intermarry and have friendships across ethnic lines.

Moreover, immigrants integrate more quickly in those countries which have official multiculturalism policies (like Canada and Australia) than in countries which do not (like the United States and France). And these immigrants are not only institutionally integrated, but also active participants in the political process, strongly committed to protecting the stability of mainstream institutions and to upholding liberal-democratic values.[10]

In short, there is no evidence at all that immigrant multiculturalism is promoting 'balkanization' or 'cultural and linguistic apartheid' or 'partial citizenship'. On the contrary, the evidence—while still preliminary—shows that multiculturalism is doing what it set out to do: namely, to promote better and fairer terms of integration for immigrant groups.

If I am right about the consistency of multiculturalism and immigrant integration, why have so many people assumed that these policies are balkanizing? One reason, perhaps, is that people confuse the situation of immigrant groups with that of metics, such as guest-workers in Germany, Austria, and Switzerland, or illegal immigrants from North Africa in Spain and Italy. Metics were not admitted as future citizens, and indeed all of these countries have no desire to acquire new immigrant citizens, and have no established process or infrastructure for integrating them. Moreover, many of these metics have either broken the law to enter the country (illegal immigrants), or broken their promise to return to their country of origin (guest-workers), and so are not viewed as worthy of citizenship. For these and other reasons, the official policy in many countries is not to try to integrate metics into the national community, but to get them to leave the country, either through expulsion or voluntary return.

We can see this policy reflected in the conception of 'multiculturalism' which has arisen for migrants who are denied access to citizenship—a conception which is very different from that in immigrant countries like Canada or Australia. In some German provinces (*lander*) for example, until the 1980s, the government kept Turkish children out of German classes, and instead set up separate classes for Turks, often taught in Turkish by teachers imported from Turkey, with a curriculum focused on preparing the children for life in Turkey. This was called 'multiculturalism', but unlike multiculturalism in Canada or Australia, it was not seen as a way of enriching or supplementing German citizenship. Rather, it was adopted precisely because these children

---

[10] For the statistical evidence, see Kymlicka 1998a: ch. 1.

were not seen as German citizens. It was a way of saying that these children do not really belong here, that their true 'home' is in Turkey. It was a way of reaffirming that they are aliens, not citizens. Multiculturalism without the offer of citizenship is almost invariably a recipe for, and rationalization of, exclusion.

But multiculturalism for immigrants is not seen as competing with, or a substitute for, citizenship. It is rather the flip side of citizenship. It is a recognition of the fact that the integration of new citizens is a two-way street. Just as immigrant citizens are expected to make a commitment to their new society, and to learn about its language, history and institutions, so too the larger society must express a commitment to its immigrant citizens, and adapt its institutions to accommodate their identities and practices. Just as immigrant citizens are expected to make a new home in the receiving country, so the receiving country must make them feel at home.

Another, more important, reason why people misjudge the impact of immigrant multiculturalism is that they ignore the big picture. They look at multiculturalism in isolation from other government policies, and so assume that multiculturalism is the only policy that bears on the decision of immigrants to integrate. But in fact multiculturalism is a relatively minor policy in the overall scheme of things. The primary pillars of government-sponsored integration are the policies on naturalization, education, and employment— and all of these pillars of integration remain fully in place.

Relatedly, people underestimate how difficult it would be for a minority actually to establish and reproduce a distinct societal culture. It requires a vast panoply of public institutions and political powers, none of which have been granted under the multiculturalism rubric, and which could only be achieved by changes in virtually all areas of public policy and in all political structures. The idea that an immigrant group might use multiculturalism policies to form and maintain a separate society only seems feasible because people ignore the big picture.

But this just pushes back the problem a level. Why do people ignore the big picture? After all, there is nothing mysterious about the way governments promote sociocultural integration. The evidence is there in plain view, available to anyone who takes even a cursory glance at naturalization laws or education policies. The answer, I think, is that many commentators have been seduced by the myth of 'ethnocultural neutrality (or of a purely 'civic nationalism') which I discussed in Chapter 1, according to which membership in the nation is just a matter of subscribing to certain political principles, and not a matter of integration into a societal culture. Since this model provides no justification for encouraging immigrants to integrate into an anglophone societal culture, commentators conveniently overlook all of the government policies that do precisely this. And having ignored all the government policies that promote integration, they then adopt an exaggerated, almost hysterical, view of the disintegrating effects of multiculturalism policies.[11] To get a balanced view of the impact of multiculturalism policies for immigrants, we need a more honest view of the role of states in promoting and diffusing national cultures.

5. The Limits of Tolerance

So far, I have argued that anxieties about the impact of multiculturalism on the integration of immigrant groups are misplaced. But integration is not the only important question raised by multiculturalism. For many people, multiculturalism also raises the question of the limits of tolerance. Does multiculturalism require us to tolerate the traditional practices of other cultures, even if these violate the principles of individual rights and sexual equality guaranteed in our constitution?

For example, should ethnic groups be allowed to perform clitorectomies on young girls; should compulsorily arranged marriages or talaq divorces be legally recognized; should husbands be allowed to cite 'culture' as a defence when charged with beating their wives? Each of these practices is permitted in some parts of the world, and may even be viewed as an honoured tradition.

Most citizens of Western democracies are unwilling to tolerate such practices, and indeed none of them is permitted in most Western countries. They have never been a part of official multiculturalism policy in any Western country. But many critics worry that the logic of multiculturalism will lead to such practices. In Gwyn's words: 'To put the problem at its starkest, if female genital mutilation is a genuinely distinctive cultural practice, as it is among Somalis and others, then since official multiculturalism's purpose is to "preserve" and "enhance" the values and habits of all multicultural groups, why should this practice be disallowed in Canada any more than singing "O Sole Mio" or Highland dancing?.'[12]

Defenders of multiculturalism have, in general, failed to answer this question clearly. Some defenders have talked in a vague way about the need to 'balance' individual rights and the rights of ethnic groups, as if it's okay to violate individual rights a little bit, but not too much. Many defenders, however, have ignored the issue entirely, and sometimes implied that only prejudiced people would even raise the question. But people have a right to ask this question, and deserve a proper answer.

However, there are limits to multiculturalism in Western democracies, and these limits are remarkably consistent across the various countries. In

---

[11] This is my best explanation for the otherwise incomprehensibly paranoid misinterpretations of immigrant multiculturalism in the works of Schlesinger, Lind, Hughes, *et al.*

[12] Gwyn 1995: 189; cf. Bissoondath 1994: 138–9.

Australia, for example, the government policy sets out certain clear limits. After laying out the principles and goals of multiculturalism, including the right of immigrants to 'be able to develop and share their cultural heritage', and the responsibility of institutions to 'acknowledge, reflect and respond to the cultural diversity of the Australian community', the policy statement immediately goes on to emphasize 'that there are also limits to Australian multiculturalism', which it summarizes this way (Office of Multicultural Affairs 1995):

• multicultural policies require all Australians to accept the basic structures and principles of Australian society—the Constitution and the rule of law, tolerance and equality, Parliamentary democracy, freedom of speech and religion, English as the national language and equality of the sexes;
• multicultural policies impose obligations as well as conferring rights; the right to express one's own culture and beliefs involves a reciprocal responsibility to accept the right of others to express their views and values;
• multicultural policies are based upon the premise that all Australians should have an overriding and unifying commitment to Australia, to its interests and future.

I do not like the third limit, at least in its present form, which overstates the sort of allegiance which states can rightfully demand from their citizens. We are citizens of a nation, but also citizens of the world, and sometimes the interests of others can—indeed should—take precedence over our national interests. An Australian who commits some of her time and resources to helping people in developing countries, or in her country of origin, or who pushes Australia to increase its foreign aid budget, may not be putting Australia's interests 'first and foremost', but she is not doing anything wrong. A better way to make the point underlying this third limit is to say that we all have an obligation to do our fair share to uphold the basic institutions of our society, and to tackle the problems which face the country. The public institutions of Australian life provide most citizens with many benefits—a remarkable degree of peace, prosperity, and individual freedom—and citizens have a responsibility to do their share to ensure that these institutions endure and function, and to ensure that all Australians enjoy these benefits, whatever their race, religion, gender or ethnicity. This is an obligation of democratic citizenship that the state should promote, and which sets a limit to multiculturalism. It does not, however, require that every Australian put the interests of Australia 'first and foremost'.

The limits on multiculturalism in Canada are similar, though not as explicit. It is not quite true to say, as Bissoondath does, that the Multiculturalism Act in Canada 'suggests no limits to the accommodations offered to distinct cultural practices' (Bissoondath 1994: 138–9). The preamble to the Multiculturalism Act begins by emphasizing human rights, individual freedom, and sexual equality. Moreover, its provisions specify that the aims of multiculturalism are to promote individual freedom, and to do so in a way that respects sexual equality. It also says that multiculturalism policy should 'strengthen the status and use' of the official languages; should 'ensure that Canadians of all origins have an equal opportunity'; and should promote the 'interaction between individuals and communities of different origins'. These limits are also implicit in the fact that the Multiculturalism Act is subordinate to the Canadian Human Rights Act, which guarantee basic individual civil and political rights for all Canadians, including gender equality rights and equal opportunity. Moreover, the Multiculturalism Act must comply with the Canadian Charter of Rights and Freedoms, and would be struck down if it imposed any restrictions on individual rights which were not 'demonstrably justified in a free and democratic society'.

So the Canadian policy works within three broad limits: (a) it works within the framework of official bilingualism, and insists that immigrants learn and accept English or French as the languages of public life in Canada; (b) it works within the constraints of respect for liberal-democratic norms, including the Charter and Human Rights Act, and insists on respect for individual rights and sexual equality; and (c) it encourages openness to and interaction with people of different origins, rather than promoting segregated and inward-looking ethnic ghettoes. Multiculturalism in Canada is the commitment that within the constraints of these three principles, the government has a positive obligation to respect and accommodate diversity.

In short, the logic of multiculturalism involves accommodating diversity within the constraints of constitutional principles of equal opportunity and individual rights. And, here too, immigrant groups fully recognize and accept this. They accept the expectation that they will abide by constitutional principles. Few immigrant groups in Canada have objected to the Charter of Rights. On the contrary, they have consistently affirmed their support for it, and have made no attempt to get their cultural practices or traditions exempted from constitutional protections of individual rights and gender equality.

If we examined immigrant multiculturalism in other Western democracies, such as New Zealand or Britain or Sweden, we would find a similar story. In each case, multicultural accommodations operate within the context of an overarching commitment to linguistic integration, respect for individual rights, and inter-ethnic co-operation.[13] And these limits are understood and accepted by immigrant groups.

---

[13] As James Jupp puts it, multiculturalism 'is essentially a liberal ideology which operates within liberal institutions with the universal approval of liberal attitudes. It accepts that all humans should be treated as equals and that different cultures can co-exist if they accept liberal values' (Jupp 1996: 40).

Yet many citizens are still confused about the limits of multiculturalism. Indeed, many feel unable to even raise the issue in public forums, for fear of being labelled racist or prejudiced.[14] People want to know that there are certain fundamental requirements of being a citizen, including respect for human rights and democratic values, yet debate on this issue has been suppressed by political elites, who suggest that anyone who criticizes multiculturalism is prejudiced. This attempt to stifle the debate over the limits of multiculturalism is counter-productive. It does not promote understanding or acceptance of the policy, but simply leads to silent resentment against it.

Of course, any attempt to promote a public debate over the limits of multiculturalism is sure to stir up feelings of prejudice. We can reliably predict that any public debate will be painful at times, as some people out of fear and ignorance label other cultures as barbaric or undemocratic. But the end-result would, I think, be worth the temporary costs.

Consider, as an example, the debate over the hijab in Quebec schools. When the debate first arose, many Quebecers automatically assumed that all Muslims were fundamentalists who were opposed to sexual equality; or that all Muslims who supported the hijab also supported clitorectomy and talaq divorces, and perhaps even supported Iranian terrorism and the death-sentence against Salman Rushdie. These various stereotypes about Muslims were all present in the back of many people's minds, and the debate over the hijab provided an opportunity for these stereotypes to emerge. The result, at the beginning, was almost certainly harmful and painful to Muslims, who must have felt that they were destined to be permanent outsiders to Quebec society. They were being defined as the ultimate 'other' to Quebec's modern, pluralist, secular society.

But the debate progressed, and the end-result was actually to challenge these stereotypes. Quebecers learned not to equate Islam with fundamentalism. They learned that not all Muslims support keeping women locked up all day in the house; not all Muslims support talaq divorces and female clitorectomy; not all Muslims support killing authors who criticize Islam. Indeed, they learned that very few Muslims in Quebec adopt any of these attitudes. In the end, they learned that the enemy was not Islam as such, but rather certain forms of extremism that can be found in many different cultures, including 'our own'. The result was, I think, a more profound understanding and acceptance of Islam than existed before.

This was a painful process, to be sure, but it was an essential one. People needed an opportunity to disentangle the various ideas that were conflated in the back of their minds. They had legitimate objections to certain practices (female clitorectomies, the fatwah against Rushdie)—things that are indeed

[14] As Gwyn notes, when ordinary Canadians asked about the limits of multiculturalism, political elites 'had no answer other than guilt-tripping' (Gwyn 1995: 189).

worth fighting against. Before they were able and willing to accommodate the hijab in schools, therefore, they had to be convinced that accepting the hijab was not going to lead to accepting clitorectomies, talaq divorces, or death threats against writers. They were willing to embrace the accommodation of diversity, but only once they were clear about the limits of this accommodation. Debating the limits of diversity made possible the greater acceptance of diversity within those limits, and Quebec society today is better off for having had that debate.

Indeed, it is often ethnic groups themselves that want to clarify the terms of integration and the limits of accommodation. As Tariq Modood notes,

the greatest psychological and political need for clarity about a common framework and national symbols comes from the minorities. For clarity about what makes us willingly bound into a single country relieves the pressure on minorities, especially new minorities whose presence within the country is not fully accepted, to have to conform in all areas of social life, or in arbitrarily chosen areas, in order to rebut the charge of disloyalty. (Modood 1994: 64)

What newcomers often most desire from their new country is a clear statement of the criteria of social and political acceptance, and a debate over the limits of multiculturalism would help provide that (Hawkins 1989: 217).

The 'logic' of multiculturalism, then, is not to undermine respect for liberal-democratic values, any more than it is to undermine institutional integration. On the contrary, multiculturalism takes these political values as given and assumes that immigrants will accept them, just as it takes integration into mainstream public institutions as given. Multiculturalism simply specifies *how* this sort of political and social integration should occur— namely, in a way that respects and accommodates diversity. Within the constraints of liberal-democratic values, and of linguistic/institutional integration, governments must seek to recognize and accommodate our increasing ethnocultural diversity. These principles are implicit in the practice of multiculturalism, and are understood and accepted by immigrant groups.

Not only is this a consistent liberal-democratic approach to ethnocultural diversity, it is arguably the only approach which is truly consistent with liberal-democratic values. This helps explain why multiculturalism has been adopted in an increasing number of Western democracies.

9

A Crossroads in Race Relations

The evidence to date strongly suggests that multiculturalism policies have not undermined the historical tendency for immigrant groups in North America to integrate. Many people worry, however, that these integrationist trends apply only to white immigrant groups, but not to non-white groups. Others worry that while some non-white groups appear to be integrating—particularly Latin-American, Asian, Arab, and East Indian groups—Blacks are not.

In this chapter, I will look more closely at the status of racial minorities in Canada and the United States.[1] I will begin by briefly comparing race relations in the United States (section 1) and Canada (section 2). In each country, there are concerns about the lack of integration of racial minorities, and about the creation of a racially defined underclass whose members are in a state of more-or-less permanent alienation from, and opposition to, the mainstream society. But there are also many profound differences between the two countries.

In the United States, most Blacks are not immigrants, but rather are descended from the African slaves forcibly brought to the United States in the eighteenth and nineteenth centuries. Recent immigrants account for only a small percentage of the Black community in the United States, and have little influence in the major African-American organizations and political movements. The situation in Canada is essentially the reverse. While slavery and segregation existed in Canada, and a Black community has existed from the earliest period of colonization, the vast majority of Blacks in Canada are recent immigrants, primarily from the Caribbean. The descendants of the earlier Black slaves or settlers in Canada account for only a small percentage of the Black community, and have little influence in the major Canadian Black organizations.

In light of these differences, we might predict that the immigrant model of integration is a realistic policy goal for Blacks in Canada, whereas a new and more complex model of accommodation will be required for African-Americans. That is indeed the argument I will make in this chapter. However,

[1] In Canada, the term 'visible minorities' is often used instead of 'racial minorities'. I will use the two terms interchangeably to refer to non-white, non-Aboriginal groups. They include Blacks, Chinese, Koreans, Filipinos, Indo-Pakistanis, West Asians and Arabs, Southeast Asians, Latin Americans, and Pacific Islanders.

as always, there are complications to be considered. Blacks in Canada, particularly immigrants from the Caribbean, face many barriers to integration not faced by other immigrants, including other non-white immigrants (section 3). While they have not endured the same experience of historical oppression as African-Americans, Blacks in Canada have been the victims of racial bias in the schools, courts, and economy, and have sought to avoid this racism by partially separating themselves from the mainstream society. As a result, the potential for the creation of a disaffected black subculture is a real one, and some disturbing signs of this trend can already be seen. I will conclude by considering some of the measures that have been proposed to improve the status of Blacks in Canada, and how they relate to comparable proposals for African-Americans (section 4).

1. Race in the United States: The Case of African-Americans

The historical treatment of racial groups in North America provides a stark reminder that integration is always a two-way street. On the one hand, it requires a willingness on the part of the minority group to adapt to certain features of the mainstream society—e.g. learning the official language, or participating in certain common institutions. But it equally requires a willingness on the part of the majority to accept the minority as equal citizens—i.e. a willingness to extend the full range of rights and opportunities to the minority, to live and work cooperatively alongside members of the minority, and to adapt mainstream institutions where necessary to accommodate the distinctive needs and identities of the minority.

The historical record shows that in many instances, the majority has lacked the sort of openness that makes it possible for minority groups to integrate. In the case of African-Americans the sort of openness which would make integration possible has been almost entirely absent. Many commentators argue that the systemic discrimination faced by African-Americans in the United States has made integration virtually impossible, or at least much more difficult than for immigrant groups.

I believe that this is true, but it is important to clarify exactly how the barriers confronting African-Americans differ from those confronting immigrant groups. It goes without saying that African-Americans have faced great prejudice and discrimination, starting from the moment they were brought to America, and even in the post-Civil War period. But that in and of itself is not the crucial factor. After all, most American immigrant groups historically have faced discrimination and prejudice, from the Irish in the 1840s to the Japanese in the 1940s. Indeed, as Kenneth Karst notes, 'virtually every cultural minority in America has had to face exclusion, forced conformity, and subordination'.[2]

It would therefore be misleading to say that integration requires that minorities be 'welcomed'. There are relatively few cases where (non-WASP) immigrants have been warmly welcomed, rather than viewed with fear and apprehension. Even when the American government has been committed to encouraging immigration, and to encouraging immigrants once here to acquire citizenship, this official policy has rarely been fully reflected in everyday public attitudes. Large elements of the American public have always viewed immigrants as a threat to their culture, or their jobs, or to political stability. Throughout their history, many Americans have believed that the health and stability of American society is dependent on maintaining the hegemony of WASP cultural traditions, and hence is threatened by widespread immigration from non-English, non-Protestant and non-white countries.[3] This nativist streak has been reflected not only in the various attempts to implement restrictive and discriminatory immigration policies, but also in widespread discrimination in housing, employment, banking, education, private clubs etc., and in the prejudicial stereotypes which were accepted and disseminated in the media.

For example, there were laws against the teaching of immigrant languages—a prohibition which was primarily aimed at German immigrant groups; there were laws prohibiting the employment of Asians in certain professions; quotas limiting the numbers of Jews in universities; restrictive covenants which prevented non-whites from buying houses in particular neighbourhoods; literacy tests that were used to prevent Hispanics and other non-Anglos from voting; and so on. At a more general level, the degree of public prejudice was such that it was very difficult for members of any of these groups to achieve elected public office. These measures were justified on the grounds that 'aliens' were stupid, lazy, irresponsible, deceitful, unclean, undemocratic, unpatriotic, etc. And these stereotypes were themselves often justified by reference to pseudo-scientific arguments about 'racial' differences. (It is important to remember that until well into the twentieth century, Eastern and Southern Europeans were viewed as separate 'races', and indeed sometimes even as 'black'. The idea that all Europeans belong to a single 'white' race is comparatively new.)[4]

Yet most immigrant groups have gradually overcome these barriers. The long history of virulent prejudice and discrimination against immigrant groups—whether Irish Catholics, Jews, Germans, Japanese, or Hispanics—deferred, but did not ultimately prevent, their integration. Why then has the integration of African-Americans proven so difficult? The explanation lies not in discrimination and prejudice *per se*, but rather in the *kind* of discrimination

---

[2] Karst 1986: 325.   [3] R. Smith 1997.   [4] Ignatiev 1995.

they faced in the post-Civil War era. With most immigrant groups, the discrimination they faced was intended to keep them in a subordinate status, but this was still subordination *within the larger society*. They were treated as second-class citizens, but they were still seen as members of the mainstream society. There was never any intention of allowing or encouraging Jews or Germans to form a separate society, alongside the mainstream society.

Since immigrant groups were included in the larger society, albeit as second-class citizens, their struggles took the form of demanding more equal inclusion within the mainstream society. Moreover, as I noted in Chapter 8, the whole idea of building a separate society is an enormous undertaking which is simply beyond the reach of immigrant groups, even in an avowedly 'multicultural' society. Hence if immigrants were to succeed in their new 'land of opportunity', it could only be through greater inclusion, rather than the building of a separate society.

Indeed, if we examine the period of highest immigration, in the early part of this century, much of the prejudice and discrimination immigrant groups faced was aimed at inhibiting any public expression of their ethnic identity, and at coercively assimilating them into the dominant 'Anglo-conformity' mould. If immigrants faced discrimination within mainstream institutions, they faced even greater hostility when they were perceived as trying to build separate ethnic enclaves. Ethnic separatism was seen as proof of 'un-American' sentiments, and was ruthlessly suppressed. As Karst put it, immigrants faced 'forced conformity and subordination'—they were forcibly Americanized, yet were only allowed to become second-class Americans.

In short, while immigrant groups in the United States often faced virulent prejudice and systemic discrimination, these restrictions none the less operated alongside a kind of societal integration. Immigrants were shunted into subordinate positions within the mainstream society—they were often prevented from occupying the elite positions within mainstream institutions, but equally they were prevented from creating separate societies.

By contrast, African-Americans were discouraged—indeed legally prevented—from integrating into the societal institutions of the mainstream. Prior to the Civil War, they were not even seen as persons, let alone equal citizens. As slaves, they were denied all civil and political rights. But even after the Civil War, they faced a system of total institutional segregation—not just in public parks and residential neighbourhoods, but in buses and trains, bars and restaurants, workplaces and unions, washrooms and drinking fountains, etc. And this extended into government services and government employment—not only were schools and hospitals segregated, but so were army units. Moreover, there were laws against miscegenation in many states, so as to prevent any intermixing of white and black races.

Given this total institutional segregation, African-Americans had no choice but to develop their own separate society. And indeed they did. They created their own schools and universities, hospitals and businesses, churches and recreational associations. This was particularly true in the South, but even in cities like Chicago black urban neighbourhoods functioned in effect as institutionally complete societies.[5] This is quite unlike the status of freed slaves in Central or South America, or in other former European colonies, where the descendants of slaves often were able to integrate into the mainstream society, even if only as disadvantaged second-class citizens.

In this respect, African-Americans are closer to the 'national minority' pattern than to the 'immigrant' pattern. Like the Aboriginals, Québécois, or Puerto Ricans, African-Americans formed an institutionally complete society alongside the dominant society. Yet it would be very misleading to equate the institutional segregation of African-Americans with that of national minorities. In the case of national minorities, a culturally distinct society, settled for centuries on its historic homeland, seeks to defend its pre-existing institutional separateness out of a desire to maintain its existence as a separate society, and to preserve its language and culture.

By contrast, the exclusion of African-Americans from mainstream institutions was coercively imposed not intentionally adopted. Moreover, the slaves did not have a common language, culture or national identity. They came from a variety of African cultures, with different languages, and no attempt was made to keep together those with a common ethnic background. On the contrary, people from the same culture (even from the same family) were often split up once in America. And even if they shared the same African language, slaves were forbidden to speak it, since slave-owners feared that such speech could be used to foment rebellion.[6]

When slavery was abolished, therefore, most African-Americans wanted to integrate into the mainstream society. Insofar as they had a national identity, it was as anglophone 'Americans'. Any previous African national identity or language had been largely expunged. Because they were coercively prevented from integrating, however, they had no choice but to build up their own separate institutions.

It is important to emphasize this point. The initial exclusion of African-Americans from mainstream institutions did not arise because they were encouraged or allowed to maintain an already existing culture. On the contrary, this exclusion went hand in hand with systematic efforts by whites to prevent the maintenance of any previous African languages, cultures, and national identities. In terms of their uprootedness, therefore, African-Americans are much closer to immigrants and refugees than to national minorities. Over time, they have developed a high degree of institutional separateness, like national minorities; yet like immigrants and refugees, they were uprooted, physically and culturally, from their homeland. Indeed, the

<hr/>

[5] Wilson 1978.   [6] Sagarin and Kelly 1985: 26–7.

nature and extent of their physical and cultural uprooting was much more violent and radical than that of any immigrant group in North America. Their subsequent institutional separateness, therefore, was not a way of maintaining an existing culture on a historic homeland, but was simply one component of a larger system of racial oppression.

None the less, the history of almost total institutional segregation helps explain why Black nationalism has, at times, been a potent force within the African-American community. The fact is that after the Civil War, Blacks did create a viable, functioning and highly-developed separate society, with its own economy, press, schools, hospitals, churches, sports leagues, music halls, etc. And these separate institutions provided avenues for meaningful accomplishments, upward mobility, and social recognition. Because their institutional segregation was complete, there were Blacks in virtually all professions and class categories—there were Black professors, lawyers, doctors, journalists, librarians, authors, scientists, musicians, engineers, etc. And there were Black newspapers that recognized their accomplishments.

The impact of desegregation, therefore, has been viewed with significant ambivalence in the African-American community. It has meant the gradual loss of these Black-focused institutions. Yet the history of racism and economic disadvantage is such that blacks lack equal opportunity in the mainstream society, and have become overwhelmingly concentrated in the lower classes. Indeed, many blacks now believe that they had a greater opportunity to become professionals within the old segregated system than within existing 'integrated' institutions. Moreover, their accomplishments have become invisible within the mainstream media. Instead, they are portrayed primarily as criminals and drug addicts.[7]

The feeling amongst Blacks that they face insuperable obstacles within the mainstream society is also influenced by the apparent success of subsequent immigrant groups. It is important to note that the success of these immigrant groups is not viewed by most African-Americans as evidence that non-white groups can succeed in America. On the contrary, it is seen as proof of how much the odds are stacked against them. Anglo-Saxon whites who have resolutely avoided genuine educational or residential integration with Blacks have nonetheless accepted, and eventually welcomed, Jews, Irish, Italians, Asians, Arabs, or Latinos into their schools, workplaces and homes. Many Blacks believe that the success of these groups has come at their expense, and they resent it. This is reflected in the conflict between Blacks and Hispanics in Miami, between Blacks and Asians in Los Angeles, between Blacks and Jews in New York, or between Blacks and Irish in Boston.

As a result of all these factors, many Blacks have come to look with some nostalgia at the era of separate institutions, and have come to believe that

---

[7] Addis 1993.

Black success in America can only be achieved through turning Blacks into a self-governing nation within the United States. Indeed, various attempts have been made to redefine African-Americans as a national minority. Some African-Americans, sceptical of the possibility of integration, have adopted the language of nationalism, and sought a form of territorial self-government. The idea of creating a 'Black state' in the south had some support in the 1930s (it was even endorsed by the American Communist Party), and resurfaced briefly in the 1960s.

But that idea was never realistic, not only because Blacks and whites are intermingled throughout the south, but also because African-Americans are no longer concentrated in the South, having migrated throughout the country. As a result, there is no state where African-Americans form a majority. In any event, most Blacks do not have or want a distinct national identity. They see themselves as entitled to full membership in the American nation, even if whites deny them that birthright, and so have fought for full and equal participation within the mainstream society.

To achieve this, many Americans have hoped that the immigrant model of integration can be made to work for African-Americans. Thus John Ogbu wants to 'help [African-Americans] understand and adopt the immigrant minorities' model'.[8] Nathan Glazer expresses the hope that if we firmly enforced anti-discrimination laws, Blacks could become 'the same kind of group that the European ethnic groups have become':

with proper public policies to stamp out discrimination and inferior status and to encourage acculturation and assimilation, [Blacks] will become not very different from the European and Asian ethnic groups, the ghost nations, bound by nostalgia and sentiment and only occasionally coalescing around distinct interests.[9]

Similarly, Michael Walzer says that separatism would not be tempting if Blacks had the 'same opportunities for group organization and cultural expression' available to white immigrant groups. He too hopes that this model of integration which is 'adapted to the needs of immigrant communities' can nonetheless 'successfully be extended to the racial minorities now asserting their own group claims'.[10]

This was the underlying presupposition of the American civil rights movement in the 1960s. Greater protection against discrimination would make it possible for Blacks to follow the immigrant path to integration and economic success. But that too has proved unrealistic, given the profound historical differences between immigrants and African-Americans. The legacy of

---

[8] Obgu 1988:164–5.

[9] Glazer 1983: 184, 284. It is interesting to note that Glazer himself has recently changed his position, and acknowledged that the immigrant model will not work for African-Americans. See the interesting discussion in Glazer 1997.

[10] Walzer 1995: 153–4.

centuries of slavery and segregation has created barriers to integration which immigrants simply do not face. As a result, despite the legal victories of the civil rights movement, Blacks remain disproportionately at the bottom of the economic ladder, even as more recent (non-white) immigrants have integrated (e.g. Asian-Americans).

The needs and aspirations of African-Americans do not match those of either immigrant groups or national minorities. Indeed, this is part of the problem: we have no clear theory or model for understanding or meeting the needs of African-Americans. Neither the model of multination federalism for national minorities, nor the model of multicultural integration for immigrant groups, is adequate here.

In light of these complex circumstances and tragic history, African-Americans have raised a complex, unique, and evolving set of demands. As a result, it is increasingly recognized that a *sui generis* approach will have to be worked out for African-Americans, involving a variety of measures. These may include historical compensation for past injustice, special assistance in integration (e.g. affirmative action), guaranteed political representation (e.g. redrawing electoral boundaries to create Black-majority districts), and support for various forms of Black self-organization (e.g. subsidies for historical Black colleges, and for Black-focused education). These different demands may seem to pull in different directions, since some promote integration while others seem to reinforce segregation, but each responds to a different part of the complex and contradictory reality which African-Americans find themselves in, and the contradictory relationship they have had to American nation-building.[11] The long-term aim is to promote the integration of African-Americans into the American nation, but it is recognized that this is a long-term process that can only work if existing Black communities and institutions are strengthened. A degree of short-term separateness and colour-consciousness is needed to achieve the long-term goal of an integrated and colour-blind society.[12]

It is difficult to specify precisely which principles should be used to evaluate these demands, all of which are controversial. As with most other groups, there are both moral and prudential factors to be considered. African-

---

[11] Like metics in many countries (e.g. Turks in Germany), African-Americans were historically excluded from becoming members of the nation. But unlike metics, the justification for this was not that they were citizens of some other nation to which they should return. Blacks in America can hardly be seen as 'foreigners' or 'aliens', since they have been in the US as long as the whites, and have no foreign citizenship. Instead, they were effectively denationalized— they were denied membership in the American nation, but nor were they viewed as belonging to some other nation which could provide the basis for some alternate conception of nationhood.

[12] For proposals along these lines, see Brooks 1996; For helpful discussions of the status and claims of African-Americans, and their connection to liberal-democratic norms, see Spinner 1994, Gutmann and Appiah 1996; Cochran 1999; Vall, 1999.

Americans have suffered perhaps the greatest injustices of all ethnocultural groups, both in terms of their historical mistreatment and their current plight. Morally speaking, then, we have an urgent obligation to identify and remedy these injustices. Moreover, the result of this ongoing exclusion has been the development of a separatist and oppositional subculture in which the very idea of pursuing success in 'white' institutions is viewed by many Blacks with suspicion. The costs of allowing such a subculture to arise are enormous, both for the Blacks themselves, who are condemned to lives of poverty, marginalization, and violence, and for society at large, in terms of the waste of human potential, and the escalation of racial conflict. Given these costs, it would seem both prudent and moral to adopt whatever reforms are needed to prevent such a situation.

It is interesting to note that the immigrant model has in fact worked for many Blacks who really are *immigrants* to the United States—for example, recent immigrants from the Caribbean have done quite well, and second-generation Caribbean-Americans do better than average on many criteria.[13] But these immigrant Blacks see themselves (and are seen by other Americans, both white and Black) as separate from the historical African-American community, and the relative success of the former has not eased the burdens of the latter.

3. Visible Minorities in Canada

The experience of racial minorities in Canada does not match that of African-Americans. To be sure, there are some important similarities. For example, there was slavery in Canada from 1689 to 1834, both under French rule and after the British conquest. This primarily involved Indian slaves, but historians estimate that there also existed up to 1,000 slaves of African descent. Indeed, there was a period of time when slavery was legal in Canada but illegal in the northern United States, and some slaves left Canada for the US to gain their freedom. Moreover, as in the United States, the abolition of slavery led not to racial equality, but to a system of segregated institutions for Blacks in Canada. Indeed the last segregated school in Ontario only closed in 1965.[14]

These facts are useful reminders about the depth of racism in Canada's past. However, they are not really the root of Canada's race relations problems today, since these long-settled Blacks form only a small minority of the visible minorities who live in Canada today. Indeed, they form only a small minority of those who define themselves as 'Black'.

---

[13] Foster 1996: 318–19; Henry 1994: 18.   [14] D. Williams 1989: 7–14, 17–18.

The Black community in Canada in the eighteenth and nineteenth centuries—the descendants of former slaves and Black United Empire
Loyalists—was never very large, compared to the African-American population in the United States. Moreover, it shrunk dramatically between 1870 and
1930 as Blacks moved back to the United States. There were several waves of
Black emigration, first between 1870 and 1902, and then again in the 1920s
and 1930s, as Blacks pursued greater opportunities to the south. Indeed, the
overall population of Blacks in Canada decreased by two-thirds in Canada
over this period.[15]

As a result, the largest group of Blacks in Canada today is recent immigrants from the Caribbean. For example, 80 per cent of Blacks in Montreal are
from the Caribbean—primarily Haiti, but also from various British
Caribbean islands, particularly Jamaica and Trinidad. Descendants of long-
settled Blacks form only a small minority—under 20 per cent.[16] The same
general trend applies to Toronto, although there the largest group is
Jamaicans rather than Haitians. Amongst the major Canadian cities, it is only
in Halifax where the long-settled Black population remains more significant
than recent Caribbean immigration.

So the history of slavery and segregation in Canada, while more similar to
the US than most Canadians realize, is not the source of contemporary race
relations problems. The numbers of Blacks who experienced these conditions was relatively small, and their descendants are now massively outnumbered by immigrants from the Caribbean or Africa.

This has two important consequences. First, the idea of Black nationalism
has never taken hold in Canada. Because the Black community was small during the period of official segregation and discrimination, it never developed
the same degree of institutional completeness as in the United States. As
Dorothy Williams puts it,

Widespread discrimination in the United States had created two parallel societies.
American Blacks lived in a fully segregated society from top to bottom, that had its
own Black universities, businesses, lawyers, newspapers, hospitals, tradesmen and
labourers. But in Canada, where opportunities were purported to be equal, most
Blacks, regardless of skills, tended to fit into one level of society—*the bottom*.[17]

There were a few Black-focused institutions in Canada which provided
avenues for Black mobility and achievement—e.g. in journalism. And it is
possible to find some people expressing mild nostalgia for this period.[18] But
the size of the Black community was so small, and territorially dispersed, that
the idea of developing a complete and separate Black society was never seri-

---

[15] D. Williams 1989: 30, 45.
[16] Ibid. 80–1. On the extent to which recent Caribbean immigrants have 'hijacked' the race
agenda in Canada, see Foster 1996: 25–6.
[17] D. Williams 1989: 44.   [18] See e.g. Shadd 1994: 14.

ously contemplated. The only viable option for Blacks to participate in modern life in Canada was through inclusion in the mainstream society.

Second, the fact that most Blacks today are recent immigrants means that they can build upon the success of earlier non-WASP immigrants. Unlike in the United States, the success of Jews, Greeks, and Asians is not perceived as having come at the expense of Blacks in Canada, but rather has helped to establish the principle of a pluralistic, non-discriminatory multicultural society.

Indeed, one could argue that the obstacles facing many visible minorities in Canada today are comparable to those facing immigrant groups in the past. To be sure, visible minorities today face enormous prejudice and discrimination. But so did earlier immigrants. Current stereotypes about violence and criminality amongst Jamaicans are not very different from the historical stereotypes about the Irish; current misperceptions about the 'clannish' and 'ghettoized' nature of the Chinese community are not very different from earlier misperceptions about the Italians and Ukrainians; current fears about the dangers of religious extremism amongst Muslims and Sikhs are not very different from earlier fears about the dangers of Catholicism and Judaism.

There is reason to believe that visible minorities today can overcome these barriers to integration, just as earlier immigrant groups have done. Or at least it is premature to conclude otherwise. After all, most visible minorities have arrived in Canada in the last thirty years. It often took non-WASP immigrants three or more generations to fully integrate, and we simply do not yet know how the grandchildren of Jamaicans or Vietnamese immigrants will fare. Indeed, even today, we can see evidence that some visible minorities are doing quite well in Canada. For example, 1986 Census statistics show that Arab-Canadians have a higher per-capita income than British-Canadians, and that South Asian-Canadians have a higher average income than either South European-Canadians or French-Canadians.[19]

Similarly, many non-white immigrant groups in the United States are integrating well. This is particularly true of some Asian-American groups, who have moved 'from pariahs to paragons', as a recent commentator put it.[20] But it is also true to some extent of newer Black immigrants to the US, including Caribbean immigrants. As I noted earlier, they too are following the general immigrant pattern of integration, although only by deliberately distancing themselves, physically and culturally, from African-Americans. It would seem, therefore, that African-Americans form a very special case, and that their tragic situation need not presage the fate of other non-white minorities in Canada or the United States.

[19] Fleras and Elliot 1996: 105.   [20] Rose 1989.

4. Towards a Multiracial Society in Canada

However, while we may be reasonably optimistic that racial minorities in Canada will successfully integrate, we should not be complacent about the level of racism in Canadian society. In particular, there are serious concerns about the future of the Black community in Canada. As Stephen Lewis noted in his controversial 1992 *Report on Race Relations in Ontario*, Blacks in Canada face obstacles that other non-white groups do not:

What we are dealing with, at root, and fundamentally, is anti-Black racism. While it is obviously true that every visible minority community experiences the indignities and wounds of systemic discrimination throughout Southwestern Ontario, it is the Black community which is the focus. It is Blacks who are being shot, it is Black youth who are unemployed in excessive numbers, it is Black students who are being inappropriately streamed in schools, it is Black kids who are disproportionately dropping-out, it is housing communities with large concentrations of Black residents where the sense of vulnerability and disadvantage is most acute, it is Black employees, professional and non-professional, on whom the doors of upward equity slam shut.[21]

Measuring racism is a difficult task, but there appears to be ample scientific and anecdotal evidence that Blacks are subject to particularly harsh prejudice, compared to other visible minorities. This is reflected in statistics on housing and job discrimination;[22] or in the negative portrayal of Blacks in the media;[23] or in the way Blacks are punished more severely for breaking the rules in schools or in jails;[24] or in surveys of how comfortable Canadians feel around different ethnic groups, in which Blacks are ranked near the bottom (well below the Chinese or Japanese, for example).[25]

More subtly, it is also reflected in the way many people assume that a particular crime is likely to have been committed by a Black; or in the way many people criticize Blacks for trying to understand their African heritage, or for giving their children African names, yet tolerate or even applaud Irish-Canadians for celebrating their ethnic heritage.[26] Even more subtly, anti-Black racism is reflected in the widespread assumption that all Blacks must be recent immigrants, thereby ignoring the long history and contributions of Blacks in Canada.[27]

None of these forms of prejudice needs to involve what Elliot and Fleras call 'red-necked racism'—that is, the explicitly avowed belief that one race is

[21] Lewis 1992: 2.   [22] See e.g. Henry 1994: ch. 5.
[23] See Henry 1994: 219–22; Foster 1996: 189; Fleras 1994.
[24] For a discussion of double-standards regarding punishment in jails, see Commission on Systemic Racism 1995: 48–9. On the schools, see Toronto Board of Education 1988: 33, and appendix E, p. 4.
[25] Breton *et al.* 1990: 199–201.   [26] For interesting examples, see Codjoe 1994: 235.
[27] See Shadd 1994: 11; D. Williams 1989: 4.

genetically superior to another. Nor need it involve 'polite racism', where people who believe in racial superiority avoid saying so in public. Instead, these can all be seen as examples of what they call 'subliminal racism'. This sort of racism is found in people who genuinely and sincerely accept egalitarian values, but who nonetheless, often unconsciously, invoke double-standards when evaluating or predicting the actions of different racial groups. This sort of racism is particularly difficult to identify, or to eliminate, since it is found in people who consciously and sincerely reject all racist doctrines.[28]

This raises an important point about racial dynamics in Canada. As I noted earlier, there have been considerable historical variations in people's perceptions of who is 'white' and who is 'black'. For example, the idea that all Europeans are white is relatively recent—a process studied in books such as 'How The Irish Became White'.[29] We can see this dynamic at work today in South Africa, where the (mixed-race) 'Coloureds', who used to be considered black, are increasingly seen as (almost) white.

These shifts in the colour line have made it possible for various visible minorities to gain equality with whites in North America. Indeed, we can measure a group's success at integrating by examining how it has moved on the colour line. Just as the Irish have become white, so I think that Latin Americans and Arabs are increasingly seen as white by many Canadians. And some day I suspect that the Japanese will be seen as white.

. The problem, however, is that each of these groups have 'become white' precisely by gaining some distance from 'blacks'. They have come to be seen as 'respectable', like whites, in contrast to the 'unruly' Blacks.[30] They are seen as decent, hard-working and law-abiding citizens, as opposed to the promiscuous, lazy, and criminal Blacks.

This raises questions about the term 'visible minorities', which is widely used in Canada to refer to all non-white groups. The adoption of this term was premised on the assumption that the fundamental divide in Canada is between whites and non-whites. That probably was true thirty years ago, but I think it is quite misleading today. Our society remains racially divided, but the fundamental divide is less and less white/non-white, and more white/black.

Where do groups which are neither white nor black—like Latinos, Asians, Pacific Islanders and Arabs—fit in this new racial divide? The term 'visible

[28] On 'subliminal racism' in Canada, and how it differs from red-necked and polite racism, see Fleras and Elliot 1996: 71–78. They describe subliminal racism as reflecting a contradiction between the values of social equality and individual freedom. This seems quite unhelpful to me. So far as I can tell, it is rather a contradiction between people's general beliefs about freedom/equality and their more specific habits, dispositions, and emotions.

[29] Ignatiev 1995.

[30] For a discussion of how the changing status of Coloureds in South Africa is related to a racialized discourse of 'respectability', see Seekings and Jung 1997.

minorities' presupposes that for sociological and public policy purposes, these non-white groups are closer to the 'black' side than to the 'white' side of the dichotomy. But in reality many of these groups are slowly being seen as (almost) white. The term 'visible minorities' may be blinding us to this important trend.

I don't want to exaggerate this phenomenon. For example, while Latinos and East Asians (e.g. Chinese, Japanese) are increasingly accepted by white Canadians, and indeed are now reaching the same level of acceptance as white ethnic groups, Arabs and South Asian Muslims (e.g. Indo-Pakistanis) face greater resistance, and their level of acceptance is closer to that of West-Indian Blacks.[31] But these results may reflect religious prejudice as much as racial prejudice. White Canadians may assume that Arabs and South Asians are Muslims or Sikhs, whom they see as prone to violence and fundamentalism. By contrast, most Canadians have no similar fears about East Asian religions. In other words, Canadians may be made uncomfortable more by the religion of these groups than by their skin colour.[32]

It is an interesting question how exactly we should describe this phenomenon. Are Asians and Arabs in Canada (or Coloureds in South Africa) in fact being perceived as 'white'? Or is it rather that whites continue to see 'brown' people as non-white, but now draw greater distinctions amongst different kinds of non-white groups, emphasizing the difference between brown and black? Put another way, is the fundamental racial divide between whites and non-whites, so that being accepted in Canada requires being seen as white? Or is the fundamental divide between Blacks and non-Blacks, so that being accepted does not require that one be white—one could be brown, yellow or red and still be one of 'us'—so long as one is not Black.

I am unsure how best to analyse this phenomenon. But it seems to exist, and I think it has potentially serious consequences for the integration of Blacks in Canada. While there is reason for optimism about the status of some visible minorities in Canada, it may be that their admission into Canadian society has not in fact opened the door for Blacks. Insofar as visible minorities gain acceptance in Canada by distancing themselves from Blacks—by becoming white—then perhaps very little has in fact changed in the racial psyche of Canadians. (I don't mean to suggest that these groups have deliberately sought to distance themselves from Blacks, although some have. It is more a matter of how whites perceive the distinctions between these various groups). This doesn't mean that all of the people who are currently perceived as Black will face this sort of prejudice. However, while the

[31] Berry and Kalin 1995: 301–20; Driedger 1996 264.

[32] It would be interesting, for example, to see whether the acceptance of Lebanese Christians is closer to that of whites or blacks. (So far as I know, such a question has not been asked in surveys of Canadians' ethnic attitudes). My guess is that Arabs are increasingly seen as 'white', racially, even if Arab Muslims remain subject to religious prejudice.

category of 'black' may change and perhaps shrink, prejudice against 'blacks' may prove very difficult to dispel.

The existence of this anti-Black racism creates a serious potential for racial conflict in Canada. It raises the possibility that Blacks in Canada will adopt an oppositional stance towards the mainstream society in which the very idea of pursuing success in mainstream institutions is viewed as 'acting white'. And indeed there is some evidence that this is already happening amongst Caribbean students in some Toronto high schools, as it has amongst many African-Americans students in the United States,[33] leading to unusually high drop out rates.[34]

An even more disturbing trend is the emergence of almost conspiracy-like fears about the police and the courts amongst some Blacks in Canada. This too is imported from the United States, and seems to be as much influenced by American events (Rodney King, O. J. Simpson) as by events here. Whatever the reality of discrimination by police and courts—and it is real— it is clear that some Blacks have exaggerated its scope, drawing on African-American rhetoric about 'white justice' and 'government plots'. Andrew Hacker argues that such conspiracy-type fears are pivotal in explaining the existence and persistence of a separatist and oppositional subculture amongst Blacks in the United States, and Cecil Foster worries that a similar phenomenon is developing in Canada.[35] If these perceptions of injustice and fears about conspiracy are not addressed in Canada, we are in very great danger indeed of falling into the American pattern of race relations.

Yet it is unclear how widespread this tendency towards adopting an oppositional subculture is. It seems primarily found amongst Blacks from the Caribbean, rather than immigrants from Africa (who remain a relatively small percentage of the overall Black population). Moreover, it is unclear whether this tendency applies primarily to Blacks born in the Caribbean, or whether it is also being passed on to native-born Blacks. There is some evidence to think that native-born Blacks are less likely to adopt this oppositional stance.[36] And other commentators stress the extent to which Black students still are committed to the idea that success in mainstream institutions is possible, and worth pursuing.[37]

---

[33] For evidence regarding African-Americans, see Ogbu 1988: 164–5.

[34] Solomon 1994: 191. Indeed, as Solomon notes, the drop-out rate actually underestimates the problem, since many Blacks stay in school only for the sports, without any real interest or concern about academic achievement (p. 189). Solomon argues that students within this 'sports subculture' have de facto 'dropped out'.

[35] Hacker 1992; Foster 1996: 115.

[36] See Henry 1994: 144. Unfortunately, in other places, Henry discusses 'Black youth' in a way that makes it unclear whether the trends apply to both Caribbean-born and native-born Blacks.

[37] See, for example, Toronto Board of Education 1988.

It would seem that we are at a pivotal point in the history of race relations in Canada. With meaningful reforms, Caribbean Blacks could overcome the barriers of racism, and follow the historical pattern of immigrant integration. But if nothing is done, the drift towards the sort of oppositional subculture found amongst some African-Americans could snowball.

The history of race relations in the United States suggests that once such a separatist and oppositional subculture is created, it is difficult to break out of. As I noted earlier, the costs of allowing such a subculture to arise are enormous, both for the Blacks themselves and for society at large. Given these costs, it would seem rational—indeed imperative—to adopt whatever reforms are needed to prevent such a situation. I do not have the space or expertise to assess which policies and programmes would be most effective, but I would like briefly to consider two issues—black-focused schools, and affirmative action. My aim is not to defend either unconditionally, but rather to emphasize the need to think seriously, and with an open mind, about possible strategies for dealing with an urgent situation.

Black-Focused Schools

Some Black groups in Toronto have supported the establishment of black-focused schools, which are open to students of all races, but which are designed with the educational needs of Blacks in mind. Many Canadians fear that this is the first step towards a more comprehensive Black separatism and nationalism. This concern makes some sense in the American context, since, as I noted earlier, the idea of black nationalism has some historical and sociological relevance. The promotion of 'Afrocentric' public schools could be seen as part of a larger project for building a separate society, which would include reviving or recreating segregated black universities, businesses, media, etc. In the United States, the prospect of a separate Black societal culture is coherent, if ultimately unrealistic, and proposals for Black-focused schools will inevitably be viewed in that context.

My own sense is that most African-American defenders of Afrocentric schools in the US are not in fact seeking to recreate or extend institutional separateness. They are instead seeking long-term integration, and see Black-focused schools as a transitional step, needed to reduce drop-out rates, and thereby enable more African-Americans to acquire the skills and credentials needed to succeed in mainstream institutions.

In any event, the idea that Black-focused schools could lead to comprehensive Black separatism is clearly off-base in the Canadian context. Unlike in the United States, there is no history of Black universities in Canada, and no one has proposed creating them. Demands for Black-focused public schools, therefore, are like the demand for bilingual classes for immigrant children. They can only be seen as a transitional step towards long-term integration into mainstream educational, economic, and political institutions in Canada.[38]

Indeed, far from promoting separatism, Black-focused schools may be the last, best chance for avoiding the creation of a separatist, oppositional Black subculture. A series of studies has consistently concluded that integrated schools in Toronto are inhospitable to Caribbean Blacks, due to the low numbers of Black teachers and guidance counsellors, the invisibility of Black authors and history in the curriculum, the failure of school authorities to crack down on the use of racial epithets by fellow students, double-standards in disciplinary decisions, and the disproportionate streaming of Blacks into dead-end non-academic classes.[39] This is leading to heightened drop-out rates, and reinforcing the sense that success in 'white society' is impossible.[40]

Some of these problems can and should be resolved by aggressively attacking racism within the integrated schools. But two decades of studies and reforms have apparently had little effect in improving the performance of Blacks, and it is worth considering the possibility that Black-focused schools can help as a transition step towards long-term integration.

Whether or not they would help reduce the drop-out rate and improve long-term integration is, of course, an empirical question. And so any move in the direction of developing black-focused schools should take the form of pilot projects, with rigorous monitoring of their actual results.

But one reason why they might work is that they could deal more effectively with the tricky issue of Caribbean dialects.[41] Studies show that many Caribbean students suffer in schools because they have not learned Canadian English. Students realize this, and know that they need to learn Canadian English in order to succeed in Canadian society.

However, they feel insulted by the way their dialects are treated within the school system. They are often told that they do not speak or write 'proper' English, as if Jamaican English were somehow an inferior or less accurate

---

[38] On the differences between Canadian and American models of black-focused schools, see Foster 1996: 130–4.

[39] See Toronto Board of Education 1988; Henry 1994: ch. 6; Lewis 1992: 20–1; Solomon 1994; Braithwaite 1989; Dei 1994, 1995.

[40] I don't mean to imply that racism in Canada is the only, or even primary, explanation for the difficulties facing young Caribbean Black adults today. For one thing, some of those who are in greatest difficulty (e.g. those caught up in crime, drugs, gangs) are recent arrivals in Canada, and in fact received most of their education in schools in Jamaica, with Black teachers and a curriculum adopted by Black educators. It would be implausible to argue that it is the one or two years of schooling they've had in Canada which are solely responsible for such outcomes. In at least some of these cases, the roots of the problem started before their arrival in Canada, with the attitudes and aptitudes they acquired in Jamaica, and the worst that can be said is that Canadian schools have failed to rescue people who were already in danger of falling through society's cracks.

[41] For a discussion of this issue, see Toronto Board of Education 1988: 33–4; appendix E, pp. 4–5.

form of English than Canadian English. They have pride in their own language, and resent the implication that it is inferior (a perception which they see as reflecting a subtle form of racism). As a result, some of them refuse to speak in class, rather than be faced with ridicule for their language.

Most school administrators now accept that teachers should not describe Jamaican English as an inferior or inaccurate form of English. It is instead simply a different form of English—one of many World Englishes—no better or worse than Canadian English. Caribbean students need to learn Canadian English not because it is superior, but simply because it is the form of English used within Canadian society. In this sense, Jamaicans are in the same boat as any other immigrant group that does not speak Canadian English—they must learn English as a Second Language. Hence they are sometimes encouraged to take ESL classes.

The problem, however, is that most Caribbean students do not like being lumped in with non-English-speaking immigrants in the same ESL class. After all, they do speak (a form of) English, and indeed the immigration system awards them points for their mastery of English. Insisting that they take ESL classes is perceived as denigrating their language. Moreover, even when schools create special 'English as a Second Dialect' classes to remedy this problem, Caribbean blacks perceive (plausibly) that their dialect is treated with less respect, and is accorded less status, than the dialects of those from, say, Newfoundland or India.

This may seem like a rather trivial point. But in fact there is widespread evidence that while immigrants want to learn (Canadian) English, they also bitterly resent any implication that their mother-tongue is inferior. And denigrating the immigrants' mother-tongue (in the hope of encouraging the learning of Canadian English) has proven to be counter-productive. Immigrants learn English best when they believe that their native tongue is respected within the larger society, and when their attachment to their mother-tongue is accepted as valid.

As I noted, school administrators have acted to promote the view that Jamaican English, for example, should be treated with respect rather than denigrated. But the very fact that Jamaican English is so close to Canadian English makes this balancing act much more difficult than for other immigrant groups. Correcting the English usage of a Vietnamese person will not be seen as a reflection on the value of her mother-tongue; but 'correcting' the English of a Jamaican may be seen that way. To date, we have few models of how public schools should respond to the issue of non-Canadian English dialects. A Black-focused school might have more flexibility to come up with innovative solutions to this problem.

Whether Black-focused schools would in fact succeed is an empirical question. But we need to avoid the simplistic assumption that integrated schools inherently promote integration whereas Black-focused schools inherently promote separation. The simple fact is that integrated schools are currently generating a separatist and oppositional subculture, and Black-focused schools might help reverse that trend.

Black-focused schools are no more *inherently* separatist than girl-only classes in math or science. Whether such classes encourage more girls to go on to study science in university is a complicated question, but it is perfectly clear that they are intended to promote this kind of long-term integration, not to promote any kind of comprehensive sexual separatism. Everyone expects that the girls who attend girl-only science classes will go on to work alongside men in their later education and subsequent employment, and in most cases to live with and marry men in their personal lives. Similarly, there is no reason to assume the students who go through Black-focused schools will not go on to live and work beside (and perhaps even marry) whites. These schools are indeed intended precisely to make it more likely for Blacks to succeed in the mainstream.

Whether such schools would actually promote integration depends on many factors, including the details of their organization and curriculum. The decision to attend such a school must of course be optional, and the pedagogical materials used must meet appropriate government standards. In particular, it would be important to ensure that such schools did not rely solely on materials used in American 'Afrocentric' schools. Indeed, one vital purpose of the project would be to provide Black youth with accurate information about Blacks in Canada, so that they don't rely so heavily on American media for their vocabulary and models of race relations, as occurs now.

Needless to say, these schools could never be a complete solution to the issue of racism in schooling. For one thing, many Black parents will not want their children to attend such schools. Moreover, Blacks in many parts of Canada are too dispersed to form the numbers needed to sustain such schools. So it is not a question of choosing *either* to create Black-focused schools *or* to fight racism within integrated schools. Whether or not Black-focused schools are adopted, reforming integrated schools remains an essential task.

And if we succeed in eliminating racism in integrated schools, then we can predict that the demand for Black-focused schools will diminish. As in the United States, most Black parents want their children to attend integrated schools, just as they want to live in integrated neighbourhoods, so long as they think they are safe from racism. But racism in schools seems peculiarly stubborn, and in the meantime we should take seriously proposals for Black-focused schools.

Affirmative Action

Another programme which is intended to promote the integration of Blacks is affirmative action. Yet this too is currently under attack in various parts of Canada on the grounds that it is both unfair and divisive.

It is certainly true that affirmative action for Blacks in Canada, unlike in the United States, cannot be defended on grounds of compensation for historical injustices. Since most Blacks in Canada are members of immigrant communities, issues of historical compensation are not generally relevant here, except in places like Halifax, where indeed there is a serious debate about compensation for the unjust resettlement of the historic Africville community.

But compensation is not the only basis for affirmative action. Its primary justification in the Canadian context, I think, is that it can help undermine the belief that everything is stacked against Black Canadians. Indeed affirmative action has enormous symbolic value in the Black community precisely for this reason. It is seen as one of the few signs that whites have a genuine, good-faith commitment to equality. It is one of the few cases where whites have put their money where their mouth is, backing up their pronouncements about the sanctity of equality with some tangible action. It shows that whites are willing to pay a price—albeit a small one—to promote racial equality. As Stephen Lewis put it, affirmative action 'is a kind of cause celebre of visible minority communities everywhere. They see it as the consummate affirmation of opportunity and access'.[42]

Affirmative action does not just have symbolic value. Studies show that a crucial link that explains the emergence of a racial underclass is the fact that many families of Caribbean origin in Canada are headed by a single parent. Teenage girls from the Caribbean have a disproportionate tendency to get pregnant, drop out of school, and remain unmarried. These families tend to be very poor. The precise causes for the phenomenon are complex, but there is reason to believe that the poor economic prospects of Blacks (particularly Black men) are a factor.[43] If young people had the expectation that they would be able eventually to support a family comfortably, they might delay having children until completing their education and getting established in jobs or careers.

I don't mean of course that teenage girls consciously choose to get pregnant. Teenage pregnancies are almost always unplanned, and so the immediate explanation for the pregnancy is usually inadequate or inappropriate sex education and birth control. But at another level, poor prospects may partly explain why unmarried teenage pregnancies have come to some extent to be accepted and expected as normal, an expectation which surely in turn influences the decisions girls make about schooling, or about birth control.

---

[42] Lewis 1992: 17.   [43] For a discussion of this issue, see Henry 1994: ch. 4.

This means that fighting poverty within the Caribbean community requires improving the job prospects of its members. And affirmative action is one of the few policies in place that can promote that goal. To eliminate affirmative action could simply deepen the sense that Blacks have little or no economic prospects, and so perpetuate the cycle of poor, single-parent families.

However, if Blacks face barriers to integration that other visible minorities in Canada do not face—as I believe they do—then the target groups of Canadian affirmative action programmes need to be revised. If Arab-Canadians have a higher average income than British-Canadians, it is not clear why they need preferential access to jobs. The same could be said about immigrants from Hong Kong. These groups cannot claim compensation for historical injustice; nor can they claim to suffer from a cycle of poverty; and there is no danger that they will adopt an oppositional subculture.

So I see no pressing need or valid justification for including all 'visible minorities' in affirmative action programmes. Indeed, it seems quite unfair that the child of highly-educated and wealthy Chinese immigrants, living amidst the prosperous Asian community in Vancouver, should have preferential access to jobs over the child of poor and uneducated whites living in economically distressed fishing villages in Newfoundland. This is one case where multiculturalism has gone beyond the requirements of fair integration, to give at least some immigrants an unjust privilege.

A similar objection can be raised to affirmative action programmes in the United States, which also give preferential treatment to non-white immigrant groups, even those that are not disadvantaged. In the American case, this over-extension of affirmative action was the result of a gradual widening of the target groups. Originally, African-Americans were the sole target group. Some people argued that many Chicanos in the South-West had been subject to comparable historical injustices—e.g. being denied the vote, being subject to educational segregation and job discrimination. But no attempt was made to distinguish the Chicanos who had faced this historic discrimination from other Hispanics, many of whom were recent immigrants from Latin America. (And perhaps there was no feasible way to make this distinction.) So the programme was extended to include all Hispanics. But then members of other non-white immigrant groups asked why Hispanic immigrants were given preferential treatment? Why should a Spanish-speaking immigrant from Peru get preferential treatment, but not a Portuguese-speaking immigrant from Brazil, or a Tagalog-speaker from Philippines, or a Tamil-speaking immigrant from Sri Lanka? So the programme was expanded to include all non-white immigrant groups. One can see the logic in this progression, but in my view, the policy would have been more effective, and more defensible, if it was limited to African-Americans. To be sure, there are other groups that have faced serious historic discrimination (such as the Chicanos, or American Indians), and who may therefore be entitled to certain compensatory programs and policies. But these could have been handled separately, rather than folding all such groups into a single omnibus programme.

In both the United States and Canada, therefore, there are good reasons for focusing our attention and efforts on Blacks. I don't mean to trivialize the reality of ongoing prejudice against Asians or Arabs in Canada or the United States. But we can think of the glass as either half-full or half-empty. Prejudice against Asians and Arabs is real, but not I think all that different from the sort of prejudice faced by Irish, Jews, or Poles when they arrived in Canada. Prejudice against Blacks, however, seems more deeply-rooted.

In any event, even if all visible minorities continue to be included in Canadian affirmative action programmes, Blacks should form their own category, with their own targets. According to a widely-circulated story, when the federal affirmative action programme was announced, banks went out and hired enough Asians to meet their quota of 'visible minorities', thereby avoiding the need to hire any Blacks. This story is probably apocryphal, but it points up a genuine issue. Insofar as we view affirmative action as a way of helping the least advantaged in our society, and of overcoming the danger of racial exclusion and separatism, then it is crucial to make sure that it is indeed helping the group which is most in need. And amongst Canada's visible minorities, that is surely Blacks.

I don't want to exaggerate the impact that affirmative action has on improving the prospects of poor Blacks in Canada. In the end, relatively few people benefit from affirmative action, and we know that the beneficiaries tend to be those members of the target group (whether it is women or visible minorities) who are already comparatively well-off.

Affirmative action, therefore, is only a modest part of a much larger strategy for addressing inequalities in society. It is not a question of choosing either affirmative action or race-neutral anti-poverty programmes. The latter are essential, partly because poverty is not confined to racial minorities, and partly because affirmative action can only benefit a small segment of the Black community. But I think that affirmative action is potentially important for its symbolic value. It is a concrete manifestation of the commitment by Canadians to ensure equal opportunity for Blacks, and a tangible refutation of the conspiracy-type fears that generate an oppositional subculture.

As with black-focus schools, my aim is not to defend affirmative action unconditionally, but rather to encourage an open-minded debate about its possible role in Canada. In my view, Canada faces the worrisome prospect of the emergence and consolidation of an oppositional subculture amongst Caribbean Blacks in Canada. If affirmative action and black-focus schools can help, aren't they worth considering? And if we reject these proposals, what are the alternative strategies for dealing with this urgent situation? It is easy to point to the limitations and drawbacks of these proposals, but unless we have some coherent alternatives ready to put in place, the refusal to even consider these proposals is tantamount to putting one's head in the sand.

PART III

Misunderstanding Nationalism

10

From Enlightenment Cosmopolitanism to Liberal Nationalism

The idea of progress was central to many Enlightenment theorists, such as the Marquis de Condorcet. One prominent feature of Condorcet's conception of progress is the emancipation of individuals from ascribed roles and identities. Individuals should be free to judge for themselves, in the light of their own reasoning and experience, which traditional beliefs and customary practices are worth maintaining. Modernity liberates people from fixed social roles and traditional identities, and fosters an ideal of autonomous individuality that encourages individuals to choose for themselves what sort of life they want to lead.

Condorcet thought that cosmopolitanism would be the natural and inevitable outcome of this emancipation of the individual. While people are born into particular ethnic, religious, or linguistic communities, and some might choose to remain within them, emancipated individuals would not see their options as limited or defined by membership in their inherited cultural group. As more and more individuals explored the options available outside their group, and as cultural membership thereby became purely voluntary and optional, ethnocultural identities would gradually lose their political importance, replaced by a more cosmopolitan identity. Smaller groups would gradually assimilate into larger and larger ones. Condorcet's belief in the emergence of a universal language can be seen as the logical culmination of this process of assimilating smaller groups into larger ones, as eventually all cultures are merged into a single cosmopolitan society.

In reality, this process has been much slower than Condorcet predicted, and indeed has sometimes stalled completely. The appeal of cosmopolitanism has often proved weaker than the pull of more particularistic identities. In our century, cosmopolitanism has repeatedly run up against the power of nationalism, and whenever the two have collided, nationalism has usually won out.

Since Condorcet was writing before the age of nationalism, he did not foresee this conflict. However, it is perhaps the most pressing issue facing the heirs of the Enlightenment. What is the appropriate role of nations—of national boundaries and national cultures—in the scheme of Enlightenment values? Many heirs of the Enlightenment have assumed that nationalism is an irrational and illiberal attachment to an ascriptive group identity which is inconsistent with the modern ideal of autonomous individuality, and which therefore would—or at least should—fade as modernization progresses. On this view, nationalism is inherently inimical to Enlightenment values.

Over the past few years, however, an increasing number of theorists have been challenging this view, arguing that national cultures and polities provide the best context for promoting Enlightenment values of freedom, equality, and democracy. What we increasingly see, therefore, is not a debate between liberal cosmopolitanism and illiberal particularism, but rather a debate between liberal cosmopolitanism and liberal nationalism.

This is the debate I wish to focus on. I will begin by trying to identify the actual points of conflict between cosmopolitanism and nationalism (section 1). I will then discuss several reasons why national societies might provide the best context for Enlightenment values of freedom and democracy (sections 2–4). Paradoxically, I think that some of Condorcet's own comments about the role of language should have alerted him to the value of national identity in these regards (section 5). However, this is not to reject all cosmopolitan principles. I conclude the paper with some suggestions about how to reconcile liberal nationalism with the more attractive features of Condorcet's cosmopolitanism (section 6).

1. Cosmopolitanism versus Nationalism

As Max Boehm has noted, 'the form which cosmopolitanism assumes is in general conditioned by the particular social entity or group ideal from which it represents a reaction' (Boehm 1931: 458). In the past, cosmopolitanism was a reaction against the privileging of the local city, class, or religious sect. But in today's world, cosmopolitanism is almost always defined in contrast to nationalism. Cosmopolitans are, almost by definition, people who regret the privileging of national identities in political life, and who reject the principle that political arrangements should be ordered in such a way as to reflect and protect national identities.

While the contrast between cosmopolitanism and nationalism is commonplace, even clichéd, the precise points of conflict between them are often misunderstood, usually because the nature of nationalism has itself been misunderstood. I will start, therefore, with a brief account of modern nationalism, and then try to pinpoint where it comes into conflict with cosmopolitanism.

It is often said that we live in an age of nationalism. But what does this mean? For the purposes of this paper, it refers to the tenacity with which ethno-national groups have fought to maintain their distinct identity, institutions, and desire for self-government. This is a striking fact of twentieth-century history: there are few examples of national minorities—that is, national groups who share a state with larger national groups—voluntarily assimilating into the larger society.

Cosmopolitans did not predict this resilience of national identities. They assumed that the members of smaller groups would willingly assimilate into larger and larger groups, so long as their individual rights were respected. For Voltaire, people would feel bound to, and at home in, whichever country respected their individual liberty, and would not expect or demand that the state also protect their national identity.[1] Condorcet's belief in the emergence of a universal language can be seen as the logical culmination of this process of assimilating smaller groups into larger ones, as eventually all cultures are merged into a single cosmopolitan society (1795:197–9). Nor was this belief unique to Condorcet. The ideal of a universal language was also endorsed by cosmopolitans from Descartes and Liebniz to Franklin, Voltaire, d'Alembert, and Turgot (Schlereth 1977: 42–3).

Enlightenment cosmopolitans disagreed amongst themselves about how this cosmopolitan society based on a universal language would be achieved. Some thought it would involve the invention and diffusion of a new, more rational, language; others thought that French would gradually become a universal language. Some thought that the emergence of a world culture would be accompanied by political unification, through the emergence of a single world government or world federation; others argued that it would occur even if existing political boundaries were maintained, so long as the relations between political units were regulated by some form of international law. Some thought that the emergence of a world culture could be pushed along by the judicious and enlightened use of colonialism; others (like Condorcet) felt that its emergence would (and should) be the result of consensual exchange and learning between peoples, not the coercive imposition of a dominant culture on subordinated groups. But they all shared the assumption that, sooner or later, minority and 'backward' groups would assimilate into larger and more 'advanced' groups, and that it was in their interests to do so.

The dream of a universal language died out in the nineteenth century. But the underlying assumption that national identities would weaken did not. Echoes of this assumption can be found among nineteenth-century liberals and socialists. According to J. S. Mill,

Experience proves it is possible for one nationality to merge and be absorbed in another: and when it was originally an inferior and more backward portion of the human race the absorption is greatly to its advantage. Nobody can suppose that it is

---

[1] For Voltaire, one's country should be 'where one feels secure and knows liberty'. The role of the state 'was not to bestow upon a man his national character, but to assure him of his fundamental liberties as a human individual' (Schlereth 1977: 105, 109).

not more beneficial to a Breton, or a Basque of French Navarre, to be brought into the current of the ideas and feelings of a highly civilised and cultivated people—to be a member of the French nationality, admitted on equal terms to all the privileges of French citizenship . . . than to sulk on his own rocks, the half-savage relic of past times, revolving in his own little mental orbit, without participation or interest in the general movement of the world. The same remark applies to the Welshman or the Scottish Highlander as members of the British nation (Mill 1972 : 395).

We can find almost identical quotes in the work of Marx and Engels (e.g. Engels 1952). For both liberals and Marxists in the nineteenth century, the great nations, with their highly centralized political and economic structures, were the carriers of historical development. The smaller nationalities were backward and stagnant, and could only participate in modernity by abandoning their national character and assimilating to a great nation. Attempts to maintain minority languages were misguided, for German was 'the language of liberty' for the Czechs in Bohemia, just as French was the language of liberty for the Bretons, and English was the language of liberty for the Québécois in Canada.

This sort of view was very widespread in the nineteenth century. Indeed, Hobsbawm claims that it is 'sheer anachronism' to criticize Mill or Marx for holding it, since it was shared by virtually all theorists in the nineteenth century, on both the right and left. This view provided a justification not only for assimilating minorities within European states, but also for colonizing other peoples overseas.[2]

The assumption that progress involves assimilating 'backward' minorities to 'energetic' majorities is still with us, although the labels have changed. Indeed, until very recently, most theorists of modernization argued that national identities would wither away, particularly in the case of smaller nations or national minorities. These smaller groups face strong economic and political pressures to assimilate into larger nations, and modernization theorists assumed that the members of these groups would accept this process, rather than fight to maintain themselves as culturally distinct societies at the price of economic well-being or social mobility.

It is this assumption—shared by eighteenth-century Enlightenment theorists, nineteenth-century socialists and twentieth-century modernization theorists—which has been decisively disproved in our age of nationalism. Nationalism has so far defeated the cosmopolitan expectation of the withering away of national identities, and the emerging of a world culture based on a universal language.

However, this expectation was not the only—or perhaps even the most important—component of Condorcet's Enlightenment cosmopolitanism. If

---

[2] Hobsbawm 1990: 35. On the way this attitude toward minority cultures supported European colonialism, see Parekh 1994, and Todorov 1993: ch. 3.

we examine Condorcet's other predictions, many of them have proven remarkably prescient. For example, we have witnessed the multiplication of global economic trade and the increasing liberalization of global markets, which Condorcet viewed as the primary means for creating peaceful relations between peoples. We have also witnessed the universal diffusion of science and technology, the increase in global communications, and the multiplication of transnational institutions of international law, international mediation, and human rights—all of which Condorcet predicted. And, perhaps most importantly, we have seen the adoption throughout the West of the principle of free and equal citizenship, reflected in the spread of mass education and liberal-democratic constitutions. This commitment to free and equal citizenship has reached the point where virtually no other form of government has any perceived legitimacy in the eyes of citizens.

As a result of these processes, we can now say that all national groups within Western democracies share a common civilization—i.e. they all share a modern, urban, secular, consumerist, literate, bureaucratic, industrialized, democratic civilization, in contrast to the feudal, agricultural, and theocratic world of our ancestors. In these respects, the cosmopolitanism thesis is true. It has taken longer than Condorcet expected—pockets of quasi-feudal and quasi-theocratic agrarian societies existed in the West well into this century—and there are many parts of the world which have not yet industrialized or democratized. But at least within the West, we can see the diffusion of the sort of common civilization that Condorcet envisaged. In terms of their basic forms of social organization, the Catalans, Flemish, Germans, French, Greeks, Québécois, and Americans have never been so similar. And this common civilization has, in part, emerged in the way Condorcet envisaged. While imperialist coercion played an important role at some times and places, the emergence of this common civilization was also the result of cultural exchange, and the consensual adoption of common forms of science and politics.

Condorcet's great mistake, however, was in thinking that the diffusion of a common *civilization* would lead to the emergence of a common *culture*— that is, to the diminishing of national identities, and the assimilation of smaller national groups into larger ones. On the contrary, national minorities have fought to maintain themselves as separate and self-governing societies, living and working in their own languages, even as they modernize and liberalize their historical cultures.[3] They accept the common civilization, but

---

[3] Since one of the *OED* definitions of 'culture' is 'civilization', we can say, if we like, that Western societies share the same culture. But in another sense, national groups which share a common civilization belong to different cultures—that is, different societies, with different languages and institutions, and different histories. And it is these separate national cultures which nationalism seeks to protect.

wish to participate in it as distinct and self-governing cultures, and mobilize along nationalist lines to pursue this aim.

2. National Identity and Individual Freedom

How are we to explain and assess this desire of smaller national groups to maintain themselves as distinct societal cultures, rather than integrating into a larger nation? Cosmopolitans typically argue that this commitment to cultural maintenance reflects an illiberal preference for ascriptive group identity over individual choice—a preference that is incompatible with the modern ideal of autonomy. If this is correct, then one possible explanation for the persistence of minority nationalism is that Enlightenment theorists overestimated the value of autonomy. And indeed there is a lively debate within contemporary political philosophy about the value of autonomy. Scepticism about autonomy has typically been associated with conservative or communitarian critics of liberalism (e.g. Sandel 1982). But even liberals have increasingly questioned the privileging of autonomy. After all, the idea that people should critically reflect on their inherited roles is not universally accepted, even within liberal societies. In particular, it is rejected by isolationist religious groups, like the Amish, or fundamentalist groups, whether Christian, Jewish, or Muslim. To ground liberal theory on the value of autonomy, many liberals worry, is 'sectarian'—it will alienate such groups, and lead them to view the liberal state as a threat, and its authority as illegitimate (Galston 1995; Rawls 1993a).

My own view is that these concerns about the privileging of autonomy are overstated. The idea that we have an interest in being able to assess and revise our inherited conceptions of the good is very widely shared in Western democratic societies, and is arguably a defining feature of modernity (Coser 1991). Moreover, I think we can defend the claim that our lives really do go better when we have the capacity rationally to assess and revise our conceptions of the good (Kymlicka 1989).[4]

In any event, the assumption that minority nationalism necessarily involves an abdication of individual autonomy is, I believe, profoundly mistaken. To be sure, some nations and nationalist movements are deeply illiberal. Far from enabling autonomy, they simply assign particular roles and duties to people, and prevent people from questioning or revising them. Other cultures allow this autonomy to some, while denying it to others, such as women, lower castes, or visible minorities. In order to preserve their

---

[4] To be sure, there are some insulated minorities who resist the spread of autonomy, but they are the exceptions, and should be treated as such. For discussions of the distinctive status of such groups, see Spinner 1994: ch. 3; Kymlicka 1995a: ch. 8. See also Ch. 16 below.

'authentic' cultural traditions, they may seek to isolate themselves from other peoples and cultures.

We are all familiar with this picture of nationalism as culturally xenophobic, ethnically exclusionary, anti-democratic, even territorially expansionist and prone to violence. This is the image of nationalism that was shaped by the experience of Europe during the World Wars, and recent developments in the Balkans have reinforced it. But minority nationalisms within liberal democracies—whether in Quebec, Catalonia, Flanders, Scotland, or Puerto Rico—are not usefully seen in these terms. These are the sorts of nationalist movements that I will focus on in this paper. They represent a very distinctive form of nationalism, I believe, and we can not understand them if we start with the assumption that they are necessarily inconsistent with autonomy.

For one thing, this assumption does not explain why many nationalists in Quebec or Flanders or Catalonia have also been liberal reformers. They have fought for self-government while simultaneously fighting to liberalize their society. Why were these liberal reformers also nationalists? Because they believed that participation in a national culture, far from inhibiting individual choice, is what makes individual freedom meaningful. On this view, freedom involves making choices amongst various options, and one's societal culture not only provides these options, but also makes them meaningful to one. Hence the gradual erosion of one's societal culture—a prospect confronting national minorities which lack strong self-government rights—leads to gradual erosion of one's individual autonomy.[5]

I think this view of the connection between individual freedom and cultural membership is essentially correct, though difficult to articulate. I won't explore it in detail, since I have tried to do so elsewhere (Kymlicka 1995a: ch. 5). The basic idea is this: modernity is defined (in part at least) by individual freedom of choice. But what does individual choice involve? People make choices about the social practices around them, based on their beliefs about the value of these practices. And to have a belief about the value of a practice is, in the first instance, a matter of understanding the meanings attached to it by our culture. Societal cultures involve 'a shared vocabulary of tradition and convention' which underlies a full range of social practices and institutions (Dworkin 1985: 231). To understand the meaning of a social practice, therefore, requires understanding this 'shared vocabulary'—i.e. understanding the language and history which constitute that vocabulary. Whether or not a course of action has any significance for us depends on whether, and how, our language renders vivid to us the point of that activity. And the way in which language renders vivid these activities is shaped by our history, our 'traditions

---

[5] By societal culture, I mean a territorially concentrated culture, centred on a shared language which is used in a wide range of societal institutions, in both public and private life (schools, media, law, economy, government, etc.). See Ch. 1 for a more detailed explanation.

and conventions'. Understanding these cultural narratives is a precondition of making intelligent judgements about how to lead our lives. In this sense, our culture not only provides options, it also 'provides the spectacles through which we identify experiences as valuable' (Dworkin 1985: 228). The availability of meaningful options depends on access to a societal culture, and on understanding the history and language of that culture—its 'shared vocabulary of tradition and convention' (Dworkin 1985: 228, 231). For meaningful individual choice to be possible, individuals need not only access to information, the capacity to reflectively evaluate it, and freedom of expression and association. They also need access to a societal culture.

For this reason, the foundational liberal commitment to individual freedom can be extended to generate a commitment to the ongoing viability and flourishing of societal cultures. And in multination states, this leads to the rise of minority nationalisms—i.e. to the demand for language rights and self-government powers. These rights and powers ensure that national minorities are able to sustain and develop their societal cultures into the indefinite future.

3. The 'Cosmopolitan Alternative'

This account of the relationship between individual freedom and membership in a national culture has been explicitly developed by several recent defenders of liberal nationalism, including Yael Tamir (1993), Avishai Margalit and Joseph Raz (1990), Charles Taylor (1992a), Jeff Spinner (1994) and David Miller (1995).[6] But not everyone has been convinced. In a recent provocative article, Jeremy Waldron challenges this view, and defends what he calls the 'cosmopolitan alternative' (Waldron 1995). According to this cosmopolitan alternative, people can pick and choose 'cultural fragments' that come from a variety of ethnocultural sources, without feeling any sense of membership in or dependence on a particular culture. In the modern world, people live 'in a kaleidoscope of culture', moving freely amongst the products of innumerable cultural traditions. Each person's life incorporates a melange of such cultural fragments, including, say, Innuit art, Italian opera, Chinese food, German folklore, and Judaeo-Christian religion (1995: 95).

Indeed, Waldron questions whether there really are such things as distinct cultures. The extent of cultural interchange—due to the globalization of trade, the increase in human mobility, and the development of international institutions and communications—has made it impossible to say where one culture begins and another ends. The only way to preserve a distinct culture

[6] For further discussion of the link between individual freedom and national cultures, see Ch. 11.

intact, he argues, would be to cut it off artificially from the general course of human events. The only way to preserve the 'authenticity' or 'integrity' of a particular culture would, paradoxically, be to adopt a wholly inauthentic way of life—one which denied the overwhelming reality of cultural exchange and global interdependence (1995: 101).

It is not clear, however, if Waldron's 'cosmopolitan alternative' is really all that different from the liberal nationalism he claims to be attacking. After all, Waldron's primary concern is to reject the idea that our choices and self-identity are defined by our ethnic descent. For example, he suggests that a Québécois who eats Chinese food and reads Roman mythology to her child, or an Irish-American who likes Innuit art and listens to Italian opera on a Japanese stereo, is living in 'a kaleidoscope of cultures', since these cultural practices originated in different ethnic groups.

But this sort of cultural mélange—which is indeed a characteristic of modernity—does not involve moving between societal cultures. It is simply a case of enjoying opportunities provided by the pluralistic societal culture that characterizes contemporary French-speaking Quebec society, or contemporary English-speaking American society. Liberal nationalists define cultures as historical communities that possess a societal culture—that is, which possess a set of institutions, operating in a common language, covering both private and public life. On this view, the Québécois form a distinct culture in North America because they are a historical community with a more or less complete set of societal institutions operating in the French language. There is nothing in the idea of a societal culture that precludes the incorporation of new ideas and practices from other parts of the world. The fact that some Québécois now eat Mexican food and practise Zen Buddhism does not mean that they cease to form a distinct culture, living and working in French-language institutions. It simply means that the societal culture they belong to is an open and pluralistic one, which borrows whatever it finds worthwhile in other cultures, integrates it into its own practices, and passes it on to the subsequent generations.

On any liberal view, this sort of cultural interchange is a good thing. Liberals cannot endorse a notion of culture that sees the process of interacting with and learning from other cultures as a threat to 'purity' or 'integrity', rather than as an opportunity for enrichment. Liberals want a societal culture that is rich and diverse, and much of the richness of a culture comes from the way it has appropriated the fruits of other cultures. So we don't want to build closed walls around cultures, to cut them off from 'the general movement of the world', as John Stuart Mill put it in the passage I quoted earlier. But that is neither the aim nor the effect of the sort of language rights and self-government being sought by national minorities in the West.

Waldron ignores this possibility because he assumes that the aim of minority nationalists is to protect the 'authenticity' of their culture. This may be an accurate characterization of certain illiberal nationalisms in Eastern Europe. But liberal nationalists do not seek to preserve their 'authentic' culture, if that means living the same way that their ancestors did centuries ago, unable to learn from other peoples and cultures. As I noted earlier, they want to live in modern democratic societies, and to share in a common Western civilization. What the Québécois or Flemish want, for example, is to preserve their existence as a culturally distinct group—always adapting and transforming their culture, of course, but resisting the pressure to abandon entirely their group life and assimilate into the larger society. In short, these minority cultures wish to be cosmopolitan, and embrace the cultural interchange Waldron emphasizes, without accepting Waldron's own 'cosmopolitan alternative', which denies that people have any deep bond to their own language and cultural community.

4. National Identity and Democratic Citizenship

National societies may be important for Enlightenment principles in another way. Enlightenment theorists like Condorcet were not just committed to individual autonomy, but also to democratization, and to the right of the masses to use their reason in political deliberation. But this sort of shared political deliberation is only feasible if participants understand and trust one another, and there is good reason to think that such mutual understanding and trust requires some underlying commonalities. Some sense of commonality or shared identity may be required to sustain a deliberative and participatory democracy.

But what sort of shared identity? If we examine different existing democracies to see what sorts of commonalities have proved necessary for deliberative democracy, I think we would find that deliberative democracy does *not* require a common religion (or common lifestyles more generally); a common political ideology (e.g. right vs. left); or a common racial or ethnic descent. We can find genuinely participatory democratic forums and procedures that cut across these religious/ideological/racial cleavages.

When we turn to language, however, things are more complicated. There are several multilingual democracies—Belgium, Spain, Switzerland, and Canada. Each of these countries contains at least one sizeable national minority whose distinctive language has some official status. But if we look at how democratic debates operate within these countries, we find that language is increasingly important in defining the boundaries of political communities, and the identities of political actors.

There is a similar dynamic which is taking place in all of these countries, by which (*a*) the separate language groups are becoming more territorialized—that is, each language has become ever-more dominant within a particular region, while gradually dying out outside that region (this phenomenon—known as the 'territorial imperative'—is very widespread);[7] and (b) these territorialized language groups are demanding increased political recognition and self-government powers through federalization of the political system. (These processes of territorialization and federalization are closely linked—the latter is both the cause and the effect of the former.) Political boundaries have been drawn, and political powers redistributed, so that territorialized language groups are able to exercise greater self-government within the larger federal system.

In short, language has become an increasingly important determinant of the boundaries of political community within each of these multilingual countries. These countries are becoming, in effect, federations of self-governing language groups. Like other national minorities, these self-governing language groups often describe themselves as 'nations', and mobilize along nationalist lines, and so we can call these countries 'multination states'.

There are good reasons to think that these 'national' linguistic/territorial political communities—whether they are unilingual nation-states or linguistically distinct subunits within multination states—are the primary forums for democratic participation in the modern world. They are primary in two senses. First, democracy within national/linguistic units is more genuinely participatory than at higher levels that cut across language lines. Political debates at the federal level in multination states, for example, or at the EU, are almost invariably elite-dominated.

Why? Put simply, democratic politics is politics in the vernacular. The average citizen only feels comfortable debating political issues in their own tongue. As a general rule, it is only elites who have fluency with more than one language, and who have the continual opportunity to maintain and develop these language skills, and who feel comfortable debating political issues in another tongue within multilingual settings. Moreover, political communication has a large ritualistic component, and these ritualized forms of communication are typically language-specific. Even if one understands a foreign language in the technical sense, without knowledge of these ritualistic elements one may be unable to understand political debates.[8] For these

---

[7] As Grin notes, apart from a few municipalities, 'there is no official bilingualism at the local level in Switzerland. Switzerland may be quadrilingual, but to most intents and purposes each point of its territory can be viewed as unilingual. Correspondingly, living in Switzerland means living entirely in German, in French or in Italian' (Grin 1999: 6). On the territorial imperative in Belgium, see Lejeune 1994, and Senelle 1989; on Switzerland, see Mansour 1993: 109–11, Grin 1999. For a more general theoretical account of the 'territorial imperative' in multilingual societies, see Laponce 1987, 1993.

[8] In other words, the sort of fluency needed to debate political issues is far greater than the sort of knowledge needed to handle routinized business transactions, or for tourist purposes.

and other reasons, we can expect—as a general rule—that the more political debate is conducted in the vernacular, the more participatory it will be.

There are of course 'public spaces' and forms of civil society that cut across language lines. However, these tend to be issue-specific and/or elite-dominated. If we look for evidence of a genuinely popular process of 'collective will formation'—or for the existence of a mass 'public opinion'—we are likely to find these only within units which share a common language (and a common media using that language). John Stuart Mill, writing in 1861, argued that genuine democracy is 'next to impossible' in multilingual states, because if people 'read and speak different languages, the united public opinion necessary to the workings of representative institutions cannot exist' (Mill 1972: 392). The evidence from Europe suggests that linguistic differences remain an obstacle to the development of a genuine 'public opinion'. As Dieter Grimm notes, it is the presence of a shared mass media, operating in a common language, 'which creates the public needed for any general opinion forming and democratic participation at all', and

the absence of a European communication system, due chiefly to language diversity, has the consequence that for the foreseeable future there will be neither a European public nor a European political discourse. Public discourse instead remains for the time being bound by national frontiers, while the European sphere will remain dominated by professional and interest discourses conducted remotely from the public.[9]

There is a second sense in which these 'national' units are primary—namely, they are the most important forum for assessing the legitimacy of other levels of government. Members of these national units may wish to devolve power upwards—to the federal level in multination states, or to the EU—just as they may wish to devolve power downwards to local or municipal governments. As I noted earlier, such upward (or downward) devolutions of power are to be expected, since they will often be in the national interest of these collectivities. But the legitimacy of these devolutions of power is generally seen as dependent on the (ongoing) consent of the national unit. (And this consent will only be given if these devolutions of power do not undermine the ability of the national unit to maintain itself as a viable, self-governing society). Decisions made by larger units—whether they are federal policies in multination states, or EU policies—are seen as legitimate only if they are made under rules and procedures that were consented to by the national unit. And changes to the rules are only legitimate if they are debated and approved by the national unit. Members of these national collectivities debate amongst themselves, in the vernacular, how much power they wish to devolve upwards or downwards, and periodically

[9] Grimm 1995: 296. This same dynamic can be seen even *within* the various multilingual states in Europe, where it has become increasingly obvious that 'public opinion' is divided on language lines.

reassess, at the national level, whether they wish to reclaim some of these powers. The legitimate authority of higher-level political bodies depends on this ongoing process of debate and consent at the national level. And these decisions are made on the basis of what serves the national interest (and not on the basis of what serves the interests of, say, Europe as a whole).[10]

So the evidence suggests that language is profoundly important in the construction of democratic political communities. It has in fact become increasingly important in defining political communities, and these language-demarcated political communities remain the primary forum for participatory democratic debates, and for the democratic legitimation of other levels and forums of government. Insofar as this is true, then the desire of national minorities to maintain themselves as distinct societal cultures does not conflict with Enlightenment values of individual freedom or democratic equality, but rather provides the best context for these values. We can put the same point another way. The Enlightenment ideal is a society of free and equal individuals, but what is the relevant 'society'? For most people it seems to be their nation. The sort of freedom and equality they most value, and can make most use of, is freedom and equality within their own societal culture. And they are willing to forego a wider freedom and equality to ensure the continued existence of their nation.

For example, few citizens in liberal democracies favour a system of open borders, where people could freely cross borders and settle, work, and vote in whatever country they desire. Such a system would dramatically increase the domain within which people would be treated as free and equal citizens. Yet open borders would also make it more likely that people's own national community would be overrun by settlers from other cultures, and that they would be unable to ensure their survival as a distinct national culture. So we have a choice between, on the one hand, increased mobility and an expanded domain within which people are free and equal individuals, and, on the other hand, decreased mobility but with a greater assurance that people can continue to be free and equal members of their own national culture. Most people in liberal democracies favour the latter. They would rather be free and equal within their own nation, even if this means they have less freedom to work and vote elsewhere, than be free and equal citizens of the world, if this means they are less likely to be able to live and work in their own language and culture.

And most theorists in the liberal tradition have implicitly agreed with this. Many eighteenth-century Enlightenment theorists endorsed the principle of open borders, but few major liberal theorists since then have done so, or even

[10] In other words, the existence of political authority at higher levels is not seen as morally self-originating or self-justifying, but rather as conditional on the consent of the constituent national units. By contrast, the right of the national unit to self-government is seen as inherent, and as not requiring the consent of any other level of government.

seriously considered it.[11] They have generally accepted—indeed, simply taken for granted—that the sort of freedom and equality which matters most to people is freedom and equality within one's societal culture. Like Rawls, they assume that 'people are born and are expected to lead a complete life' within the same 'society and culture', and that this defines the scope within which people must be free and equal (1993a: 277).

In short, liberal theorists have generally, if implicitly, accepted that cultures or nations are basic units of liberal political theory. In this sense, as Tamir puts it, 'most liberals are liberal nationalists' (1993: 139)—i.e. liberal goals are achieved in a liberalized societal culture or nation.

5. Condorcet on Vernacular Languages

Despite Condorcet's defence of a universal language, it is interesting to note that he was quite aware of the democratic value of vernacular languages. As Keith Baker notes, Condorcet viewed language as the 'social technology' of man, and so viewed the reform of society as heavily bound up with the reform of language (K. Baker 1975: 361). This was not just the banality that without language, humans would be incapable of any meaningful form of individual agency or social progress. Rather Condorcet emphasized that it matters who speaks *which* language. Inequalities in access to a privileged language were a major source of other social inequalities. Social equality could only be achieved by equality in the learning and use of language.

According to Condorcet, the greatest threat to progress was the monopolization of truth-claims by a closed elite using an esoteric language (e.g. priests). This monopoly was first challenged by the development of an alphabet, which allowed secular men of science to participate in the production and assessment of knowledge. But so long as this secular discourse was conducted in Latin, the result remained a kind of oligarchy of truth-claims from which the masses were excluded. It is only when vernacular languages displaced Latin that science became accessible to all educated persons. As Condorcet put it, to have continued using a language other than the vernacular 'would have divided men into two classes, perpetuated error and prejudice, and placed an irrevocable obstacle in the way of true equality in the use of reason and in the acquisition of necessary truths' (Condorcet 1795: 118). This is analogous to the argument I made in section 4. Just as politics is only truly democratized when it is conducted in the vernacular, so science is only democratized when it is conducted in the vernacular.

---

[11] For Enlightenment defenders of open borders, see Schlereth 1977: 105. For a discussion of contemporary liberal views on open borders, see Carens 1987.

If Condorcet was aware of the democratic value of the use of the vernacular, why then did he seek to create a universal language? Condorcet believed that once mass public education undermined the distinction between the educated and the masses, the shift to a universal language would not divide world into those with the key to knowledge and those without (K. Baker 1975:365). If a proper system of mass education were in place, then a new universal language could be learned by all, regardless of their social class, 'as easily as their own language' (Condorcet 1795:198). This new language would then give people 'a precision and a rigour that would make knowledge of the truth easy and error almost impossible' (1795: 199).

We now know that this is unrealistic. Various efforts have been made to encourage personal bilingualism, particularly in multination states, but they have failed. The goal was that Belgian citizens, for example, would read a Flemish newspaper in the morning, and watch the French news on television at night, and be equally conversant with, and feel comfortable contributing to, the political debates in both languages. However, these efforts have been uniformly unsuccessful. This sort of easy personal bilingualism is more or less restricted to intellectuals, while the vast majority of the population clings stubbornly to their own tongue. We can bemoan this fact, but I do not think it is likely to change in the foreseeable future.

For one thing, Condorcet—like many intellectuals today—underestimates the problems that many people have in learning a second language. Even when people understand a second language, they rarely acquire the same facility in it as in their mother-tongue. Moreover, Condorcet neglects the expressive interests people have in their mother-tongue. Language is one of the fundamental markers of people's identity, and so people view any denigration in the public status of their mother-tongue as an assault on their identity.[12]

This is particularly important given the link that was forged in the nineteenth century between language and national identity. Condorcet was writing before the age of mass literacy and mass democracy (although he favoured both), and so perhaps he could not predict what the impact would be of educating the masses and enabling them to participate politically in their vernacular. He thought that promoting democratic politics in the vernacular would just be a transitional phase towards cosmopolitan democracy in a universal language. But we now know that the combination of mass literacy and mass democracy helped create powerful national identities, symbolized in the use of the vernacular, which bestowed on citizens a new-found dignity—identities which remain with us to this day.

[12] For the distinction between the instrumental and expressive interests in one's mother-tongue, see Réaume 1991.

It is important to remember that in earlier periods of European history, elites tried to dissociate themselves as much as possible from 'the plebs' or 'the rabble', and justified their powers and privileges precisely in terms of their alleged distance from the masses. The rise of nationalism, however, valorized 'the people'. Nations are defined in terms of 'the people'—i.e. the mass of population on a territory, regardless of class or occupation—who become 'the bearer of sovereignty, the central object of loyalty, and the basis of collective solidarity' (Greenfeld 1992: 14). National identity has remained strong in the modern era in part because its emphasis on the importance of 'the people' provides a source of dignity to all individuals, whatever their class. Mass education and mass democracy conducted in the vernacular are concrete manifestations of this shift towards a dignity-bestowing national identity. The use of the language of the people is confirmation that the political community really does belong to the people, and not to the elite. So it should not be surprising that most people have a deep emotional attachment to the vernacular which goes beyond their purely instrumental interest in using a language that they are already familiar with. Whereas cosmopolitans are inclined to see people's commitment to the vernacular as evidence of an illiberal attachment to an ascriptive group identity, it may instead reflect a deep attachment to Enlightenment values of free and equal citizenship.

Given the instrumental and expressive interests which people have in their vernacular, it was naive of Condorcet to expect citizens to relinquish it in the name of a more cosmopolitan identity. Cosmopolitanism may eventually triumph, but for the foreseeable future, and for good reasons, the desire for individual freedom and democratic participation will be pursued within the context of national cultures.

6. Conclusion: Reconciling Nationalism and Cosmopolitanism

In this chapter, I have defended liberal nationalism against traditional Enlightenment cosmopolitanism. However, it is important not to exaggerate the conflict between the two, or to ignore their many commonalities. At the level of international relations, liberal nationalists have typically shared Condorcet's commitment to a world order founded on free trade, the development of international law, including universal respect for human rights, and prohibitions on territorial aggression. At the domestic level, liberal nationalists have typically shared Condorcet's commitment to liberal democratic constitutionalism, equality of opportunity, religious tolerance, and more generally, openness to pluralism and cultural interchanges.

The dispute between Enlightenment cosmopolitans and liberal nationalists, therefore, is quite limited. The most basic disagreement, it seems to me, concerns the role of the state in protecting and affirming national identities, through such things as language rights, public holidays, and self-government rights. Enlightenment thinkers viewed the state simply as a protector of individual liberties, not the defender of national cultures or identities (Schlereth 1977: 109). For liberal nationalists, however, it is a legitimate and essential task of government to protect the ongoing viability of national cultures, and, more generally, to express people's national identities. As Tamir puts it, political institutions should be 'carriers of the national identity', and 'should reflect the unique character and draw on the history, the culture, the language, and at times the religion of the national group, thereby enabling its members to regard it as their own' (1993:74).[13]

This basic dispute leads to another subsidiary dispute over immigration. Most Enlightenment cosmopolitans favoured what is essentially an 'open borders' policy—that is, unlimited rights of free mobility across borders (Schlereth 1977:105). Moreover, they often viewed this as a 'natural right'. For liberal nationalists, however, as I noted earlier, there is a trade-off between the benefits of mobility and the desire to ensure the viability of one's national culture. At the moment, immigrants are almost always a source of enrichment, both culturally and economically, to national societies. But that is because the numbers of immigrants are limited, and those who are admitted are encouraged to integrate into the existing national culture. A policy of open borders, however, could lead to tens of millions of new immigrants entering a country, exceeding the capacity of existing national institutions to integrate them. This is particularly a concern for national minorities (e.g. immigrants settling in the traditional homelands of indigenous peoples).[14] On the liberal nationalist view, states have a legitimate right to limit the numbers of immigrants, and to encourage their integration, in order to protect the viability of existing national cultures.

So there are definite points of conflict between liberal nationalism and traditional Enlightenment cosmopolitanism. However, it would be misleading,

---

[13] The Enlightenment assumption that the state could simply protect individual liberties, without adopting or advancing any particular national identity, is in any event incoherent. After all, the state must decide on the language of public education and public services, as well as on the drawing of the boundaries of internal political subunits, and the recognition of public holidays—all of which unavoidably express and promote a particular national culture. See Kymlicka 1995a: ch. 6.

[14] See the discussion in Ch. 15. One could argue that this is a realistic danger to majority groups only because Western countries refuse their obligations of justice to share their wealth with poorer countries. As a result, many inhabitants of poorer countries see emigration to the West as their best hope to have a decent life for themselves and their children. If greater justice in the international distribution of resources were achieved, there would be much less migration between countries, and those who do choose to move would presumably be doing so precisely in order to join a culture that they admire. Under these circumstances, an open borders policy would probably not jeopardize the viability of societal cultures.

I think, to describe liberal nationalism as a rejection of cosmopolitanism as such. Given the many commonalities between liberal nationalism and Enlightenment cosmopolitanism, and given their shared commitment to universal values of freedom and equality, I would prefer to say that liberal nationalism involves a *redefinition* of cosmopolitanism.

I noted earlier that cosmopolitanism is always defined in reaction to a particular social grouping. In the modern era, cosmopolitanism has almost always been defined in contrast with nationalism. I think this is unfortunate, since nationalists need not, and often do not, disagree with basic cosmopolitan values of human rights, tolerance, cultural interchange, and international peace and co-operation.[15]

Instead, cosmopolitanism should be defined by contrast with its real enemies—xenophobia, intolerance, injustice, chauvinism, militarism, colonialism, etc. To be sure, some nationalists exhibit these vices, but being a nationalist is neither a necessary or sufficient condition for possessing them. As Thomas Schlereth notes, cosmopolitanism is best understood as a state of mind, exhibited in a rejection of xenophobia, a commitment to tolerance, and a concern for fate of humans in distant lands (Schlereth 1977: p. xi). As I have tried to show, there is no reason why liberal nationalists cannot embody these cosmopolitan virtues.

[15] Indeed, there is some evidence that minority nationalist parties are actually more supportive of international aid than anti-nationalist parties. See Breuning 1999 for Belgium, but I think the same is true of Quebec and Catalonia.

11

Cosmopolitanism, Nation-States, and Minority Nationalism

(CO-AUTHORED WITH CHRISTINE STRAEHLE)

1. Introduction

According to John Rawls, a theory of liberal justice should apply to 'the basic structure of society'. But what is the relevant 'society'? For Rawls, 'society' is defined in terms of the nation-state. Each nation-state forms one (and only one) society, and Rawls's theory applies within the boundaries of each nation-state.

Rawls is hardly alone in his focus on the nation-state. Most modern political theorists have taken for granted that the theories they develop should operate within the boundaries of the nation-state. When theorists develop principles of justice to evaluate economic systems, they focus on national economies; when theorists develop principles of rights to evaluate constitutions, they focus on national constitutions; when theorists develop an account of the appropriate virtues and identities required for democratic citizenship, they ask what it means to be a good citizen of a nation-state; when theorists discuss what 'political community' can or should mean, they are asking in what sense nation-states can be seen as political communities.

This focus on the nation-state is not always explicit. Many theorists talk about 'the society' or 'the government' or 'the constitution' without specifying what sort of society, government, or constitution they are referring to. But on inspection, they almost always have nation-states in mind. And this shows how widespread the paradigm is. The assumption that political norms apply within nation-states, conceived as single integrated 'societies', is so pervasive that many theorists don't even see the need to make it explicit.

To be sure, theorists are dimly aware that there are forms of governance which exist both above the level of the nation-state, in transnational institutions like the European Union or the United Nations, and also below the level of the nation-state, in local or regional political institutions. But these have been seen as of secondary importance, supplementing but never challenging or displacing the centrality of national political institutions.

It is surprising, therefore, that until very recently so little had been written about the role of nationhood in political theory. As Bernard Yack puts it, 'there are no great theoretical texts outlining and defending nationalism. No Marx, no Mill, no Machiavelli. Only minor texts by first rate thinkers like Fichte, or major texts by second rate thinkers like Mazzini.'[1]

This situation has changed significantly in the last few years, starting with the publication of Yael Tamir's *Liberal Nationalism* (1993), David Miller's *On Nationality* (1995), and Margaret Canovan's *Nationhood and Political Theory* (1996). There has indeed been a veritable explosion of articles, symposiums, and books on the political theory of nationalism in the last few years.[2] In this chapter, we will survey some of the main lessons that can be gleaned from this literature about the appropriate units or levels of political theory. We have summarized these lessons under three main headings.

First, these works have helped to explain why nationhood and nation-states have played such a central (albeit implicit) role in Western political theory. We have learned a great deal about why the theory and practice of democracy, justice, legitimacy, and citizenship have become tied to national institutions. According to several recent authors, often referred to as 'liberal nationalists', it is only within nation-states that there is any realistic hope for implementing liberal-democratic principles. We will discuss some of these liberal nationalist arguments in section 2 below.

Much of this literature can be seen as a defence not just of nation-states as they exist in the West, but also of *nationalism*. By nationalism, we mean those political movements and public policies that attempt to ensure that states are indeed 'nation-states' in which the state and nation coincide. According to liberal nationalists, it is not just a happy accident that nation-states happen to exist: rather, it is legitimate to use certain measures to try to bring about a greater coincidence of nation and state.

However, nationalist movements have attempted to make nations and states coincide in two very different and conflicting ways. On the one hand, states have adopted various 'nation-building' policies aimed at giving citizens a common national language, identity and culture; on the other hand, ethnocultural minorities within a larger state have mobilized to demand a state of their own. We can call the first 'state nationalism' and the second 'minority nationalism'.

Both of these nationalist strategies have tended to create serious conflict whenever a country contains national minorities. By 'national minorities' we mean ethnocultural groups that think of themselves as nations within a larger state. Confronted with state nationalism, these groups have typically resisted pressure to assimilate into the majority nation, and have instead

---

[1] Quoted in Ronald Beiner, 'Introduction', in Beiner 1999.

[2] Miller 1995; Tamir 1993; Canovan 1996; Beiner 1999; Miller *et al.* 1996; McKim and McMahan 1997; Moore 1998; Couture *et al.* 1998; Lehning 1998; Gilbert 1998.

mobilized along minority nationalist lines to form their own self-governing political community, either as an independent state or as an autonomous region within the larger state.

These sorts of conflicts between state nationalism and minority nationalism have been a pervasive feature of twentieth-century history. Moreover, contrary to most predictions, we have seen no abatement in such conflicts. Quite the contrary. The conflict between state nationalism and minority nationalism remains the most powerful dynamic in (and obstacle to) the newly democratizing countries of post-Communist Europe. And even in well-established Western democracies, minority nationalism has been intensifying, not diminishing, in Quebec, Scotland, Catalonia, Flanders, and Puerto Rico.

This raises an obvious question: if liberal nationalists are correct in arguing that liberal democracy works best within national political units, does this provide a defence of state nationalism, or of minority nationalism, or of both? And what should we do when the two forms of nationalism conflict?

Much of the liberal nationalist literature has tended to sidestep this critical issue, and to downplay the potential conflict between these two competing forms of nationalism. However, several authors have argued that liberal nationalism, by its own logic, should support minority nationalism. According to this view, there are legitimate reasons why ethnonational groups will continue to mobilize as 'nations', seeking 'national' rights of self-government and perhaps even secession. Here too important work has been done recently in explaining the power and durability of minority nationalism. We discuss these reasons in section 3. This is the second main lesson we draw from the literature.

This literature has yielded genuine insights into the centrality of nation-states, nationhood, and nationalism. Yet this literature has a distinctly 'owl of Minerva' feel to it. We seem to be gaining an understanding of the centrality of nationhood just as it is being challenged and displaced by other forces. In particular, many people argue that this focus on the nation-state and on minority nationalism must be replaced with a more cosmopolitan conception of democracy, focused on supranational or international institutions. These institutions are evolving, and increasingly influential, but traditional political theory tells us very little about the sort of democratization, rights, virtues, and identities appropriate to them. Important work has been done exploring at least the first steps in such a theory of 'cosmopolitan democracy', and we discuss these developments in section 4. The need for such a theory is the third main lesson in the literature.

In sum, the recent literature teaches us three lessons: (a) why nation-states have been so central to modern political theory; (b) why minority nationalism has been such an enduring feature of liberal-democratic life; and (c) why we need to at least partly displace or supplement this focus on nations and nation-states with a more cosmopolitan democracy. Needless to say, these three lessons pull in somewhat different directions. They do not sit comfortably with each other, and it is difficult to reconcile them in a single theory. Many theorists, therefore, have insisted that one of these is the 'real' lesson to be learned, and that the others are overstated. For example, some defenders of cosmopolitan democracy have argued, not only that transnational institutions are becoming as important as nation-states, but that the latter are increasingly obsolete, and that we are indeed witnessing 'the end of the nation-state' (Guéhenno 1995). Similarly, defenders of the nation-state have often disputed the significance of minority nationalisms; while defenders of minority nationalism often dismiss ideas of cosmopolitan democracy as utopian.

In our view, however, there is a kernel of truth in all three of these lessons. This suggests that we need a much more complex and multilevel conception of political theory than we have to date, one which does justice to minority nations, nation-states and to transnational institutions. Our aim in this article is not to develop such a theory, but perhaps to identify some of its potential building-blocks.

2. The Centrality of the Nation

In retrospect, we can see two powerful trends in the last two centuries in the West: (a) the almost universal reordering of political space from a confusing welter of empires, kingdoms, city-states, protectorates and colonies into a system of nation-states, all of which have embarked on 'nation-building' policies aimed at the diffusion of a common national identity, culture, and language;[3] and (b) the almost universal replacement of all forms of pre-liberal or non-democratic forms of government (e.g. monarchies, oligarchies, theocracies, military dictatorships, Communist regimes, etc.) with systems of liberal democracy. Common sense suggests that there must be some important affinity between nation-states and liberal democracy. But what is the nature of this affinity? As we noted earlier, there has been surprisingly little written by political theorists about this linkage. Political theorists have tended to implicitly assume that they are writing for a world of nation-states—as if the existence of nation-states was simply a fact of life—rather than exploring whether or why nation-states provide a good home for liberal democracy.

---

[3] For example, in the 18th century the Holy Roman Empire consisted of 1,800 distinctive 'territories', ranging from large states like Austria to tiny ecclesiastical and princely estates (Gagliardo 1980: 4).

However, the last few years have seen the emergence of a new school of thought—often called 'liberal nationalism'—that seeks to explain the link between liberal democracy and nationhood. We can think of liberal democracy as involving three connected but distinct kinds of principles: (*a*) social justice; (*b*) deliberative democracy; and (*c*) individual freedom. According to liberal nationalists, all three of these principles can best be achieved—or perhaps only be achieved—within *national* political units. We will say a few words about each of these linkages.

(a) Social Justice

Liberal democratic theorists differ amongst themselves about the precise requirements of social justice. Some left-liberals favour a dramatic redistribution of resources so as to achieve some conception of 'equality of resources' or 'equality of capabilities'. But even those on the centre-right of the liberal spectrum would generally agree that distributive justice requires: (i) equal opportunity to acquire the skills and credentials needed to participate in the modern economy, and to compete for valued jobs; (ii) a system of social entitlements to meet people's basic needs, and to protect people against certain disadvantages and vulnerabilities (e.g. health care, pensions, unemployment insurance, family allowances).

Why think social justice in these senses has any intrinsic connection to nation-states? Liberal nationalists suggest two sorts of reasons. First, a welfare state requires us to make sacrifices for anonymous others whom we do not know, will probably never meet, and whose ethnic descent, religion and way of life differs from our own. In a democracy, such social programmes will only survive if the majority of citizens continue to vote for them. History suggests that people are willing to make sacrifices for kin and for co-religionists, but are only likely to accept wider obligations under certain conditions. In particular, there must be some sense of common identity and common membership uniting donor and recipient, such that sacrifices being made for anonymous others are still, in some sense, sacrifices for 'one of us'. Also, there must be a high level of trust that sacrifices will be reciprocated: i.e. that if one makes sacrifices for the needy today, that one's own needs will be taken care of later. Liberal nationalists argue that national identity has provided this common identity and trust, and that no other social identity in the modern world has been able to motivate ongoing sacrifices (as opposed to episodic humanitarian assistance in times of emergency) beyond the level of kin groups and confessional groups (Miller 1995; Canovan 1996).

Second, the commitment to equality of opportunity, by definition, requires equal access to training and jobs. As the economy industrialized, jobs have come to require a high degree of literacy, education and the ability to communicate (compared to work in a peasant economy). According to

lner, the diffusion of mass education in a common language was a
requirement of the modernization of the economy. On Gellner's
ionalization' of education was not initially done in order to pro-
mo.. .. ality of opportunity for all citizens, but was simply a way of ensuring an adequate labour force (Gellner 1983). However, the nationalization of
education was quickly adopted by left-liberals and social democrats as a crucial tool for greater equality in society. National systems of education, providing standardized public education in a common standardized language,
succeeded in integrating backward regions and the working class into a common national society, and made it possible (in principle) for children from all
regions and classes to gain the skills needed to compete in a modern economy. Indeed, in many countries, equality of opportunity is often measured
precisely by examining the success of different groups within these common
national educational institutions.

For both of these reasons, various 'nation-building' policies by states can
be seen as promoting social justice, by promoting the solidarity needed to
motivate redistribution, and by promoting equal access to common educational and economic institutions.

(b) Deliberative Democracy

Liberal democracy is, by definition, committed to democratization. But for
liberals, democracy is not just a formula for aggregating votes: it is also a system of collective deliberation and legitimation that allows all citizens to use
their reason in political deliberation. The actual moment of voting (in elections, or within legislatures) is just one component in a larger process of
democratic self-government. This process begins with public deliberation
about the issues that need to be addressed and the options for resolving them.
The decisions which result from this deliberation are then legitimated on the
grounds that they reflect the considered will and common good of the people
as a whole, not just the self-interest or arbitrary whims of the majority.

Why think deliberative democracy in this sense has any intrinsic connection to nation-states? Here again, liberal nationalists suggest two sorts of reasons. First, as with social justice, deliberative democracy requires a high level
of trust. People must trust that others are genuinely willing to consider one's
interests and opinions. Moreover, those who lose out in one election or
debate are only likely to abide by the results if they feel that they might win
next time, and that others will abide by the results if and when they do win.
And, as we've seen, liberal nationalists argue that only a common national
identity has succeeded in securing this sort of trust.

Second, collective political deliberation is only feasible if participants
understand one another, and this seems to require a common language. In
principle, one could imagine extensive translation facilities amongst people

of different languages, but this can quickly become prohibitively expensive and cumbersome. When nation-states promote a common national language, therefore, they can be seen as enabling a more robust form of deliberative democracy. For liberal nationalists, national political forums with a single common language form the primary locus of democratic participation in the modern world, and are more genuinely participatory than political forums at higher levels that cut across language lines.[4]

(c) Individual Freedom

The link between individual freedom and nationalism is more complicated than that of social justice and deliberative democracy. The latter two are collective enterprises, and it is clear why they might require some sense of community. Whether nationhood provides the appropriate sort of communal basis for justice and democracy is a separate question, to which we will return, but they clearly imply some communal boundedness. By contrast, it may be less clear how nationalism can be seen as promoting liberal principles of individual freedom. After all, nationalism tends to assume that people's identity is inextricably tied to their nation, and that people can only lead meaningful lives within their own national culture. Yet is this not precisely the sort of valourization of ascriptive group identities that the liberal ideal of autonomous individuality was intended to challenge?

According to liberal nationalists, however, the relationship between individual autonomy and national culture is more complex. Participation in a national culture, they argue, far from inhibiting individual choice, is what makes individual freedom meaningful. People make choices about the social practices around them, based on their beliefs about the value of these practices. And one's national culture not only provides these practices, but also makes them meaningful to one. As Avishai Margalit and Joseph Raz put it, membership in a national culture provides meaningful options, in the sense that 'familiarity with a culture determines the boundaries of the imaginable'. Hence if a culture is decaying or discriminated against, 'the options and opportunities open to its members will shrink, become less attractive, and their pursuit less likely to be successful' (Margalit and Raz 1990: 449).

For this reason, the foundational liberal commitment to individual freedom can be extended to generate a commitment to the ongoing viability and flourishing of national cultures. This does not explain why people prefer their *own* national culture, rather than to integrate into some other, perhaps more flourishing, national culture. Liberal nationalists offer a number of reasons, however, why it is difficult for the members of a decaying culture to integrate into another culture. According to Margalit and Raz, for example, the option

---

[4] For a more detailed exposition of this point, see Ch. 10.

of integrating is difficult not only because it is 'a very slow process indeed', but also because of the role of cultural membership in people's self-identity. Cultural membership has a 'high social profile', in the sense that it affects how others perceive and respond to us, which in turn shapes our self-identity. Moreover, national identity is particularly suited to serving as the 'primary foci of identification', because it is based on belonging not accomplishment. Hence cultural identity provides an 'anchor for [people's] self-identification and the safety of effortless secure belonging'. But this in turn means that people's self-respect is bound up with the esteem in which their national group is held. If a culture is not generally respected, then the dignity and self-respect of its members will also be threatened (Margalit and Raz 1990: 447–9). Charles Taylor (1992a) and Yael Tamir (1993: 41, 71–3) give similar arguments about the role of respect for national membership in supporting dignity and self-identity.

Tamir also emphasizes the extent to which cultural membership adds an 'additional meaning' to our actions, which become not only acts of individual accomplishment, but also 'part of a continuous creative effort whereby culture is made and remade'. And she argues that where institutions are 'informed by a culture [people] find understandable and meaningful', this 'allows a certain degree of transparency that facilitates their participation in public affairs'. This in turn promotes a sense of belonging and relationships of mutual recognition and mutual responsibility (Tamir 1993: 72, 85–6). James Nickel emphasizes the potential harm to valuable intergenerational bonds when parents are unable to pass on their culture to their children and grandchildren (Nickel 1995). Benedict Anderson and Chaim Gans emphasize the way national identity enables us to transcend our mortality, by linking us to something whose existence seems to extend back into time immemorial, and forward into the indefinite future (Anderson 1983; Gans 1998). For all of these reasons, liberal nationalists argue, people's sense of individual freedom and meaningful autonomy is typically tied up with participation in their own national culture.

In sum, liberal nationalists give a variety of reasons why nation-states provide the appropriate units of liberal political theory. Liberal-democratic values of social justice, deliberative democracy, and individual autonomy, they argue, are best achieved in a nation-state—i.e. in a state which has diffused a common national identity, culture, and language amongst its citizens. As Margaret Canovan puts it, nationhood is 'the battery' which makes liberal democratic states run (Canovan 1996: 80).[5] Insofar as these liberal nationalist

---

[5] We should emphasize that Canovan, unlike the other authors we have mentioned in this section, is not really endorsing the liberal nationalist position. Indeed, in some respects she thinks it quite regrettable that liberal democracy is so tied to nationhood. But she argues that this connection has indeed been a strong one, and that it is not clear what the alternative bases for liberal democracy would be.

arguments are sound, it helps explain why, as Tamir puts it, 'most liberals are liberal nationalists' (1993: 139), and why the liberalization and nationalization of political life in the West have gone hand in hand.[6]

3. Nationalizing States and Minority Nations

There are many points in this liberal nationalist argument which can be questioned, particularly in an era of globalization, and we will examine some of these questions shortly. Before doing so, however, there is an ambiguity in the liberal nationalist argument that needs to be explored.

Liberal nationalists argue that various benefits arise when people within a political community share a sense of nationhood. But we know that this sense of common nationhood is not 'natural', and did not always exist. In many nation-states, the idea that all residents of the territory do, or should, share the same national identity is comparatively recent, at most a few centuries old, and it took a long time for it to take hold in the popular imagination. Put another way, nation-states did not come into being at the beginning of time, nor did they arise overnight: they are the product of careful nation-building policies, adopted by the state in order to diffuse and strengthen a sense of nationhood. These policies include national educational curriculums, support for national media, the adoption of national symbols and official language laws, citizenship and naturalization laws, and so on. For this reason, it is perhaps better to describe these as 'nation-building states' or as 'nationalizing states' rather than as 'nation-states'.[7] The successful diffusing of a common national identity is, in many countries, a contingent and vulnerable accomplishment—an ongoing process, not an achieved fact.

To be sure, in some countries, these nation-building policies have been strikingly successful. Consider France or Italy. Who could have predicted in 1750 that virtually everyone within the current boundaries of France or Italy would share a common language and sense of nationhood? In many countries, however, these nation-building policies have been resisted by sizeable, territorially-concentrated minorities, particularly when these minorities historically exercised some degree of self-government which was stripped from them when their homeland was incorporated into the larger state. As we noted earlier, these minorities often see themselves as 'nations within', and mobilize along nationalist lines to gain or regain rights of self-government.

---

[6] It also helps explain the paradox noted by Richard Sakwa: 'Liberalism is the most universal of ideologies yet, paradoxically, it is the most national in form—a feature recognized by John Stuart Mill, Jules Michelet and Guiseppe Mazzini as they became the intellectual proponents of liberal nationalism' (Sakwa 1998).

[7] See Brubaker 1996 for a sustained development of this argument.

Such minority nationalisms often directly conflict with state nationalism, since the latter aims to promote a common national identity throughout the state. Indeed, such minority nationalisms are often the first target of state nationalism and of nation-building policies. After all, members of the majority typically already feel some sense of shared nationhood, which is reflected in the public culture, and may not need any encouragement or pressure in order to identify with it. Nation-building policies are sometimes intended to help bring disadvantaged or marginalized members of the nation into the mainstream, but these policies are also typically aimed at those people who do not think of themselves as members of the larger nation at all—i.e. at national minorities—and at trying to eliminate their sense of forming a distinct nation within the larger state.

This raises the question captured nicely in the title of Walker Connor's famous article: are nation-states 'Nation-Building or Nation-Destroying?' (Connor 1972). In truth, they are both. Nation-states have typically sought to build a common nationhood by destroying any pre-existing sense of distinct nationhood on the part of national minorities. We can see this in the massive coercion used by the French government in the nineteenth-century against Bretons and Basques, and we can see it today in the policies adopted by the former Slovak government against the ethnic Hungarians, or by the Latvian government against the ethnic Russians.

And this raises an important question that has been remarkably neglected in the political theory literature, even amongst those who emphasize the centrality and importance of national identity to liberal-democracy. What should we do in states which contain two or more nations, and in which state nationalism comes into direct conflict with, and seeks to undermine, minority nationalism? Should we endorse state nation-building if it involves minority nation-destroying?

Putting the question this way presupposes that liberal nationalists are not just defending nation-states as they happen to exist, but also defending the legitimacy of nation-building programmes. This is not always clear in the texts: some writers take the existence of nation-states as a given, without saying anything about what, if anything, can be done to bring them into existence. However, as we noted earlier, the essence of nationalism is precisely about political movements and public policies that actively attempt to ensure that states are indeed 'nation-states' in which the state and nation coincide. Any theory of nationalism, liberal or otherwise, must therefore address the question about what measures are legitimate to try to bring about a greater coincidence of nation and state.[8] And in thinking about that question, we

[8] Wayne Norman has argued at length that the real task for political theorists in theorizing nationalism is not to evaluate the merits of nation-states as institutions, but rather to evaluate the merits of nation-building as a political practice. He argues that this aspect of nationalism has been almost entirely ignored by political theorists (Norman 1996; 1999). For example,

need to recognize that state nation-building is often connected to minority nation-destroying.

One might think that this conflict is not as severe as we've presented it. After all, the examples we've just given of state nationalism are hardly examples of the sort of nation-building supported by contemporary liberal nationalists. In both the case of nineteenth-century France and Slovakia in the 1990s, nation-building policies were being pursued in a coercive way, violating people's basic civil and political rights (e.g. rights to free association and freedom of the press, the right to run for political office, etc.). It is hardly surprising that these forms of state nationalism are nation-destroying. But contemporary liberal nationalists would only support state nation-building policies that respect people's basic human rights, and one might hope that these more moderate and liberal forms of state nationalism are not 'nation-destroying'.

Unfortunately, the conflict between state nationalism and minority nationalism does not disappear even when state nationalism works within the limits of human rights. As noted in Chapter 4, there are several ways in which national minorities can be systematically disempowered by the state without the violation of their individual civil and political rights. These include settlement/migration policies, manipulating the boundaries and powers of internal political subunits, and official language policy. Such policies have been a common element in the 'nation-building' programmes which Western states have engaged in.[9] Policies designed to settle minority homelands, undermine their political and educational institutions, and impose a single common language have been important tools of state nation-building. And while they are less coercive than the policies in nineteenth-century France, and do not involve violating basic individual rights, they are no less 'nation-destroying' in their intentions or results.

The fact that state nation-building can be minority nation-destroying even when conducted within the constraints of a liberal-democratic constitution helps to explain why minority nationalism remains a powerful force within Western democracies, and why secession remains a live issue in several regions (e.g. Flanders; Quebec; Catalonia; Scotland). National minorities will not feel secure, no matter how strongly their individual civil and political

Craig Calhoun notes that while many 19th-century liberals endorsed nation-states, they 'failed to address the processes by which national identities came into being and by which the populations living in any one territory were encouraged (or forced) to adopt more or less similar identities, languages and lifestyles' (Calhoun 1997: 87). The same is generally true of today's theorists of nationalism. See also Ch. 1.

[9] And, in a different way, in the Communist bloc. See Walker Connor's account of how Communist leaders dealt with the issues of settlement policy, gerrymandering, and linguistic policies, all of which were key policy tools in the Communist approach to national minorities. See Connor 1984.

rights are protected, unless the state explicitly renounces forever any intention of engaging in these sorts of state nation-building policies. This means, in effect, that the state must renounce forever the aspiration to become a 'nation-state', and accept instead that it is, and will remain, a 'multination state'.

So liberal nationalists cannot escape the conflict between state nationalism and minority nationalism. And so the question remains: is state nation-building permissible when it involves minority nation-destroying? As we noted earlier, there has been remarkably little written addressing this question. In one sense, it is understandable that this question has been ignored. The conflict between state nationalism and minority nationalism puts defenders of liberal nationalism in a major bind. If it is indeed desirable for states to be nation-states, then this seems to leave two unattractive options in countries where there are two or more national groups: either split up multination states so as to enable all national groups to form their own nation-state, through secession and the redrawing of boundaries; or enable the largest or most powerful national group within each multination state to use state-nationalism to destroy all competing national identities. The former is obviously unrealistic in a world where there are many more nations than possible states, and where many national groups are intermingled on the same territory, and it would be catastrophic to try to implement it.[10] But the latter seems arbitrary and unjust, and hardly consistent with the underlying principle that national identities are worthy of respect and recognition.

Faced with this dilemma, liberal nationalists have responded in various ways. Some simply ignore the problem. Others bite the bullet and argue that indeed multination states should, wherever possible, be split up into nation-states (e.g. Walzer 1992c). Yet others have argued that, if accorded some level of respect by the larger society, national minorities can be persuaded to relinquish their sense of 'nationhood', and to integrate into the dominant nation (e.g. Miller 1995). The evidence to date suggests that this is an unrealistic hope. Throughout the Western democracies (and indeed around the world) national minorities have become more insistent, not less, on their status as nations and their national rights. This hope is unrealistic precisely for the reasons which liberal nationalists have themselves advanced: namely, that people have a deep attachment to their own national identity and culture; and a deep desire to participate in politics in their vernacular. Indeed, if we re-examine the liberal nationalist arguments discussed in section 2, all of them seem to apply with equal force to minority nations as to dominant nations.

---

[10] We are here passing quickly over a very complicated question—namely, the right of secession—which has been the subject of much recent debate. See e.g. Buchanan 1991; Lehning 1998; Moore 1998.

Moreover, the minimal condition of according 'respect' to national minorities is to protect them against the sort of unjust nation-destroying policies discussed above. But the sorts of measures needed to protect against these policies are precisely those that involve reaffirming a sense of distinct nationhood amongst the minority. To prevent unjust settlement policies, for example, national minorities may make certain land claims—insisting that certain lands be reserved for their exclusive use and benefit. Or they may demand that certain disincentives be placed on immigration. For example, migrants may need to pass lengthy residency requirements before they can vote in local or regional elections. Or they may not be able to bring their language rights with them—that is, they may be required to attend schools in the local language, rather than having publicly-funded education in their own language. Similarly, the courts and public services may be conducted in the local language. These measures are all intended to reduce the number of migrants into the homeland of the national minority, and to ensure that those who do come are willing to integrate into the local culture. Similarly, to avoid being disempowered politically, national minorities need guaranteed rights to such things as self-government, group-based political representation, veto rights over issues that directly affect their cultural survival, and so on. And to avoid linguistic injustice, national minorities may demand that their language be accorded official language status, at least within their own region.

All of these demands, which are at the heart of minority nationalism around the world, provide the concrete evidence of whether a state has renounced the aspiration to a common nationhood and accepted instead its multinational reality. They all involve, in effect, the right of a national minority, not only to opt out of state nation-building policies, but also to engage in its own competing form of minority nation-building, so as to maintain itself as a distinct and self-governing society alongside the dominant national group. And the evidence is clear that national minorities will not feel secure within larger states unless these sorts of demands are met. So the idea that national minorities can be persuaded to integrate into the dominant nation appears quite naive. Minority nationalism will remain as resilient as state nationalism, and for much the same reasons.

Where does that leave the liberal nationalist? Liberal nationalists have typically argued that because national identity is important to people's freedom and self-respect, and because a common national identity serves many legitimate liberal-democratic values, therefore it is morally desirable for nations and states to coincide. However, this position now seems self-defeating. To promote a common national identity by destroying minority nationality seems hypocritical (and often unrealistic). Yet we cannot hope to grant all national minorities their own state.

In our view, this does not require abandoning the insights of liberal nationalism, but it does require reformulating the goal. National identities are important, and there are benefits to creating political units within which national groups can exercise self-government. However, the relevant 'political units' cannot be states. We need to think of a world, not of nation-states, but of multination states. If liberal nationalism is to be a viable and defensible approach in today's world, we need to renounce the traditional aim of liberal nationalism—namely, the aspiration to common nationhood within each state—and instead think of states as federations of self-governing peoples, in which boundaries have been drawn and powers distributed in such a way as to enable all national groups to exercise some degree of self-government.

We could call this new goal that of 'multination federalism', and we can see clear movement towards such a model in many Western democracies (e.g. Spain, Belgium, Britain, Canada). However, as of yet, virtually nothing has been written about the political theory of such a multination federation. There is no political theory about the appropriate way to draw boundaries or divide powers within multination states, or about the forms and limits of self-government which national minorities should exercise.[11]

4. The Need for a More Cosmopolitan Conception of Political Theory

So far, we have examined the reasons why nation-states have formed the traditional units of liberal political theory, and why minority nationalism will remain a powerful force into the future. But even if we accept these arguments, this is not to deny the obvious fact that we need international political institutions that transcend linguistic/national boundaries. We need such institutions to deal not only with economic globalization, but also with common environmental problems and issues of international security. This fact is widely accepted even by those who continue to emphasize the centrality of nationhood and national identities in the modern world.

At present, these transnational organizations exhibit a major 'democratic deficit', and have little public legitimacy in the eyes of citizens. They are basically organized through intergovernmental relations, with little if any direct input from individual citizens. Moreover, these institutions have evolved in an *ad hoc* way, each in response to a particular need, without any underlying theory or model about the kinds of transnational institutions we want, or how they should be governed, or how they should relate to each other, or what sorts of principles should regulate their structures or actions.

In short, while we have an increasing number of transnational institutions, which exercise an increasing influence over our lives, we have no political

---

[11] For tentative first steps towards such a theory, see Norman 1994; Baubock 2000; Tully 1995; cf. Ch. 5 above.

theory of transnational institutions. We have well-developed theories about what sorts of principles of justice should be implemented by the institutions of the nation-state; well-developed theories about what sorts of political rights citizens should have vis-à-vis these national institutions; and well-developed theories about what sorts of loyalties and commitments citizens should have to these institutions. By contrast, few people have any clear idea what principles of justice or standards of democratization or norms of loyalty should apply to transnational institutions.

It is increasingly clear, therefore, that we can no longer take the nation-state, or minority nations, as the sole or dominant context for political theory. We need a more cosmopolitan conception of democracy and governance that explicitly addresses these issues. Perhaps the most important work in this field is David Held's model of 'Cosmopolitan Governance' (Held 1995). Held's cosmopolitan argument can be structured along three concerns: (*a*) the principle of individual autonomy; (*b*) political legitimacy; and (*c*) the democratic public law. He argues that a nation-state framework can no longer assure these three principles. We will first sketch the argument made for each point, before discussing the difficulties facing such a cosmopolitan political theory.

(a) Individual Autonomy

Held's argument starts from the premiss that the goal of normative political theory is to assure the autonomy of the individual in her political context. Autonomy should be understood as 'the capacity of humans to reason self-consciously, to be self-reflective and to be self-determining' (Held 1995: 151). He agrees with liberal nationalists that the historical predominance of the liberal democratic nation-state within political theory can be explained in part by its capacity to assure individual political participation and freedom through procedures of representative and limited government, which in turn enable individual autonomy. However, Held argues that the capacity of the nation-state to protect individual autonomy is now gone. Instead, nation-states have become integrated into transnational economic, military, and legal regimes. On a less institutionalized level, Held also notes an increasing international interdependence in the form of the globalization of culture, media, and communication. This transnational interdependence has increased to such an extent that the ability of the nation-states to determine crucial questions about their members' life-chances can no longer be taken for granted. And so relying on the nation-state, and participation in its internal democratic structures and procedures, is no longer sufficient to assure individual autonomy.

(b) Political Legitimacy

Liberal nationalists argue that one virtue of nation-states is that the process of national elections and national political deliberation provides a strong basis for the legitimation of the exercise of political power by the nation-state. However, as Held notes, given that nation-states are integrated into transnational regimes to such an extent that national parliaments no longer have the final say in many policy decisions, then the crucial legitimation process for these decisions is jeopardized. There is no process of collective deliberation or common will-formation that precedes, shapes and hence helps legitimate such decisions. In order to re-establish the democratic requirements of accountability and hence legitimacy, the relevant political community has to be reconsidered. As transnational regimes gain in relevance, political legitimacy can only be restored by developing forms of citizen representation and participation in them.

Unlike what he calls 'hyper-globalizers', Held accepts that the nation-state will not fade away. His model of cosmopolitanism includes a place for nation-states, and gives them an important role in representing their members. However, Held insists that they must share political space with other decision-making centres based on NGOs, INGOs, International Organizations and so on, each of which would provide the site for democratic political action.

(c) Rights and Democratic Public Law

As we noted earlier, the need for transnational institutions is widely accepted, as is the need to somehow make them more accessible and accountable to citizens. However, it is far from clear how we can go about 'democratizing' these institutions, and even a cursory consideration of the obstacles to this democratization can quickly lead to pessimism.

Held does not answer this question directly, but approaches it indirectly, by focusing on the rights necessary to assure individual autonomy. These rights form the basis of what he calls 'the democratic public law', which should regulate all political institutions, national or transnational. According to Held, rather than ask how to democratize existing national or transnational institutions, we should first ascertain the content of these rights and of the democratic public law, and then ask what forms of institutions and of participation are consistent with the fundamental value of individual autonomy.

In most political theory, and certainly in liberal nationalist theory, rights are typically understood as citizenship-rights, and hence are tied to the state as the provider or guarantor of rights. Held, however, suggests that rights should be understood as 'empowering rights and entitlement capacities' (Held 1995: 223). These can be related to a nation-state, but also to transnational institutions. These rights are understood as providing individual autonomy in seven related and sometimes overlapping 'sites of power' (Held 1995: 176 ff.):

- the *body*, referring to the physical and emotional wellbeing of the individual;
- *welfare*, referring to goods and services accessible to the individual in the community;
- *culture and cultural life* as the expression of public interest, identity, local customs and communal dialogue;
- *civic associations* referring to the institutions and organizations of civil society;
- *economy*, referring to the organization of the production, distribution, exchange and consumption of goods and services;
- the domain of *coercive relations and organized violence* which in the framework of the nation-state rested with the state in order to guarantee peace and order in the community;
- the sphere of *regulatory and legal institutions* as describing the coordination of different subunits in one societal framework.

The aim of rights is to ensure an equitable or 'symmetrical' distribution of power in each of these 'sites'. Power in this context is defined as 'the capacity of social agents, agencies and institutions to maintain and transform their environment'. If power relations are asymmetrical, then individual autonomy is eroded. As Held puts it, 'the asymmetrical production and distribution of life-chances limit and erode the possibilities of political participation' (Held 1995: 170–1). In order to ensure that autonomy is upheld in any given site of power, Held imposes a number of conditions: access to each power site must be open, opportunities within it must be guaranteed and outcomes of each power structure ought not to be biased in favour of certain groups or interests.

How does all of this help us to conceptualize a more cosmopolitan democracy? Consider the spheres of the individual body and the economy. It is common knowledge that industrialization of the economy brought about one of the main challenges to individual autonomy, namely social class and social stratification based on capital, which (pre-)determined individual capacities to political participation. However, according to Held, the challenges posed by the economy to political equality today, in an era of globalization, are more comprehensive then the immediate impact of economic inequalities. For example, the institutionalization of free markets, either through free trade agreements (like NAFTA) or monitoring organizations like the IMF or the WTO, can seriously erode democracy. Besides the obvious constraints put on national governments of debtor countries by the IMF, Held argues that national governments are under pressure not to interfere too heavily with capital accumulation. In the age of globalization, large employers can circumvent most national policies restricting capital accumulation simply by relocating to foreign markets with cheaper production and labour costs. By contrast, labour is typically less mobile. This not only threatens political legitimacy, for the reasons discussed earlier, but also creates asymmetrical power relations between economic agents.

A closer look at the site of power of the body, on the other hand, illustrates other ways in cosmopolitan governance is needed. This sphere refers to the provision and pursuit of bodily needs and pleasures and the domain of biological reproduction, of which one crucial part is the right to choose or deny parenthood. One clearly asymmetrical structure would be if women were denied the right and means to decide whether to mother a child or not. Hence access to contraception is crucial, as is, in other contexts, the possibility to have more then one child. It is the latter that has been made difficult for women in highly populated countries such as China or some African countries. Spaces in day-care may be restricted to one child per family, hence obliging the parents to either rely on extended family structures or one of the parents, traditionally the mother, to stay home to provide for the second child. Although highly acclaimed by international organizations, given the overpopulation in these regions, such policies nevertheless involve stripping individual women of their right to take crucial decisions autonomously.

This suggests that the individual has to be taken into account if the democratic public law is to be effective. This also suggests that relying on nation-states to represent their members in the international sphere does not ensure the democratization of this sphere. Giving more representation or veto rights to nation-states within international organizations may do little to better the democratic circumstances their citizens live in.

In order to assure autonomy therefore, rights have to be established according to each site of power. The democratic public law responds to the new conditions of power and interdependence of each site of power, and seeks to create a system of rights that prevents asymmetrical power from arising.

This is just a brief sketch of Held's approach, leaving out many of the institutional specifics, but enough has been said perhaps to see where the strengths and weaknesses lie, at least in comparison with the liberal nationalist approach. The main strength of Held's model, we think, is that it recognizes the reality that democratic political agency must transcend the level of nations if citizens are to have any meaningful say over the circumstances of their lives.

The main difficulty, however, is that Held provides no real account of the preconditions which make such democratic political agency possible. As we have seen, one of the main arguments made by liberal nationalists is that nationhood still functions as the basis for solidarity among members because it 'constitutes a collective political subject—a 'we'—with the capacity to act collectively over long periods of time' (Canovan 1996: 72). Nationhood functions as a 'battery' for the nation-state, a generator of power (Canovan 1996: 80). It provides the solidarity and trust needed to sustain relations of redistribution and of democratic rule. According to the liberal nationalist account, every entity that aims at providing the framework of a liberal-democratic welfare state needs this kind of communal spirit to be effective.

The model of cosmopolitan governance proposed by Held is for the most part silent on these questions of collective identity and social justice. There are genuine transnational identities, grounded in the individual sense of belonging to the global community. Consider members of Greenpeace protesting against the resource exploitation in the Antarctic because of the environmental harm this may cause. When acting in this way, these individuals do not perceive themselves as particular nationals, but rather as members of Greenpeace, hence of a global organization lobbying against damage done to the global environment. We can think of other issue-specific transnational identities, evident in adherence to values like the protection of the environment or the advocacy of human rights. Richard Falk for example describes groups like Amnesty International and their work as an expression of a transnational civil society with a genuine identity (Falk 1995).

One option, therefore, would be to try to build on these issue-specific transnational identities, as the foundation for the sort of solidarity and trust required by justice and democracy. The problem, however, is that democracy requires us to trust, and to make sacrifices for, those who do not share our interests and goals. The emergence of issue-specific transnational identities may explain why Greenpeace members are willing to make sacrifices for the environment around the world, but it doesn't explain why Greenpeace members are willing to make sacrifices for, say, ethnocultural minorities around the world, particularly those who may demand the right to engage in practices harmful to the environment. Democracy requires the adjudication of conflicting interests, and so works best when there is some sort of common identity that transcends these conflicting interests. Within nation-states, a common national identity ideally transcends differences between pro-development and pro-environment groups, and enables some level of trust and solidarity between them. It is difficult to see what serves this function at the transnational level.

A second option for democratizing transnational institutions is to rely upon existing national identities, and to find ways to hold international institutions more accountable through nation-states. This is the pattern followed by the United Nations and related international organizations, and one could imagine ways to strengthen the accountability of transnational institutions to nation-states (e.g. by giving nation-states veto powers over the decisions of transnational institutions, or by requiring that the decisions of transnational institutions be debated publicly within each national context). In this way, citizens could feel that they had some control over transnational institutions through the normal processes of national political participation.

However, we have to remember that many nation-states are not very democratic. Although the nation-state may provide fertile conditions for nurturing liberal democracy, the mere fact of being a nation-state does nothing to assure liberal democratic procedures. Hence if citizens can only influence transnational institutions through their nation-states, this may not really democratize the system, given that the world is composed primarily of autocratic states (Bobbio 1995).

A third option for the democratization of the transnational system is to expand the scope of the agents who have 'a seat at the table'. Instead of the state-centred approach to representation in international organizations, Held proposes that a second chamber of the United Nations be established in which for example NGOs, INGOs, and ethnocultural minorities could be represented.[12] By expanding the decision-making group, individuals could better be represented. As a result, the ultimate concern with individual autonomy would be reinforced by giving the individual a means to politically participate beyond the nation-state. Moreover, this would help to counter the concern that nation-states often fail to represent many of their own citizens. This is a particular concern with undemocratic states, but even democracies have been known to systematically ignore the interests of some of their minorities in international settings. The attractiveness of this model lies in its combination of subnational, national, and transnational components. However, the problem remains how can we develop the sort of common identity and solidarity needed to establish and sustain this sort of cosmopolitan democracy.

5. Conclusion

In this chapter, we have discussed the claims made regarding the importance of three separate levels of political community and political agency: sub-state minority nations, nation-states, and transnational institutions. In our view, we need a theory which does justice to all of these levels (and to others as well).[13] To date, few theorists have succeeded in combining these levels, in part because they are often taken as inherently competing for power, resources, and loyalty. People who wish to defend the importance of minor-

---

[12] See the related proposals in Franck 1997 and Archibugi 1995.

[13] We have said nothing in this article, for example, about the importance of municipal governments, which have also been strikingly ignored by political theorists. For a critique of political theorists for this neglect, see Magnusson 1996; cf. Young 1990: ch. 8.

ity nationalism, for example, often assume that this requires downplaying the importance of nation-states or of transnational institutions.

In reality, however, these levels are often mutually reinforcing rather than mutually competing. For example, Mary Kaldor argues that any attempt to resolve the conflict in the Balkans with (nineteenth-century) ideas of the nation-state is doomed to failure from the outset. If all sides to the conflict operate with outdated notions of the sovereign nation-state, it becomes almost a matter of life or death whether one's group controls the state, and the result is that neither state structures nor national minorities are safe. She argues instead for a solution in a broader framework like that of the European Union (Kaldor 1995). In such a framework, transnational institutions help to reduce the threat that states pose to minorities, and vice versa.

Put another way, each level of political community/agency can help to ensure the legitimacy of the other. As we've seen, nation-states can no longer protect the interests of their citizens on their own, and this is leading people to question the legitimacy of the state. Establishing well-functioning transnational institutions, capable of resolving the problems which transcend nation-states, should not necessarily be seen as weakening nation-states, but rather as restoring legitimacy to them, by enabling them to focus on those goals which they can successfully pursue. Similarly, self-government for national minorities need not be seen as a threat to states, but rather as a precondition for the long-term stability of states.

Identifying these potential forms of symbiosis might help us to overcome the zero-sum mentality which still unconsciously governs much of the debate about minorities, states and transnational institutions, and encourage the development of a political theory which does justice to the multilayered nature of politics today.

12

Misunderstanding Nationalism

A striking fact of twentieth-century history is the tenacity with which ethno-national groups have maintained their distinct identity, institutions, and desire for self-government. There are few examples this century of national minorities—that is, national groups who share a state with larger national groups—voluntarily assimilating into the larger society.

North Americans often overlook this fact, because they fail to distinguish immigrants from national minorities. Immigrants choose to leave their original culture and homeland, and move as individuals or families to a new country. They know that this uprooting will only be successful if they adapt to their new country, including learning its language and customs. For the last 150 years, large numbers of immigrants from other countries have voluntarily assimilated into the mainstream American society, so that they, and particularly their children, will become full participants in its economic and political institutions.

Immigrant groups rarely give rise to nationalist movements. They do not think of themselves as separate nations alongside the mainstream society, and do not seek to establish their own autonomous homelands and self-governing political institutions within the United States. This is true even of proponents of a more 'multicultural' America, since they are primarily demanding greater accommodation of ethnic identity *within* mainstream institutions. These demands are evidence not of growing nationalism, although some paranoid critics have suggested this, but of a new, more pluralistic conception of integration within the American nation (see Ch. 8).

The only reason an immigrant group would adopt a nationalist agenda is if it was prevented from integrating into the mainstream society, through mandatory segregation and legal discrimination. So nationalism will not arise if immigrant groups are guaranteed equal civil and political rights.

But that is not true of non-immigrant minorities—that is, groups whose historic homeland has been incorporated into a larger state, through colonization, conquest, or voluntary federation. These are the sorts of groups giving rise to nationalist conflict in Europe. They are rarely satisfied with

A review of Liah Greenfeld, *Nationalism: Five Roads to Modernity* (Harvard University Press, 1992); Michael Ignatieff, *Blood and Belonging: Journeys into the New Nationalism* (Farrar, Straus, and Giroux, 1993); William Pfaff, *The Wrath of Nations: Civilization and the Furies of Nationalism* (Simon and Schuster, 1993); Yael Tamir, *Liberal Nationalism* (Princeton University Press, 1993).

individual civil and political rights. They want self-government, either through regional autonomy or complete secession.

The inadequacy of the immigrant model for national minorities is clear even in North America. The Québécois, Indian tribes, Puerto Ricans, and native Hawaiians have all fought for (and gained) some measure of self-government and local autonomy. Groups which are incorporated into a larger state, not because they left their homeland and moved here, but because their homeland was conquered or annexed, often develop a distinct national consciousness, even though they may be free to assimilate.

In short, while there are virtually no cases of immigrants becoming nationalists, there are also few recent cases of national minorities accepting assimilation. If we focus on territorial nations, rather than immigrants, nationalism has been a constant factor of twentieth-century history.

Yet nationalism remains poorly understood, and Western leaders have been continually caught off-guard by nationalist movements abroad, or indeed within their borders. For this reason, the appearance of these four books is welcome. Unfortunately, much of the recent writing on nationalism obscures as much as it reveals.

This is particularly true of Michael Ignatieff's *Blood and Belonging* and William Pfaff's *The Wrath of Nations*, which offer similar analysis of nationalism. At the heart of both books is the distinction between 'ethnic' and 'civic' nationalism. 'Ethnic' nations, like Germany, define membership in terms of shared descent, so that people of a different racial or ethnic group (eg. Turkish guest-workers in Germany) cannot acquire citizenship no matter how long they live in the country. 'Civic' nations, like the United States, are in principle open to anyone who lives in the territory. Ethnic nationalism is exclusive, civic nationalism is inclusive. Both Ignatieff and Pfaff argue that only civic nationalism is compatible with liberalism, democracy, and peace.

This is a familiar distinction, invoked by many recent authors on nationalism. To take one other example, Thomas Franck distinguishes between a 'romantic tribal nationalism', which he describes as a kind of virus or 'craze' which has infected many parts of the world, and an earlier form of nationalism, typified by American and French revolutionary nationalism, which was based, not on common blood or culture, but on political principles, particularly principles of freedom and equality. Whereas romantic tribal nationalism is an illiberal, exclusive and defensive reaction to modernity, the American–French form of nationalism is liberal, inclusive and forward-looking (Franck 1997).

This sort of distinction is almost a cliche in the literature, but it needs to be handled carefully, and can easily be misinterpreted or misapplied. For example, all these authors equate 'ethnic' nationalism with 'cultural' nationalism. Cultural nationalism defines the nation in terms of a common culture, and the aim of the nationalist movement is to protect the survival of that culture.

Examples of cultural nationalism include the Québécois or the Catalans in Spain. This sort of concern with cultural survival is a common feature of almost all minority nationalisms around the world. Ignatieff defines all such minority cultural nationalisms as 'ethnic' nationalisms.

But that is clearly wrong. Both the Québécois and tha Catalans accept immigrants as full members of the nation, so long as they learn the language and history of the society. They define membership in terms of participation in a common culture, open to all, rather than on grounds of ethnic descent. The shift from an ethnic to a cultural conception of the nation is these cases has been a slow and painful one, but it is now firmly entrenched in citizenship laws and mainstream public opinion (see Ch. 15 below).

Pfaff and Ignatieff also overlook the fact that 'civic nationalism' has a cultural component. They say that membership in a civic nation is based, not on descent or culture, but on allegiance to certain political principles of democracy and freedom. This is obviously false of the 92 per cent of Americans who are native-born, since their citizenship has nothing to do with their political beliefs. They automatically acquire citizenship by descent, and cannot be stripped of it if they turn out to be fundamentalists or fascists. And it is only half-true of immigrants to America. The US government does require immigrants to swear allegiance to the constitution, but it also requires them to learn the English language and American history. These legal requirements of gaining citizenship are intended to integrate immigrants into the common societal culture.

French and American nationalisms were not just concerned with political principles; they were also concerned with creating a common identity, in part by imposing a common language. In the French case, this language was quite brutally imposed on the Basques, Bretons, and other linguistic minorities, through prohibitions on publications in minority languages, as well as legal requirements that the language of all education, army units and government employment be French. A similar process occurred in the United States. When the United States annexed the Southwest from Mexico in 1848, various language rights were guaranteed to the Spanish-speaking population in the Treaty of Guadelupe Hidalgo, but these treaty obligations were quickly violated. And when Puerto Rico was taken over from Spain in 1898, attempts were made to replace the Spanish-language schools with English-language schools. One can find many other examples where the US government imposed English on a non-English-speaking population.[1]

So American nationalism, like French nationalism, has been concerned not only with promoting freedom and equality, but also with promoting a common language. I think that these two goals were seen as related—that is, people believed that promoting a common language would provide the nec-

[1] For a history of language rights in the United States, see Kloss 1977.

essary basis for a society of free and equal citizens. The best and most stable form of a democratic republic was one that was unified by a common language.

The idea that civic nationalisms are 'forward-looking', unlike 'backward-looking' ethnic nationalisms, also requires qualification. There is an important historical element in both American and French nationalism. History is emphasized, not in the form of a historical folk culture, but rather as a way of emphasizing an historical commitment to certain institutions and procedures which embody principles of equality and freedom. After all, principles of freedom and equality, by themselves, are vague, and under-determine political institutions. They do not tell us where to draw political boundaries, or how to distribute powers between different levels of government, or what sort of electoral system to adopt. These sorts of questions could lead to serious conflict in a society, even if people agreed on basic principles. However, promoting a common sense of history is a way of ensuring that people identify, not just with abstract principles, but with *this* political community, with its particular boundaries, institutions, procedures, and so on. A forward-looking commitment to universal principles of freedom and equality is balanced, if you like, with a backward-looking emphasis on the historical specificity and particularity of the American (or French) instantiation of these principles. In short, a common language and a common sense of history are deliberately promoted, not *instead of* freedom and equality, but rather as a way of defining and unifying this particular society of free and equal citizens.[2]

So membership of the American nation, just as of the Québécois nation, involves participation in a common societal culture. It is a legal requirement for children to learn the English language and American history in schools, and all levels of American government have instisted that there is a legitimate governmental interest in promoting a common language.

This is not necessarily wrong or oppressive. After all, the societal culture which American immigrants must integrate into is capacious, leaving ample room for the expression of a particular ethnic or religious identity. And learning a common language and shared history helps ensure that immigrants are not disadvantaged in the mainstream economy or polity.

Conversely, the assumption that minority cultural nationalisms are a defensive and xenophobic reaction to modernity is often overstated. This may be true of the current situation in Rwanda or Bosnia, but I think there

---

[2] As Calhoun notes, American and French revolutionary ideas of 'the people' 'depended in turn on the growth of ideas about non-political social organization. Whether expressed as "nation" or "people", reference to some recognizably bounded and internally integrated population was integral to modern notions of popular will and public opinion. In other words, it was important that "the people" be (or at least be seen as) socially integrated, not dispersed like so many grains of sand or divided into smaller communities and families. Politics depended in new ways upon culture and society' (Calhoun 1997: 71).

are many cases of minority nationalisms around the world today which are not all that different from French and American revolutionary nationalism, in the sense that they too are forward-looking political movements for the creation of a society of free and equal citizens. They seek to create a democratic society, defined and united by a common language and sense of history. I think this is what most Québécois nationalists seek, as well as most Catalan, Scottish, and Flemish nationalists. They are not trying to avoid modernity; they are precisely trying to create a modern democratic society.

This is reflected not only in their increasing openness to immigration, but also in their economic policy. Nationalist regions are often firm proponents of economic liberalization and free trade. Support for the North American Free Trade Agreement was higher in Quebec than in the rest of Canada, and support for the European Union is higher in Catalonia and Scotland than elsewhere in Spain or Britain. These minority groups see free trade and globalization as a crucial part of the modern society they wish to build.[3] So these movements are not a defensive reaction against modernity. They are open societies—open to immigration and free trade, and to interacting with others more generally. In some cases, they are more open than majority groups.

Of course, some minority nationalisms are deeply illiberal. And indeed some members of the groups I've been discussing are illiberal. There are illiberal strands within the Québécois, Flemish, Catalan, and Scottish nationalist movements. We can see a struggle going on in all of these societies between the liberal nationalists and the reactionary or radical nationalists. I don't want to deny or downplay the existence of illiberal elements in these minority nationalisms. But I don't think we can get a handle on these conflicts unless we see that there is also a very powerful liberal strand to these movements— a strand which is committed, like American and French nationalism, to the creation of modern societies of free and equal citizens. And in some cases, the liberal strand is winning. In any event, the balance between liberal and illiberal strands is something that can only be determined empirically, not presupposed in advance.[4]

The point is that all nationalisms have a cultural and historical component. Of course, the way culture and history is interpreted varies from nation to nation. Some nations define their culture in racial and religious terms, others do not. These variations are crucial to understanding why some nationalism are xenophobic, authoritarian, and expansionist, while others peaceful, liberal, and democratic. Unfortunately, since Pfaff and Ignatieff downplay the

---

[3] For a survey of the attitudes of minority nationalists-secessionists towards free trade, see Davis 1994.

[4] See Shafir 1995 for a recent study of the extent to which different minority nationalisms are open to immigrants.

cultural component of nationalism, they shed no light on the variations in how culture is interpreted.

For the same reason, they provide no real explanation of why people value their national identity. Pfaff says that national identity reflects a 'primordial' desire for 'community'. But even if people have such a primordial desire, why does this take the form of a bond to their *national* community, rather than their church, city, or workplace? Pfaff offers no explanation of this.

Ignatieff explains the affirmation of national identity in Eastern Europe as a response to the power vacuum created by the collapse of Communism. But that puts the cart before the horse, since nationalist movements predated, and helped cause, the collapse of Yugoslavia and the Soviet Union. To be sure, the disintegration of the state made violence more likely, by leaving groups at each other's mercy. But the feeling of national identity underlying those groups preceded the collapse of Communism.

These weak explanations for the tenacity of national identity should not be surprising. Pfaff and Ignatieff treat nationalism as a matter of either political principle (civic nationalism) or ethnic descent (ethnic nationalism). But insofar as both civic and ethnic nationalisms are cultural phenomenon, any plausible account of national identity must examine people's attachment to their culture, which Pfaff and Ignatieff largely ignore.

Similarly, both misinterpret the nature of nationalist conflict. They argue that ethnic nationalism is the cause of nationalist conflict, because of its ethnic exclusiveness. In fact, nationalist conflict is often due to attempts by civic nationalists to forcibly incorporate national minorities. Consider the Kurds. The problem is not that Turkey refuses to accept Kurds as Turkish citizens. The problem is precisely its attempt to force Kurds to see themselves as Turks. Turkey refuses to accept that Kurds are a separate national group (the government calls them 'mountain Turks'), and until 1990 banned the use of the Kurdish language in an attempt to coercively assimilate the Kurds. The violence in Kurdistan—one of the longest-running nationalist conflict in the world—is not because of ethnic exclusion, but through the forcible inclusion of a national minority into a larger national group.

The same process has occurred in America. The American government forcibly incorporated Indian tribes, native Hawaiians, and Puerto Ricans into the American state, and then attempted to coercively assimilate each group into the common American culture. They banned the speaking of Indian languages in school, and forced Puerto Rican and Hawaiian schools to use English not Spanish or Hawaiian. The explicit aim was to make these groups see themselves as members of the American nation, not as members of a separate and self-governing nation. These groups resisted (often violently) the assimilationist policies, and today a measure of self-government is granted to each group.

It is essential to see that this aggressive expansionism was quite consistent with civic nationalism. After all, the aim was to turn Indians and native

Hawaiians into American citizens, with the same rights as other American citizens. Civic nationalism in the United States has historically justified the conquering and colonizing of national minorities, and the coercive imposition of English-language courts and schools.

Much of the nationalist conflict around the world is the result of attempts by majority nations to coercively assimilate national minorities. This aggression is often rationalized precisely on the grounds that the majority nation is non-ethnic. Since Indians will be treated as equal citizens of the American nation, just as Kurds will be equal citizens of the Turkish nation, what harm is done by abolishing their separate institutions and forcing them to join the larger nation?

The motivation of Québécois, Latvian, Flemish, Kurdish, or Slovak nationalists is not a fear of being excluded from a larger nation on ethnic grounds, but a desire to maintain themselves as separate nations. To treat ethnic exclusiveness as the sole, or even main, source of nationalist conflict is a striking mistake.

Ignatieff also misinterprets the relation between nationalism and democracy. He claims that civic nationalism is 'necessarily democratic, since it vests sovereignty in all of the people'. But consider virtually any country in Latin America. Most of these countries have a strong sense of national identity that is non-ethnic. Peru and Brazil, for example, are extraordinarily multiethnic societies, granting equal citizenship to whites, blacks, Indians, and Asians. Yet there is nothing 'necessarily democratic' about them. Civic nations can be military dictatorships as easily as liberal democracies.

Pfaff and Ignatieff are right to insist on the distinction between civic and ethnic nationalism. However, virtually every claim they make about this distinction—and its relationship to culture, violence, and democracy—is overstated. They present themselves as having seen through the myths of nationalism, but they propagate their own mythical conception of civic nationalism as inherently good, peaceful, and democratic.

Each book has some redeeming features. Pfaff has some interesting things to say about the deleterious impact of nationalist ideas in Asia and Africa. Ignatieff's book includes an account of his journeys to Yugoslavia, Kurdistan, Ukraine, Quebec, Germany, and Ulster, and his talks with the people affected, from workers and students to nationalist rebels and government ministers. He is a good interviewer, and their stories of broken dreams, resentments, fears, and hopes are often compelling. The book was written to accompany a BBC series of the same name, broadcast on PBS in 1994, which is worth watching. Unfortunately, while the interviews are interesting, Ignatieff's analysis of the events or feelings he encounters is seriously flawed.

While these books are not very informative about nationalism, they do tell us something about the psychology of cosmopolitan liberals at the end of the twentieth century. Pfaff is an expatriate American columnist for the

International Herald Tribune living in France; Ignatieff an expatriate Canadian living in England. They are multilingual citizens of the world whose ambitions took them beyond their country's border, and for whom borders are largely irrelevant. Confronted by nationalists who care deeply about borders, and indeed who often wish to redraw them so as to create smaller political units, many cosmopolitan liberals feel threatened and confused. Moreover, unlike liberals in the nineteenth century or the 1950s, liberals today no longer are confident that history is on the side of cosmopolitanism. These books provide revealing examples of the sense of anxiety and confusion engulfing cosmopolitan liberals today. For an explanation of nationalism, however, readers must look elsewhere.

For the historical origins of nationalism, Liah Greenfeld's book is a useful starting point. According to Greenfeld, the national idea first arose among elites, rather than among the middle or lower classes. Yet, she notes, this raises a puzzle, for nations are defined in terms of 'the people'—i.e. the mass of population on a territory, including the members of different classes and occupations. Why would elites accept an ideal that viewed the people 'as the bearer of sovereignty, the central object of loyalty, and the basis of collective solidarity'? Elites traditionally tried to dissociate themselves as much as possible from 'the plebs' or 'the rabble'. How then did they come to identify with the people?

Some recent theorists have argued that 'nation-building' was a functional requirement of modernization. Modern economies required a literate educated workforce, which in turn required integrating the lower classes into a common culture, through standardized public education. However, Greenfeld insists that the national idea arose before modernization, in response to more contingent factors. She argues it first arose in England in the early sixteenth century, adopted by Henry VIII to support his battle with Rome, and then by Parliament in its battle with James I. Similarly, she argues, the emergence of nationalism in France, Russia, Germany, and the United States all predated industrialization. In each case, the idea of 'the nation' served the interests of a particular elite group—e.g. the French and Russian nobility's battle with absolutist monarchs; the German intellectuals' desire for social acceptance.

Greenfeld tracks the rise of the word 'nation' and its correlates ('people', 'country') with meticulous care, showing when it came into usage in each country, by whom, for what purposes. The result is an impressive, but also daunting, work of scholarship. I suspect that only specialists will want to wade through the 20 pages detailing the various orders of the French aristocracy, or the 9-page synopsis of an obscure work by the German Romantic Carl Moritz.

Greenfeld reminds us of the contingent origins of nations. But her book doesn't explain their tenacious persistence. Her narrative ends at the beginning of the nineteenth-century, by which time national ideals had been entrenched amongst elites in the five countries she examines. She does not address how these national ideals became diffused to the masses, or why national minorities have held on to their identity, despite powerful economic and political incentives to join larger nations.

This is not a criticism of her book, which succeeds admirably in the task it set. Greenfeld is addressing the question of why feudal elites abandoned their traditional prenational identity for a national identity. She is not addressing the modern-day question of how to understand conflict between two or more groups whose national identities are already firmly rooted.

Greenfeld does touch on this issue at the end of her book. She argues that national identity has remained strong in the modern era because its emphasis on the importance of 'the people' provides a source of dignity to all individuals, whatever their class. But (as she admits), this does not explain why any *particular* national identity is important, or why people are unwilling to abandon their original identity for another national identity that also would guarantee them dignity. Why should the Kurds not be happy to be members of the Turkish nation?

To understand this, we need a clearer account of why national identity matters to people. The great virtue of Yael Tamir's book—one of the few full-length philosophical discussions of nationalism—is that she tackles this question head on. Tamir is an Israeli philosopher, and the book reflects her attempt to reconcile Zionist convictions with liberal beliefs in individual rights and personal autonomy.

Tamir begins by noting that nations—civic or ethnic—are cultures which provide their members with meaningful ways of life across the full spectrum of human activity (economic, political, educational, recreational, religious, etc.). Following Anthony Smith, we can call these 'organizational cultures', to signify that they form institutionally integrated societies, not simply lifestyle subgroups or advocacy movements within a society. The value of national identity, then, is tied to the value of cultural membership. Why is cultural membership important? Tamir starts from the liberal assumption that people are capable of making autonomous choices about their aims in life. But the ability to make these choices depends on 'the presence of a cultural context', so that individual liberty is dependent on membership in a cultural community. Over time, individuals can put these cultural contexts themselves in question, and choose which culture they wish to live in.

Being able to express one's cultural identity is important for many reasons: cultural membership is a precondition of autonomous moral choices, and itself reflects an autonomous cultural choice that is worthy of respect; it is a 'constitutive' aspect of one's identity which affects one's sense of status and self-respect; actions performed in a cultural context are 'endowed with additional meaning' because they can be seen both as acts of individual achievement and as contributions to the development of one's culture; and shared membership in a culture promotes a sense of belonging and relationships of mutual recognition.

This is a sensible account of the value of national identity, similar to the view of many nineteenth-century liberals. Tamir then argues that expressing one's cultural identity requires some degree of 'national self-determination'. Since Tamir defines nations as the bearers of distinct cultures, she construes the right to national self-determination as the right to ensure the continued existence and development of that distinct culture. This, she argues, does not require that each nation have its own sovereign 'nation-state', which is in any event impossible. Instead, the right to develop one's national culture can be ensured by autonomy within multination states, through mechanisms such as federalism or consociational democracy.

The exact form of self-determination, she argues, is not important. What matters is that the culture have some 'public expression'. Without this public component, the existence of a nation as a distinct social unit would be jeopardized. Hence the state should serve an 'expressive' role, actively reflecting a particular national identity in its symbols and institutions.

Tamir's defence of nationalist politics rests heavily on this claim regarding the need for the 'public expression' of a culture. But her argument is not very clear. Why isn't freedom of speech and association sufficient to allow people to express their cultural identity? Why is the state needed for people to 'share a language, memorise their past, cherish their heroes, live a fulfilling national life'? If people can collectively express their religious identity through freedom of association while still maintaining a strict separation of church and state, why shouldn't we maintain a separation of state and nation?

In places, Tamir implies that state involvement is simply unavoidable. She rightly argues that the state cannot avoid expressing a cultural identity when it adopts official languages and public holidays. On this view, state expression of a national identity is more regrettable than desirable, but since it is unavoidable, justice requires that we compensate national minorities for disadvantages this creates, and protect them from pressures to assimilate.

Yet at other times, Tamir implies that it is a positive good that states express a national identity, and that existing liberal democracies should do more to develop the 'cultural essence of the state'. She says that the 'yearning for self-determination' is to see political institutions as 'carriers of the national identity'. On this view, political arrangements 'should reflect the unique character and draw on the history, the culture, the language, and at times the religion of the national group, thereby enabling its members to regard it as their own'. The argument here is not about the survival of the culture, but about the desire for political affirmation of self-identity, and the desire to have a sense of ownership of government through one's nation.

Tamir's last chapter is entitled 'Making A Virtue Out of Necessity', which captures the two strands in her thought. But it is unclear why liberals should see the political expression of national identity as a virtue to be promoted. In most nationalist conflicts over devolution of powers, boundaries, political representation, language rights, etc., the ambitions of nationalists generally far exceed what is required to ensure the continued existence of the nation as a distinct society. Yet they all increase the public expression of the national culture, and promote national identification with the state. Tamir's theory provides no way to resolve these conflicts, in part because she provides no clear basis for judging whether nationalist politics are a necessity to be minimized, or a virtue to be promoted.

In my view, it can be a mistake to make a virtue out of necessity. The boundaries of state and nation rarely if ever coincide perfectly, and so viewing the state as the possession of a particular national group can only alienate minority groups. The state must be seen as belonging equally to all people who are governed by it, regardless of their nationality.

But it would be an even more serious mistake to ignore the ways in which states necessarily privilege particular national cultures. This is obvious in decisions regarding the language of schools, courts, and government services. Given the centrality of the state to modern life, a group without such language rights will face enormous pressures to assimilate. Decisions regarding immigration and naturalization also affect the viability of national cultures. Immigration can strengthen a national group, so long as the numbers are regulated and immigrants are encouraged (or required) to learn the nation's language and history. But if immigrants in a multination state integrate into the majority culture, then national minorities will be increasingly outnumbered and so increasingly powerless in political life. Moreover, states often encourage immigrants (or migrants from other parts of the country) to settle in lands traditionally held by national minorities, reducing them to a minority even within their historic territory. (Consider the fate of Indian tribes and Chicanos in the American South-West). Decisions about public holidays and school curriculum also typically reflect and help perpetuate a particular national culture.

In short, there are many ways that government decisions play a crucial role in sustaining national cultures. If a national group has full language rights, and control over immigration, education, and resource development policy, then its long-term viability is secured. If it lacks these rights and powers, its long-term viability is in grave jeopardy. So if national minorities do not wish to assimilate, they must struggle to gain those rights and powers, either through secession or regional autonomy. Since national majorities have historically been very reluctant to accept the demands of national minorities, the result is long-standing national divisions, sometimes flaring into nationalist violence.

This is true even in states which consciously avoid an 'expressive' role. Tamir would like states to be more explicit about affirming a national identity—e.g. entrenching an official language in their constitution. But even in a country like the United States that avoids this symbolic trapping of nationalism, the problem for national minorities remains. What matters are not symbols, but the facts on the ground—i.e. whether a national minority has sufficient control over decisions regarding language, education, immigration, and economic development to ensure its long-term viability (see Ch. 4).

The failure of liberalism to understand nationalism is directly related to its failure to acknowledge these unavoidable connections between state and culture. The myth that the state can simply be based on democratic principles, without supporting a particular national identity or culture, has made it impossible to see why national minorities are so keen on forming or maintaining political units in which they are a majority. Indeed, as Ernest Gellner noted, once we recognize the inevitable links between state and culture, the question is not so much why nationalist movements arise, but why there aren't more of them.

13

The Paradox of Liberal Nationalism

Nationalists are renowned for seeing plots against their national honour and national interests, and for assuming that others are insensitive to their national aspirations. Quebec nationalists are no exception to this. The former premier of Quebec, Lucien Bouchard, has developed this paranoia into an art form, finding an insult to Quebec in virtually any statement or policy of the federal government, however innocuous on the surface. But as the old saying goes, 'just because you are paranoid doesn't mean they aren't out to get you'. I would not say that most English-speaking Canadians are out to 'get' Quebec, but I do believe that most English-speaking Canadians are indeed insensitive to, or uncomprehending of, Quebec nationalism. Most English-speaking Canadians do not take seriously the implications of the fact that the Québécois view themselves as a 'nation'.

This failure became clear to me, surprisingly enough, when I was working on the staff of the Canadian Royal Commission on New Reproductive Technologies. The Commission received hundreds of submissions from the across the country—from professional medical organizations, women's groups, infertile couples, Catholic and pro-life groups, community health organizations, groups representing people with disabilities, and so on—and I had the task of reading through all of them. This quickly became rather tedious, because pro-life activists say the same thing whether they come from Moncton, Toronto, or Vancouver, as do community health advocates or patients' support groups. The rhetoric, the reasoning and the recommendations of each of these groups was utterly consistent from one end of the country to the other.

Except for Quebec. Outside of Quebec, there was a virtually unanimous desire for federal regulation of new reproductive technologies, such as in vitro fertilization, donor insemination, or embryo experimentation. In Quebec, by contrast, most groups assumed that provincial governments should set the basic rules. This disagreement over jurisdiction reflected an even deeper difference in attitudes towards federalism. Most groups from English-speaking Canada paid no attention to the fact that Canada is a federal system. For them, the assumption that NRTs should be regulated at the national level was not even seen as controversial. English-speaking Canadians

A review of Joseph Carens (ed.) *Is Quebec Nationalism Just? Perspectives from Anglophone Canada* (McGill-Queen's University Press, Montreal, 1995).

simply took it for granted that since NRTs raise important social and ethical issues, they ought to be dealt with at the national level, rather than having each province set its own policy. Few groups made any effort to show that the federal government had any legitimate jurisdiction over this area, even though health care is in fact one of the clearest cases of provincial jurisdiction.

What this shows, I think, is that most English-speaking Canadians have no real commitment to federalism in the classic sense—that is, to a system in which provincial and federal governments are co-equal, in that both have inherent sovereign powers which the other level of government cannot intervene in. In a true federal system, there are certain issues on which the federal government simply has no legitimate authority. Yet English-speaking Canadian groups never questioned whether the federal government had the authority to establish the sort of national licensing scheme for the providers of NRTs that already exists in Britain or France. Groups debated the merits of different regulatory schemes, but the idea that the federal government might be constitutionally prohibited from establishing such a scheme was never even considered. Of course, one might think it unreasonable for such groups to be familiar with the arcane points of federal jurisdictions. But the fact that these jurisdictional issues seem arcane to many English-speaking Canadians is itself evidence of how far the federalist ideal has receded from their political consciousness.

When most English-speaking Canadians think about federalism, they typically think of it simply as a form of decentralization. Because Canada is a large and diverse country, we have decentralized certain decisions to lower levels, including provincial governments. But this distribution of powers is largely seen as a matter of efficiency, rather than entrenched principle. Moreover, decentralization may work best by giving powers to local governments rather than provincial governments. Indeed many of those groups who favoured national standards for NRTs also favoured a radical decentralization of health care administration away from provincial bureaucracies to regional or community health councils, leaving provincial governments with little role in either establishing or administering policy. For most English-speaking Canadians, then, powers are contingently decentralized in various ways, but the federal government is assumed to have a kind of ultimate authority over all issues. So if something really important arises—like NRTs—it is right and proper for the federal government to intervene and establish national standards.

The Royal Commission itself, to its credit, recognized that the jurisdictional issues were more complicated. Yet it too endorsed a federal regulatory regime. The Commission's argument involved an extraordinary interpretation of the 'peace, order and good government' clause of the old BNA Act, which allows federal intervention in provincial affairs in cases of urgent and overriding national importance. This convoluted legal argument can be seen, generously, as a bold attempt to respond to the overriding desire of Canadians (outside Quebec) to have national regulation of NRTs. But it also reflects the typical English-speaking Canadian indifference to federalist principles. Federalism, from this point of view, is a legal formality whose anachronistic barriers can always be overcome by marshalling ingenious legal arguments.

It is this attitude towards federalism that drives Quebec nationalists up the wall. And they see this same attitude in many other areas—most notably, in the repatriation of the constitution and the adoption of the Charter of Rights in 1982 without Quebec's consent. The debate in Quebec is often described as a conflict between 'federalists' and 'nationalists'. But many Quebec nationalists argue, with some justification, that they are the only true federalists left. They argue that federalism could have provided a satisfactory form of national self-determination for Quebec, but that the English-speaking Canadian indifference towards (true) federalism has made sovereignty the only way to ensure respect for Quebec's national aspirations.

Does this attitude amongst English-speaking Canadians reflect a desire to oppress Quebec, or to impose English-Canadian values on the Québécois? I don't think so. Most English-speaking Canadians assume that the Québécois share the same basic concerns and principles. Hence adopting national standards, even in areas of provincial jurisdiction, is seen as promoting shared values, not as imposing one group's values on another. And, in a sense, English-speaking Canadians are correct to make this assumption. For example, there was no evidence whatsoever in the Commission's public consultations that Quebecers differed from other Canadians in their attitudes regarding the appropriate use of NRTs. Fifty years ago, one would have expected Quebecers to adopt a distinctive attitude towards reproductive technologies, based on Catholic teaching regarding the evils of contraception, abortion, and donor insemination. But not today. And indeed none of the Quebec groups who favoured provincial jurisdiction did so in the name of cultural differences. If Quebec were to adopt its own regulatory regime regarding NRTs, there is every reason to think it would be based on the same norms and principles as in English-speaking Canada. How then can a single national regulatory regime be seen as oppressive to Quebec, rather than uniting all Canadians through the promotion of shared values?

And here we get to the paradox which is at the heart of the Quebec–Canada relationship, and which is the background for the essays in Carens's volume. Quebec nationalists have become more and more preoccupied with maintaining and enhancing their provincial jurisdiction even as they have become more and more similar to other Canadians in their basic values. They have become more and more insistent on recognition as a 'distinct society', even as they in fact become less and less distinct. Quebecers now live in the same secularized, liberal-democratic, pluralist, urbanized, consumerist culture as English-speaking Canadians, worshipping the same ideals of individual liberty and democratic equality. Public opinion polls have repeatedly shown that there are no statistically significant differences between Quebecers and other Canadians in basic values, including 'moral values, prestige ranking of professions, role of the government, workers' rights, aboriginal rights, equality between the sexes and races, and conception of authority' (Dion 1991: 301). If anything, Quebecers actually score higher on measures of individualism than English-speaking Canadians (Webber 1994: 50). How then can national policies based on these shared values—whether relating to NRTs or to the Charter of Rights—be seen as oppressive or insulting to Quebec?

It is this 'paradox' which explains, at least in part, the impasse in Canada–Quebec relations. Apart from a few bigots, the overwhelming majority of English-speaking Canadians have no desire to 'get' Quebec, or to insult Quebecers. But they simply do not understand why Quebecers would feel insulted by the adoption of a common national NRT policy—or a common Charter of Rights—so long as these are based on shared values.

Faced with this paradox, two responses are possible. One is to avoid the paradox by assuming that Quebec nationalism must, after all, be illiberal. On this view, the apparent shift in Quebec political culture towards secular liberal pluralism is simply skin-deep, and the demand for greater provincial autonomy reveals a deeper, covert desire to retreat from modernity and recreate a more closely-knit and intense communal life, based on shared ethnicity, history and religion. This view denies that a truly liberal nationalism is possible—the desire for national recognition and autonomy by Quebec proves that they do not in fact share the liberal values of other Canadians.

The other response is to accept that the paradox of liberal nationalism is real, and will not go away. The essays in Carens's collection all adopt this second response. They accept that Quebec nationalism is fundamentally driven by a forward-looking conception of Quebec as a pluralistic, liberal modern society, rather than a backward-looking communitarian or conservative ideology.

The claim that modern Quebec nationalism is a fundamentally liberal movement is hardly novel. However, the essays in this collection go beyond this familiar claim in two ways. First, they aim to delineate more carefully how liberal and national principles interact in a liberal nationalist movement such as Quebec's. Second, they aim to explain why the existence of shared liberal values has not solved, or even reduced, the conflicts between Quebecers and the rest of Canada.

Some of the essays focus on particular issues in which liberal and national values interact—for example, Joseph Carens discusses Quebec's immigration policy ('Immigration, Political Community, and the Transformation of Identity: Quebec's Immigration Policies in Critical Perspective'); Howard

Adelman focuses on refugee policy ('Canada, Quebec and Refugee Claimants'), and on secession ('Quebec: The Morality of Secession'); and Reg Whitaker focuses on Aboriginal rights in Quebec ('Quebec's Self-Determination and Aboriginal Self-Government: Conflict and Reconciliation?'). In each case, the authors show that Quebec nationalists are guided by the project of building a 'distinct society' based on the 'French Fact'—that is, building and reproducing a prosperous and institutionally complete society whose public life is conducted in French. Yet in each case, the pursuit of this goal is shaped and limited by liberal principles.

For example, as Carens notes, immigrants are expected to learn French, and indeed this is an important criterion by which they are selected. But this applies only to public life, leaving ample room for the expression of heritage languages in private life and ethnic associations. Indeed the Quebec government encourages and funds this use of heritage languages. Moreover, the acceptance of French as a public language does not entail accepting any moral claim about the necessity of 'la survivance'. While French is the language of political debate, one of the things that can be publicly debated is precisely whether or not to continue endorsing the project of building a distinct society. And while Quebec can select immigrants who speak French, it does not employ racially or religiously discriminatory criteria in order to select francophone immigrants from groups which are perceived to be more assimilable to Québécois society (e.g. choosing Christians over Muslims, or whites over blacks). In all of these cases—and others that Carens discusses—liberal principles have constrained the pursuit of national goals in immigration policy (cf. Ch. 15). Promoting the distinct society might be more successful if language laws applied to private life, or if naturalization depended on swearing allegiance to Québécois nationalist ideals, or if racial or religious discrimination were used in the selection of immigrants. But a liberal society is premised on freedom of conscience, principles of non-discrimination, and a robust zone of privacy, and a liberal nationalism must respect these limits.

Adelman's account of refugee policy provides another instructive example. As he notes, while the Quebec government has sought greater power over the selection of immigrants, it has not demanded jurisdiction over the acceptance of refugees who arrive seeking asylum. Yet these refugees account for 15 per cent of overall immigration. Why then hasn't Quebec sought to establish its own refugee policy, akin to its immigration policy, in order to better promote its distinct society? The answer, according to Adelman, is that Quebecers accept that the human rights of refugees take precedence over the pursuit of national goals. Genuine refugees who arrive on our shores are entitled to asylum, and it would simply be immoral for Quebec to accept or reject them based on whether they are seen as likely contributors to the 'distinct society' project. Since the granting of asylum is not an appropriate arena for pursuing national goals, Quebec has not sought jurisdiction over this issue.

Of course, no one can deny that there are residual illiberal elements within Quebec society, as there are in the rest of Canada. But according to Carens, Adelman, and Whitaker, if we examine the policies and pronouncements of mainstream Quebec nationalists towards a range of issues, they fit this pattern of pursuing national goals within the constraints of liberal norms.

But if Quebec nationalists are motivated by liberal norms, why has it proved so difficult to accommodate Quebec nationalism? If we all share the same basic liberal democratic principles, why are we constantly in danger of falling apart as a country? Some commentators argue that Quebec nationalism has eroded the basis of Canadian federalism. Demands that Quebec be recognized as a 'nation' or a 'distinct society', not simply as one province amongst others, are seen as inconsistent with basic federalist principles of provincial equality. However, the essays by Robert Vipond ('From Provincial Autonomy to Provincial Equality [Or, Clyde Wells and the Distinct Society]') and Janet Ajzenstat ('Decline of Procedural Liberalism: The Slippery Slope to Secession') suggest that the erosion of Canadian federalism occurred earlier, and at the hands of the federal government and English-speaking Canada. Vipond and Ajzenstat argue, as I suggested earlier, that it was the rest of Canada which abandoned earlier federalist principles in favour of a more unified conception of the Canadian political community.

According to Vipond, an earlier doctrine of 'provincial autonomy', which emphasized the independent and inherent powers of provinces as parties to the agreement of federation, has been replaced in English-speaking Canada by a doctrine of 'provincial equality', which emphasizes the importance of equal representation for provinces in the Senate, and of equal legislative powers for all provinces. The earlier doctrine emphasized equality between the provinces and the federal government—in the sense that neither level of government was subordinate to the other—but was relatively unconcerned about differences between provinces. Indeed, such differences were to be expected in light of the very different circumstances facing each province, and the broad autonomy that each province exercised. The latter doctrine emphasizes equality amongst provinces—in the sense that each province should be identical in its rights and powers—but is relatively unconcerned about asserting provincial jurisdiction vis-à-vis the federal government. Indeed, influential exponents of provincial equality (e.g. Clyde Wells) have sometimes favoured a strongly centralized federation. Vipond suggests that this new rhetoric of provincial equality has radically changed (and 'hobbled') constitutional debate in Canada. According to Vipond, the 'older understanding of liberal federalism' had the right focus. It emphasized the need for the federal government to respect provincial autonomy, and for the provincial government to respect individual rights, but was tolerant of the inevitable differences which arose between provinces in their legislative representation and powers. The newer understanding of provincial equality, by contrast, shifts attention away from the importance of provincial autonomy, and focuses instead on relations between provinces. Moreover, it turns all of these differences between provinces—including those special provisions for Quebec which date back to Confederation—into sources of 'privilege' and 'inequality'. It thereby turns federalism into a tool for opposing Quebec's national aspirations, rather than a possible vehicle for accommodating them.

Janet Ajzenstat provides a different, though complementary, account of the erosion of Canadian federalism. She focuses on the gradual erosion of what she calls 'the procedural constitution'—that is, the idea that the constitution should simply set the ground rules for political debate, but should not entrench any particular political programme or ideology. The demand by Quebec nationalists for recognition as a 'distinct society' is an example of this erosion, since it involves an attempt to inscribe a certain substantive and controversial nationalist ideology in the constitution. But as Ajzenstat notes, this demand is itself a response to an earlier event—namely, the attempt by Pierre Trudeau to inscribe his pan-Canadian, anti-nationalist ideology in the Constitution, through the 1982 Constitution Act. According to Ajzenstat, the debate between Quebec nationalists who favoured territorial bilingualism and Quebec anti-nationalists who favoured sea-to-sea bilingualism used to be seen as a debate which was properly left to ongoing democratic debate. In 1982, however, Trudeau's anti-nationalist vision was given 'constitutional imprimatur'. And indeed many defenders of the 1982 Act defended it precisely because it would have this symbolic value of placing a pan-Canadian, anti-nationalist ideology above and beyond the fray of everyday politics. But once the door was opened to using the Constitution as a vehicle for advancing one's ideological views, the inevitable result was that many other groups—including Quebec nationalists—insisted that their vision also be given constitutional validation. The result was not only the 'distinct society' clause, but also the 'Canada clause', and then endless debates about how these clauses relate to each other, and to Trudeau's original Charter.

According to Ajzenstat, the net result of all this has been to undermine any confidence in the very idea of a neutral constitution that allows various political ideologies and interests to compete fairly and openly for public allegiance. Rather than seeing the constitution as standing above these political disputes, it is now seen as the most important forum for pursuing them. And since these competing ideologies cannot in fact all sit comfortably within the same constitution, the result has been endless constitutional frustration for Quebec nationalists, who now see secession as the only way to ensure that the constitutional rules of the game are not biased against them.

In effect, then, both Vipond and Ajzenstat argue that the demand for national recognition by Quebec has been made more urgent because English-speaking Canadians have abandoned an earlier understanding of federalism which was more accommodating of their national aspirations. They both express the hope that we could return to these earlier understandings, but are not optimistic that this will happen.

All of these articles are helpful in exploring the nature and limits of Quebec's liberal nationalism, and the conflicts it gives rise to. But, at another level, these articles do very little to resolve the paradox of liberal nationalism. Even if English-speaking Canadians have become largely indifferent to true federalism, why do Quebecers still care about it? If Quebecers now share the same liberal values as other Canadians, why object to national policies and political structures that embody these shared values? Why seek recognition as a distinct society when they no longer endorse distinct political principles?

This question is partially addressed in Wayne Norman's important article ('The Ideology of Shared Values: A Myopic Vision of Unity in the Multi-Nation State'). According to Norman, Quebec's liberal nationalism appears paradoxical because we've misunderstood the role of 'shared values' in unifying political communities. The assumption that shared values are the foundation of political unity is remarkably widespread. As Norman shows, it is found not only in general public debate, but also in academic political theory. And it has provided the foundation of the federal government's nation unity strategy for the last few years. (Recall the 1991 *Shared Values: The Canadian Identity* pamphlet which accompanied its constitutional proposals—Government of Canada 1991). Focusing attention on all the values we share in common is supposed to make Canadians—English, French, or Aboriginal—happy to be a part of the same political community.

But as Norman notes, if we look around the world, this strategy is simply a non-starter. Shared political principles by themselves do not provide a reason for two or more national groups to stay together in one country. For example, there is a remarkable convergence of political principles between the citizens of Norway and Sweden, but is this any reason for them to regret the secession of Norway in 1905? Norman does not think so. The fact that they share the same principles doesn't, by itself, explain why they should want to live together under one state. After all, each nation can pursue those principles in its own nation-state—remaining separate states does not require them to abandon their shared principles.

Similarly, the fact that Quebecers and other Canadians share the same principles of justice is not a strong reason to remain together, since the Québécois rightly assume that their own national state could respect the same principles. The same applies to national minorities throughout the Western world. Consider Flanders in Belgium, or Catalonia in Spain, or Puerto Rico in the United States. In all of these places, national minorities have essentially adopted the same political values that characterize the majority culture. Yet in none of these cases has the presence of shared values diminished nationalist movements.

This suggests that shared political principles are not sufficient for political unity. The fact that two national groups share the same principles of liberal justice does not necessarily give them any strong reason to join (or remain) together, rather than remaining (or splitting into) two separate countries. If two national groups want to live together under a single state, then sharing political principles will obviously make it easier to do so. But sharing political principles is not, in and of itself, a reason why two national groups should want to live together.

What then does underlie political unity? Norman suggests that the key to political unity is not *shared political values*, but a *shared political identity*. People decide who they want to share a country with by asking who they identify with, who they feel solidarity with. What holds Americans together, despite their many disagreements, is the fact that they share an identity as Americans. Conversely, what keeps Swedes and Norwegians apart, despite their shared political principles, is the lack of a shared identity.

What then is the basis of shared identity? Unfortunately, Norman does not pursue this question. The answer presumably involves a mix of factors relating to language, territory, and historical bonds. The shared values account of political unity, with its emphasis on people's principles, is much too cerebral and rationalistic. In reality, political identity is much more contingent and affective. It develops over long periods of time, integrating groups of people on a particular piece of territory into a common political identity.

And the historical reality is that Quebecers have developed a strong sense of political identity. As a result, they want to act together as a political community—to undertake common deliberations, make collective decisions, and cooperate in political goals. They want to make these decisions with each other, not because their goals are different from other Canadians, or from Americans or Belgians, but because they have come to see themselves as members of the same society, and hence as having responsibilities to each other for the ongoing wellbeing of that society.

Indeed, Adelman suggests that this sense of political identity is so strong that, in an important sense, many Quebecers have already seceded from Canada. Many Quebecers, perhaps most, see their provincial political community as having the legitimate moral right to exercise sovereign authority over all areas of jurisdiction. They have exercised this sovereign authority in part by delegating powers upwards to other levels of government, such as the federal government or the UN, and downwards to municipal and regional governments. But for many Quebecers, the legitimate authority of these other levels of government depends on the ongoing consent of Quebecers as a provincial community, which retains the moral right to revoke the delegation and reassert its inherent sovereignty.[1] According to Adelman, insofar as many Quebecers view their province as forming this sort of sovereign political community, morally if not legally, then they have already *de facto* seceded from Canada, even though they remain legal citizens of Canada.

Understanding the nature and strength of this political identity is, I think, the crucial step towards resolving the paradox of liberal nationalism. It may seem puzzling that Quebecers have such a strong sense of political identity. But once we recognize the fallacy of the 'shared values' approach to political unity, then we can see that the same question can be asked of English-speaking Canadians. Why, for example, are English-speaking Canadians so keen to have national standards relating to NRTs? The answer can't be that they share common political values, since that doesn't in fact explain why they prefer federal to provincial regulation. Provinces can act on these shared values just as easily as the federal government can.

Instead, the answer surely is that English-speaking Canadians have over time developed their own strong sense of forming a (pan-Canadian) political community. And so they want to act collectively as a political community, not simply as separate provinces. They want to deliberate together, and to make collective decisions, and to create and uphold collective institutions. That is, they too want to act as a nation.

Of course, the national identity that English-speaking Canadians have developed is pan-Canadian, including Quebec. Few English-speaking Canadians would describe their nation as being 'English Canada'. And this is why English-speaking Canadians view federal legislation as pivotal to expressing their national identity. Federal regulation of NRTs would allow English-speaking Canadians to express their collective political identity, and to fulfil their deeply felt sense of collective responsibility for each other and for their shared society. The problem, of course, is that (true) federalism puts serious limits on the extent to which English-speaking Canadians can act on this national identity. The only way for English-speaking Canadians to act collectively in an area like NRTs is to undermine the federal principles that have made it possible for Quebecers to act collectively.

In other words, the impasse in Quebec–Canada relationships is not simply that Quebecers have developed a strong sense of political identity that is straining the bonds of federalism. The problem is also that Canadians outside Quebec have developed a strong sense of pan-Canadian political identity that strains the boundaries of federalism. Moreover, both of these political identities are complex and deeply-rooted psychological phenomena, grounded in

---

[1] As I discussed in Ch. 5, this perception of legitimacy is likely to be a feature of many multi-nation federations. In a genuinely multination federation, the constituent national groups are likely to see the legitimacy of the central government as dependent on their historic and ongoing consent. This attitude does not reflect secession from a multination federation, but rather is part of the fabric of such federations.

history, territory and social interactions. There is a popular myth amongst many liberals that whereas Quebec's political identity is grounded in irrational factors such as language and history, English-speaking Canada's political identity is grounded in a rational commitment to principles of freedom and democracy. But the fact that English-speaking Canadians share a commitment to freedom and democracy does not explain their deeply felt desire to act as a single pan-Canadian collectivity, rather than as separate provinces. This too is a contingent and affective desire rooted in a shared sense of belonging and membership that has transcended provincial boundaries.[2]

This suggests that if we are to unravel the paradoxes of Quebec's national identity, we need to look more honestly at the development of English-speaking Canada's political identity. For both of these identities are now straining the bonds of federalism. It also suggests that if we are to find a lasting settlement to our constitutional predicament, we need to find a political arrangement that accommodates both of these political identities. We need to find a form of federalism that allows Quebec to act on its sense of national political identity, without preventing English-speaking Canadians from acting on their equally deeply felt desire to act collectivity, and not simply as discrete provinces.

---

[2] The same dynamic exists amongst the majority groups in other multination states as well. Thomas Franck lays the blame for the conflicts in multination states primarily on the minorities that are seeking greater autonomy and greater protection for their languages. He says that, by and large, minorities in democratic societies no longer face any injustice. While the Québécois suffered unjust discrimination fifty years ago, and while the Catalans suffered under Franco, they no longer have any basis for complaint. To pursue greater autonomy now, therefore, is simply an irrational form of identity-politics (Franck 1997). I disagree. I would argue that it is often the majority that exhibits an irrational commitment to an unrealistic and obsolete identity, refusing to accept the reality that they live in a multination state. The majority often clings to the myth of being a 'nation-state' whose citizens all share the same national identity. In all multination states, the identity politics of the majority is just as salient as the identity politics of the minority.

14

American Multiculturalism in the International Arena

Like citizens in many other countries, Americans have been debating issues of multiculturalism for several years. But the debate in the United States has a special importance because of the profound influence of American ideas around the world. Unfortunately, the international influence of American debates has not been entirely propitious. It has been beneficial for some issues, but unhelpful for others, serving to exacerbate rather than remedy important injustices. I'll try to explain why in this paper, and how this danger can be minimized.

1. American Multiculturalism

A wide range of views has been expressed in the American debate about multiculturalism, but I think we can see an emerging consensus, or at least a dominant paradigm, centred on the following three claims:

(a) Some or other form of multiculturalism is now unavoidable ('we are all multiculturalists now', as Nathan Glazer (1997) puts it), and that the interesting debate is not whether to adopt multiculturalism, but rather what kind of multiculturalism to adopt.

(b) the appropriate form of multiculturalism must be fluid in its conception of groups and group boundaries (i.e. it must accept that new groups may emerge, older groups may coalesce or disappear); voluntary in its conception of group affiliation (i.e. it must accept that individuals should be free to decide whether and how to affiliate with their community of descent); and non-exclusive in its conception of group identity (i.e. it must accept that being a member of one group does not preclude identification with another group, or with the larger American nation). Only such an open-ended, fluid and voluntary conception of multiculturalism fits with the fluid and open nature of American society, and its deep respect for individual freedom and choice.

(c) the greatest challenge to creating such a fluid conception of multiculturalism remains the disadvantaged and stigmatized status of African-

Americans. Being 'Black' is an ascribed identity which is difficult for most African-Americans to escape or renounce. The child of a Greek–Arab mixed marriage can choose whether to think of herself as a Greek-American or Arab-American or both or neither; the child of a Greek–African American mixed marriage will be seen by others as 'Black', whether or not that is how she wants to be seen. Moreover, the result of this ascribed identity is a greater degree of social exclusion and segregation than for other ethnic groups (i.e. Blacks are more likely to live in segregated neighbourhoods, attend segregated schools, and so on). The main challenge for American multiculturalism, therefore, is to reduce the ascriptive, stigmatizing and segregating elements of 'Black' identity, so that being Black can come to resemble the open, voluntary and fluid nature of other ethnic identities in America.

I accept these three claims. However, I worry about the way in which they have been defended. Too often, this open, fluid and voluntary conception of American multiculturalism has been explained and defended *in contrast to minority nationalism*. That is, when American authors explain what a closed, static, and involuntary conception of multiculturalism would look like, they typically point to cases of minority nationalism, whether in Quebec or Flanders, Yugoslavia, or Sri Lanka. This contrast confuses, rather than clarifies, debates about multiculturalism in America. More importantly, it is having a pernicious influence in other countries, inhibiting efforts to understand and accommodate minority nationalisms.

2. Hollinger's Postethnic America

Consider the recent work of David Hollinger, whose *Postethnic America* is the most sophisticated defence of the consensus view (Hollinger 1995). Hollinger distinguishes two kinds of multiculturalism: a 'pluralist' model which treats groups as permanent and enduring, and as the subject of group rights; and a 'cosmopolitan' model which accepts shifting group boundaries, multiple affiliations and hybrid identities, and which is based on individual rights. As he puts it: 'pluralism respects inherited boundaries and locates individuals within one or another of a series of ethno-racial groups to be protected or preserved. Cosmopolitanism is more wary of traditional enclosures and favours voluntary affiliations. Cosmopolitanism promotes multiple identities, emphasizes the dynamic and changing character of many groups, and is responsive to the potential for creating new cultural combinations' (3).

Hollinger strongly defends the latter cosmopolitan form—with its 'ideal according to which individuals decide how tightly or loosely they wish to affiliate with one or more communities of descent' (165)—while criticizing the former. He argues that this cosmopolitan model has worked well for white European immigrants to America in the past, and that it continues to work well for more recent immigrants from Latin America, Africa, and Asia. He recognizes that it will be more difficult to bring African-Americans (the descendants of the slaves, as distinct from new immigrants from Africa or the Caribbean) under this 'post-ethnic' umbrella. However, he insists that this sort of inclusion is what most Blacks want, and what justice requires, and that it remains an achievable goal, although certain special measures may be required (e.g. more targeted forms of affirmative action).

I am sympathetic to Hollinger's view about the appropriate form of multiculturalism in America. And I think it can work for immigrant groups in many other countries as well. Indeed, the official 'multiculturalism policy' adopted by the federal government in Canada in 1971 is largely inspired by this conception of how immigrant ethnicity should be handled. Some critics of this policy have argued it falls into Hollinger's 'pluralist' category, treating immigrant groups as fixed and self-contained entities. However, on inspection, it is clear that the multiculturalism policy in Canada, both in its intentions and its consequences, is much closer to Hollinger's 'cosmopolitan' version. It explicitly treats immigrant ethnocultural affiliation as voluntary, and encourages the members of different immigrant groups to interact, to share their cultural heritage, and to participate in common educational, economic, political and legal institutions. The long-term result of this approach has been a significant increase over the last thirty years in rates of interethnic friendships and intermarriages— higher than in the United States— and to the proliferation of shifting, multiple and hybridic identities.[1]

Like Hollinger, I think that the integration of immigrants into this fluid and hybridic form of multiculturalism is desirable, and quite a success story. And, like Hollinger, I think that this process can work not only for the older white immigrants from Europe, but also for more recent Arab, Asian, and Caribbean immigrants to the United States and Canada (see Ch. 9). I have defended this model of immigrant integration myself both in Canada (where it is already fairly strongly entrenched) and in Europe (where it remains strongly resisted). So on this issue, Hollinger's account of a post-ethnic America is a good model for other countries, and countries like Austria or Belgium could learn a great deal from it about the successful integration of immigrants.

My worry, however, is about the applicability of this model to non-immigrant groups, and in particular to those groups which have been conquered or colonized, like the Québécois or indigenous peoples in Canada. These 'nations within' were originally self-governing, and like other conquered or colonized peoples around the world, have consistently fought to gain (or rather regain) their autonomy, so as to maintain themselves as separate

---

[1] See Kymlicka 1998a for a defence of this claim; cf. Ch. 8.

and self-governing societies. They call themselves 'nations', and assert national rights. And indeed both the indigenous peoples and the Québécois do have substantial autonomy within Canada: the former through the system of self-governing Indian bands; the latter through the system of federalism.

Hollinger never explicitly addresses the question of the rights of colonized or conquered peoples within liberal democracies, or the legitimacy of the forms of minority nationalism adopted by such groups. But it is clear that he does not support minority nationalism, which he equates with the 'pluralist' conception of multiculturalism. For example, he says that his model rejects 'the notion of legally protected territorial enclaves for nationality groups' (91). He also states that pluralism differs from cosmopolitanism 'in the degree to which it endows with privilege particular groups, especially the communities that are well-established at whatever time the ideal of pluralism is invoked' (85). These passages implicitly reject the essence of minority nationalism in Canada or elsewhere. After all, the Québécois and indigenous peoples in Canada claim legally recognized rights of self-government over their traditional territories, and the justification for these claims is precisely that these societies were 'well established' prior to British dominion. Hollinger's theory seems to rule such nationalist claims out of court.

Hollinger is not just implicitly rejecting minority nationalism, he explicitly criticizes it as well. For example, he describes Québécois nationalism as the extreme form of 'pluralist' multiculturalism, since it treats the Québécois as a permanent and enduring group, and as the bearer of group rights. Indeed, he says it is a form of 'ethnic nationalism' (134), whose claims to self-determination are logically equivalent to racial segregation in the United States (131).

I think this reflects a misunderstanding of the nature of minority nationalism. To see this, it is helpful to first examine how minority nationalisms have historically been dealt with in Western democracies, including the United States.

3. Accommodating Minority Nationalism

How have Western democracies responded to such minority nationalisms? Historically, democracies have tried to suppress them, often ruthlessly. At various points in the eighteenth and nineteenth centuries, for example, France banned the use of the Basque and Breton languages in schools or publications, and banned any political associations which aimed to promote minority nationalism; Britain tried to suppress the use of Welsh; Canada stripped the Québécois of their French-language rights and institutions, and redrew political boundaries so that the Québécois did not form a majority in any province; Canada also made it illegal for Aboriginals to form political associations to promote their national claims. These measures were intended to disempower national minorities, and to eliminate any sense of their possessing a distinct national identity. This was justified on the grounds that minorities that view themselves as distinct 'nations' would be disloyal, and potentially secessionist.

However, attitudes towards minority nationalism have changed dramatically this century, from suppressing to accommodating their national claims. We can see this shift in most Western democracies that contain national minorities. For example, Canada adopted a federal system which gives the Québécois significant language rights and regional autonomy; both Canada and the Scandinavian countries accord self-government rights to indigenous peoples; and Belgium, Spain, and Britain have also moved recently in the direction of giving regional autonomy to their national minorities. In all of these countries, the goal of eliminating minority national identities has been abandoned, and it is now accepted that these groups will continue into the indefinite future to see themselves as separate and self-governing nations within the larger state.

In short, an increasing number of Western democracies that contain national minorities accept that they are 'multination' states, rather than 'nation-states'. They accept that they contain two or more nations within their borders, and recognize that each constituent nation has a valid claim to the language rights and self-government powers necessary to maintain itself as a distinct societal culture. And this multinational character is often explicitly affirmed in the country's constitution. Several multination states are also recognizing that these national rights are best protected through some form of federalism, since federalism allows the creation of regional political units, controlled by the national minority, with substantial (and constitutionally protected) powers of self-government. What we see emerging within several Western democracies, therefore, is a new form of 'multinational federalism'—i.e. a model of the state as a federation of regionally concentrated peoples or nations, in which boundaries have been drawn, and powers distributed, in such a way as to ensure that each national group is able to maintain itself as a distinct and self-governing societal culture. And, as I noted in Chapter 5, these multination federations are successful by basic liberal criteria: peace, democracy, individual freedom, economic prosperity, etc.

So Hollinger's critique of minority nationalism is out of step with the practice of other democracies. Nor does it reflect the American experience with minority nationalism. The US includes several groups which were colonized, and which think of themselves as 'nations within': e.g. Puerto Rico, the Chamoros of Guam, and American Indians. These are the paradigm cases of minority nationalism within the United States. (I do not include African-Americans, the descendants of slaves brought to America, as national minorities. Hollinger argues, and I agree, that most Blacks in the United States have never thought of themselves as a separate nation, but rather have fought for inclusion into the American nation.)

In dealing with its 'nations within', the US government has followed the same pattern we have seen in other Western democracies. In the nineteenth and early twentieth centuries, efforts were made to suppress these minority nationalisms. For example, when the United States conquered Puerto Rico, it tried to replace Spanish-language schools with English-language schools; and made it illegal to join political parties promoting independence. Similarly, Indian tribes endured a long series of policies (e.g. the Dawes Act) aimed at undermining their traditional institutions, and at breaking open Indian lands for colonizing settlers.

Today, however, these national minorities are treated in effect as 'nations'. Political units have been created in such a way as to enable them to form a local majority, and to exercise substantial rights of self-government on a territorial basis. They all possess a distinct political status (e.g. the Commonwealth of Puerto Rico; the domestic dependent nation status of Indians) not exercised by, or offered to, other territories or subunits of the United States.[2] In short, the US has dealt with minority nationalisms in much the same way other Western democracies have: first by attempting to suppress them, then by accommodating them through various forms of territorial self-government and special political status.

Hollinger says little about these cases of minority nationalism in the United States. This is understandable, since they are relatively peripheral, both geographically and numerically, in the American context. Yet they are important theoretically, because they represent the clearest cases where the US has confronted minority nationalism. And with respect to these groups, the US is indeed a multination state, a federation of distinct nations. The US treats these groups as permanent and enduring, and as the subject of group rights.

4. Post-ethnic Multiculturalism and Minority Nationalism

This raises a puzzle. If Hollinger is right that minority nationalisms are 'ethnic nationalisms' based on the primacy of blood and descent, why have liberal democracies started to accommodate them? The short answer is that Hollinger has misinterpreted the nature of these nationalist movements.

Consider Quebec. Quebec administers its own immigration programme, actively recruiting immigrants, most of whom are non-white. These immig-

---

[2] For discussion and references to national minorities in the US, see Ch. 5.

rants are not only granted citizenship under relatively easy terms, but are encouraged by Quebec's own 'interculturalism' policy to interact with the members of other ethnic groups, to share their cultural heritage, and to participate in common public institutions. The result is just the sort of fluid hybridic multiculturalism within Quebec that Hollinger endorses. Quebec is not unique in this. As I discuss in Chapter 15, the clear trend throughout most Western democracies is towards a more open and non-racial definition of minority nationalism.

Hollinger's argument reflects a common misconception about minority nationalism. There is a tendency to assume that minority nationalism is the extreme form of 'pluralist' multiculturalism, and hence diametrically opposed to cosmopolitan multiculturalism. In reality, however, these doctrines operate at different levels. Nationalism is a doctrine about the boundaries of political community, and about who possesses rights of self-government. Minority nationalists assert that as 'nations within', they have the same rights of self-government as the majority, and form their own self-governing political community. It is consistent with that view to insist that all nations—minority and majority—should be post-ethnic civic nations. This indeed is one way to understand the idea of *liberal* nationalism: liberal nationalism is the view that nations have rights of self-government, but that all nations, majority or minority, should be post-ethnic.

Insofar as it is guided by a liberal conception of nationhood, minority nationalism does not reject cosmopolitan multiculturalism: rather it is a doctrine about the unit within which cosmopolitan multiculturalism should operate. Should cosmopolitan multiculturalism operate within Canada as a whole, or Quebec? Within Spain as a whole, or Catalonia? Within the United States as a whole, or Puerto Rico? In none of these cases is the debate about the merits of post-ethnic multiculturalism; nor is it a debate between civic and ethnic nationalism. All of these nations, majority and minority, share a civic, post-ethnic model in Hollinger's sense. The debate is whether there is just one civic nation within the state, or more.

Hollinger's view seems to be that cosmopolitan multiculturalism should operate at the level of the state as a whole, not Puerto Rico, Quebec, or Catalonia. But he offers no reasons for this preference, perhaps because he has never considered the possibility that minority nations can also promote and embody a civic, post-ethnic form of nationalism.

Some people might argue that the appropriate unit for cosmopolitan multiculturalism is neither the state nor a sub-state level, but rather the world as a whole. On this view, states should have fully open borders, and put no obstacle to the mixing of peoples across state lines. This would be a genuinely 'cosmopolitan' form of multiculturalism. Hollinger himself rejects that view on the grounds that Americans form a nation, cherish their national identity, and have a right to maintain it into the indefinite future. That is, he treats

Americans as a permanent and enduring group which exercises rights of self-government, and insists that his 'cosmopolitan' conception of multicultural-ism operate within the stable boundaries of American nationhood. (In this respect, his preferred model of multiculturalism is more accurately called 'pan-American' than 'cosmopolitan'.) He denies that there is any contradic-tion in affirming a fluid and shifting form of multiculturalism within the stable and enduring boundaries of a nation.

I agree with Hollinger that 'the cosmopolitan element in multiculturalism is compatible with a strong affirmation of American nationality' (151). But it is also compatible with the strong affirmation of Puerto Rican or Québécois nationality. If Québécois nationalism is 'pluralist' because it implies that mul-ticulturalism should operate within the stable and enduring boundaries of a Quebec nation, then so too is the American nationalism that Hollinger defends. Both involve the same combination of fluid multiculturalism within stable national boundaries. And I can see no possible liberal justification for saying that Americans have a right to national existence, but not Puerto Ricans or Québécois.

5. Does it Matter?

But why does this matter? After all, minority nationalism is peripheral to Hollinger's book, mentioned only in a few passing references. Moreover, the book was written for a domestic audience, like many other recent American books that make passing references to minority nationalism. These refer-ences may be misleading or inaccurate, but have they really influenced other countries?

I believe they have. Let me give two examples: Canada and Eastern Europe. English-speaking Canadians have been heavily influenced by American debates, and one consequence of this has been a reluctance to accord the Québécois the sort of public recognition of their national identity that they seek.[3] The American influence has made it more difficult to come to an acceptable settlement with Quebec, even though, as I noted earlier, the United States itself was quite willing to extend this sort of national recogni-tion to Puerto Rico. If American writers had emphasized that it was a part of

---

[3] In a recent article, David Bromwich suggested that Charles Taylor's essay on 'Multiculturalism and the Politics of Recognition' is 'in some ways a Canadian sermon to Americans' (Bromwich 1995: 96). I think this is a misunderstanding. Taylor's lecture is better understood as a sermon to (Americanized) English-speaking Canadians, and his argument is not that American-style liberalism is wrong for most groups in the US, but rather that it is wrong for countries like Canada whose central dilemma is how to deal with minority nation-alisms.

the American practice to accommodate minority nationalisms, then I believe that Quebecers today would not be so close to seceding from Canada.

The situation in Eastern Europe is even more serious. If Quebec were to secede, the result would probably be two relatively stable liberal democracies in the northern half of the continent, instead of one. In Eastern Europe, however, the inability to accommodate minority nationalism is a threat, not just to existing boundaries, but to democracy itself, and to the existence of a peaceful civil society. There is strong correlation between democratization and minority nationalism: those countries without significant minority nationalisms have democratized successfully (Czech Republic; Poland; Hungary; Slovenia); those countries with powerful minority nationalisms are having a much more difficult time (Slovakia; Ukraine; Romania; Serbia; Macedonia).

Given this context, the influence of American debates has been unhelpful in two ways. First, it has helped to marginalize the liberal intellectuals within these countries, who often look to American liberals for guidance. Influenced by American models, these liberals have little to say about the accommodation of minority nationalism, except to chant the mantra that the solution to ethnic conflict is 'individual rights not group rights'. This is an unhelpful slogan since it tells us nothing about how to resolve the issues raised by minority nationalism. The current conflict in Kosovo, for example, revolves around whether political power should be centralized in Belgrade or whether the regional government in Kosovo should have extensive autonomy. The slogan 'individual rights not group rights' provides no guidance about this conflict. Without any clear conception of what justice requires in a multination state, liberals have become passive spectators in the struggles between majority and minority nationalists.

Second, American debates have, paradoxically, been invoked by majority nationalists to justify suppressing minority nationalisms. Nationalist governments in these countries have not only studied, but also largely adopted the American rhetoric that a good liberal democracy should be a 'civic nation'. They adopt the language of liberal democracy and civic nationalism partly to impress foreign observers, but also because it provides an excuse to crush minority nationalism, and to strip national minorities of their separate public institutions and rights of self-government. We see this trend in Slovakia, Romania, Serbia, and Russia. It may be surprising to hear majority nationalists adopt the language of civic nationalism, but they do. And they do so precisely *because* it legitimizes policies that inhibit national minorities from expressing a distinct national identity and demanding national rights.

What we see in Eastern Europe, therefore, is an unholy alliance of liberal intellectuals and majoritarian nationalists, both of whom invoke American models to justify rejecting the claims of national minorities. As I noted earlier, attempts to suppress minority nationalism can only be achieved by coercion, and the result has been to create fear amongst the minorities, to exacerbate interethnic relations, and to strengthen authoritarian tendencies within both the majority and minority nationalist movements.

Of course, American writers have not endorsed coercive policies aimed at suppressing minority nationalism in Eastern Europe. On the contrary, American foreign policy has often encouraged states to accept some minority claims. Indeed, the American government is currently pressing Serbia to accord autonomy to Kosovo. But Milosevic understandably sees this as hypocrisy, as yet another case of America trying to impose a settlement on weaker countries that it would never accept at home. After all, don't Americans say that we should fight against ethnic minority nationalism and instead seek to build a single, shared civic nation within each state?

The American position on Kosovo might have more credibility if Americans emphasized that they have accommodated their own minority nationalisms. This is just one of many examples in which the transition to democracy in the multination states of Eastern Europe would have been smoother had American writers and statesmen emphasized that accommodating minority nationalism was part of the American reality. I am not suggesting that American theorists of multiculturalism put issues of minority nationalism at the centre of their theories. The situation of Blacks is, and should be, at the heart of American debates about multiculturalism. But I wish that, if only in passing, Americans would admit that accommodating minority nationalism, far from being un-American or undemocratic, is one (small) part of the American experience.[4]

---

[4] For a more in-depth discussion of how Western models for accommodating minority nationalism relate to Eastern Europe, see Kymlicka and Opalski: 2001.

15

Minority Nationalism and Immigrant Integration

Virtually every recent discussion of minority nationalism has begun by emphasizing that its survival and resurgence was not predicted by theorists of modernization and globalization. Globalization was supposed to extinguish minority national identities, to be replaced either by a supra-national cosmopolitan identity, or by a post-national civic or constitutional identity. This prediction has been clearly proven wrong. Most minority nationalisms are as strong now as ever before, and show no sign of losing steam. Indeed, minority nationalism is today a truly global phenomenon, found in every corner of the globe. As Walker Connor puts it, powerful minority nationalisms can be found:

in Africa (for example, Ethiopia), Asia (Sri Lanka), Eastern Europe (Romania), Western Europe (France), North America (Guatemala), South America (Guyana), and Oceania (New Zealand). The list includes countries that are old (United Kingdom) as well as new (Bangladesh), large (Indonesia) as well as small (Fiji), rich (Canada) as well as poor (Pakistan), authoritarian (Sudan) as well as democratic (Belgium), Marxist-Leninist (China) as well as militantly anti-Marxist (Turkey). The list also includes countries which are Buddhist (Burma), Christian (Spain), Moslem (Iran), Hindu (India), and Judaic (Israel) (Connor 1999: 163–4).

There are still those who deny that minority nationalism is compatible with modernity, and who view these manifestations of minority nationalism as the last gasp of pre-modern values, fighting a defensive rearguard action against the inevitable forces of globalization (e.g. Franck 1997). But it is increasingly realized, I think, that minority nationalism has survived and thrived because it has proved able to adapt itself to modernity, and to accommodate and satisfy modern needs and aspirations. Indeed, minority nationalism has proved to be an effective vehicle by which national groups can modernize their societies, and participate more actively in the global economy and in the increasingly dense networks of international law and civil society.

To be sure, globalization does raise many new challenges for minority nationalism, and this chapter will focus on one of these: the impact of immigration. Discussions of globalization typically focus on the dramatic increase in the global movement of goods and capital, and perhaps also on the global circulation of ideas. But a less noted aspect of globalization is the movement of people, particularly the significant increase in the numbers of economic migrants. This has indeed been called the 'age of migration', as people from poorer countries, or from rural areas within a country, migrate to the burgeoning cities in the West which are the nexus of the global economy (Castles and Miller 1993). And some of these cities are located in the heartland of national minorities: Montreal (Quebec), Barcelona (Catalonia), Bilbao (Basque Country), Glasgow (Scotland), Brussels (Flanders), Geneva (French-speaking Switzerland). Some of these cities have been magnets for immigrants for decades, others are only recently seeing significant numbers of immigrants. But immigration is becoming an increasingly important reality of the major cities within the territory of national minorities.

How does the presence of these immigrants affect minority nationalist movements? There has been a great deal of discussion of both minority nationalism and immigration in recent years. As a result, we have learned a number of important lessons about the challenges that these two forms of ethnocultural diversity pose for the theory and practice of liberal democracy. However, these two topics have generally been discussed in isolation from each other; the interaction between them has received much less attention.

Since both minority nationalism and immigration challenge the traditional model of a culturally homogeneous 'nation-state', they are often treated as complementary but separate processes of deconstructing the nation-state. In reality, however, they are often intimately connected, and not always in complementary ways. Consider typical cases of minority nationalism in the West: Catalans, Basques, Puerto Ricans, Scots, Québécois, and Flemish. Each of these groups sees itself as a distinct and self-governing nation within a larger state, and has mobilized along nationalist lines to demand greater regional self-government and national recognition. However, the presence of significant numbers of immigrants into the minority's region is affecting the sort of national identity, and nationalist mobilization, which is feasible and/or desirable. Many minority nationalists have seen these changes as regrettable, and have viewed immigrants as a threat, rather than potential benefit, to the national minority.

Immigration, therefore, is not only a challenge to traditional models of the nation-state; it is also a challenge to the self-conceptions and political aspirations of those groups that see themselves as distinct and self-governing nations within a larger state. Indeed, some commentators insist that all forms of minority nationalism are by definition 'ethnic' or exclusionary, and hence inherently antagonistic to immigrants. This chapter will offer a more nuanced view of the relationship between immigration and minority nationalism. I will attempt to outline some of the issues that arise when immigrants settle in areas of a country dominated by a national minority. When are the claims of immigrants in conflict with the aspirations of national minorities, and when are they compatible or even mutually reinforcing? Since my background is in political theory, my main interest is in exploring the normative issues raised by this coexistence of immigration and minority nationalism. That is, I am interested not only in how the claims of immigrants and national minorities relate to each other, but also in how they relate to the underlying principles of liberal democracy, such as individual freedom, social equality, and democracy. Which sorts of accommodations or settlements amongst immigrants and national minorities are most consistent with liberal-democratic norms of justice and freedom, and which settlements would be unjust and in violation of these norms?

A growing number of liberal theorists defend both the claims of national minorities to self-government, and the claims of immigrant groups for greater accommodation of their ethnocultural identities and practices. However, as I noted, relatively little has been written discussing the potential conflict between these two sorts of claims. Yet these claims can and often do come into conflict: indeed, immigration of any sort has typically been seen as a threat to minority nationalism (section 1). Some commentators argue that this conflict is inherent and intractable, since minority nationalisms are by definition forms of 'ethnic nationalism' which are ethnically exclusive. I will argue that this view is empirically inaccurate regarding many minority nationalisms within the West, and rests on a misunderstanding of the nature of minority nationalism. Many minority nationalisms today welcome immigrants, and allow them to maintain and express their ethnic identity, while simultaneously encouraging their integration into the minority nation (section 2). Some minority nationalisms, in short, are as 'civic' or 'post-ethnic' as majority nationalisms. However, the likelihood that a national minority will adopt such a post-ethnic model of minority nationalism seems to depend on a number of factors. In particular, it may require a range of policies (e.g. regarding language, education, and employment) which give the minority some control over the process of immigrant integration, and which establish or protect the pre-eminence of the minority's language on its historic territory (section 3). And this creates a potential dilemma. For these linguistic and educational policies may be illiberal. The very policies that make a post-ethnic form of minority nationalism possible may themselves be inconsistent with liberal norms and values. If so, is it permissible to adopt illiberal policies in order to create the conditions under which civic forms of minority nationalism can emerge? I conclude with some tentative reflections on this question, but do not offer any definitive answers.

1. The Conflict between Immigrant Multiculturalism and Minority Nationalism

As I noted in Chapter 3, there is a clear trend in the West towards accepting the legitimacy of both minority nationalism and immigrant multiculturalism.

This is part of a larger movement towards liberal culturalism. And because both challenge the traditional model of a culturally homogeneous 'nation-state', they are often seen as allies, at least at the level of theory. They are both participants in the new politics of identity, both fighting to expand the room within which citizens can express their identities and diversities, and so share a commitment to principles of pluralism and the recognition of difference.

However, on the ground, the relation between the two is more complicated. As I noted earlier, the forces of globalization have meant that many multination states have experienced significant levels of immigration into the homeland of a national minority (e.g. Quebec, Flanders, Catalonia, Basque Country, Scotland). This has raised the question whether minority nationalisms can accommodate immigrant multiculturalism. Are national minorities capable of including immigrants in their self-conception, and thereby becoming themselves 'multicultural'?

At first glance, the answer may seem to be 'no'. The relation between national minorities and immigrants has historically been fraught with tension. Large-scale immigration has typically been seen as a threat to national minorities. For one thing, there is a strong temptation for immigrants to integrate into the dominant culture (which usually offers greater mobility and economic opportunities). Many immigrants to Quebec, for example, would opt to learn English rather than French, if given the choice. (This was certainly the historical pattern, until the Quebec government made it more difficult for immigrants to choose English.) And if immigrants in a multination state integrate into the majority group, the national minority will become increasingly outnumbered and so increasingly powerless in political life. Moreover, states have often deliberately encouraged immigrants (or migrants from other parts of the country) to settle in lands traditionally held by national minorities, as a way of swamping and disempowering them, reducing them to a minority even within their historic territory (see Ch. 4).

Moreover, the fact that immigrants seem able and willing to integrate into the dominant society is often used as grounds for insisting that national minorities also integrate. If immigrants can successfully integrate, the majority often asks, why not national minorities? If immigrants are satisfied with modest forms of multicultural accommodations within the larger society, rather than seeking self-government in order to maintain themselves as separate and distinct societies, why not national minorities?

In addition, immigrants are unlikely to understand or share the mentality of 'la survivance' which national minorities typically have developed in their many years (or centuries) of struggle to maintain their distinct language, culture and political autonomy. So even if immigrants do learn the minority's language and integrate into the minority's society, they are still unlikely to support nationalist mobilizations. They may join the minority nation, but they are unlikely to become minority nationalists.[1]

For these and other reasons, there has been a pronounced tendency for national minorities to adopt a defensive and exclusionary attitude towards immigrants. As a result, minority nationalisms have often taken the form of 'ethnic' nationalisms which privilege bonds of blood and descent, which are deeply xenophobic and often racist, and which seek to exclude immigrants.

Given this history, the idea that minority nationalism and immigrant multiculturalism are allies in the pursuit of a more pluralist or tolerant form of cultural politics seems odd. Rather than challenging or decentring pretensions of national homogeneity, minority nationalism seems, if anything, to be a reversion to a premodern, illiberal form of nationalism, even less tolerant of diversity than the sort of nationalism and national identity promoted by Western states.

This connection between minority nationalism and ethnic nationalism is so strong that many commentators view minority nationalism as *inherently* based on ethnic exclusiveness, and as inherently opposed to 'civic' nationalisms based on shared political principles. For example, Thomas Franck argues that minority nationalisms are illiberal and exclusive forms of 'tribal' nationalism, diametrically opposed to the liberal and open forms of civic American and French nationalism (Franck 1997). Similarly, David Hollinger equates minority nationalisms with illiberal 'pluralist' forms of multiculturalism which assign people to categories on the basis of blood, and which are therefore logically equivalent to racial segregation (Hollinger 1995). And Michael Ignatieff says that minority nationalisms are 'ethnic' nationalisms defined by race and blood, and therefore incompatible with liberalism, democracy and peace (Ignatieff 1993). These three authors differ in many respects, but what is striking is that all automatically assume that minority nationalists are ethnic nationalisms based on blood and race (see my discussion of these authors in Chs. 12 and 14).

For all of these authors, then, minority nationalism is an obstacle, not an ally, in the quest for a more tolerant and inclusive form of political community. It is not a partner with immigrants in the building of new forms of post-ethnic or post-national democracy, but rather is fighting a rearguard action to maintain an outdated form of ethnic nationhood.

---

[1] This is the situation in Quebec today. As a result of the policies described later in the chapter, Quebec has been quite successful in integrating immigrants into the French-speaking society. Moreover, many of these immigrants have come to think of themselves as 'Québécois', and feel a stronger sense of identification with Quebec than with Canada. But even these immigrants who identify as Québécois are extremely unlikely to support independence, and indeed in the 1995 referendum voted overwhelmingly against secession.

2. Can They be Reconciled?

This equation of minority nationalism and ethnic nationalism is understandable given the historical tensions I've mentioned earlier. But the assumption that minority nationalisms are inherently ethnic nationalisms is, I think, mistaken, and increasingly inadequate as an account of minority nationalisms in the West.

Consider Quebec. According to Franck, contemporary minority nationalisms exhibit a xenophobic desire to exclude those who are different. In reality, Quebec has a very pro-active immigration policy: its per-capita immigration is roughly the same as that of the United States. Control over immigration is one of the powers Quebec nationalists have sought and gained, and the province administers its own immigration programme, actively recruiting immigrants, most of whom are non-white. It seeks immigrants from all over the world as a way of building what it calls its 'distinct society'. Quebec knows that, due to declining birth rates and an aging population, it needs immigrants in order to succeed as a modern society. The Quebec government encourages immigrants to learn French, of course, just as the American government encourages immigrants to learn English. If they do learn French, they are seen as full members of Quebec society.[2]

To be sure, the issue of whether or how to integrate immigrants was a contentious one in Quebec for many years. But the approach it has developed since the 1970s—known as 'interculturalism'—is similar to the multiculturalism policy in many Western states: it seeks to affirm and accommodate ethnocultural identities and practices within common institutions, subject to three important principles:

- Recognition of French as the language of public life.
- Respect for liberal democratic values, including civil and political rights and equality of opportunity.
- Respect for pluralism, including openness to and tolerance of others' differences.

These three principles form the bedrock of the 'moral contract' between Quebec and immigrants that specify the terms of integration.[3] They are virtually identical to the principles underlying both the Australian and Canadian

[2] For a careful evaluation of Quebec's immigration policy, see Carens 1995b. He argues that Quebec's immigration policy 'is morally legitimate and fully compatible with liberal democratic principles'. Indeed, he concludes by saying that it may 'provide a model for other liberal democratic societies, particularly in Europe, of a way to combine a strong sense of national identity with a deep commitment to liberal democratic values' (p. 74).

[3] For a clear statement of these three principles, and the moral contract more generally, see Government of Quebec 1990.

multiculturalism policies, which are widely (and rightly) seen as two of the most successful models of immigrant multiculturalism in the world.[4]

Under this approach, immigrants are not only granted citizenship under relatively easy terms, but are encouraged by Quebec's own 'interculturalism' policy to interact with the members of other ethnic groups, to share their cultural heritage, and to participate in common public institutions. The result is just the sort of fluid 'cosmopolitan' multiculturalism within Quebec that Hollinger endorses. (Indeed, the level of acceptance of interracial marriage is considerably higher in Quebec than in the United States.) Far from trying to preserve some sort of racial purity, Quebec nationalists are actively seeking people of other races and faiths to come join them, integrate with them, intermarry with them, and jointly help build a modern, pluralistic distinct society in Quebec.

Quebec is not unique in this. Consider Catalonia. It has had a very high immigration rate, mainly from other regions in Spain. These immigrants have been welcomed and accepted as members of the Catalan society, and are seen as a vital part of the project of Catalan 'renaixença'. It is too early to tell how well the more recent immigrants from North Africa, who (unlike migrants from the rest of Spain) are neither European nor Catholic, will integrate. But it is the official policy of the Catalan government to promote the integration of all residents, whatever their religion or skin-colour, and this non-racialist conception of nationhood is backed by popular opinion.[5]

Or consider Scotland. It has not had the same level of immigration as Quebec or Catalonia, but here too a non-racialist conception of nationhood is firmly entrenched in both the platform of the main nationalist party (the SNP) and in popular opinion. Migrants from elsewhere in Britain have integrated well, and it is accepted that the more recent immigrants from Asia and Africa must also be accepted as 'Scots'.

Or consider Puerto Rico. It has had relatively few immigrants in the past, but now receives increasing number of people from the Caribbean. For most of these immigrants, Puerto Rico is initially seen as a stepping-stone to the continental US, but some stay and integrate into the Puerto Rican society. The idea of a non-racialist nation is, in this case, quite natural, since Puerto Rican society (unlike mainland US) has always been a self-consciously *mestizo* society with high levels of intermarriage between white settlers, blacks, and Indians (Portillo 1997).

---

[4] Compare with the discussion of Australian and Canadian multiculturalism in Ch. 8. For a more detailed comparison of Canadian multiculturalism and Quebec's interculturalism, see Juteau *et al.* 1998; Kymlicka 1998*a*: ch. 4. Of course, the Australian policy specifies English as the language of public institutions, and the Canadian federal policy defines both English and French as the languages of public life, and hence of schooling and advancement.

[5] For a discussion of attitudes to immigrants in Catalonia, see Medrano 1995, esp. 158–61.

All of these nationalisms are post-ethnic in Hollinger's sense. To be sure, not all minority nationalisms are post-ethnic: racialism remains a stronger force in both Basque and Flemish nationalism. In these cases, there is an ongoing struggle between a liberal/inclusive conception of nationhood and the racialist/exclusive conception, and this struggle is reflected both within the nationalist political parties and in popular opinion.[6] The liberal/inclusive conception, though a strong force in Flemish and Basque nationalism, is not yet hegemonic, as it has become in Quebec, Catalonia, or Scotland. We can find similar struggles between liberal/inclusive and racialist/exclusive conceptions in many cases of nationalist mobilization among indigenous peoples.

In short, the extent to which a particular form of minority nationalism is ethnic/racialist or post-ethnic/civic can only be determined by examining the facts, not by conceptual fiat or armchair speculation. And the clear trend throughout most Western democracies is towards a more open and non-racial definition of minority nationalism. In the case of Quebec, for example, the overwhelming majority of Quebecers forty years ago believed that to be a true 'Québécois' one had to be descended from the original French settlers; today, fewer than 20 per cent accept this view (Crête and Zylberberg 1991). This is a dramatic change in the nature of Québécois identity, which has indeed incorporated immigrants into its self-conception, and turned itself into a post-ethnic, multicultural nation. And this openness is recognized by immigrants, who are now much more inclined to integrate into Québécois society. For example, whereas the overwhelming majority of second-generation immigrants in Quebec used to become anglophones, now most think of themselves as 'Québécois', and are more likely to speak French than English at home. Unfortunately, most theorists of nationalism have not yet recognized this change: indeed, it has been rendered invisible by the assumption that minority nationalisms are inherently ethnic nationalisms.

Why has this shift towards a post-ethnic form of minority nationalism occurred? For essentially the same reasons it has occurred within majority

---

[6] For changes in Basque perceptions of immigrants, see Medrano 1995: 78–83, 150. In Flanders, the liberal/inclusive wing is represented by the Volks Unie party, the illiberal/exclusivist wing is represented by the Vlams Blok. Of course, the nature of the immigration differs in Flanders. Flanders has few migrants from other parts of Belgium (unlike Catalonia or Scotland), or indeed from elsewhere in Europe. Since most of the migrants to Flanders are from North Africa, they differ in their language, religion, and race from the native-born Flemish. By contrast, most migrants to Catalonia came from elsewhere in Spain, and so shared the same Catholic religion as the native-born Catalans, and were fellow (white) 'Europeans', differing primarily in their language. And in Scotland, most migrants came from England or Wales, so they shared a Protestant religion and English language with the Scots, as well as being seen as fellow Europeans. The integration process is easier when one or more of race, religion, and language is shared between the immigrants and the national minority. In this sense, the Flemish had the most difficult task of these various national minorities.

nations. Like majority nations, national minorities often need immigrants to fill economic niches, or to counterbalance negative demographic trends (i.e. an aging population and declining birth rate). Moreover, it has become clear that migration is difficult if not impossible to fully control, and that a certain level of immigration is certain to continue. Hence there is increasing interest amongst national minorities in the question of how to integrate immigrants into their 'nation'. This of course is the same question majority nations have had to face—e.g. how to integrate immigrants into the Dutch, Spanish, or Italian nation. And the answer that national minorities increasingly come up with is very similar to the approach adopted by majority nations. Both majority and minority nations are moving towards a conception of national identity which is post-ethnic and multicultural; both emphasize the linguistic and institutional integration of immigrants, while simultaneously accepting and accommodating the expression of immigrant ethnicity.

3. Rethinking the Terms of the Debate

The fact that minority nationalisms can be, and increasingly are, post-ethnic nationalisms that are open to immigrants raises a number of important policy questions, which I will discuss in section 4. But it also suggests that we need to dramatically rethink the way we think and talk about minority nationalism. We do not yet have the sort of conceptual framework we need to make sense of these new forms of post-ethnic minority nationalisms: too often we continue to rely instead on outdated myths and misconceptions.

For example, there is a tendency in the literature to assume that the conflicts raised by minority nationalisms within Western democracies are conflicts between a civic (post-ethnic) nationalism promoted by the state, and an ethnic (racialist) nationalism promoted by the national minority. In reality, however, in most Western democracies, these conflicts are between two competing forms of civic/post-ethnic nationalism. Both state nationalism and minority nationalism are defined in post-ethnic, non-racialist terms.[7] And insofar as these conflicts are between two forms of post-ethnic nationalism, I can no see no reason why liberals should automatically privilege majority or state nationalism over minority nationalism.

Second, there is a tendency to assume that if the majority nation is not defined in ethnic terms, but rather is a nation open to all regardless of ethnic descent, then minority nationalisms become inherently unnecessary and

[7] In some countries of Eastern Europe, by contrast, both sides to the conflict are forms of ethnic nationalism: state nationalism and minority nationalism are both defined in terms of ethnic descent. It is relatively rare to find a civic nationalism opposed to an ethnic nationalism: what we find are either civic vs. civic conflicts; or ethnic vs. ethnic conflicts.

pointless, except for those groups obsessed with racial purity. For example, Rogers Brubaker claims that:

it is difficult to assert a status as national minority in states such as the United States that do not have clear dominant ethnocultural nations. If the nation that legitimates the state as a whole is not clearly an ethnocultural nation but a political nation, open, in principle, to all, then the background condition against which the claim of national minority status makes sense is missing (Brubaker 1996: 60 n. 6)

The example of Puerto Rico in the United States—or of Quebec in Canada, Scotland in Britain, Corsica in France—shows that this analysis is deeply flawed. National minorities do not seek to maintain themselves as distinct societies because they are excluded on ethnic grounds from membership in the dominant nation. Rather, they mobilize as nations because they cherish their own national identity and national institutions, and wish to maintain them into the indefinite future. National minorities organize to defend their distinct society and culture whether or not they are eligible for inclusion in the dominant nation. We cannot make any headway in understanding minority nationalism within Western democracies unless we understand that it is not necessarily, or even typically, adopted as a compensation for exclusion from the majority nation. Rather, it is adopted because of an intrinsic commitment to the maintenance of the minority's own national identity, culture and institutions. Hence the fact that the majority nation is post-ethnic does nothing, in and of itself, to resolve or eliminate the claims of national minorities.

Third, there is a tendency to assume that because minority nationalism is concerned with ensuring the survival of a partcular national language and societal culture, it is diametrically opposed to what Hollinger calls 'cosmopolitan' or 'post-ethnic' multiculturalism where group identities and membership are fluid, hybridic and multiple. In reality, however, minority nationalism and cosmopolitan multiculturalism operate at different levels. Insofar as it is guided by a liberal conception of nationhood, minority nationalism does not reject cosmopolitan multiculturalism: rather it is a doctrine about the unit within which cosmopolitan multiculturalism should operate. Should cosmopolitan multiculturalism operate within Canada as a whole, or Quebec? Within Spain as a whole, or Catalonia? Within Britain as a whole, or Scotland? Within the United States as a whole, or Puerto Rico? In none of these cases is the debate about the merits of post-ethnic multiculturalism; nor is it a debate between 'civic' and 'ethnic' nationalism. All of these nations, majority and minority, share a post-ethnic model in Hollinger's sense. The debate is whether there is just one post-ethnic nation within the state, or more.

Fourth, there is a tendency in the literature to conflate two separate claims. The first claim is that in order to be legitimate, nationalisms must be post-ethnic. I agree with this claim, and have defended it myself. It is one of the defining features of a liberal nationalism. The second claim, however, is that a post-ethnic model of civic nationalism is inherently incompatible with the recognition of minority nationalism. This second claim is, I think, mistaken, and inconsistent with the practice of most Western democracies, including the United States.

Finally, we need to rethink the cliché that minority nationalisms are defensive protests against globalization and modernization. This cliché cannot account for the way some national minorities actively seek immigrants, or for the fact that national minorities often express greater support for free trade than majority groups. These movements are not defensive reactions against modernity. They are open societies—open to immigration and free trade, and to interacting with others more generally (see Ch. 12).

In short, the inherited view that minority nationalisms represent an illiberal, exclusive and defensive reaction to modernity is multiply mistaken, at least in the context of Western democracies. Some minority nationalisms represent a liberal, inclusive, and forward-looking embrace of modernity and globalization, and are potentially just as 'civic'/post-ethnic and cosmopolitan/hybridic as majority nationalisms. And as I noted earlier, liberal-democratic theory, as of yet, provides us with no clear guidelines for assessing or resolving conflicts between competing civic nationalisms within a state.

4. Unresolved Tensions

To say that many minority nationalisms are now post-ethnic is not to say that there aren't particular difficulties concerning the integration of immigrants into a minority nation. Indeed, it may be that special circumstances must be in place for such a post-ethnic multicultural form of minority nationalism to arise. First, it requires that the national minority exercise some control over the *volume* of immigration, to ensure that the numbers of immigrants are not so great as to overwhelm the ability of the society to integrate them. This is particularly important because, as I noted earlier, states have often encouraged immigrants (or migrants from other parts of the country) to move into the historical territory of the national minority. Such large-scale settlement policies are often deliberately used as a weapon against the national minority, both to break open access to their territory's natural resources, and to disempower them politically, by turning them into a minority even within their own traditional territory (McGarry 1998). To protect against these unjust policies, national minorities need and demand some control over the numbers of immigrants.

Second, it requires that the national minority exercise some control over the *terms of integration*. As I noted earlier, immigrants have obvious incentives to integrate into the majority society, if given the choice, and in many countries have historically tended to do so. This means that special policies may be needed to encourage or pressure immigrants to integrate into the minority's culture. For example, national minorities may demand that immigrants send their children to schools in the minority's language, rather than having the choice of majority or minority-language schooling. Similarly, the courts and public services may be conducted in the local language. These measures are intended to ensure that immigrants or migrants who settle in the region are willing to integrate into the local culture.

The measures to encourage integration may go even further. In Quebec, for example, a law was passed banning the use of languages other than French on outdoor commercial signs. This was intended to give Quebec a particular 'visage linguistique', in order to make clear to immigrants that French was indeed the language of public life. (This law was subsequently relaxed so that other languages in addition to French are allowed, but the law still requires that French be included on all commercial signs.)

These policies are sometimes criticized as illiberal. And perhaps they are. But here we reach a genuine dilemma. For such illiberal policies may be required if national minorities are to successfully integrate immigrants. Studies suggest that immigrants will only learn the minority language if it is seen as a 'prestige' language, as the language of economic success, political advancement or high culture. Immigrants will not learn a minority language if it is seen as the language of the working-class or of the countryside, as French was in Quebec prior to the 1960s. (Although anglophones were a minority in Quebec, they formed the business and media elite until the 1960s.) Immigrants will only integrate into a minority-language group if they see that the minority language is the language of business, politics, law, and high culture. The Quebec government has therefore systematically gone about increasing the 'prestige' of the French language. This has been done in part by subsidizing French-language services, education, and media; but also by stronger forms of pressure and coercion, including laws restricting access to English-language schooling; laws requiring the use of French on commercial signs; and laws giving employees the right to speak French in the workplace. The provincial government has set about creating a francophone elite in business, law, education, culture, and politics, precisely so as to make it attractive for immigrants to integrate into the francophone rather than anglophone societies.

These policies have often been interpreted as evidence of ethnic nationalism, as an attempt to create an ethnic hierarchy in which the descendants of the original French colonists stand above all other ethnic groups. But that is quite misleading. In reality, these policies have been adopted, at least in part, precisely in order to shift Québécois nationalism from an ethnic to a post-ethnic form of nationalism. The nationalist leaders wanted to attack the older ethnic model of nationhood, and wanted Quebecers to accept the necessity and desirability of attracting immigrants, and of becoming a post-ethnic, multicultural society. These leaders reasoned, correctly I believe, that the shift from an ethnic to post-ethnic definition of Québécois nationhood could only occur if Quebecers were persuaded that immigrants would contribute to Québécois society, rather than integrating into the anglophone society, and that immigrants would not dramatically change the balance of power between English and French in Canada. And this required establishing a range of incentives and pressures to ensure that the majority of immigrants would indeed become part of the francophone society in Quebec.

This was a bold strategy. And, as I noted earlier, the evidence suggests that it has worked. The overwhelming majority of Quebecers now adopt a post-ethnic definition of Québécois nationalism; and the majority of immigrants to Quebec now seek to integrate into the francophone society. One could argue, then, that these policies were not the expression of ethnic nationalism, but rather were the last nails in the coffin of ethnic nationalism in Quebec. I think we can see the same situation in Catalonia. Here too the willingness to adopt a post-ethnic conception of minority nationalism has depended on the existence of a range of policies which enhance the prestige of the minority language and which pressure immigrants to integrate into the minority society. By contrast, the residual strength of an ethnic conception of Basque and Flemish nationalism may be due, in part, to the fact that Basque and Flemish have not achieved the same prestige status in the eyes of immigrants.[8]

This suggests an interesting dilemma. Many commentators commend Quebec nationalism for abandoning an ethnic definition of nationhood, but criticize it for its illiberal policies on education and commercial signs. If I am right, however, we cannot separate out these aspects of Quebec nationalism. The illiberal policies on schools and signs are precisely what have made it possible for Quebecers to shift from an ethnic to a post-ethnic definition of nationhood. And if so, then we face a hard choice. Should we insist on a rigorous adherence to liberal norms of individual choice, knowing that this will stop and perhaps reverse the shift from an ethnic to post-ethnic definition of Québécois nationalism? Or should we accept some limited deviation from liberal norms in order to consolidate and extend the shift to a civic form of minority nationalism?[9]

---

[8] Shafir argues that part of the explanation for the Catalans' greater openness to immigrants, compared to the Basques, is the greater prestige of the Catalan language (Shafir 1995). See also Arel 2000 for a good analysis of how national minorities deal with the 'fear of minorisation', and how greater security regarding immigrants can encourage a more open and liberal redefinition of national identity.

[9] Parenthetically, I think that this is what Charles Taylor should have argued in his influential 'Politics of Recognition' paper (Taylor 1992a). Taylor defended Quebec's sign law on the grounds that it involved only a minor deviation from liberal norms in order to enable

I have no definite answer to this question. It surely depends on how great the violation of liberal norms would be. Restricting the language of commercial signs is one thing; restricting the language of newspapers, churches, or private schooling (as sometimes happens in Eastern Europe) is another. However, I would offer a qualified defence of the permissibility of using some illiberal policies in order to overcome ethnic nationalism, for two reasons: (*a*) the majority of immigrants themselves seem to think that this is an acceptable trade-off. Many immigrants in Quebec have not in fact objected to the principle that schools are publicly funded only in the minority language, in part because they see how this principle is connected to a broader strategy for making Quebec a more inclusive society (Norris 1998). They see these policies, not as a rejection of their participation and inclusion in Québécois society, but rather as clarifying the terms of integration; (*b*) ethnic nationalism is such a dangerous phenomenon, capable of such violence and hatred, that I am inclined to look favourably on any policies which would help to dislodge and dispel it, even if they are mildly illiberal. Some commentators view the sign law in Quebec as the first step on a slippery slope towards much greater interference in freedom of speech. My concern is different. I have no fear that Quebecers will relinquish their basic commitment to free speech. I am, however, concerned about the potential contained within all forms of ethnic nationalism for racism, xenophobia, and ethnic cleansing. And if the potential for these evils is increasingly remote in Quebec, it is in part because of mildly illiberal policies which have created the conditions under which a post-ethnic, multicultural form of Québécois identity could emerge and gradually displace the older ethnic definition of nationhood.

5. Conclusion

I have tried in this chapter to raise some questions about the challenge which immigration raises for minority nationalism in an era of globalization. Is it acceptable for a national minority to impose more stringent integration requirements for immigrants than a majority does? Is it acceptable for a national minority to expect or require immigrants to come to share their nationalist identity and goals? More generally, what is a morally legitimate and defensible attitude for national minorities to take towards immigrants? To what extent is it morally required that national minorities become 'multi-

Quebecers to pursue their distinctively communitarian vision of the common good. In reality, Quebecers are no more communitarian than other Canadians, and do not share a conception of the common good. I would defend minor deviations from liberal norms, not in order to make room for communitarianism, but rather to make it possible to shift from an ethnic to post-ethnic nationalism.

cultural'? To what extent can immigrants be expected, or required, to identify with the nationalist project? I have not tried to provide a definitive answer to any of these questions. I am not myself sure how the claims of minority nationalism and immigrant multiculturalism should be reconciled, or what a morally permissible balance between the goals of 'la survivance' and accommodation of immigrant ethnicity would be.

However, I am persuaded that we need to rethink these issues, and that in order to do so, we need to set aside many of the prejudices and myths which have informed the debate so far. Minority nationalisms are not inherently illiberal, pre-modern, or xenophobic. Some are, some are not. We need to look at each case of minority nationalism on its own terms, and examine the nature of its self-understandings and aspirations. We may find that the conflict between minority nationalism and immigrant multiculturalism is not as serious as it looks at first glance.

However, there will almost certainly be some conflict, even under the best of circumstances. Given that national minorities feel vulnerable to the majority, and may view immigrants as likely to defect to the majority, it will be more difficult for them to adopt multiculturalism policies that accommodate the identities of immigrants. Immigrant multiculturalism and minority nationalism are not necessarily enemies, but nor are they easy allies. The sorts of policies required to achieve a successful form of multicultural integration may be more complicated, and in some ways less liberal, than those which the majority can adopt. And this raises difficult questions which political theorists are only beginning to address.

PART IV

Democratic Citizenship in Multiethnic States

16

Education for Citizenship

It is widely accepted that a basic task of schooling is to prepare each new generation for their responsibilities as citizens. Indeed, the need to create a knowledgeable and responsible citizenry was one of the major reasons for establishing a public school system, and for making education mandatory. Education for citizenship includes, but also goes far beyond, classes in 'civics'. Citizenship education is not just a matter of learning the basic facts about the institutions and procedures of political life; it also involves acquiring a range of dispositions, virtues, and loyalties that are intimately bound up with the practice of democratic citizenship. Children acquire these virtues and loyalties not just (or even primarily) in civics classes. Rather, they are inculcated throughout the educational system. The aim of educating citizens affects what subjects are taught, how they are taught, and in what sorts of classrooms. In this sense, education for citizenship is not an isolated subset of the curriculum, but rather is one of the ordering goals or principles which shapes the entire curriculum.

In this chapter, I will discuss some of the issues raised by citizenship education. I will begin by considering what citizenship means in modern democratic societies, and what sorts of capacities and dispositions it requires (section 1). I hope to show that liberal democratic citizenship is more complicated than is often realized, and that even 'minimal' conceptions of citizenship impose significant obligations and constraints on individual and group behaviour. I will then discuss why schools must play a role in educating children for citizenship (section 2). It would be unrealistic to expect schools by themselves to develop the skills and virtues needed for democratic citizenship. People learn to be responsible citizens not only in schools, but also in the family, neighbourhood, churches, and many other groups and forums in civil society. Schools are not the only, or perhaps even the primary, forum for learning citizenship, but they are, I believe, indispensable. These other institutions supplement, but cannot replace, the provision of citizenship education in schools.

The rest of the chapter will then consider three interrelated areas of controversy that arise within ethnoculturally diverse societies: whether citizenship education requires common schooling (section 3); whether promoting responsible citizenship requires promoting personal autonomy (section 4); and whether promoting a shared civic identity requires teaching not only shared political values or principles but also promoting particular national or cultural identities (section 5). These three issues are not exhaustive of the range of controversies that arise, but they suggest the centrality of education for citizenship to both political theory and educational philosophy.

1. The Nature and Importance of Citizenship

There has been an explosion of interest in the concept of citizenship amongst political theorists. In 1978, it could be confidently stated that 'the concept of citizenship has gone out of fashion among political thinkers' (van Gunsteren 1978: 9). Fifteen years later, citizenship has become the 'buzz word' amongst thinkers on all points of the political spectrum (Heater 1990: 293). Interest in citizenship has been sparked by a number of recent political events and trends throughout the world—increasing voter apathy and long-term welfare dependency in the United States, the resurgence of nationalist movements in Eastern Europe, the stresses created by an increasingly multicultural and multiracial population in Western Europe, the backlash against the welfare state in Thatcher's England, the failure of environmental policies that rely on voluntary citizen co-operation, etc.

These events have made clear that the health and stability of a modern democracy depends, not only on the justice of its 'basic structure',[1] but also on the qualities and attitudes of its citizens: e.g. their sense of identity, and how they view potentially competing forms of national, regional, ethnic, or religious identities; their ability to tolerate and work together with others who are different from themselves; their desire to participate in the political process in order to promote the public good and hold political authorities accountable; their willingness to show self-restraint and exercise personal responsibility in their economic demands, and in personal choices which affect their health and the environment. Without citizens who possess these qualities, democracies become difficult to govern, even unstable.[2]

Many classical liberals believed that a liberal democracy could function effectively even in the absence of an especially virtuous citizenry, by creating checks and balances. Institutional and procedural devices such as the separation of powers, a bicameral legislature and federalism would all serve to block would-be oppressors. Even if each person pursued her own self-interest, without regard for the common good, one set of private interests

---

[1] Rawls says that the 'basic structure' of society is the primary subject of a theory of justice (1993: 257–89).

[2] This may account for the recent interest in citizenship promotion amongst governments (e.g. Britain's Commission on Citizenship, *Encouraging Citizenship* 1990; Senate of Australia, *Active Citizenship Revisited* 1991; Senate of Canada, *Canadian Citizenship: Sharing the Responsibility* 1993).

would check another set of private interests. Kant, for example, thought that the problem of good government 'can be solved even for a race of devils' (quoted in Galston 1991: 215). However, it has become clear that procedural-institutional mechanisms to balance self-interest are not enough, and that some level of civic virtue and public-spiritedness is required.

Consider the many ways that public policy relies on responsible personal lifestyle decisions: the state will be unable to provide adequate health care if citizens do not act responsibly with respect to their own health, in terms of maintaining a healthy diet, exercising regularly, and limiting their consumption of liquor and tobacco; the state will be unable to meet the needs of children, the elderly or the disabled if citizens do not agree to share this responsibility by providing some care for their relatives; the state cannot protect the environment if citizens are unwilling to reduce, reuse and recycle in their own consumer choices; the ability of the government to regulate the economy can be undermined if citizens borrow immoderate amounts or demand excessive salary increases; attempts to create a fairer society will flounder if citizens are chronically intolerant of difference and generally lacking in a sense of justice. Without co-operation and self-restraint in these areas, 'the ability of liberal societies to function successfully progressively diminishes' (Galston 1991:220).[3] In short, we need 'a fuller, richer and yet more subtle understanding and practice of citizenship', because 'what the state needs from the citizenry cannot be secured by coercion, but only cooperation and self-restraint in the exercise of private power' (Cairns and Williams 1985:43). Yet there is growing fear that the civility and public-spiritedness of citizens of liberal democracies may be in serious decline (Walzer 1992a: 90).[4]

Certain virtues are needed in virtually any political order, whether it is liberal and democratic or not. These would include general virtues, such as courage and law-abidingness, as well as economic virtues, such as the capacity to delay self-gratification or to adapt to economic and technological change.[5] But there are also certain virtues which are distinctive to a liberal

---

[3] Hence recent theories of citizenship emphasize that citizenship requires a balance of rights and responsibilities. For a survey of recent work on citizenship theory, which I am drawing on in this section, see Kymlicka and Norman 1994. For useful collections of recent articles, see Beiner 1995; Shafir 1998. For a more historical survey of citizenship theory, see Walzer 1989, and the readings collected in Clarke 1994.

[4] According to a recent survey, only 12 per cent of American teenagers said voting was important to being a good citizen. Moreover, this apathy is not just a function of youth—comparisons with similar surveys from the previous fifty years suggest that 'the current cohort knows less, cares less, votes less, and is less critical of its leaders and institutions than young people have been at any time over the past five decades' (Glendon 1991: 129). The evidence from Great Britain is similar (Heater 1990: 215).

[5] For a helpful discussion and typology, see Galston 1991: 221–4.

democracy, relating to the basic principles of a liberal regime, and to the political role citizens occupy within it, and it is these which I wish to focus on.

I will consider four such virtues:

- public-spiritedness, including the ability to evaluate the performance of those in office, and the willingness to engage in public discourse;
- a sense of justice, and the capacity to discern and respect the rights of others, and to moderate one's own claims accordingly;
- civility and tolerance;
- a shared sense of solidarity or loyalty.

Many commentators argue that the fourth virtue is inapplicable to liberal democracies, or perhaps more accurately, is redundant, since it supervenes on the first three. On this view, whatever sense of shared loyalty is required in a liberal democracy simply involves loyalty to principles of tolerance, justice and democracy. Shared commitment to these basic political principles is a sufficient foundation for a shared political identity or loyalty. I think that is mistaken, and will return to this point in section 5 below.

For the moment, however, I want to focus on the first three, starting with 'public-spiritedness'. This includes the ability and willingness to engage in public discourse about matters of public policy, and to question authority. These are perhaps the most distinctive aspects of citizenship in a liberal democracy, since they are precisely what distinguish 'citizens' within a democracy from the 'subjects' of an authoritarian regime.

The need to question authority arises in part from the fact that citizens in a representative democracy elect representatives who govern in their name. Hence an important responsibility of citizens is to monitor those officials, and judge their conduct. The need to engage in public discourse arises from the fact that the decisions of government in a democracy should be made publicly, through free and open discussion. But the virtue of public discourse is not just the willingness to participate in politics, or to make one's views known. Rather, as William Galston notes, it 'includes the willingness to listen seriously to a range of views which, given the diversity of liberal societies, will include ideas the listener is bound to find strange and even obnoxious. The virtue of political discourse also includes the willingness to set forth one's own views intelligibly and candidly as the basis for a politics of persuasion rather than manipulation or coercion' (Galston 1991: 227).

Stephen Macedo calls this the virtue of 'public reasonableness' (Macedo 1990). Liberal citizens must give reasons for their political demands, not just state preferences or make threats. Moreover, these reasons must be 'public' reasons, in the sense that they are capable of persuading people of different faiths and nationalities. Hence it is not enough to invoke Scripture or tradition. Liberal citizens must justify their political demands in terms that fellow citizens can understand and accept as consistent with their status as free and equal citizens. It requires a conscientious effort to distinguish those beliefs that are matters of private faith from those that are capable of public defence, and to see how issues look from the point of view of those with differing religious commitments and cultural backgrounds. As I discuss below, this is a stringent requirement that many religious groups find difficult to accept

The virtue of public reasonableness is less relevant for citizens who do not wish to participate in political affairs, and there will always be a portion of the population who have little or no desire to be politically active. Some people will find their greatest joys and projects in other areas of life, including the family, or the arts, or religion. A liberal democracy must respect such diverse conceptions of the good life, and should not compel people to adopt a conception of the good life that privileges political participation as the source of meaning or satisfaction.[6] For these more or less apolitical people, the virtue of public reasonableness may be less important.

Some commentators would argue that most people in contemporary democracies will fall into this apolitical camp—that meaningful political participation is almost inevitably confined to elites. According to T. H. McLaughlin, this is one of the important points of division between 'minimal' and 'maximal' conceptions of citizenship. On the minimal view, citizenship for most people primarily involves passive respect for laws, not the active exercise of political rights. By contrast, maximal conceptions of democracy insist that a true democracy, or that political justice, must aim for more widespread participation (McLaughlin 1992a).

Justice clearly requires that everyone have the opportunity to become active citizens, if they so choose, which means eliminating any economic or social barriers to the participation of disadvantaged groups, such as women, the poor, racial and ethnic minorities, etc. But whether we should encourage all individuals to choose to be active political participants is another matter. Whether active citizenship should be encouraged depends, I think, on the second virtue listed above—namely, a sense of justice. To have a sense of justice does not simply mean that we do not actively harm or exploit others. It also involves the duty to prevent injustice, by creating and upholding just institutions. So if there are serious injustices in our society which can only be rectified by political action, then citizens should recognize an obligation to

---

[6] This is why liberals cannot endorse a strong version of 'civic republicanism'. In one sense, civic republicanism refers to any view which highlights the importance of civic virtues, and the extent to which the functioning of a democracy requires certain virtues and identities amongst its citizens. In this sense, as I have argued, liberals must be republicans. But in another stronger sense, civic republicanism refers to the view that the best life—the most truly human life—is one which privileges political participation over other spheres of human endeavour. This sort of position is defended by Oldfield (1990b), Pocock (1992), Beiner (1992), Skinner (1992), amongst others. However, it is inconsistent with liberalism's commitment to pluralism, and in any event is implausible as a general account of the good life for all persons. See Kymlicka and Norman 1994: 361–2.

protest against that injustice. Or if our political institutions are no longer functioning, perhaps due to excessive levels of apathy, or to the abuse of power, then citizens have an obligation to protect these institutions from being undermined. To sit passively by while injustices are committed, or democratic institutions collapse, in the hope that others will step in, is to be a free rider. Everyone should do their fair share to create and uphold just institutions.

The extent of injustice, and the health of political institutions, will vary from society to society. In some times and places, though perhaps only in rare and fortunate circumstances, our natural duty of justice will not require us to participate actively. Where a society is basically well ordered, and its institutions healthy, then individuals should be free to follow their own conceptions of the good, even if these give little or no weight to political participation. So there will be times and places where minimal citizenship is all that we can or should require. And for minimal citizens, the stringent demands of 'public reasonableness' will be less significant. But even here, the requirements of liberal citizenship are by no means trivial. The obligations of minimal citizenship are often described in purely negative terms—i.e. the obligation not to break the law, and not to harm others, or restrict their rights and liberties. Minimal citizenship, in short, is often seen as simply requiring non-interference with others.

But that ignores one of the most basic requirements of liberal citizenship, albeit one that is often neglected in theoretical discussions. This is the virtue of 'civility' or 'decency', and it is a virtue that even the most minimal citizen must learn, since it applies not only to political activity, but also—indeed, primarily—to our actions in everyday life, on the street, in neighbourhood shops, and in the diverse institutions and forums of civil society. Civility refers to the way we treat non-intimates with whom we come into face-to-face contact. To understand civility, it is helpful to compare it with the related requirement of non-discrimination. The legal prohibition on discrimination initially only applied to government actions. Government laws and policies that discriminated against people on the basis of race or gender have gradually been struck down in Western democracies, since they violate the basic liberal commitment to equality of opportunity. But it has become clear that whether individuals have genuinely equal opportunity depends not only government actions, but also on the actions of institutions within civil society—corporations, schools, stores, landlords etc. If prejudiced shop-owners or real estate agents discriminate against people, they will be denied equal citizenship, even if the state itself does not discriminate. Hence legal requirements of non-discrimination have increasingly been applied to 'private' firms and associations.

This extension of non-discrimination from government to civil society is not just a shift in the scale of liberal norms, it also involves a radical extension in the obligations of liberal citizenship. For the obligation to treat people as equal citizens now applies to the most common everyday decisions of individuals. It is no longer permissible for businesses to refuse to hire black employees, or to serve black customers, or to segregate their black employees or customers. But not just that. The norms of non-discrimination entail that it is impermissible for businesses to ignore their black customers, or treat them rudely, although it is not always possible to legally enforce this. Businesses must in effect make blacks feel welcome, just as with white customers. Blacks must, in short, be treated with *civility*. The same applies to the way citizens treat each other in schools or recreational associations, even in private clubs.

This sort of civility is the logical extension of non-discrimination, since it is needed to ensure that all citizens have the same opportunity to participate within civil society. But it now extends into the very hearts and minds of citizens. Liberal citizens must learn to interact in everyday settings on an equal basis with people for whom they might harbour prejudice. The extent to which this requirement of civility can (or should) be legally enforced is limited. It is easier to compel businesses to be non-discriminatory in hiring than to compel them to treat black customers with civility. But the recent spread of laws and regulations against sexual and racial harassment, both in society generally and within schools and businesses, can be seen as an attempt to ensure a level of civility, since they include forms of offensive speech as well as physical intimidation, And while it is obviously impossible to compel civility between citizens in less formal settings—e.g. whether whites smile or scowl at an Asian family in the neighbourhood park—liberal citizenship none the less requires this sort of civility.

It is easy to trivialize this requirement of civility as being simply 'good manners'. Philip Rieff, for example, dismisses the insistence on civility as a superficial façade that simply hides a deeper indifference to the needs of others. As he puts it, 'We have long known what "equality" means in American culture: it means . . . a smile fixed to the face, demanding you return a smile' (quoted in Cuddihy 1978: 6). John Murray Cuddihy views civility as the imposition of a Protestant (and bourgeois) sense of 'good taste' on other religious groups. He argues that Catholics and Jews (and now Muslims) have had to abandon their conception of true faith, which required the public expression of contempt for other religions, to conform to this 'religion of civility'.

It is true that liberal societies have reinforced, and thereby partially conflated, the moral obligation of civility with an aesthetic conception of 'good manners'. For example, the expectation of civility is sometimes used to discourage the sort of forceful protest that may be needed for an oppressed group to be heard. For a disadvantaged group to 'make a scene' is often seen as 'in bad taste'. This sort of exaggerated emphasis on good manners can be used to promote servility. True civility does not mean smiling at others no matter how badly they treat you, as if oppressed groups should be nice to their oppressors. Rather, it means treating others as equals on the condition that they extend the same recognition to you. While there is some overlap between civility and a more general politeness, they are none the less distinct—civility involves upholding norms of equality within the public life of a society, including civil society, and thereby upholding essential liberal values.[7]

2. The Need for Citizenship Education in Schools

Even the most minimal conception of liberal citizenship, therefore, requires a significant range of civic virtues. But are schools the appropriate arena to teach these virtues, given that this would involve inculcating substantive (and controversial) moral beliefs? I believe the schools have an unavoidable role, in part because no other social institution can take their place.

To be sure, other institutions can play a supplementary role in promoting civic virtue. For example, theorists of the 'New Right' often praise the market as a school of virtue. Many Thatcher/Reagan reforms of the 1980s aimed to extend the scope of markets in people's lives—through freer trade, deregulation, tax cuts, the weakening of trade unions, and reducing welfare benefits—in part in order to teach people the virtues of initiative and self-reliance. Moreover, markets are said to encourage civility, since companies which refuse to hire black employees, or serve black customers, will be at a competitive disadvantage. However, the limits of the market as a school of civic virtue are clear. Many market deregulations arguably made possible an era of unprecedented greed and economic irresponsibility, as evidenced by the savings-and-loan and junk bond scandals in America. Markets teach

---

[7] My discussion here draws extensively on Jeff Spinner's account of civility (1994: ch. 3). It also draws on Patricia White's account of civility, or what she calls 'decency' (1992), although I disagree in part with her emphasis. She seems primarily concerned with improving the overall level of 'decency' in society, rather than with eliminating glaring instances of incivility aimed at identifiable groups. For example, she compares the smiling and co-operative waiters in a Canadian cafe with the surly and uncooperative waiters in a Polish cafe (1992: 208), and argues that we should educate children to be friendly with strangers rather than surly. While I agree that it's a good thing for people to display this sort of decency, and that a minimal level of it is a precondition of a functioning democracy, I do not think this is the fundamental problem for citizenship education. From my point of view, waiters who are only minimally cheerful to all their customers are morally preferable to waiters who are generally very cheerful but who are surly to black customers. The latter may display more decency overall, but their behaviour towards an identifiable group threaten the most basic norms of liberal citizenship. However, I agree with White that it is important to be sensitive to the cultural variations in norms of civility (White 1992: 215). Iris Young makes a similar point about cultural variations in norms of public reasonableness (Young 1993a).

initiative, but not a sense of justice or social responsibility (Mulgan 1991: 39). And so long as a sizeable portion of the population harbours prejudices towards certain groups, then businesses will have an economic incentive to serve that market, by creating goods and services that exclude these groups.[8] In any event, the market cannot teach those civic virtues specific to political participation and dialogue—e.g. the virtue of public reasonableness.

Following Rousseau and J. S. Mill, many 'participatory democrats' assume that political participation itself will teach people responsibility and toleration. As Adrian Oldfield notes, they place their faith in the activity of participation 'as the means whereby individuals may become accustomed to perform the duties of citizenship. Political participation enlarges the minds of individuals, familiarizes them with interests which lie beyond the immediacy of personal circumstance and environment, and encourages them to acknowledge that public concerns are the proper ones to which they should pay attention' (Oldfield 1990a: 184). Unfortunately, this faith in the educative function of participation seems overly optimistic. Emphasizing participation does not yet explain how to ensure that citizens participate responsibly— i.e. in a public-spirited, rather than self-interested or prejudiced, way (Mulgan 1991: 40–1). Empowered citizens may use their power irresponsibly by pushing for benefits and entitlements they cannot ultimately afford; or by voting themselves tax breaks and slashing assistance to the needy; or by 'seeking scapegoats in the indolence of the poor, the strangeness of ethnic minorities, or the insolence and irresponsibility of modern women' (Fierlbeck 1991: 592). Successful political participation requires the ability to create coalitions, which encourages a partial development of the virtues of justice and public reasonableness. No one can hope to succeed in political life if they make no effort to listen to or accommodate the needs and views of others. But in many cases, a winning coalition can be built while ignoring the claims of marginalized groups. Indeed, if a significant portion of the population is prejudiced, then ignoring or attacking such group may be the best route to political success.

'Civil-society theorists' emphasize the necessity of civility and self-restraint to a healthy democracy, but deny that either the market or political participation is sufficient to teach these virtues. Instead, it is in the voluntary organizations of civil society—churches, families, unions, ethnic associations,

---

[8] For example, real-estate agents have an economic incentive to maintain segregated housing. In any event, New Right reforms arguably violated the requirements of liberal justice, since cutting welfare benefits, far from getting the disadvantaged back on their feet, has expanded the underclass. Class inequalities have been exacerbated, and the working poor and unemployed have been effectively disenfranchised, unable to participate in the social and political life of the country (Fierlbeck 1991: 579). So even if the market taught civic virtue, laissez-faire capitalism violates the principle that all members of society have an equal opportunity to be active citizens.

co-operatives, environmental groups, neighbourhood associations, support groups, charities—that we learn the virtues of mutual obligation. As Michael Walzer puts it, 'The civility that makes democratic politics possible can only be learned in the associational networks' of civil society (Walzer 1992a: 104). Because these groups are voluntary, failure to live up to the responsibilities that come with them is usually met simply with disapproval, rather than legal punishment. Yet because the disapproval comes from family, friends, colleagues, or comrades, it is in many ways a more powerful incentive to act responsibly than punishment by an impersonal state. It is here that 'human character, competence, and capacity for citizenship are formed', for it is here that we internalize the idea of personal responsibility and mutual obligation, and learn the voluntary self-restraint which is essential to truly responsible citizenship.

The claim that civil society is the 'seedbed of civic virtue' (Glendon 1991: 109) is essentially an empirical claim, for which there is little hard evidence one way or the other.[9] It is an old and venerable view, but it is not obviously true. It may be in the neighbourhood that we learn to be good neighbours, but neighbourhood associations also teach people to operate on the 'NIMBY' (not in my backyard) principle when it comes to the location of group homes or public works. Similarly, the family is often 'a school of despotism' that teaches male dominance over women (Okin 1992: 65); churches often teach deference to authority and intolerance of other faiths; ethnic groups often teach prejudice against other races, and so on.

Walzer recognizes that most people are 'trapped in one or another subordinate relationship, where the "civility" they learned was deferential rather than independent and active'. In these circumstances, he says, we have to 'reconstruct' the associational network 'under new conditions of freedom and equality'. Similarly, when the activities of some associations 'are narrowly conceived, partial and particularist', then 'they need political correction'. Walzer calls his view 'critical associationalism' to signify that the associations of civil society may need to be reformed in the light of principles of citizenship (Walzer 1992a: 106–7).

But this may go too far in the other direction. Rather than supporting voluntary associations, this approach may unintentionally license wholesale intervention in them. Governments must of course intervene to protect the rights of people inside and outside the group, if these rights are threatened. But do we want governments to reconstruct churches, for example, to make them more internally democratic, or to make sure that their members learn to be critical rather than deferential? And, in any event, wouldn't reconstructing churches, families, or unions to make them more internally demo-

---

[9] Putnam (1993) argues that the reason why some Italian regional governments function better than others is the number and vitality of civic associations in each region. This claim is hotly disputed.

cratic start to undermine their essentially uncoerced and voluntary character, which is what supposedly made them the seedbeds of civic virtue?

Indeed, it would be unreasonable to expect churches to teach the virtue of public reasonableness. Public reasonableness is essential in political debate, but is unnecessary and sometimes undesirable in the private sphere. It would be absurd to ask church-goers to abstain from appealing to Scripture in deciding how to run their church. Civil-society theorists demand too much of voluntary associations in expecting them to be the main school for, or a small-scale replica of, democratic citizenship. While these associations may teach civic virtue, that is not their *raison d'être*. The reason why people join churches, families, or ethnic organizations is not to learn civic virtue. It is rather to honour certain values, and enjoy certain human goods, and these motives may have little to do with the promotion of citizenship. To expect parents or priests to organize the internal life of their groups so as to maximally promote citizenship is to ignore why these groups exist in the first place. (Some associations, like the Boy Scouts, are designed to promote citizenship, but they are the exception not the rule.)

It seems then that we cannot rely on the market, the family, or the associations of civil society to teach civic virtue. People will not automatically learn to engage in public discourse, or to question authority, in any of these spheres, since these spheres are often held together by private discourse and respect for authority. This suggests that schools must teach children how to engage in the kind of critical reasoning and moral perspective that defines public reasonableness. And indeed, as I noted earlier, promoting these sorts of virtues was one of the fundamental justifications for mandatory education. But using schools to promote civic virtue raises many controversies, of which I will briefly examine three—the role of separate schools, the teaching of autonomy, and the relationship between civic and cultural identities.

3. Citizenship and Separate Schools

The need for citizenship education raises questions about the role of separate schools in a liberal democracy, particularly religious schools. Various religious groups have sought to establish separate schools, partly in order to teach their religious doctrine, but also to reduce the exposure of their children to the members of other religious groups. Most liberal states have accepted this demand, as a way of respecting parental rights and religious freedom, but have insisted that such schools teach a core curriculum, including citizenship education.

It is not clear, however, that this compromise position—separate schools with a common curriculum—provides the appropriate sort of citizenship education. Such schools are obviously capable of teaching basic facts about government. But as I noted earlier, citizenship education is not simply a matter of knowledge of political institutions and constitutional principles. It is also a matter of how we think about and behave towards others, particularly those who differ from us in their race, religion, class, etc. Liberal citizenship requires cultivating the habit of civility, and the capacity for public reasonableness, in our interaction with others. Indeed, it is precisely these habits and capacities which most need to be learned in schools, for they are unlikely to be learned in smaller groups or associations, like the family, neighbourhood, or church, which tend to be homogenous in their ethnocultural backgrounds and religious beliefs.

Some critics argue that separate religious schools cannot provide an adequate education in either civility or public reasonableness. For these virtues are not only, or even primarily, learned through the explicit curriculum. For example, common schools teach civility not just by telling students to be nice, but also by insisting that students sit beside students of different races and religions, and co-operate with them on school projects or sports teams (Gutmann 1987: 53). Similarly, common schools teach public reasonableness not only by telling students that there are a plurality of religious views in the world, and that reasonable people disagree on the merits of these views. They also create the social circumstances whereby students can see the reasonableness of these disagreements. It is not enough to simply tell students that the majority of the people in the world do not share their religion. So long as one is surrounded by people who share one's faith, one may still succumb to the temptation to think that everyone who rejects one's religion is somehow illogical or depraved. To learn public reasonableness, students must come to know and understand people who are reasonable and decent and humane, but who do not share their religion. Only in this way can students learn how personal faith differs from public reasonableness, and where to draw that line. This sort of learning requires the presence within a classroom of people with varying ethnocultural and religious backgrounds (Callan 1995).

In these ways, religious schools are limited in their capacity to provide an adequate citizenship education. Of course, it is important not to idealize common schools, which suffer their own deficiencies. For example, while common schools in North America typically contain a diversity of religions, they are more segregated than religious schools by class, race, and academic talent (Gutmann 1987: 115–17). Yet divisions of class and race are equally important obstacles to civility and public reasonableness as religious divisions. Indeed, one could argue that the greatest failure of liberal citizenship in the United States is not the division between religious groups, but the increasing desire of middle-class whites to distance themselves (both physically and emotionally) from inner-city blacks, or the poor more generally. In terms of teaching students how to have a public dialogue with the disadvantaged, religious schools may well do better than a common school in the suburbs full of well-off (but religiously diverse) whites.

Moreover, it is important to distinguish temporary or transitional separate schooling from permanent separation. The requirements of liberal citizenship suggest that common schooling is necessary—or at least highly desirable—at some point in the educational process. But there is no reason why the entire process should be integrated. Indeed, there are good reasons for thinking that some children may do best by having their early schooling in separate schools, beside others who share their background, before moving into a common school later in the process. For example, this may be true of historically disadvantaged groups (girls, blacks) who can best develop their self-esteem in an environment free of prejudice (McLaughlin 1992b: 122). More generally, schooling within a particular ethnocultural or religious setting may provide virtues unavailable within the common schools. If common schools do a better job promoting a shared sense of justice, separate schools may do better at providing children with a clear sense of what it is to have a stable sense of the good. They may provide a better environment for developing the capacity for in-depth engagement with a particular cultural tradition, and for loyalty and commitment to particular projects and relationships. There is more than one starting point from which children can learn liberal citizenship (Callan 1995: 22–3; McLaughlin 1992b: 123–4).

The requirement of common schools—even if limited to the later stages of children's education—will be rejected by some religious groups, who insist on keeping their children separate and apart from the rest of society. Should a liberal state impose integrated common schools, in the name of citizenship education? In answering this, it is worth distinguishing two kinds of religious groups that might seek exemption from common schooling. Some groups, like the Amish, voluntarily isolate themselves from the larger society, and avoid participating in either politics or the mainstream institutions of civil society. They do not vote, or hire employees, or attempt to influence public policy (except where a proposed policy would jeopardize their isolation), and seek only to be left alone. We can call this 'isolationist multiculturalism', as distinct from the pluralizing or hybridic immigrant multiculturalism discussed in Chapter 8, which involves accommodations within common institutions.

What is the impact on democratic citizenship of enabling such isolationist groups to withdraw their children from common schools and other public institutions? Allowing groups to, in effect, opt out of the public life of the country clearly impedes, rather than promotes, the sort of habits and virtues needed for good democratic citizenship. To be sure, by protecting the associational life of the Amish, isolationist multiculturalism promotes many non-political virtues. For example, the Amish are widely admired for their work ethic, law-abidingness, family loyalty, and religious devotion. But the Amish show no interest in the political virtues of citizenship. They do not learn the ability to evaluate the performance of those in elected office—indeed, they take no interest in elections, and neither vote nor run for elected office. Nor do they learn to engage in public discourse, or to interact civilly with others in the institutions of civil society. Indeed, the very idea of interacting extensively with non-Amish is strongly discouraged. (When this sort of interaction is unavoidable, it is done through paid intermediaries.) And this sort of multiculturalism does not promote a shared sense of solidarity or loyalty. Isolationist multiculturalism, in effect, absolves the Amish from their responsibilities as citizens to deal with the country's problems. It absolves them from any responsibility to think about the problem of inner-city neighbourhoods, or how to pay off the national debt, or of how to respond to injustices overseas.

But while this sort of multiculturalism does not promote democratic citizenship, nor is it very harmful to the overall functioning of liberal democracies, precisely because the Amish are so politically passive and socially isolated. It is not that the Amish participate in politics in an irresponsible or selfish manner, it is simply that they don't participate at all. Similarly, it is not that the Amish discriminate against others in civil society, it is rather that they don't enter the larger society. They are, to use Jeff Spinner's term, 'partial citizens' (Spinner 1994: 98). They have, in effect, waived both the rights and responsibilities of democratic citizenship. They do not accept their civic responsibilities, but nor do they exercise their political rights or seek political office.

Spinner argues that such groups should be tolerated, and their special exemptions granted, so long as they remain socially withdrawn and politically passive, and so long as members are free to leave. Since they do not participate in either politics or civil society, it is less urgent that they learn the virtues of civility and public reasonableness. Because they have relinquished the right to participate, they can also be absolved of the responsibilities that accompany that right, including the responsibility to learn and practice civility and public reasonableness. Hence he supports their right to withdraw their children from school at the age of 14, before they would have to learn about the larger society, or interact with non-Amish children. [10] Assuming that such groups are small, and sincerely committed to their self-imposed isolation, they pose no threat to the practice of liberal citizenship in society generally. Such groups should not be encouraged, since they accept no responsibility to work together with other citizens to solve the country's

---

[10] My own view is that we should continue to respect the special exemptions that were historically promised to certain groups (particularly when it was the promise of such exemptions that led these groups to settle where they are now). However, I do not believe that liberal democratic states have any obligation to make it possible for new groups to acquire this status (e.g. Christian fundamentalist survivalist groups). See Kymlicka 1995a: 116–20.

injustices and problems. They are free riders, in a sense, benefiting from a stable liberal order that they do nothing to help maintain.[11] But a liberal state can afford a few such free riders.[12]

By contrast, other religious groups seeking exemption from integrated schools are active participants in both civil society and politics, and seek to influence public policy generally. This would include fundamentalist Christians in the United States, or Muslims in Britain. In these cases, one could argue that, having chosen to exercise their rights as full citizens, they must accept the sort of education needed to promote responsible citizenship, including the obligation to attend common schools at some point in the educational process.

4. Citizenship and Personal Autonomy

A related question is whether schools, be they separate or common, should promote the capacity for individual autonomy. 'Autonomy' means different things to different people. I am using the term to refer to the capacity to rationally reflect on, and potentially revise, our conceptions of the good life. An autonomous person is capable of reflecting on her current ends, and assessing whether they are worthy of her continued allegiance. Autonomy, on this view, is consistent with people endorsing their inherited way of life, if they reflectively prefer it to the alternatives. But it is inconsistent with an uncritical attitude towards inherited traditions, or with an unquestioning acceptance of the pronouncements of parents, priests or community leaders regarding the worth of different ways of life.[13]

---

[11] I am here disagreeing with those who defend the exemption for the Amish by arguing that their separate schools provide adequate citizenship education. This was the view of the American Supreme Court, which said that the Amish education system prepared Amish children to be good citizens, since they became productive and peaceful members of the Amish community (*Wisconsin v. Yoder* 406 US 205 (1972)). However, as I noted earlier, liberal citizenship requires more than being law-abiding and economically self-sufficient. For a critique of *Yoder*'s account of civic responsibilities, see Arneson and Shapiro 1996.

[12] As Spinner notes, there are unlikely to be many such groups, since the price of 'partial citizenship' is to cut oneself off from the opportunities and resources of the mainstream society (Spinner 1994: ch. 5).

[13] I mean to distinguish this account of autonomy from two other interpretations. On one (Kantian) view, the exercise of choice is intrinsically valuable, since it is the most distinctly human attribute. On another (Millian) view, the exercise of choice is valuable insofar as it leads to greater 'individuality'—that is, insofar as it leads individuals to reject traditional ways of life, and construct their own unique way of life. People who reject these views may none the less accept the more modest idea that informed choice is valuable because our current beliefs about the good may be mistaken, and so it is important for people to be able to assess the value of alternative ways of life. On this, see Kymlicka 1989: ch. 2.

I did not include autonomy in my list of the basic virtues of liberal citizenship in section 1, and I do not think that autonomy, in and of itself, is necessary for the practice of democratic citizenship. However, there are good reasons to think that autonomy will be indirectly promoted by citizenship education, since it is closely associated, both conceptually and developmentally, to various civic virtues. For example, responsible citizenship involves the willingness to hold political authorities accountable. Hence schools should teach children to be sceptical of the political authorities who govern in our name, and to be cognizant of the dangers of the abuse of power. As Amy Gutmann puts it, children at school 'must learn not just to behave in accordance with authority but to think critically about authority if they are to live up to the democratic ideal of sharing political sovereignty as citizens'. People who 'are ruled only by habit and authority . . . are incapable of constituting a society of sovereign citizens' (Gutmann 1987:51).

This democratic virtue is exercised in public life, and promoting it does not entail or require encouraging children to question parental or religious authority in private life. As Galston puts it, the need to teach children how to evaluate political leaders 'does not warrant the conclusion that the state must (or may) structure public education to foster in children sceptical reflection on ways of life inherited from parents or local communities' (Galston 1991: 253). But there will likely be some spillover effect. Indeed, there is strong evidence that adolescents' attitudes towards authority tend 'to be uniform across all the authority figures they encounter', so that encouraging scepticism of political authority will likely encourage questioning of familial or religious authority (Emler and Reicher 1987). Galston himself admits that it is not easy for schools to promote a child's willingness to question political authority without undermining her 'unswerving belief in the correctness' of her parents' way of life.

Citizenship education not only involves promoting a certain sort of critical attitude towards authority, it also involves developing habits of civility and the capacity for public reasonableness. Both of these indirectly promote autonomy, since they encourage children to interact with the members of other groups, to understand the reasonableness of other ways of life, and to distance themselves from their own cultural traditions. Consider civility. In section 1, I emphasized that norms of civility and non-discrimination protect ethnic and religious groups from prejudice and discrimination. This means that groups wishing to maintain their group identity and cultural practices will face fewer legal barriers or social stigmas. But civility also increases the interaction between the members of different groups, and hence the likelihood that individuals will learn and adopt new ways of life. Historically, cultural boundaries have often been maintained by the visible expression of prejudice towards outsiders; people stayed within their group because they were not welcome elsewhere. The spread of civility in social institutions (including schools) means that these boundaries tend to break down. Members of one group are more likely to co-operate with and befriend children of other groups, and so learn about other ways of life, and possibly adopt new identities and practices.

Simply by teaching and practising civility, schools make this sort of mingling and fraternizing between the members of different groups more likely, and hence make the breakdown of cultural barriers more likely. In some cases, adopting other ways of life may be done in an unreflective way, simply imitating one's peers, and hence does not count as the exercise of autonomy. But schools also promote a more reflective process, by teaching the virtue of public reasonableness. Because reasonable people disagree about the merits of different religions and conceptions of the good life, children must learn to distinguish reasons based on private faith from reasons that can be publicly accepted in a diverse society. To develop this capacity, children must not only learn how to distance themselves from beliefs that are taken for granted in their private life, but they must also learn to put themselves in other people's shoes, in order to see what sorts of reasons might be acceptable to people from other backgrounds. The virtue of public reasonableness does not require that children come to admire or cherish other ways of life. But it does require that children be exposed to competing ways of life, and be encouraged to view them as the expressions of coherent conceptions of value which have been sincerely affirmed by other reasonable people. Learning to view other ways of life in this way does not inevitably lead to the questioning of one's own way of life, but it surely makes it more likely, since it requires a sort of broad-mindedness which is hard to combine with an unreflective deference to traditional practices or authorities.

For all these reasons, education for democratic citizenship will almost unavoidably, albeit indirectly, promote autonomy. Through citizenship education children both become aware of alternative ways of life, and are given the intellectual skills needed to understand and appreciate them. As Gutmann puts it, citizenship education involves 'equipping children with the intellectual skills necessary to evaluate ways of life different from that of their parents', because 'many if not all of the capacities necessary for choice among good lives are also necessary for choice among good societies' (Gutmann 1987: 30, 40). Democratic citizenship and personal autonomy, while distinct, are interconnected at various levels.

As a result, those groups that rely heavily on an uncritical acceptance of tradition and authority, while not strictly ruled out, are bound to be discouraged by the critical and tolerant attitudes which civic education encourages (Macedo 1990: 53–4). This indeed is why religious groups often seek to establish separate schools, even when they have to teach a common curriculum. They fear that if their children attend common schools, they will be more likely to question traditional practices, even if the school curriculum does not directly promote this sort of autonomous attitude. To preserve an uncritical deference to communal traditions, children can only be exposed to a minimal level of citizenship education, one that teaches facts about government, but not civility, public reasonableness, or critical attitudes to political authority.

I should note two qualifications here. First, citizenship education historically has often discouraged, rather than encouraged, autonomy. The aim of citizenship education, in the past, was to promote an unreflective patriotism, one which glorifies the past history and current political system of the country, and which vilifies opponents of that political system, whether they be internal dissidents or external enemies (Nelson 1980). This sort of civic education, needless to say, promoted passivity and deference, not a critical attitude towards political authority or broad-mindedness towards cultural differences. Today, however, educational theorists and policy-makers increasingly reject this model of civic education, in favour of one that promotes more active and reflective forms of citizenship.[14] The earlier form of civic education can still be found, of course, and some people continue to defend it (see Galston 1991: 244; AASA 1987: 26). However, if our aim is to produce self-governing democratic citizens, rather than passive subjects of an authoritarian government, a different sort of civic education is required, one which is much more likely to promote autonomy.

Second, I have suggested that the promotion of personal autonomy should be seen as the indirect consequence of civic education, not as its direct or explicit purpose. I do not mean to deny, however, that there might be other reasons for directly promoting personal autonomy. Indeed, a strong case could be made that promoting autonomy is an integral part of an adequate education for modern life. While autonomy may not be needed to fulfil the social role of citizen, it may be needed if children are to enjoy life to the greatest extent possible. If so, then children may have a right to an autonomy-promoting education, even where their parents resist it. To pursue this question however would raise issues that go far beyond this chapter. While I am myself attracted to the view that schools should promote autonomy, it would be misleading to defend this as a precondition of democratic citizenship. Autonomy, I think, is valuable not because it makes people better citizens, but because it enables people to lead more fulfilling lives, quite independently of their role as citizens.[15]

[14] We can mark this shift by comparing two accounts of the relationship between civic education and moral reasoning. Writing in 1980, Jack Nelson objected that contemporary accounts of civic education promoted passive deference, and so conflicted with the sort of autonomy which he felt was required by true moral agents. By 1991, however, William Galston was arguing that contemporary accounts of civic education excessively promote critical reflectiveness, and so undermined the sort of moral identity and moral commitment underlying many religious groups.

[15] I am skipping lightly over a very deep division within liberal political philosophy. There is an important debate between 'political' or 'pragmatic' liberals and 'comprehensive' or

5. Citizenship and National Identity

Finally, I want to briefly address the issue of identity. As I noted earlier, many commentators argue that social unity in a liberal democracy rests not on a shared identity, but rather on shared allegiance to political principles. As Rawls puts it, 'although a well-ordered society is divided and pluralistic . . . public agreement on questions of political and social justice supports ties of civic friendship and secures the bonds of association' (Rawls 1980: 540; Strike 1994:8). On this view, by teaching certain common political principles—like principles of justice, tolerance and civility—citizenship education provides the foundation for national unity as well.

I think this is a mistake. Shared political principles obviously are helpful to maintain social unity, and indeed deep conflict over basic principles can lead to civil war. But shared principles are not sufficient. Throughout the West, an increasing convergence on liberal values has gone hand in hand with contin-ued, even increasing, demands for self-government by national minorities. The fact that two national groups share the same principles of justice does not necessarily give them a strong reason to remain together, rather than splitting into two separate countries, since each national group can imple-ment those principles in its own separate state.[16]

Social unity, then, requires not only shared principles, but also a sense of shared membership. Citizens must have a sense of belonging to the same community, and a shared desire to continue to live together. Social unity, in short, requires that citizens identify with their fellow citizens, and view them as 'one of us'. This sense of shared identity helps sustain the relationships of trust and solidarity needed for citizens to accept the results of democratic decisions, and the obligations of liberal justice (Miller 1995).

What underlies this shared national identity? In non-liberal states, shared identity is typically based on a common ethnic descent, religious faith, or conception of the good. However, these cannot provide the basis for social unity in a liberal state, since none of them are shared in modern pluralist

'ethical' liberals over the role of autonomy with liberal theory. Political liberals, like John Rawls and Charles Larmore, argue that because many groups within society do not value autonomy, liberals must look for a way of justifying liberal institutions that does not appeal to such a 'sectarian' value (Rawls 1993; Larmore 1987). Comprehensive liberals, like Joseph Raz, argue that liberal institutions can only be defended by appealing to the value of autonomy (Raz 1986). I discuss this debate, and defend the comprehensive liberal option, in Kymlicka 1995a: chap. 8. See also Callan (1996), who argues that the distinction between political and comprehensive liberalism cannot be sustained in the educational context. However, for a cri-tique of the emphasis on autonomy, and a defence of Muslim demands for a separate school system that restricts the development of autonomy, see Halstead 1990; 1991.

[16] For a more detailed development of this argument, see Norman 1995. For a related cri-tique of the idea that shared principles underlie social unity, see Paris 1991. See also Ch. 13.

states. What then makes citizens in a liberal state feel that they belong together, that they are members of the same nation? The answer typically involves a sense of shared history, and a common language. Citizens share a sense of belonging to a particular historical society because they share a language and history; they participate in common social and political institutions which are based on this shared language, and which manifest and perpetuate this shared history; and they see their life-choices as bound up with the survival of this society and its institutions into the indefinite future. Citizens can share a national identity in this sense, and yet share very little in terms of ethnicity, religion, or conceptions of the good.[17]

The need for this sort of common national identity raises many questions for citizenship education. I will focus on two, regarding the teaching of languages, and the teaching of history, both of which are fundamental to the construction of a national identity. First, what should be the language of the school system? This is a remarkably neglected question in liberal theory.[18] The need for a common national identity suggests that states should inculcate a common language. And indeed the definition, standardization, and teaching of an official language has been one of the first tasks of 'nation-building' throughout the world .

But whether imposing a common language promotes social unity depends on the circumstances. The historical evidence suggests that voluntary immigrant groups are willing to adopt the language of the mainstream society. They have already uprooted themselves from their original homeland, and know that the success of their decision to emigrate depends on some measure of integration into their host society. Insofar as they demand education in their mother-tongue, it is in addition to, or as a means of facilitating, learning the common language, not as a substitute. Much of the opposition to bilingual education for immigrant groups is, I think, misguided, but liberal states have a legitimate interest in ensuring that these programmes do ultimately lead to competence in the language of the mainstream society.

The case of territorially concentrated language groups whose homeland has been incorporated into larger states—like the Québécois, Puerto Ricans, or Flemish, or indigenous peoples around the world—is very different. They have strongly—even violently—resisted the attempt to have the majority language imposed on them. This reflects the fact that they typically view themselves as forming their own 'nation' or 'people', and so have their own sense

[17] This is a thumbnail sketch of the nature of national identity in a liberal state, and its role in promoting political stability and relationships of trust and solidarity. For accounts of liberal nationalism, see Chs. 10 and 11 .

[18] As Brian Weinstein put it, political theorists have had a lot to say about 'the language of politics'—that is, the symbols, metaphors and rhetorical devices of political discourse—but have had virtually nothing to say about 'the politics of language'—that is, the decisions about which languages to use in political, legal, and educational forums (Weinstein 1983: 7–13).

of national identity, with their own language, history, and encompassing social institutions. States with such groups are not nation-states, but multination states, and attempts to impose a single national identity on these national minorities are likely to undermine rather than promote social unity. Multination states are most stable if they are seen as a federation of peoples, each with their own historic territories, language rights, and powers of self-government, including their own schools (Gurr 1993; Hannum 1990).

What is the impact on democratic citizenship of allowing national minorities to control their own schools and other public institutions? Obviously, the project of maintaining a separate and self-governing society, with its own complete set of institutions operating in its own distinct language, does not promote horizontal connectedness amongst citizens. On the contrary, the almost inevitable result is to make democratic co-operation between the members of distinct nation groups more difficult. The problem here, unlike the case of the Amish, is not that national minorities lack the virtues of public reasonableness or civic engagement. The problem, rather, is that they see themselves as belonging to a separate political community, and as having only a secondary, and often ambivalent, bond to the larger state. After all, most national minorities were involuntarily incorporated into the larger state, and even those that do not actively seek secession none the less insist that the authority of the larger state over them is limited.

One could say, therefore, that accommodating minority nationalism is 'balkanizing'. But this is to beg the question. For the whole point of minority nationalism is to insist that national minorities form separate political communities, with the right to govern themselves. Their concern is with the democratic functioning of their own political community, and minority nationalist policies are intended precisely to promote trust and solidarity within their own national society. They care about democratic virtues, but their concern is, in the first instance, with promoting these virtues within their own polity, and they see minority nationalism as building the common institutions and public spaces within which civic engagement can take place, and within which democratic virtues can be developed.

This raises an important point. The claim that interaction and co-operation in common institutions promotes democratic virtues may be true, but as with most claims about democracy, it tells us nothing about where the relevant boundaries of the democratic unit should be. Democracy is the rule of 'the people', and the evidence suggests that democracy functions best when 'the people' are engaged in civil society. But what if there are two or more peoples in the state, each with the right to rule themselves, and each with its own civil society? In such multination states, the impact of minority nationalism on democratic citizenship is to be evaluated not just by its effect on democracy at the federal level, but also by its effect on democracy at the level of the self-governing national community.

Put this way, it seems likely that minority nationalism promotes democracy at the level of the self-governing nation, but renders democratic co-operation more difficult at the federal level. Québécois nationalism has led to a flourishing francophone civil society within Quebec, but has not promoted the participation of Quebecers in the pan-Canadian anglophone civil society. To reject minority nationalism on the grounds that it impedes democratic co-operation at the federal level, therefore, is to assume precisely what national minorities dispute—namely, that for the purposes of evaluating democratic functioning, the country as a whole forms a single 'people', rather than two or more peoples each with the right to govern itself. Of course, one might respond that national minorities are wrong to think that they have a right to govern themselves. I cannot address that objection here, except to say that in situations where national minorities have been involuntarily incorporated into a larger state through conquest or colonization or the imperial cession of territory, I think that they do have a very powerful right to self-government (see Chapter 4). Indeed, to oppose minority nationalism under such circumstances on the grounds that it interferes with democratic co-operation at the federal level is not a defence of democracy, but of colonialism.

In multination states, then, citizenship education typically has a dual function—it promotes a national identity within each constituent national group, defined by a common language and history, but it also seeks to promote some sort of transnational identity which can bind together the various national groups within the state. Unfortunately, recent developments in multination states—e.g. the breakdown of Yugoslavia and Czechoslovakia, the constitutional crises in Belgium and Canada—suggest that it is very difficult to construct and maintain this transnational identity. And indeed schools have little idea how to go about promoting this identity.

This points to an important gap in political and educational theory. Most liberal accounts of civic identity argue that shared political principles are the basis of civic identity. Implicitly, however, they typically assume that citizens share not only principles, but also a common language and sense of membership in a national community. The problem is that neither the explicit emphasis on principles, nor the implicit emphasis on shared language and history, can explain social unity in multination states. If schools are to fulfil their responsibilities regarding citizenship education, we need an entirely new account of the basis of shared identity in multination states.

Insofar as a common national identity rests on identifying with a shared history, as well as a common language, this raises important questions about the teaching of history. One way—a particularly effective way—to promote identification with a group's history is to deliberately misrepresent that history. As William Galston puts it, in reference to the United States, 'rigorous historical research will almost certainly vindicate complex "revisionist" accounts of key figures in American history. Civic education, however, requires a nobler, moralizing history: a pantheon of heroes who confer legitimacy on central institutions and are worthy of emulation' (Galston 1991: 244). Similarly, Andrew Oldenquist argues that information about the American nation and government

should be taught so as to provide grounds for developing pride and affection . . . If instead we start nine-year-olds with a litany of evils and injustices, they will be likely to learn cynicism and alienation. A teacher may respond, 'But I teach about problems and injustices because I want to make my country better; if I did not have concern and affection for it I would not care about reforming it'. Precisely. The teacher did not acquire affection for our country by being told that we exterminated Indians, lynched Blacks, and slaughtered Vietnamese. The teacher's concern and affection survived this knowledge because of prior training and experience, and the pupils, like the teacher, need to acquire a basis for good citizenship before they are plunged into what is ugly. (AASA: 1987: 26)

This raises a number of troubling questions about citizenship education. For one thing, this way of promoting a national identity may undermine another goal of citizenship education—ie. the development of the capacity for independent and critical thought about society and its problems. Moreover, the proper development of civic virtue may require an honest appreciation of how those virtues were lacking in our history. It seems unlikely that children can learn the true meaning of civility and public reasonableness when historical figures who were in fact insensitive to great injustices are held up as exemplars of civic virtue (Callan 1994).

Also, it seems clear that the sanitized version of history that Galston and Oldenquist defend can itself be a cause of disunity. An account of history that focuses on the 'pantheon of heroes', while ignoring the historical mistreatment of women, blacks, Indians, Jews, etc., is essentially an account of the history of upper-class white men. And it is precisely this view of history that many minorities find so offensive. They are insulted by the way their struggles are rendered invisible in school books.

For these reasons, schools should, I think, teach history truthfully. But that doesn't mean that history should not play a special role in the curriculum. There is, I think, a legitimate role for schools to promote an emotional identification with our history. Students should view the nation's history as their history, and hence take pride in its accomplishments, as well as shame in its injustices. This sense of identification with the nation's history is one of the few means available to maintain social unity in a pluralistic state, and may be needed if citizens are to embrace their responsibilities for upholding just institutions, and rectifying historical injustices.[19]

---

[19] For a sensitive exploration of this issue, see Callan 1994.

This shows, yet again, that citizenship education is not simply a matter of teaching the basic facts about governmental institutions or constitutional principles. It is also a matter of inculcating particular habits, virtues, and identities.

17

Citizenship in an Era of Globalization: Commentary on Held

The literature is replete with discussions of the impact of globalization on us as workers, consumers, investors, or as members of cultural communities. Less attention has been paid to its impact on us as citizens—as participants in the process of democratic self-government. This is a vitally important issue, for if people become dissatisfied with their role as citizens, the legitimacy and stability of democratic political systems may erode.

David Held is one of the few theorists who has tried to systematically explore the implications of globalization on citizenship, both at the domestic level and at the level of transnational or global institutions (Held 1995: 1999). In effect, Held argues that globalization is eroding the capacity for meaningful democratic citizenship at the domestic level, as nation-states lose some of their historic sovereignty and become 'decision-takers' as much as 'decision-makers'. If meaningful citizenship is to exist in an era of globalization, therefore, it will require democratizing those transnational institutions which are increasingly responsible for important economic, environmental and security decisions.

While I agree with much of his analysis, I'd like to suggest that there is more room for optimism regarding the prospects for domestic citizenship than he suggests, but perhaps fewer grounds for optimism about global citizenship.

1. Domestic Citizenship

First, then, let me consider the impact of globalization on citizenship at the domestic level. Like many commentators, Held argues that globalization is reducing the historic sovereignty of nation-states, and so undermining the meaningfulness of participation in domestic politics. There is obviously some truth in this, but how extensive is the problem? Held gives a nuanced account of this process of globalization, and explicitly distances himself from the more exaggerated claims about the 'obsolescence' of the nation-state which

This was written as a commentary on David Held's 'The Transformation of Political Community: Rethinking Democracy in the Context of Globalization', in Ian Shapiro and Casiano Hacker-Cordon (eds.), *Democracy's Edges* (Cambridge University Press, 1999), pp. 84–111.

are made by the 'hyper-globalizers' (Held 1999: 97). Yet I think that Held too, in his own way, may overstate the situation.

It is certainly true that industrialized nation-states have less elbow room regarding macro-economic policy today than they did before. (It is doubtful whether Third World states ever had much elbow room in this area). This became painfully clear to Canadians when a left-wing government was elected in Canada's largest province (Ontario), and announced a policy of reflationary public spending to reduce unemployment. The response from international financial markets (and bond-rating services) was rapid and severe, and the government quickly dropped the proposal. This made all Canadians aware of how truly dependent we had become on the 'men in red suspenders', as our finance minister called Wall Street brokers.

But there are two possible explanations for this phenomenon. Some people see the loss of control by nation-states over macro-economic policy as an inherent and permanent feature of the new world order, which we simply have to learn to live with. This, implicitly at least, is Held's view. But other people argue that the dependence on international financial markets is not an inherent feature of globalization, but rather a contingent result of inter-national indebtedness. On this view, states that run up large foreign debts lose control over their macro-economic policy. We are now so accustomed to gov-ernments running up billions of dollars in deficits every year that we take it as normal, even inevitable, that governments owe hundreds of billions of dol-lars in debt to people outside the country. But it is insane to think that a coun-try can run up such debts for twenty years, and not have it affect their fiscal autonomy. If you put yourself in massive debt to other people, you lose some control over your life.

We will shortly be in a position to test these two hypotheses, since we are witnessing a steep decline in international indebtedness in many countries. What we see in Canada today, for example, as in many other countries, is a shift towards balanced budgets, and a reduction in the debt-to-GDP ratio. As a result, Canada is less dependent on foreign capital today than it has been for any time in the last fifteen years. As of 1998, the Canadian government no longer has to borrow money from the men in red suspenders, and in 1999 actually had a budget surplus. I believe that Canada is now regaining much (though not all) of its earlier macro-economic autonomy, including the option of adopting a jobs-creation programme, which is being seriously debated in Canada.

I think that Held also exaggerates the issue of capital mobility—i.e. the fear that companies will move their operations to whatever country offers the lowest taxes or wages. This is supposed to put dramatic limits on the extent to which countries can adopt more generous unemployment insurance pro-grammes, health and safety legislation, parental leaves, or minimum wages. Here again, there is obviously some truth to this concern, but we need to keep it in perspective. A reporter in a major American city recently selected at random a number of companies in the Yellow Pages and asked each of them whether they had thought about relocating to another country. The number who said yes was negligible. The option of moving overseas is irrelevant for large sectors of the economy—health care, education and training, construction, most retail, most services, agriculture, and so on. The issue of capital mobility is most relevant for mid-to-large manufacturing companies employing low-skilled workers. This is not an insignificant portion of the economy, but it has been a declining percentage for a long time. And it is difficult to see how Third World countries can ever develop except by competing in this sector. The loss of some of these low-skilled manufacturing jobs is inevitable, and perhaps even desirable from the point of view of international justice so long as there are fair transition programmes for those people thrown out of work. But there is no reason to think that large numbers of companies in other sectors will pack up and leave if the government tells them to provide better parental leaves to their workers.

So there remains considerable scope for national policy-making. Moreover, and equally importantly, countries continue to exercise their autonomy in very different ways, reflecting their different political cultures. Even if globalization puts similar pressures on all countries, they need not—and do not—respond in the same way. In his survey of social policy in OECD countries, Keith Banting notes that globalization puts great pressure on nation-states both to respond to the social stresses created by economic restructuring and to the demands of international competitiveness. None the less, despite fears of a race to the bottom or an inexorable harmonization of social programmes, the share of national resources devoted to social spending continues to inch upwards in OECD nations. And while all welfare states are under pressure, 'the global economy does not dictate the ways in which governments respond, and different nations are responding in distinctive ways that reflect their domestic politics and cultures' (Banting 1997: 280). I believe that citizens often care deeply about maintaining these national differences in social policy, and they provide considerable motivation for political participation in domestic politics. For example, the differences between Canadian and American approaches to social policy are increasing, not decreasing, and for Canadian citizens, these differences are worth keeping, and fighting for.

This points to another overstatement in Held's analysis. He argues that globalization is undermining the sense that each nation-state forms 'a political community of fate' (Held 1999: 102). I think he is vastly overstating the situation here. It is certainly true that 'some of the most fundamental forces and processes which determine the nature of life chances' cut across national boundaries (Held 1999: 103). But what determines the boundaries of a 'community of fate' is not the forces people are subjected to, but rather how they respond to those forces, and, in particular, what sorts of collectivities they identify with when responding to those forces. People belong to the same community of fate if they *care* about each other's fate, and want to *share* each other's fate—that is, want to meet certain challenges together, so as to share each other's blessings and burdens. Put another way, people belong to the same community of fate if they feel some sense of responsibility for one another's fate, and so want to deliberate together about how to respond collectively to the challenges facing the community. So far as I can tell, globalization has not eroded the sense that nation-states form separate communities of fate in this sense.

For example, as a result of NAFTA, North Americans are increasingly subjected to similar economic 'forces and processes'. But there is no evidence that they feel themselves part of a single 'community of fate' whose members care about and wish to share each other's fate. There is no evidence that Canadians now feel any strong sense of responsibility for the well-being of Americans or Mexicans (or vice-versa). Nor is there any evidence that Canadians feel any moral obligation to respond to these challenges in the same way that Americans or Mexicans do (or vice-versa). On the contrary, Canadians want to respond to these forces *as Canadians*—that is, Canadians debate amongst themselves how to respond to globalization, and they do so by asking what sort of society Canadians wish to live in, and what sorts of obligations Canadians have to each other. Americans ask the same questions amongst themselves, as do the Mexicans. The economic forces acting on the three countries may be similar, but the sense of communal identity and solidarity remains profoundly different, as has the actual policy responses to these forces. Despite being subject to similar forces, citizens of Western democracies are able to respond to these forces in their own distinctive ways, reflective of their 'domestic politics and cultures'. And most citizens continue to cherish this ability to deliberate and act as a national collectivity, on the basis of their own national solidarities and priorities.

So I do not accept the view that globalization has deprived domestic politics of its meaningfulness. Nation-states still possess considerable autonomy; their citizens still exercise this autonomy in distinctive ways, reflective of their national political cultures; and citizens still want to confront the challenges of globalization as national collectivities, reflective of their historic solidarities, and desire to share each other's fate. These facts all provide meaning and significance to domestic political participation.

I would not deny that many citizens in Western democracies feel dissatisfied with their political participation. But I would argue that the main sources of dissatisfaction with citizenship in Western democracies have little to do with globalization, and in fact long predate the current wave of globalization. In Canada, for example, we have an electoral system that systematically deprives smaller regions of effective political representation in Canadian political life. We have also been unable to regulate effectively campaign financing, with the result that the political process is increasingly seen as heavily skewed towards wealthy individuals and pressure groups. Nor have we changed party nomination procedures to reduce the systematic under-representation of women, Aboriginals, visible minorities, or the working class.

Moreover, Canada has a ridiculously centralized legislative process, in which the real power rests in the hands of a few people in the inner cabinet. We have no meaningful separation between the executive and legislative functions of government, and we have rigid party discipline. As a result, individual Members of Parliament, whether they are in the governing party or the opposition, have no real input into legislation—at least, much less influence than their counterparts in the American Congress. Parliamentary committees are supposed to provide a forum for input into the legislative process, but they are widely seen as a joke. For most Canadians, therefore, their elected MP is important only for constituency service, not as a conduit to the legislative process. What is the point in making one's views known to one's MP, when individual MPs seem to have no role in the legislative process?

These are the real problems with the political process in Canada—these are at the root of people's increasing sense that they have no real voice in political life. So far as I can tell, they have little to do with globalization. Globalization is not the cause of these problems, nor is there anything in globalization which prevents us from dealing with them. Consider the fate of the recent Canadian Royal Commission on Electoral Reform and Party Financing, which studied these issues in depth, and which issued a number of perfectly sensible recommendations about how to make our political system more equitable, and more responsive to the needs and opinions of Canadians (RCERPF 1991). There is nothing in the discipline of economic globalization or the rules of international regulatory agreements that prevent us from acting on these recommendations. There is nothing in NAFTA, or in our commitments to the UN or the WTO, which prevents us from adopting these recommendations tomorrow.

Yet little has been done to implement them. This is partly because it is rarely in the interest of governing parties to reform a process that put them in power. But it is also partly because we citizens have not demanded that government make it a priority. Whether as individual citizens, members of advocacy groups, or commentators in the media, Canadians have let the government off the hook for improving the democratic process. There is much we can do to protect and enhance our role as citizens, and if we decide not to, the fault lies not in globalization, but in ourselves.

I have focused on the flaws in Canada's political process, but I think we would find very similar problems in other countries—i.e. electoral systems which systemically produce unrepresentative legislatures; over-centralized legislative decision-making; excessive role of wealth in determining power and influence; and so on. These are the real causes of citizen's dissatisfaction with the political process. Globalization is not the cause of these problems, nor does it prevent us from solving them. Indeed, far from depriving domestic citizenship of its meaningfulness, globalization may actually be helping to renew it in important respects. For example, globalization is opening up the political process to new groups. Existing legislative and regulatory processes have been captured by entrenched interest groups for a long time now, but their traditional power bases are being eroded by globalization, and previously excluded groups are jumping in to fill the void (Simeon 1997: 307).

Also, globalization, far from encouraging political apathy, is itself one of the things which seems to mobilize otherwise apathetic people. Consider the vigorous debate over free trade in Canada or the debate in Denmark over the Maastricht Treaty. This should not be surprising since decisions about how to relate to other countries are themselves an important exercise of national sovereignty. This is perhaps clearer in the European context than in North America. It is quite clear, for example, that the desire of Spain or Greece to join the EU was not simply a matter of economic gain. It was also seen as a way of confirming their status as open, modern, democratic, and pluralistic states, after many years of being closed and authoritarian societies. Similarly, the decision about whether to admit new countries from Eastern Europe to the EU will be decided not just on the basis of economic gain, but also on the basis of moral obligations to assist newly democratizing countries, and on the basis of aspirations to create a Europe free of old divisions and hatreds. In other words, decisions by national collectivities to integrate into transnational institutions are, in part, decisions about what kind of societies people want to live in. Being open to the world is, for many people, an important part of their self-conception as members of modern pluralistic societies, and they autonomously decide to pursue that self-conception through various international agreements and institutions. Such decisions are not a denial of people's national identity or sovereignty, but precisely an affirmation of their national identity, and a highly valued exercise of their national sovereignty.

The best example of this, perhaps, is the desire of former Communist countries to join European organizations. It would be a profound misunderstanding to say that the decision by Baltic states to join the Council of Europe is an abridgement of their sovereignty. On the contrary, it is surely one of the most important symbolic affirmations of their new-found sovereignty. One of the most hated things about Communism was that it prevented Baltic nations from entering into such international alliances, and acting upon their self-conception as a 'European' country. Latvia's decision to join the Council of Europe was a way of declaring: 'now we are a sovereign people, able to act on our own wishes. No longer can anyone tell us who we can and cannot associate with.' Sovereignty is valued because it allows nations to act on their interests and identities, and the freedom to enter European organizations is an enormously important example of this sovereignty for Baltic nations.

These examples show, I think, that globalization often provides options which nations value, and decisions about whether and how to exercise these options have become lively topics for national debate. Globalization does constrain national legislatures, although the extent of this is often exaggerated. But globalization also enriches national political life, and provides new and valued options by which nations can collectively promote their interests and identities.

2. Cosmopolitan Citizenship

So globalization need not undermine the scope for meaningful democratic citizenship at the national level. By contrast, I am rather more sceptical about the likelihood that we can produce any meaningful form of transnational citizenship. I think we should be quite modest in our expectations about transnational citizenship, at least for the foreseeable future.

I heartily agree with many aspects of Held's conception of 'cosmopolitan democracy'. In particular, I endorse efforts to strengthen the international enforcement of human rights, and I accept Held's idea that the rules for according international recognition to states should include some reference to democratic legitimation. Principles of democracy and human rights should indeed be seen as 'cosmopolitan' in this sense—i.e. each state should be encouraged to respect these principles. But I'm more sceptical about the idea that transnational institutions and organizations can themselves be made democratic in any meaningful sense. Can we even make sense of the idea of 'democratizing' such institutions? When thinking about this question, it is important to remember that democracy is not just a formula for aggregating votes, but is also a system of collective deliberation and legitimation. The actual moment of voting (in elections, or within legislatures) is just one component in a larger process of democratic self-government. This process begins with public deliberation about the issues that need to be addressed and the options for resolving them. The decisions which result from this deliberation are then legitimated on the grounds that they reflect the considered will and common good of the people as a whole, not just the self-interest or arbitrary whims of the majority.

Arguably, these forms of deliberation and legitimation require some degree of commonality amongst citizens. Collective political deliberation is only feasible if participants understand and trust one another, and there is good reason to think that such mutual understanding and trust requires some underlying commonalities. Some sense of commonality or shared identity may be required to sustain a deliberative and participatory democracy. As I discussed in Chapter 10, there are good reasons to think that territorialized linguistic/national political units provide the best and perhaps the only sort of forum for genuinely participatory and deliberative politics.

Held argues that globalization is undermining the territorial basis of politics, and that territory is playing a less important role in the determination of political identity (Held 1999: 99). I think this is simply untrue, at least in the context of multilingual states. On the contrary, all the evidence from multilingual states suggests that language has become an increasingly important determinant of the boundaries of political community within each of these multilingual countries, and territory has become an increasingly important determinant of the boundaries of these language groups.

This is not to deny the obvious fact that we need international political institutions that transcend linguistic/national boundaries. We need such institutions to deal not only with economic globalization, but also with common environmental problems and issues of international security. At present, these organizations exhibit a major 'democratic deficit'. They are basically organized through intergovernmental relations, with little if any direct input from individual citizens. Held suggests that this is a serious problem, which can only be resolved by promoting new forms of 'cosmopolitan citizenship' which enable individuals and non-government groups to participate directly in transnational organizations (Held 1999: 104–8). For example, in the EU, there is considerable talk about increasing the power of the Parliament, which is directly elected by individual citizens, at the expense of the Commission and Council of Ministers, which operate through intergovernmental relations.

I am not so sure that Held's suggestion is realistic. It seems to me that there is no necessary reason why international institutions should be directly accountable to (or accessible to) individual citizens. To be sure, if international institutions are increasingly powerful, they must be held accountable. But why can we not hold them accountable *indirectly*, by debating at the national level how we want our national governments to act in intergovernmental contexts?

It seems clear that this is the way most Europeans themselves wish to reconcile democracy with the growth of the EU. There is very little demand for a strengthened EU Parliament. On the contrary, most people, in virtually all European states, show little interest in the affairs of the European Parliament, and little enthusiasm for increasing its powers. What they want, instead, is to strengthen the accountability of their *national* governments for how these governments act at the intergovernmental Council of Ministers. That is, citizens in each country want to debate amongst themselves, in their vernacular, what the position of their government should be on EU issues. Danes wish to debate, in Danish, what the Danish position should be *vis-à-vis*

Europe. They show little interest in starting a European-wide debate (in English?) about what the EU should do. They are keenly interesting in having a democratic debate about the EU, but the debate they wish to engage in is not a debate with other Europeans about 'what should we Europeans do?'. Rather, they wish to debate with each other, in Danish, about what we Danes should do. To put it another way, they want Denmark to be part of Europe, but they show little interest in becoming citizens of a European demos.

This is not to say that increasing the direct accountability and accessibility of transnational institutions is a bad thing. On the contrary, I support many of Held's suggestions in this regard. I agree that NGOs should have an increased role at the UN and other international bodies (Held 1999: 107–8). And I support the idea of a global civil society, in which people seek to mobilize the citizens of other countries to protest violations of human rights or environmental degradation in their own country. But it is misleading, I think, to describe this as the 'democratization' of transnational institutions, or as the creation of democratic citizenship on the transnational level. After all, these proposals would not create any form of collective deliberation and decision-making that connects and binds individuals across national boundaries.

For example, I am a member of Greenpeace, and support their efforts to gain a seat at the table of UN organizations, and their efforts to mobilize people around the world to stop acid rain, the burning of tropical rainforests, or illegal whaling. But this does not really involve democratic citizenship at the transnational level. The fact that Greenpeace has a seat at the table of the UN or the EU, or that Canadian members of Greenpeace write letters protesting Japan's whaling policy, does not change the fact that there is no meaningful forum for democratic deliberation and collective will-formation above the level of the nation-state. I can try to influence Brazil's deforestation policy, but that doesn't mean that Brazilians and Canadians are now citizens of some new transnational democratic community. Transnational activism is a good thing, as is the exchange of information across borders. But the only forum in which genuine democracy occurs is within national boundaries.

Transnational activism by individuals or NGOs is not the same as democratic citizenship. Moreover, attempts to create a genuinely democratic form of transnational citizenship could have negative consequences for democratic citizenship at the domestic level. For example, I am not convinced that it would be a good thing to strengthen the (directly elected) EU Parliament at the expense of the (intergovernmental) EU Council. The result of 'democratizing' the EU would be to take away the veto power which national governments now have over most EU decisions. Decisions made by the EU Parliament, unlike those made by the Council, are not subject to the national veto. This means that the EU would cease to be accountable to citizens through their national legislatures. At the moment, if a Danish citizen dislikes an EU decision, she can try to mobilize other Danes to change their government's position on the issue. But once the EU is 'democratized'—i.e. once the Parliament replaces the Council as the major decision-making body—a Danish citizen would have to try to change the opinions of the citizens of every other European country (none of which speak her language). And, for obvious and understandable reasons, few Europeans seek this sort of 'democratization'. For Danish citizens to engage in a debate with other Danes, in Danish, about the Danish position vis-à-vis the EU is a familiar and manageable task. But for Danish citizens to engage in a debate with Italians to try to develop a common European position is a daunting prospect. In what language would such a debate occur, and in what forums? Not only do they not speak the same language, or share the same territory, they also do not read the same newspapers, or watch the same television shows, or belong to the same political parties. So what would be the forum for such a trans-European debate?

Given these obstacles to a trans-European public debate, it is not surprising that neither the Danes nor the Italians have shown any enthusiasm for 'democratizing' the EU. They prefer exercising democratic accountability through their national legislatures. Paradoxically, then, the net result of increasing direct democratic accountability of the EU through the elected Parliament would in fact be to undermine democratic citizenship. It would shift power away from the national level, where mass participation and vigorous democratic debate is possible, towards the transnational level, where democratic participation and deliberation is very difficult. As Grimm argues, given that there is no common European mass media at the moment, and given that the prospects for creating such a Europeanized media in the foreseeable future 'are absolutely non-existent', dramatically shifting power from the Council to the Parliament would 'aggravate rather than solve the problem' of the democratic deficit (Grimm 1995: 296).

In short, globalization is undoubtedly producing a new civil society, but it has not yet produced anything we can recognize as transnational democratic citizenship. Nor is it clear to me that we should aspire to such a new form of citizenship. Many of our most important moral principles should be cosmopolitan in scope—e.g. principles of human rights, democracy, and environmental protection—and we should seek to promote these ideals internationally. But our democratic citizenship is, and will remain for the foreseeable future, national in scope.

18

Liberal Egalitarianism and Civic Republicanism: Friends or Enemies?

Michael Sandel's *Democracy's Discontent* presents us with a domestic equivalent of Samuel Huntington's 'clash of civilizations' thesis. Huntington argues that international relations should be understood as driven by a clash between rival and incommensurable world-views—e.g. Christian, Islamic, and Confucian—each with their own conception of the person, society and polity. Sandel argues that within the Christian West—or at least within the United States—domestic politics should be understood as a clash between two rival and incommensurable worldviews—civic republicanism and procedural liberalism. According to Sandel, procedural liberalism has increasingly displaced civic republicanism, with disastrous consequences for American democracy.

Presenting American politics as a clash of two world-views makes it seem rather more exciting than an old-fashioned view of politics as a clash of innumerable and cross-cutting interests and values. But I doubt it is the most accurate or helpful way to understand politics. Since I am not an expert on American history, I will not dispute Sandel's account of the historical interaction between these two world-views. I will instead focus on the contemporary situation, and ask whether civic republicanism and procedural liberalism are allies or enemies in confronting the 'discontent' that Western democracies currently suffer from. I will argue that they are—or should be—allies, and that exaggerating their differences is philosophically suspect and politically counterproductive.

I will start by specifying more clearly what sort of procedural liberalism I wish to defend—namely, the sort of left-wing liberal egalitarianism associated with Rawls and Dworkin (section 1). I will then explain why I think Sandel exaggerates the differences between this version of procedural liberalism and civic republicanism (section 2). This is not to deny that the two approaches will sometimes generate conflicting recommendations. But in these (relatively rare) cases, I will argue that we should prefer procedural liberalism to civic republicanism—that is, promoting the collective good of self-government does not justify the unjust treatment of individuals (section 3).

It seems to me that Sandel has two different criticisms of procedural liberalism. In some places, he seems to say that procedural liberalism is wrong in principle, in the sense that it gets the wrong answer on a variety of issues, independently of its long-term sustainability. But in other places, he seems to be saying that it is desirable in principle, but unsustainable in practice. That is, it gets the right answer on issues, taken one by one, but the cumulative effect of these decisions is to undermine the viability of liberal democratic institutions.

I will focus on the first principled objection, but I will return at the end of the chapter to the second practical objection. I think this second objection raises an important issue which liberal theorists have not adequately addressed, but reflecting on it helps to clarify why liberalism and republicanism should be seen as allies, not enemies (section 4).

1. What is Procedural Liberalism?

As Sandel notes, procedural liberalism can take many forms. At one end of the political spectrum, there is the right-wing libertarianism associated with Robert Nozick and David Gauthier, which affirms the sanctity of property rights, and which is hostile to all forms of state-enforced redistribution; at the other end of the spectrum, there is the left-wing liberal egalitarianism associated with John Rawls, Ronald Dworkin, and Bruce Ackerman, which affirms the necessity of rectifying undeserved inequalities, and which gives moral priority to the well-being of the least well-off.

At first glance, these appear to be very different—even diametrically opposed—theories. But Sandel insists that at a deeper level, these different forms of procedural liberalism share certain key assumptions—in particular, a conception of the unencumbered self, and of the neutral state. And it is these shared assumptions which underlie and explain the inability of procedural liberalism, in either its right-wing or left-wing form, to deal with democracy's discontents.

I agree that there are important assumptions that are shared by right- and left-wing versions of procedural liberalism. However, the political implications of these assumptions may—and I think do—differ dramatically between right-wing and left-wing liberalism. Assumptions which have disastrous political consequences when combined with a belief in the sanctity of property rights may have quite different consequences when combined with a belief in giving moral priority to the least well-off. To properly assess the impact of procedural liberalism, therefore, we need to pick a particular version of it, and see how these assumptions about the individual and state play themselves out in that context.

Since I endorse the left-wing version of procedural liberalism, I will focus in the rest of the paper on the relationship between civic republicanism and liberal egalitarianism.[1] What then is (left-wing) procedural liberalism? Sandel uses a number of terms to describe this theory—e.g. in some places, he describes it as a 'proceduralist' or 'neutralist' theory; in other places, he describes it as giving priority to the right over the good; in yet other places, he talks about unencumbered selves, autonomy, and the priority of the self over its ends. All of these terms and phrases are ambiguous and potentially confusing, so let me specify what exactly I understand by liberal egalitarianism. I would characterize it in terms of three main claims about the self, the state, and fairness respectively. The first two are common to both left-wing and right-wing liberalism, the third is distinctive to left-wing liberal egalitarianism:

(a) Rational Revisability

Individuals are not assumed to have fixed and unchangeable conceptions of the good. Rather each individual should have the capacity to rationally reflect on the ends she currently endorses, and to revise these ends if they are no longer deemed worthy of her continued allegiance. The state must make it possible for individuals to develop and exercise this capacity for rational revisability. The state does this in part by providing children with a suitable liberal education that develops this capacity, and in part by prohibiting attempts by other individuals or groups to prevent people from exercising this capacity. (This commitment to rational revisability is the claim which Sandel sometimes refers to as the 'unencumbered self', or as 'the priority of the self over its ends'.)[2]

---

[1] Although left-wing liberalism has arguably been the less influential of the two in American politics, Sandel views Rawls's theory as the most important statement of procedural liberalism. So my focus on left-liberalism is consistent, I think, with Sandel's own emphasis.

[2] The claim that our conceptions of the good are rationally revisable does not entail, as Sandel sometimes suggests, that all of our ends are 'chosen'. On the contrary, many of our ends are inherited from our family or community. Liberals simply insist that however we originally acquired our ends, we are capable of rationally evaluating and potentially revising them. Nor does the revisability claim entail, as Sandel sometimes suggests, that our conception of the good is a matter of 'preference' rather than 'obligation'. On the contrary, conceptions of the good typically specify desirable roles and relationships, each of which carries with it various obligations. A conception of the good, in other words, is not just a list of preferences, but also a specification of obligations. However, the rational revisability view insists that we are capable of rationally reflecting on the worth of the roles and relationships entailed by our conception of the good. We can judge whether the obligation-imposing roles we have entered into are still worthy of our allegiance. In short, the crux of the view is not that our conceptions of the good are chosen rather than inherited, nor that they are matters of preference rather than obligation. The crux of the view is that our conceptions of the good are rationally revisable, and that the state should make possible the development and exercise of this capacity for rational revisability.

(b) The Non-Perfectionist State

The state should be neutral amongst conceptions of the good, in the sense that it should not justify its legislation by appeal to some ranking of the intrinsic worth of particular conceptions of the good. The role of the state is to protect the capacity for individuals to judge for themselves the worth of different conceptions of the good life, and to provide a fair distribution of rights and resources to enable people to pursue their conception of the good. The state tells people what is rightfully theirs, and what rightfully belongs to others, and insists that people adjust their conception of the good to respect the rightful claims of others. But if someone's conception of the good does respect the rightful claims of others, then the state should not be assessing the intrinsic merits of her (justice-respecting) way of life. The state does not justify its actions by reference to some public ranking of the intrinsic worth of different (justice-respecting) ways of life, for there is no public ranking to refer to. As Rawls puts it, government is neutral amongst different conceptions of the good 'not in the sense that there is an agreed public measure of intrinsic value or satisfaction with respect to which all these conceptions come out equal, but in the sense that they are not evaluated at all from a [public] standpoint'.[3] (This is the claim which Sandel sometimes refers to as the 'neutral state', or as the 'priority of justice to the good'.)

These first two claims are common to all forms of procedural liberalism. The third, however, is distinctive to left-wing liberal egalitarianism.

(c) Rectifying Morally Arbitrary Inequalities

Inequalities which are 'morally arbitrary'—that is, inequalities which are not chosen or deserved—are unjust, and should be rectified. A liberal theory of justice will insist that individuals can come to have different holdings as a result of different choices that they have made about how they wish to lead their lives (e.g. different choices about the trade-off between work and leisure; or between current consumption and long-term savings; or between aversion to risk). However, if people have unequal holdings as a result of their circumstances—rather than their own choices—then these are morally arbitrary and unjust. Sources of morally arbitrary inequalities include not only social circumstances (e.g. being born into a disadvantaged family), but also natural endowments (e.g. being born with fewer physical or mental natural talents). As Dworkin puts it, on a left-liberal conception of distributive justice, distribution should be 'choice-sensitive' but 'circumstance-insensitive'— it should allow for differences in holdings due to people's choices, but rectify inequalities due to people's natural endowments or social circumstances.

---

[3] Rawls 1982: 172.

These three claims constitute the core of left-wing procedural liberalism.[4] While I have not used precisely the same terminology that Sandel uses to describe this theory, I think (and hope) that he would agree with this basic characterization. What I now want to argue is that this left-wing version of procedural liberalism is an ally of civic republicanism on most issues, and that Sandel's attempt to paint procedural liberalism as an enemy is philosophically misguided and politically unhelpful.

One reason for my scepticism about Sandel's approach is that it fits uncomfortably well into the long and unfortunate tradition of left sectarianism. People on the left who agree on 95 per cent of the actual issues confronting our society spend all of our time arguing with each other about the 5 per cent of issues we disagree about, rather than fighting alongside each other for the 95 per cent of issues we have in common. My sense is that these internecine debates are often unnecessary and counterproductive. Sandel, however, insists that liberal egalitarianism is the cause, not the solution, of democracy's discontents. According to Sandel, progress can only be made by diminishing the hold of liberal egalitarianism on the popular imagination and popular discourse. This is what I want to challenge.

2. Is Liberal Egalitarianism the Cause of Discontent?

The heart of Sandel's objection to procedural liberalism can be put this way:

(a) Americans today are feeling discontent because of a loss of a sense of community, and a loss of a sense of mastery over their fate;
(b) This sense of discontent can only be solved by attending to issues of communal identity and civic virtue;
(c) Procedural liberalism cannot attend to either communal identity or civic virtue because of its commitment to rational revisability (the 'unencumbered self') and the non-perfectionist state ('state neutrality').

I will accept, for the moment, claims (a) and (b), and focus on claim (c). Is it true that liberal egalitarians cannot attend to issues of communal identity and civic virtue? It is true that the core principles of liberal egalitarianism, as

---

[4] These three claims are interrelated, though not logically entailed by each other. For example, the commitment to a non-perfectionist state flows naturally from a commitment to rational revisability. It seems plausible to suppose that the best way to ensure that everyone has an equal and effective capacity to rationally reflect on their ends is if the state avoids giving official sanction to some (justice-respecting) ways of life over other (justice-respecting) ways of life. However, this is not strictly logically entailed, and there are some liberals who endorse rational revisability but reject the commitment to a non-perfectionist state (e.g. Raz 1986).

I have described them above, do not say anything about these issues. It is fair to say, I think, that while liberal egalitarianism has an intrinsic and foundational commitment to a particular conception of individual agency and social justice, it has no similar intrinsic or foundational commitment to a particular conception of communal identity or civic virtue. From a liberal egalitarian point of view, communal identities and civic virtues can only play a secondary role, to be judged by the extent to which they are consistent with, or promote, foundational values of individual agency and social justice.

But to say that communal identities and civic virtues can only play a secondary role within liberal egalitarianism is not to say that they can play no role at all. On the contrary, it may turn out that they play a vital and indispensable role. It may be that liberal egalitarian values can best be achieved, or indeed can only be achieved, within societies that have certain sorts of communal identities and civic virtues. If so, liberal egalitarians would have the strongest possible reasons, from within their own theory, for attending to issues of communal identity and civic virtue. From a liberal egalitarian point of view, this is an open question, to be evaluated empirically, on a case-by-case basis.

Some critics might think that treating communal identities and civic virtues as secondary values, to be assessed in terms of their impact on liberal justice, is inadequate. Some critics will insist that they should be accorded intrinsic value, and should be promoted as such, even at the expense of liberal values of individual agency and social justice. This is indeed what classical civic republicans have often claimed, and I will return to this question below. But Sandel himself makes the rather different—and quite puzzling—claim that liberal egalitarianism cannot address these issues at all, even as secondary values. According to Sandel, procedural liberalism is precluded *in principle* from using state policies to promote any conception of communal identity or civic virtue.

I think Sandel is simply mistaken here. It seems to me that he has seriously misunderstood what the liberal commitments to rational revisability and non-perfectionism entail. According to Sandel, procedural liberalism is unable to deal with issues of identity and virtue because of its underlying commitment to state neutrality. His argument, insofar as I understand it, is that if the state is committed to neutrality amongst conceptions of the good, then it must also be neutral amongst conceptions of communal identity and civic virtue, since these are inextricably tied to particular conceptions of the good life.

Sandel never actually defends the claim that conceptions of communal identity and civic virtue are inextricably tied to particular conceptions of the good, and it is not clear what exactly is the relationship he sees between them. He often simply conflates them, as if they were one and the same thing. At times, he seems to making a definitional claim—i.e. that conceptions of identity and virtue just *are* conceptions of the good life. But in other places, he seems to be making more of an argument by analogy—i.e. that whatever reason liberals have for being neutral amongst conceptions of the good are also reasons for being neutral amongst conceptions of identity and virtue.

Since I'm not sure what exactly Sandel is claiming here, I'm not sure how best to respond to it. But let me start with the definitional claim. It is clearly not true that promoting a conception of virtue is *by definition* promoting a conception of the good. It all depends on *why* one is promoting a conception of civic virtue. If the state promotes certain virtues on the grounds that possessing these virtues will make someone's life more worthwhile or fulfilling, then clearly it is promoting a particular conception of the good. However, if the state is promoting these virtues on the grounds that possessing them will make someone more likely to fulfil her obligations of justice, then it is not promoting a particular conception of the good. It has made no claim whatsoever about what makes her life go better, or about what ends in life are rewarding or fulfilling. It may well be that possessing these virtues is actually a burden to some people. For example, people who possess a willingness to remedy the disadvantages of others may perceive the exercise of this virtue as involving a sacrifice of their own well-being for the sake of others.

Of course, some people will find the exercise of these virtues inherently rewarding and fulfilling. Moreover, insofar as the liberal state insists that people abide by the requirements of justice, then it is likely that people will try to find ways to make the fulfilment of their obligations of justice as rewarding as possible. But personal gratification need not be—and in a liberal society is not—the basis on which the state promotes civic virtues. Civic virtues are promoted because, and insofar as, they enable us to achieve liberal principles of individual agency and social justice.

In short, a virtue is not a conception of the good unless it is justified on the basis that it enriches the life of the person who possesses it. But that isn't the only possible justification for promoting civic virtues, which can instead be defended as a precondition of justice to others.

The same applies to questions of communal identity. Promoting a particular communal identity need not involve promoting a particular conception of the good life. It all depends on what sort of identity it is, and why it is being promoted. If the basis for the communal identity is a shared conception of the good, then promoting such an identity will obviously involve promoting a particular conception of the good life. However, this is not the only basis for communal identities. In many cases, the basis for communal identity is not a shared conception of the good, but rather a more diffuse sense of belonging to an intergenerational society, having a common past and sharing a common future.

This, indeed, is how national identities typically operate in modern Western democracies. Citizens think of themselves as 'American', for example, and identify with other Americans, without sharing a conception of the good. They may automatically think of other Americans as 'one of us', without knowing anything about the others' conception of the good. Americans disagree with each other (sometimes violently) about the good life, but they still recognize and identify each other as Americans, because they share a sense of belonging to an intergenerational society that has some historical reference points and a common future. They may disagree about how to interpret their past, and may have very different hopes for the future, but they recognize each other as belonging to the same society, and this sense of shared belonging underlies their national identity.

Liberal states have historically promoted this sort of 'thin' national identity. And they have done so, not in order to promote a particular conception of the good life, but rather to increase the likelihood that citizens will fulfil their obligations of justice. We know that people are more likely to make sacrifices for others if these others are viewed as 'one of us', and so promoting a sense of national identity strengthens the sense of mutual obligation needed to sustain liberal justice.[5] If the state promotes such 'thin' communal identities on the grounds that possessing them will make someone more likely to fulfil her obligations of justice, then it is not violating liberal neutrality. The identity it is promoting is not grounded in a particular conception of the good; and it is not saying that a life with this particular identity is more rewarding than a life with some other identity. It is not saying anything about what ends in life are rewarding or fulfilling. It is simply saying that we are more likely to fulfil our obligations of justice if we view others as members of 'our' society.

As these examples show, I hope, the key distinction in procedural liberalism theory is between 'the right' (or justice) and 'the good'. A liberal state upholds principles of right, but it is individuals who judge the good. Sandel knows this, of course. He emphasizes it himself at the beginning of his book. But he then misjudges where this dividing line falls. He assumes, without any explanation or argument, that virtues and identities automatically fall on the side of 'the good' rather than 'the right', and hence assumes that promoting particular virtues or identities is a matter of promoting a conception of the good, rather than upholding principles of right. He writes as if issues of rights and resources fall on the side of 'the right', whereas issues of virtues and identities fall on the side of 'the good'.

But this is a mistake. The line between the good and the right is orthogonal to the distinction between identities/virtues and rights/resources. The distinction between the good and the right is a distinction between two kinds of *justifications* for public policies, not a distinction between two kinds of

---

[5] Of course, liberal states have promoted national identities for other, less praiseworthy, goals—e.g. to encourage uncritical patriotism, and the willingness to die for one's country. For a more detailed discussion of the liberal justifications for nation-building, see Ch. 11.

objects of public policy. Liberals insist that whatever the object of public policy—whether it is legal rights, economic resources, political institutions, civic virtues, or communal identities—the aim of state policy should be to promote principles of right, not to promote particular conceptions of the good. By contrast, a perfectionist state would decide all issues of public policy—whether rights, resources or virtues—on the basis of how best to promote a particular conception of the good life which has been judged to be the most rewarding or fulfilling.

Rawls himself makes this point quite clear. In an important passage on the role of virtues within procedural liberalism, Rawls distinguishes between what he calls 'classical republicanism' and 'civic humanism'. According to classical republicanism, certain political virtues must be promoted amongst citizens in order to prevent the degeneration of liberal democracy into tyranny or religious/nationalist fanaticism. Rawls notes that this justification for promoting civic virtues is entirely consistent with procedural liberalism, since they are defended as preconditions for liberal justice. By contrast, 'civic humanism' asserts that political virtues should be promoted because our 'essential nature' is realized in political life, which is the 'privileged locus of the good life'. As Rawls notes, there is a 'fundamental opposition' between procedural liberalism and civic humanism, since civic humanists defend virtues on the basis of a particular conception of the good life, not on grounds of justice.[6]

So there is no reason in principle why liberal states cannot promote certain conceptions of virtue or identity. It all depends on what the virtues and identities are, and why they are being promoted. If these virtues and identities encourage individuals to fulfil their obligations of justice, while still leaving them free to rationally assess and revise their own conceptions of the good, then they are fully consistent with foundational liberal values of individual agency and social justice. If civic virtues and communal identities help individuals to identify and fulfil their obligations to others, then they are consistent with, and indeed promote, liberal egalitarianism.

And these are precisely the sorts of virtues and identities which liberal states (and liberal theorists) have always endorsed. Liberal states have always promoted certain virtues of responsible citizenship and certain national identities—indeed, the promotion of these virtues and identities was perhaps the key justification liberal theorists gave for mandatory education.[7]

Sandel often writes as if the term 'conception of the good life' covers all normative beliefs. But a conception of the good life is just that—i.e. a

---

[6] Rawls 1988: 272–3. Although Sandel quotes repeatedly from Rawls, it is interesting to note that he never mentions this passage, which is perhaps the most directly relevant to the argument of his book.

[7] For more on the role of public education in promoting civic virtues and national identities, see Ch. 16.

conception of what makes one's life good, of what makes one's life go better. It is a conception of what makes one's life worth living, of the activities, relationships, and goods which make one's life fuller and richer and more rewarding and satisfying. And so when liberals say that the state should be neutral amongst conceptions of the good life, they mean that the state should not rank the goodness of different ways of life. The state should leave judgements about the good life to individuals, and should seek instead to ensure a free and fair context for individuals to make these judgements.

This does not preclude the promotion of certain virtues or identities so long as they are defended as identifying the limits within which we can pursue our conception of the good life. Possessing certain virtues and identities can help us to recognize when our pursuit of our own good is violating the rightful claims of others. These virtues and identities do not tell us where our own good lies; rather, they tell us how far we can go in pursuing our own good. As Rawls puts it, 'justice draws the limit, the good shows the point'.[8] Liberals can endorse state promotion of those virtues and identities which help us 'draw the limit', but will not endorse state promotion of virtues and identities which reflect a particular conception of 'the point' of human existence.[9]

3. But is it Enough?

There is an obvious objection to what I have argued so far. Someone might argue that even if procedural liberalism can endorse *some* virtues and identities, it cannot endorse the right ones, or perhaps cannot endorse them strongly enough. This objection could be developed at either a theoretical level, in terms of what liberalism is capable in principle of endorsing, or at a more practical level, in terms of what liberalism is likely to lead to in practice.

---

[8] Rawls, 1988: 252.

[9] Sandel might reply that even if promoting certain virtues and identities is not strictly equivalent to promoting conceptions of the good, the reasons liberals have for objecting to the latter apply equally to the former. This would be true if the basis for the liberal objection to state perfectionism is simply that it is controversial, and hence likely to cause social conflict. But this cannot be the predominant objection, for as Sandel himself notes, avoiding perfectionism can be just as controversial as engaging in it. Moreover, enforcing norms of justice is also very controversial (particularly left-wing norms of justice). So liberal egalitarians can hardly be committed to minimizing controversy. Instead, the major reason why liberals object to state perfectionism is that it is seen as a threat to foundational liberal values of individual agency and social justice. State perfectionism is seen, rightly or wrongly, as likely to impede rational revisability and distort the fair distribution of resources. By contrast, the state promotion of responsible citizenship and national identities can promote, not hinder, these foundational liberal values.

Let me start with the theoretical level. As I noted earlier, liberalism treats issues of virtues and identities as dependent values, to be assessed in terms of, and constrained by, deeper liberal principles of individual agency and social justice. Perhaps Sandel would argue that we should view them as intrinsic values, and endorse them even if they conflict with the requirements of liberal justice. For example, perhaps he would argue that we should not only be Rawls's 'classical republicans', who promote political virtue in order to sustain just institutions, but also civic humanists, who promote political virtues because our 'essential nature' is realized in political life which is the 'privileged locus of the good life'.

This would be an interesting argument to pursue. Unfortunately, Sandel never really tackles this question. He spends so much time defending a platitude—namely, the view that politics must attend to issues of virtues and identities—that he doesn't get very far in developing the details of his preferred account of virtues and identities. Which virtues and identities would he promote, and how would they differ from the sorts of virtues and identities which liberal egalitarians promote?

For example, liberal theorists working on the topic of citizenship education have typically emphasized the importance of promoting virtues of civility, public reasonableness, a sense of justice, and a critical attitude towards government authority.[10] These are all defended on the grounds that they are needed to create and sustain just institutions (rather than as constituents of a particular conception of the good life). They are defended as consistent with liberal commitments to rational revisability, and with liberal prohibitions on state perfectionism. How would Sandel's conception of citizenship education differ? Are there additional virtues that he would add? And if so, would he defend them on grounds of justice or the good?

Similarly, liberal theorists working on the topic of political community have typically emphasized the importance of promoting a variety of political identities, from the local (local self-government as a school in democracy) to the national (the nation as the largest feasible unit of redistribution), and also including special protections for minority ethnocultural identities.[11] Here again, the justification for state recognition of these identities is that they help to sustain just institutions, and to rectify injustices. They are defended as consistent with liberal commitments to rational revisability, and with liberal prohibitions on state perfectionism. How would Sandel's conception of identity politics differ? Which additional identities would he promote, and would he defend them on grounds of justice or the good?

Without a more detailed answer to these questions, it is impossible to judge whether Sandel's conception of republican politics is superior to, or

[10] See the works on citizenship education by Spinner, Callan, Gutmann, Macedo, etc, discussed in Ch. 16.

[11] See the works of liberal nationalists and liberal multiculturalists discussed in Ch. 2.

even genuinely different from, the liberal egalitarian politics he claims to be objecting to. In fact, I could not locate a single instance where Sandel clearly and explicitly endorses the promotion of particular virtues or identities even when it conflicts with liberal egalitarian justice.

One can imagine cases where promoting civic humanist virtues as part of a conception of the good life (rather than as a way of sustaining just institutions) would come at the expense of liberal justice. Indeed, Sandel himself cites an example from American history, although it is not clear whether he endorses it. In the nineteenth century, many Americans argued that their conception of the good life, which viewed republican political participation as uniquely and intrinsically valuable, could only be sustained by westward expansion—that is, by conquering and displacing the American Indians. Without the promise of new land and a unifying national project of expansion, these intrinsically valuable forms of republican political participation would diminish, replaced by more mundane and instrumental forms of politics. Let us assume that this claim was true, and that an intrinsically valuable way of life bound up with political participation could only be sustained by unjust treatment of Indians. Does the promotion of a civic humanist conception of the good life justify this injustice?

Similarly, imagine that the most effective way to mobilize people to participate in politics and to think about the collective good is to create some perceived threat to national survival, either from inside the country (e.g. illegal immigrants, homosexuals, Communists, drug addicts), or outside (e.g. the Soviet Union, Islamic terrorists). Imagine, in other words, that the best or only way to mobilize people to participate in republican self-government is to declare war on some invented enemy. This is not a fanciful example. Sandel himself notes that xenophobes are often quite successful in mobilizing people, and warns us against this danger. But what if this sort of mobilization in fact creates more of what Sandel calls 'republican freedom', or the 'collective good of self-government', for a greater number of people? What if it increases most people's sense of community and collective mastery, and reduces their feelings of discontent with democracy? What if we face a trade-off between promoting republican freedom for the many, and upholding justice for the few? What if promoting civic humanism as a way of life reduces the discontent of the majority, albeit at the expense of oppressing a minority?

My guess is that in all of these cases, Sandel would side with liberal justice. However much he describes republican freedom as an alternative to liberal justice, my guess is that he would not promote the former at the expense of the latter, and that he (tacitly) views principles of justice as setting constraints on the promotion of republican freedom. I suspect that in the end he shares the liberal belief that political institutions are not to be judged primarily by how satisfying they are to participants, but by how just their results are.

Perhaps Sandel would disagree with this. Since he never explicitly addresses the question, it is difficult to say. But if so, he has provided no real argument why we should abandon the liberal view that justice is the first virtue of political institutions. Suppose we face a choice between, on the one hand, political institutions that are just but which provide few opportunities for intrinsically rewarding participation, and, on the other hand, political institutions that are unjust to the minority but which provide intrinsically rewarding participation to the majority. Faced with this choice, liberals would choose just political institutions. Political institutions that claim coercive power over all citizens should not be seen as an arena for the majority to pursue intrinsically valuable ways of life. The *raison d'être* of political institutions is to secure justice for all citizens, and the promotion of republican virtues must operate within this constraint.

Of course, in many cases, enhancing the quality of political participation would not require sacrificing liberal justice. On the contrary, most plausible suggestions for how to improve collective self-government would also involve improving liberal justice—that is, they would involve reducing undeserved inequalities in people's social status, economic resources and political influence. And that is just my point. On most real-world issues, civic republicans and liberal egalitarians should be allies. There is so much that can be done to promote both liberal equality and republican democracy that it is almost idle speculation to ask what we should do when the two conflict. But if Sandel insists that we declare where we would stand in the event of such a conflict, then I would side with the liberals, and I don't see that he has provided any argument in the book to challenge this.

But perhaps Sandel would make a more practical objection to my argument so far. He might argue that, whatever the theoretical resources of liberal egalitarianism, the fact remains that in practice procedural liberalism has failed to deal satisfactorily with issues of virtues and identities. According to Sandel, the triumph of procedural liberalism in the United States has gone hand-in-hand with an increasing reluctance to deal with issues of virtue and identity. Whether or not procedural liberalism can in principle deal with such issues, it has failed to do so in practice, and this is surely no accident—there must be some internal obstacle or inhibition within procedural liberalism that makes it difficult to address these issues.

But here, I think, we need to be cautious in talking about 'the triumph of the procedural republic', as if there were a single version of procedural liberalism which has conquered American jurisprudence and political discourse. On the contrary, as I noted earlier, there are at least two very different forms of procedural liberalism—right and left—which have different implications for issues of virtue and identity. Insofar as procedural liberalism has triumphed in the US, it is predominantly the right-wing version. The United States has a higher (and growing) level of inequality amongst citizens than other Western democracies, and the lowest (and declining) level of redistribution. Insofar as the US has been influenced by liberalism, it has been influenced by the right-wing view which rejects the principle that inequalities should be rectified (and a fortiori rejects the idea that the state should promote the sort of virtues and identities which would encourage people to fulfil obligations of egalitarian justice).

Since left-wing liberalism remains a voice in the wilderness in the US, at least compared to other Western democracies, we have no clear idea what effect it would have were it to triumph politically. Moreover, insofar as right-wing liberalism has triumphed, it is at least in part because it has formed an alliance with other, non-liberal, strands of American political thought. Sandel notes that republicanism in the United States has historically been influenced by and distorted by racism, nativism, class prejudice, sexism, fear of big government, etc. But the same is true of liberalism, and the sort of right-wing liberalism that has triumphed in the United States is a strange amalgamation of ideologies and convictions. (Consider the unholy alliance of right-wing liberals and cultural conservatives under Reagan.)

It is quite misleading, therefore, to talk as if current American institutions, or current Supreme Court jurisprudence, reflect the triumph of any one particular political theory. I agree with Sandel that political theories—what he calls 'public philosophies'—are important. They do influence political institutions. But they also influence each other, to the extent that it becomes implausible, if not impossible, to describe any particular institution or decision as the pure and unalloyed consequence of a particular political philosophy.

How then can we assess the impact of left-wing liberal egalitarianism in practice, given that it is relatively weak on the ground in the United States, and always influenced and distorted by other political theories and cultural trends? It seems to me that there are two possible routes, neither of which Sandel really pursues. The first would be to engage in cross-country comparisons. We know that other Western democracies have also been increasingly influenced by 'procedural liberalism', and for the same reasons as the United States—e.g. increasing diversity, secularization, autonomy, mobility, etc. Moreover, in most of these countries, the left-wing version of procedural liberalism is considerably stronger than in the United States. (Indeed, the influence of Rawls on public discourse has been much greater in many Western European countries than in the US). Public opinion polls have shown that citizens in most Western democracies express greater support for liberal egalitarian values than in the United States.

Of course, in each of these countries, other political ideologies and cultural characteristics have influenced left-wing liberal egalitarianism. So none of them provides a pure form of left-wing liberal egalitarianism in practice. But many of these local influences get filtered out if we focus on the general cross-country trends. And so far as I can tell, the evidence suggests that left-wing procedural liberalism in these countries has not prevented governments from adopting successful policies to promote both civic virtues and communal identities, and, more generally, from sustaining not only higher levels of political participation than in the United States, but also higher levels of satisfaction with this participation. I would hypothesize that the more influential liberal egalitarianism is in a country, the more likely it is that citizens have not only a strong sense of national identity, but vibrant local politics, and recognition of minority ethnocultural identities; also, I expect they are more likely to exhibit a willingness to make sacrifices for co-citizens, have a more equitable level of political participation, and a higher sense of efficacy regarding political participation. I don't have the evidence at hand to confirm or refute this hypothesis, but this is the sort of evidence that I think would actually be needed to properly evaluate the impact of liberal egalitarianism in practice.

This raises a concern I had about the parochialism of Sandel's book. His concern is primarily with the American experience. There is nothing wrong with this, of course, and indeed I think that the best works of political theory are always grounded in a deep understanding of a particular society. But I also think that, having studied one's own society intensively, it is important to raise one's eyes and see if the conclusions one has drawn from one's own country are validated in other countries. It is important to consider the experience of other countries, not necessarily because one has an intrinsic interest in them, but because their experience provides a way to assess the merits of one's analysis of one's own country. For example, one way to test Sandel's hypothesis about the impact of procedural liberalism on issues such as gay rights or hate speech would be to examine how other liberal democracies have dealt with these issues. If other countries that have a strong commitment to procedural liberalism have dealt with these issues in a different way—as indeed they have—that suggests Sandel's hypothesis may be mistaken. Sandel's claim is that the triumph of procedural liberalism, in both its left-wing and right-wing versions, generates discontent with democracy. But if the experience of other countries suggests that the influence of left-wing liberalism has not had this effect, then perhaps Sandel has misdiagnosed the real causes of discontent in America.

This leads to the second possible strategy for evaluating the impact of liberal egalitarianism. Rather than examining the impact of liberal egalitarianism in other countries, one could study American liberalism more closely, to see how it has been influenced or distorted by its interaction with other public philosophies and other cultural characteristics of American society. In order to identify the specific impact of liberalism, we need to understand the cultural forces which have been mixed in with liberalism in practice, and which make American liberalism distinctive from liberalism in other countries.

Many people think that what makes American liberalism distinctive is that it is highly proceduralist, and that this proceduralist liberalism is highly influential in public life. I would argue, however, that these are not particularly distinctive to America. Liberalism in many other Western democracies is equally proceduralist, and equally influential. What makes American liberalism distinctive, I would argue, is that it is disproportionately right-wing—that is, the balance between right-wing liberalism and left-wing liberalism is strongly tilted to the right in the United States. I would also argue that this right-wing American liberalism is itself strongly influenced and distorted by other non-liberal forms of right-wing ideology.

Consider various areas of policy in which the United States differs from all other liberal democracies—e.g. the lack of gun control or comprehensive public health care or laws against hate speech; the presence of capital punishment; the requirement for active voter registration; and laws criminalizing homosexuality. From my point of view, and I suspect Sandel's as well, these are all failings of American democracy. But what explains American distinctiveness on these issues? Sandel wants to argue that in at least some cases, the fault lies with procedural liberalism. But that cannot be the explanation for most of these issues, since most of them clearly violate liberal norms. Moreover, other countries, where liberal egalitarian norms are stronger, have dealt quite differently with these issues.

I suggest that what underlies these issues is something else entirely—namely, a distinctively American attitude which is close to Social Darwinism. Many Americans not only admire success, but are contemptuous of failure—they admire people who rise above their circumstances, and dislike, even fear, those people who are unable to do so. This of course is the very opposite of a liberal egalitarian impulse, which says, not that people should be able to rise above their circumstances, but rather that circumstances should be equalized.

This Social Darwinism is exacerbated by another distinctively American attitude—namely, distrust of big government. This too is in conflict with liberal egalitarianism, since the government's responsibility to rectify unequal circumstances amongst citizens can only be fulfilled by major government programmes (e.g. health care). The combination of these two attitudes, I think, helps explain many of the distinctive characteristics of American politics, including the dominance of right-wing liberalism. But, as I see it, right-wing liberalism is not the cause of these attitudes—on the contrary, right-wing liberalism is often the rationalization of underlying cultural attitudes, which are themselves often rooted in various forms of racial and class prejudice. It is these attitudes which are the most important obstacle to meaningful political and social reform, since they corrode a sense of national identity and solidarity, and rationalize highly inegalitarian political structures.

Consider the recent Supreme Court cases striking down the redrawing of Congressional boundaries in order to create black-majority electoral districts.[12] Sandel typically presents the Supreme Court as making a good-faith effort to promote basic liberal principles. If the Supreme Courts rejects the redrawing of political boundaries, even in order to help disadvantaged groups, then it must be because liberalism is unable to deal with issues of group membership. It seems clear to me, however, reading the decisions, that the Supreme Court made no attempt whatsoever to consider or apply liberal norms to this case. The Court has said, in effect, that electoral boundaries can be redrawn to increase the voting power of any social group (e.g. farmers, religious groups, suburbanites), *except blacks*—the one group which has suffered most in the past from gerrymandering, and the one group which was most underrepresented in Congress. And the Court has said that their position—i.e. that boundaries can be redrawn to help any group except blacks—is required by equality! Now it seems clear to me, reading the decisions, that the Justices personally opposed the creation of black-majority districts, and were aware that an increasingly conservative electorate also opposed then, and so looked around desperately to find some rationalization for rejecting them. The resulting decision is, I think, nonsensical. But in any event, it obviously was not motivated at all by liberal impulses. Whether or not they are a good idea, from a policy point of view, creating black-majority districts clearly does not violate any basic liberal principle—it does not restrict rational revisability of ends, or involve state perfectionism. Indeed, from a liberal egalitarian point of view, such policies that assist the disadvantaged without restricting individual liberty are not only permissible, but in fact required. The opposition to creating black-majority districts is rooted, at bottom, in a set of non-liberal attitudes, including race and class prejudice.

It seems clear to me that, in this case at least, right-wing liberalism is simply providing a vocabulary that the Court used to rationalize non-liberal opposition to policies that benefit blacks. And if one agrees that this is at least a possible interpretation of the gerrymandering cases, then it is worth re-reading other recent Supreme Court decisions, to see whether they too fit this pattern. And indeed I would argue that the Court's decisions on many issues—gay rights, hate speech, abortion, affirmative action, welfare—reflect the same pattern. Right-wing liberalism may be providing the vocabulary, but it is being used to rationalize cultural attitudes that are opposed (often for non-liberal reasons) to policies that benefit the disadvantaged or minorities, and thereby to legitimate inegalitarian social, economic, and political institutions. Perhaps I am exaggerating this phenomenon, but any analysis of American liberalism that does not take into account the way it has been influenced and distorted by illiberal cultural conservatism is bound to be seriously misleading.

[12] e.g. *Shaw v. Reno* 113 S.Ct. 2816 (1993).

From my point of view—admittedly as an outsider to American politics—Sandel's claim that liberal egalitarianism is one of the causes of America's discontent seems multiply bizarre. Left-wing liberalism has been far too weak to have such consequences, and the real causes of discontent lie in cultural attitudes which are independent of, and in contradiction to, liberal egalitarianism. While right-wing liberalism has been influential, its influence has often been to rationalize non-liberal opposition to progressive policies. And the reason it has been able to do so is that it is right-wing (i.e. because it opposes redistribution), not because it is liberal (i.e. not because of its commitment to revisability and its rejection of perfectionism). And the solution to this is surely not less liberal egalitarianism, but more. If enough Americans really believed in the liberal egalitarian principle that unequal circumstances should be rectified (rather than feeling contempt for those who cannot rise above their circumstances), then there is nothing in liberal norms of revisability and neutrality which would prevent Americans from strengthening their sense of common identity, and from enhancing the fairness and efficacy of their political system, at both the local and national levels, and from dealing in myriad other ways with their discontents.

So I see no reason to endorse Sandel's claim that we should replace liberal egalitarian arguments with civic republican arguments. But I hasten to add that I would equally oppose efforts to replace all civic republican arguments with liberal arguments. As a strategic matter, different arguments are likely to be convincing to different people. Some people who cannot be motivated to make sacrifices in the name of justice might be motivated to do so in the name of enriching the good of democratic life. Others, who do not view political participation as a privileged locus of the good life, might be untouched by republican arguments, but would be motivated by considerations of justice. Since the two approaches will generate similar conclusions on most issues, there is no reason not to invoke both arguments. From a liberal egalitarian point of view, one of the likely beneficial side-effects of promoting justice is to enrich the quality of political participation; from a civic republican point of view, one of the likely beneficial side-effects of promoting the quality of political participation is to achieve greater social justice. In the overwhelming majority of cases, these arguments are complementary, and there is no reason to insist that only one be made.

Of course, as philosophers, we may want to know which is the 'real' argument—i.e. which takes precedence should they conflict. But this is a philosopher's question, which would rarely arise in the minds of everyday political agents. It is true that in some rare circumstances, these two arguments may come apart. Promoting an intrinsically rewarding form of political participation for the majority may exacerbate an injustice to the minority. If so, then I believe that liberal egalitarianism should take precedence. But it is unnecessary, and unwise, to extrapolate from these rare moments of conflict to the conclusion that liberal egalitarianism and civic republicanism are inherently in conflict.

4. Long-Term Sustainability

I noted earlier that Sandel could be interpreted, not as objecting to the principles of liberal equality, but rather as arguing that it is unsustainable over the long-term. In particular, Sandel rightly notes that liberal egalitarianism requires some sense of bounded community—i.e. some basis for deciding to whom we have obligations of justice—and he doubts that liberal egalitarianism can sustain the underlying sense of solidarity and identity that this requires. Most of the time, he argues that liberal egalitarianism is incapable in principle of addressing the issue of identity. I have tried to show why that principled objection to liberal egalitarianism is mistaken. Liberal states have consistently, and actively, and indeed successfully, promoted a sense of national identity as a response to this problem, without undermining their foundational commitment to individual agency and their opposition to state perfectionism.

But Sandel has a second argument, I think—namely, that this liberal nation-building strategy is no longer viable, due to economic globalization and internal cultural differentiation. He argues that the nation is no longer a viable unit for the purposes of liberal justice, and that we need to develop new forms of political community and political participation. This is a complicated issue, on which we have lots of armchair speculation but relatively little well-established evidence. For what it's worth, my own sense is that the alleged decentring of national identities is vastly exaggerated, at least in most Western democracies. There is no evidence that I can see to support the claim that the primacy of national identities is being seriously challenged by either external globalization or internal cultural differentiation.[13] On the contrary, in most countries, there remains a fierce commitment to the principle that the nation should remain the primary forum for collective self-government and social justice (see Ch. 11).

Of course, this is an empirical question, and perhaps down the road the nation will lose its place as the privileged locus of political identity and social

---

[13] The situation of 'multination' states which contain large, territorially concentrated ethnolinguistic minorities—e.g. Canada, Spain, Belgium—may seem to be an exception. But in fact they are the exception that proves the rule, since these minorities view themselves precisely as 'nations' which happen to be incorporated (often involuntarily) into a larger state. They are challenging the primacy of the larger state, not because they are disputing the centrality of national identities in the modern world, but precisely because the larger state does not define their nation.

justice. If so, then liberal egalitarians will need to create or strengthen just institutions at the supranational and subnational levels, in order to fill the vacuum. And then they will have to adjust their conceptions of virtues and identities accordingly, so as to make these new institutions viable.[14] Some of this is already going on, particularly in Europe. Much of Habermas's work can be seen in this light. And as his work shows, there is nothing in the basic liberal egalitarian commitment to rational revisability, state neutrality, and egalitarian redistribution that precludes this rethinking.

In any event, none of this involves a conflict between liberal equality and civic republicanism. If the traditional liberal commitment to national institutions as the site of collective self-government and distributive justice is no longer viable, then liberals will need to create new forums of self-government, new institutions of redistribution, and corresponding new forms of identity and virtues. All of this is perfectly consistent with, and indeed required by, liberal egalitarian justice. Liberal egalitarian justice remains the criteria for assessing political institutions and policies, but liberals should have an open mind about what institutions and policies, at what levels, will best serve those principles. And on this, as on most issues, liberal egalitarians and civic republicans can and should work together to find imaginative proposals that promote both social justice and participatory democracy.

[14] For a discussion of preliminary efforts along these lines, see Ch. 11.

Bibliography

AASA (1987), See American Association of School Administrators

Addis, Adeno (1992), 'Individualism, Communitarianism and the Rights of Ethnic Minorities', *Notre Dame Law Review* 67/3: 615–76.

——(1993), '"Hell Man, They Did Invent Us": The Mass Media, Law and African Americans', *Buffalo Law Review* 41: 523–626.

Ahmed, Aftab (1993), 'Ethnicity and Insurgency in the Chittagong Hill Tracts Region: A Study of the Crisis of Political Integration in Bangladesh', *Journal of Commonwealth and Comparative Studies* 31/3: 32–66.

Aleinikoff, Alexander (1994), 'Puerto Rico and the Constitution: Conundrums and Prospects', *Constitutional Commentary* 11: 15–43.

Alfred, Gerald (1995), *Heeding the Voices of our Ancestors: Kahnawake Mohawk Politics and the Rise of Native Nationalism* (Oxford University Press, Toronto).

American Association of School Administrators (1987), *Citizenship: goal of education* (AASA Publications, Arlington).

Anaya, S. James (1996), *Indigenous Peoples in International Law* (Oxford University Press, New York).

Anderson, Benedict (1983), *Imagined Communities: Reflections on the Origin and Spread of Nationalism* (New Left Books, London).

Andrews, Geoff (1991), *Citizenship* (Lawrence and Wishart, London).

Archibugi, Danielle (1995), 'From the United Nations to Cosmopolitan Democracy', in Archibugi and Held (1995: 121–62).

——and David Held (1995), *Cosmopolitan Democracy—An Agenda for a New World Order* (Polity Press, London).

Arel, Dominique (2000), 'Political Stability in the Multination State: the Civic State and the Fear of Minorisation', forthcoming in James Tully and Alain Gagnon (eds.) *Justice and Stability in Multination States* (Cambridge University Press, Cambridge).

Arneson, Richard, and Ian Shapiro (1996), 'Democracy and Religious Freedom: A Critique of Wisconsin v Yoder', in Ian Shapiro and Russell Hardin (eds.) *Political Order: Nomos 38* (New York University Press, New York) 356–411.

Baker, Judith (1994) (ed.), *Group Rights* (University of Toronto Press, Toronto).

Baker, Keith Michael (1975), *Condorcet: From Natural Philosophy to Social Mathematics* (University of Chicago Press, Chicago).

Banerjee, Ashis (1992), 'Federalism and Nationalism', in Nirmal Mukarji and Balveer Arora (eds.) *Federalism in India: Origins and Development* (Vikas Publishing, Delhi), 41–63.

Banting, Keith (1997), 'The Internationalization of the Social Contract', in Thomas Courchene (ed.), *The Nation State in a Global/Information Era* (John Deutsch Institute for Policy Studies, Queen's University, Kingston, Ont.), 255–85.

Barreto, Amilcar A. (1998), *Language, Elites, and the State: Nationalism in Puerto Rico and Quebec* (Praeger).

Baubock, Rainer (1994), *Transnational Citizenship: Membership and Rights in Transnational Migration* (Edward Elgar, Aldershot).

——(2000), 'Why Stay Together? A Pluralist Approach to Secession and Federation', in Will Kymlicka and Wayne Norman (eds.) *Citizenship in Diverse Societies* (Oxford University Press, Oxford), 366–94.

Beiner, Ronald (1992), 'Citizenship', in *What's the Matter with Liberalism* (University of California Press, Berkeley).

——(1995) (ed.), *Theorizing Citizenship* (State University of New York Press, Albany).

——(1999), (ed.), *Theorizing Nationalism* (State University of New York Press, Albany).

Beitz, Charles (1979), *Political Theory and International Relations* (Princeton University Press, Princeton).

Belanger, Sarah, and Maurice Pinard (1991), 'Ethnic Movements and the Competition Model: Some Missing Links', *American Sociological Review* 56/4: 458–74.

Berry, J. W., and R. Kalin (1995), 'Multicultural and Ethnic Attitudes in Canada', *Canadian Journal of Behavioural Studies* 27: 301–20.

Bissoondath, Neil (1994), *Selling Illusions: The Cult of Multiculturalism in Canada* (Penguin, Toronto).

Bobbio, Norberto (1995), 'Democracy and the International System', in Archibugi and Held (1995: 17–41).

Boehm, Max (1931), 'Cosmopolitanism', *The Encyclopedia of the Social Sciences* (Macmillan, New York) iv 457–61.

Boldt, Menno (1993), *Surviving as Indians: The Challenge of Self-Government* (University of Toronto Press, Toronto).

Bonazzi, Tiziano (1998), 'Civic Nation and Ethnic Nation', in Anna Krasteva (ed.) *Communities and Identities* (Petekston, Sofia): 64–85.

Braithwaite, Keren (1989), 'The Black Student and the School: A Canadian Dilemma', in Simeon Chilungu and Sada Niang (eds.) *African Continuities/L'Heritage Africain* (Terebi, Toronto), 195–214.

Brassloff, Audrey (1989), 'Spain: the State of the Autonomies', in M. Forsyth (ed.), *Federalism and Nationalism* (Leicester University Press, Leicester), 24–50.

Breton, R., Wsevzdod Isajiw, Warren Kalbach, Jeffrey Reit (1990), *Ethnic Identity and Equality: Varieties of Experience in a Canadian City* (University of Toronto Press, Toronto).

Breuning, Maruke (1999), 'Ethnopolitical Parties and Development Cooperation: The Case of Belgium', *Comparative Political Studies*, 32/6: 724–51.

Bromwich, David (1995), 'Culturalism: The Euthanasia of Liberalism', *Dissent*, Winter 1995: 89–102.

Brooks, Roy (1996), *Separation or Integration? A Strategy for Racial Equality* (Harvard University Press, Cambridge, Mass.).

Brubaker, Rogers (1996), *Nationalism Reframed: Nationhood and the National Question in the New Europe* (Cambridge University Press, Cambridge).

Buchanan, Allen (1991), *Secession: The Legitimacy of Political Divorce* (Westview Press, Boulder, Colo.).

Burgess, Adam (1999), 'Critical Reflections on the Return of National Minority Rights Regulation to East/West European Affairs', in Karl Cordell (ed.) *Ethnicity and Democratisation in the New Europe* (Routledge, London), 49–60.

Burgess, Michael (1993), 'Federalism and Federation: A Reappraisal', in M. Burgess and A. Gagnon (eds), *Comparative Federalism and Federation* (Harvester, New York): 3–14.

Burnaby, Barbara (1992), 'Official Language Training for Adult Immigrants in Canada: Features and Issues', in B. Burnaby and A. Cumming (eds.) *Socio-Political Aspects of ESL* (OISE, Toronto), 3–24.

Cairns, Alan (1991), 'Constitutional Change and the Three Equalities', in Ronald Watts and Douglas Brown (eds.) *Options for a New Canada* (University of Toronto Press, Toronto), 77–102.

——(1993), 'The Fragmentation of Canadian Citizenship', in William Kaplan (ed.) *Belonging: The Meaning and Future of Canadian Citizenship* (McGill-Queen's Press, Montreal), 181–220.

——(1995), 'Aboriginal Canadians, Citizenship, and the Constitution', in *Reconfigurations: Canadian Citizenship and Constitutional Change* (McClelland and Stewart, Toronto), 238–60.

——and Cynthia Williams (1985), *Constitutionalism, Citizenship and Society in Canada* (University of Toronto Press, Toronto).

Calhoun, Craig (1997), *Nationalism* (University of Minnesota Press, Minneapolis).

Callan, Eamonn (1994), 'Beyond Sentimental Civic Education', *American Journal of Education* 102: 190–221.

——(1995), 'Common Schools for Common Education', *Canadian Journal of Education* 20: 251–71.

——(1996), 'Political Liberalism and Political Education', *Review of Politics* 58: 5–33.

Camilleri, Joseph (1996), 'Impoverishment and the Natonal State', in Hampson and Reppy (1996: 122–53).

Canovan, Margaret (1996), *Nationhood and Political Theory* (Edward Elgar, Cheltenham).

Carens, Joseph (1987), 'Aliens and Citizens: The Case for Open Borders', *Review of Politics* 49/3: 251–73. Reprinted in Kymlicka 1995b.

Carens, Joseph (1995a) (ed.), *Is Quebec Nationalism Just? Perspectives from Anglophone Canada* (McGill-Queen's University Press, Montreal).

——(1995b), 'Immigration, Political Community, and the Transformation of Identity: Quebec's Immigration Policies in Critical Perspective', in Carens (1995a: 20–81).

——(1997), 'Liberalism and Culture', *Constellations*, 4/1: 35–47.

——(2000), 'Citizenship and the Challenge of Aboriginal Self-Government: Is Deep Diversity Possible?', in *Culture, Citizenship and Community* (Oxford University Press, Oxford), 177–99.

Cassidy, Frank, and Robert Bish (1989), *Indian Government: Its Meaning in Practice* (Institute for Research on Public Policy, Halifax).

Castles, Stephen, and Mark Miller (1993), *The Age of Migration: International Population Movements in the Modern Age* (Macmillan, Basingstoke).

Citizen's Forum on Canada's Future (1991), *Report to the People and Government of Canada* (Supply and Services, Ottawa).

Clarke, Paul Barry (1994) (ed.), *Citizenship* (Pluto Press, London).

Claude, Inis (1955), *National Minorities: An International Problem* (Harvard University Press, Cambridge, Mass.).

Cochran, David Carroll (1999), *The Color of Freedom: Race and Contemporary American Liberalism* (State University of New York Press, Albany, NY).

Codjoe, Henry (1994), 'Black Nationalists Beware! You Could be Called a Racist for Being "Too Black and African"', in Carl James and Adrienne Shad (eds.) *Talking about Difference* (Between the Lines Press, Toronto), 231–6.

Cohen, Marshal (1985), 'Moral Skepticism and International Relations', in Charles Beitz (ed.), *International Ethics* (Princeton University Press, Princeton), 3–50.

Colas, Dominique, Claude Emeri, and Jacques Zylberberg (1991) (eds.), *Citoyenneté et Nationalité: perspectives en France et au Québec* (Presses Universitaires de France, Paris).

Commission on Systemic Racism in the Ontario Criminal Justice System (1995), *Racism Behind Bars: The Treatment of Black and Other Racial Minority Prisoners in Ontario Prison* (Interim Report, Toronto).

Condorcet, Jean (1795), *Sketch for a Historical Picture of the Progress of the Human Mind* ed. S. Hampshire (Greenwood Press, Westport, 1955).

Connolly, William (1991), *Identity/Difference: Democratic Negotiations of Political Paradox* (Cornell University Press, Ithaca, NY).

——(1995), *The Ethos of Pluralization* (University of Minnesota Press, Minneapolis).

Connor, Walker (1972), 'Nation-Building or Nation-Destroying', *World Politics* 24: 319–55.

——(1973), 'The Politics of Ethnonationalism', *Journal of International Affairs* 27 / 1: 1–21.

——(1984), *The National Question in Marxist-Leninist Theory and Strategy* (Princeton University Press, Princeton).

——(1999), 'National Self-Determination and Tomorrow's Political Map', in Alan Cairns *et al.* (eds.) *Citizenship, Diversity and Pluralism: Canadian and Comparative Perspectives* (McGill-Queen's University Press, Montreal), 163–76.

Coser, Rose Lamb (1991), *In Defense of Modernity: Role Complexity and Individual Autonomy* (Stanford University Press, Stanford).

Couture, Jocelyne, Kai Nielsen, and Michel Seymour (1998) (eds.), *Rethinking Nationalism* (University of Calgary Press, Calgary).

Crête, Jean and Jacques Zylberberg (1991), 'Une problématique floue: l'autoreprésentation du citoyen au Québec', in Colas *et al.* (1991: 423–33).

Cuddihy, John Murray (1978), *No Offense: Civil Religion and Protestant Taste* (Seabury Press, New York).

da Cunha, Manuela (1992), 'Custom Is not a Thing, It Is a Path: Reflections on the Brazilian Indian Case', in Abdullah Ahmed An-Na'aim (ed.) *Human Rights in Cross-Cultural Perspective* (University of Pennsylvania Press, Philadelphia), 276–94.

Daes, Erica-Irene (1993), 'Consideration on the Right of Indigenous Peoples to Self-Determination', *Transnational Law and Contemporary Problems* 3: 1–11.

Daly, Herman, and John Cobb Jr. (1989), *For the Common Good: Redirecting the Economy toward Community, the Environment and a Sustainable Future* (Beacon Press, Boston).

Daudelin, Jean (1993), 'L'environment comme Cheval de Troie? Le Cas de l'Amazonie brésilienne' (paper presented to the annual meetings of the Canadian Political Science Association, Ottawa, June 1993).

Davis, Bob (1994), 'Global Paradox: Growth of Trade Binds Nations, but It Also Can Spur Separatism', *Wall Street Journal*, 30 June 1994: A1.

de Onis, Juan (1992), *The Green Cathedral: Sustainable Development of Amazonia* (Oxford University Press, New York).

de Sousa Santos, Bonaventura (1996), *Toward a New Common Sense* (Routledge, London).

de Varennes, Fernand (1996), *Language, Minorities and Human Rights* (Kluwer, The Hague).

Dei, George (1994), 'Reflections of an Anti-Racist Pedagogue', in Lorna Edwin and David MacLennan (eds.), *Sociology of Education in Canada* (Copp Clark Longman, Toronto), 290–310.

——(1995), '(Re)Conceptualizing Black Studies in Canadian Schools', *Canadian and International Education* 24/1: 1–19.

Dion, Stéphane (1991), 'Le Nationalisme dans la Convergence Culturelle', in R. Hudon and R. Pelletier (eds.) *L'Engagement Intellectuel: Melanges en l'honneur de Léon Dion* (Les Presses de l'Université Laval, Sainte-Foy), 291–311.

——(1994), 'La fédéralisme fortement asymétrique', in Seidle (1994), 133–52.

Dobson, Andrew (1990), *Green Political Thought* (Unwin Hyman, London).

——(1991), *The Green Reader* (Mercury House, San Francisco).

Donaldson, Susan (1995), *Un-LINC-ing Language and Integration* (MA Thesis, Department of Linguistics and Applied Language Studies, Carleton University).

Donner, Wendy (1996), 'Inherent Value and Moral Standing in Environmental Change', in Hampson and Reppy (1996: 52–74).

Donelly, Jack (1990), 'Human Rights, Individual Rights, Collective Rights', in J. Bertin *et al.*, *Human Rights in a Pluralist World* (London, Meckler).

Dreidger, Leo (1996), *Multi-Ethnic Canada: Identities and Inequalities* (Oxford University Press, Toronto).

Dupuy, René-Jean (1980), *The Right to Development at the International Level* (Sijthoff & Noordhoff: Alphen aan den Rijn).

Dworkin, R. (1981), 'What is Equality? Part II: Equality of Resources', *Philosophy and Public Affairs* 10/4: 283–345.

——(1985), *A Matter of Principle* (Harvard University Press, London).

Dworkin, R. (1992), 'Deux Conceptions de la Démocratie', in Lenoble and Dewandre (1992) 111–35.

Eckersley, Robyn (1992), *Environmentalism and Political Theory* (State University of New York Press, Albany).

ECMI (1998), 'From Ethnopolitical Conflict to Inter-Ethnic Accord in Moldova' (European Centre for Minority Issues, Report #1, Flensburg, Germany),

Eisenberg, Avigail (1998), 'Individualism and Collectivism in the Politics of Canada's North', in Joan Anderson, Avigail Eisenberg, Sherril Grace, and Veronica Strong-Boag (eds.), *Painting the Maple: Essays on Race, Gender and the Construction of Canada* (University of British Columbia Press, Vancouver).

Elazar, Daniel (1987*a*), *Exploring Federalism* (University of Alabama, Tuscaloosa).

——(1987*b*), 'The Role of Federalism in Political Integration', in D. Elazar (ed.), *Federalism and Political Integration* (Turtledove Publishing, Ramat Gan, Israel).

——(1994), *Federalism and the Way to Peace* (Institute of Intergovernmental Affairs, Queen's University, Kingston, Ont.).

Elkins, David (1992), *Where Should the Majority Rule? Reflections on Non-Territorial Provinces and Other Constitutional Proposals* (Centre for Consitutional Studies, University of Alberta).

Emler, N., and S. Reicher (1987), 'Orientations to Institutional Authority in Adolescents', *Journal of Moral Education* 16/2: 108–16.

Engel, J. Ronald (1988), 'Ecology and Social Justice: The Search For a Public Environmental Ethic', in Roger Hatch and Warren Copeland (eds.), *Issues of Justice: Social Sources and Religious Meanings* (Mercer University Press).

Engels, Friedrich (1952), 'Hungary and Panslavism' (1849), in Paul Blackstock and Bert Hoselitz (eds.), *The Russian Menace to Europe* (Free Press, Glencoe).

Falk, Richard (1995), 'The World Order between Inter-State Law and the Law of Humanity: The Role of Civil Society Institutions', in Archibugi and Held (1995: 163–79).

Favell, Adrian (1999), 'Applied Political Philosophy at the Rubicon', *Ethical Theory and Moral Practice* 1/2: 255–78.

Feit, Harvey (1980), 'Negotiating Recognition of Aboriginal Rights: History, Strategies and Reactions to the James Bay and Northern Quebec Agreement', *Canadian Review of Anthropology* 1/2: 159–72.

Fierlbeck, Katherine (1991), 'Redefining responsibilities: the politics of citizenship in the United Kingdom', *Canadian Journal of Political Science* 24/3: 575–83.

Fleras, Augie (1994), 'Media and Minorities in a Post-Multicultural Society', in Berry and Laponce (1994: 267–92).

——and Jean Elliot, *Unequal Relations: An Introduction to Race, Ethnic and Aboriginal Dynamics in Canada*, 2nd edn. (Prentice Hall, Scarborough).

Forst, Rainer (1997), 'Foundations of a Theory of Multicultural Justice', *Constellations* 4/1: 63–71.

Forsyth, Murray (1989), 'Introduction', in M. Forsyth (ed.), *Federalism and Nationalism* (Leicester University Press, Leicester).

Foster, Cecil (1996), *A Place Called Heaven: The Meaning of Being Black in Canada* (HarperCollins, Toronto).

Franck, Thomas (1997), 'Tribe, Nation, World: Self-Identification in the Evolving International System', *Ethics and International Affairs* 11: 151–69.

Fraser, Nancy (1995), 'From Redistribution to Recognition? Dilemmas of Justice in a 'Post-Socialist' Age', *New Left Review* 212: 68–93.

Frideres, James (1997), 'Edging into the Mainstream', in S. Isajiw (ed) *Multiculturalism in North America and Europe: Comparative Perspectives on Interethnic Relations and Social Incorporation* (Canadian Scholar's Press, Toronto): 537–562.

Gagliardo, John (1980), *Reich and Nation: The Holy Roman Empire as Idea and Reality* (Indiana University Press).

Gagnon, Alain-G. (1993), 'The Political Uses of Federalism', in Michael Burgess and Alain-G. Gagnon (eds.) *Comparative Federalism and Federation: Competing Traditions and Future Directions* (University of Toronto Press, Toronto), 15–44.

——and Joseph Garcea (1988), 'Quebec and the Pursuit of Special Status', in R. D. Olling and M. W. Westmacott (eds.) *Perspectives on Canadian Federalism* (Prentice-Hall, Scarborough), 304–25.

Galenkamp, Marlies (1993), *Individualism and Collectivism: The Concept of Collective Rights* (Rotterdamse Filosofische Studies, Rotterdam).

Galston, William (1991), *Liberal Purposes: Goods, Virtues, and Duties in the Liberal State* (Cambridge University Press, Cambridge).

——(1995), 'Two Concepts of Liberalism', *Ethics* 105/3: 516–34.

Gans, Chaim (1998), 'Nationalism and Immigration', in *Ethical Theory and Moral Practice* 1/2: 159–80.

Garet, Ronald (1983), 'Communality and Existence: The Rights of Groups', *Southern California Law Review* 56/5: 1001–75.

Gellner, Ernest (1983), *Nations and Nationalism* (Blackwell, Oxford).

Gilbert, Paul (1998), *Philosophy of Nationalism* (Westview, Boulder, Colo.).

Glazer, Nathan (1983), *Ethnic Dilemmas:1964–1982* (Harvard University Press, Cambridge, Mass.).

——(1997), *We Are All Multiculturalists Now* (Harvard University Press, Cambridge, Mass.).

Glendon, M. A. (1991), *Rights Talk: The Impoverishment of Political Discourse* (Free Press, New York).

Goodin, Robert (1990), 'International Ethics and the Environmental Crisis', *Ethics and International Affairs* 4: 91–105.

Government of Canada (1991), *Shared Values: The Canadian Identity* (Supply and Services, Ottawa).

Government of Quebec (1990), *Let's Build Quebec Together: Vision: A Policy Statement on Immigration and Integration* (Quebec City).

Greenfeld, Liah (1992), *Nationalism: Five Roads to Modernity* (Harvard University Press, Cambridge, Mass.).

Grimm, Dieter (1995), 'Does Europe Need A Constitution?', *European Law Journal* 1/3: 282–302.

Grin, Francois (1999) 'Language Policy in Multilingual Switzerland: Overview and Recent Developments', ECMI Brief #2 (European Centre for Minority Issues, Flensburg).

Guéhenno, Jean-Marie (1995), *The End of the Nation-State* (University of Minnesota Press, Minneapolis).

Gurr, Ted (1993), *Minorities at Risk: A Global View of Ethnopolitical Conflict* (Institute of Peace Press, Washington, DC).

Gutmann, Amy (1987), *Democratic Education* (Princeton University Press, Princeton).

——(1993), 'The Challenge of Multiculturalism to Political Ethics', *Philosophy and Public Affairs* 22/3: 171–206.

——and Anthony Appiah (1996) *Color Conscious* (Princeton University Press).

Gywn, Richard (1995), *Nationalism without Walls: The Unbearable Lightness of Being Canadian* (McClelland and Stewart, Toronto).

Habermas, Jürgen (1992), 'Citizenship and National Identity: Some Reflections on the Future of Europe', *Praxis International* 12/1: 1–19.

Hacker, Andrew (1992), *Two Nations: Black and White, Separate, Hostile and Unequal* (Ballantine, New York).

Halstead, J. M. (1990), 'Muslim Schools and the Ideal of Autonomy', *Ethics in Education* 9/4: 4–6.

Halstead, Mark (1991), 'Radical Feminism, Islam and the Single-Sex School Debate', *Gender and Education* 3/1: 263–78.

Hamilton, Alexander, James Madison, and John Jay (1982), *The Federalist Papers* (Bantam, New York).

Hampson, Fen, and Judith Reppy (eds.) (1996), *Earthly Goods: Environmental Change and Social Justice* (Cornell University Press, Ithaca, NY).

Hannum, Hurst (1990), *Autonomy, Sovereignty, and Self-Determination: The Adjudication of Conflicting Rights* (University of Pennsylvania Press, Philadelphia).

——(1993), (ed.), *Documents on Autonomy and Minority Rights* (Martinus Nijthoff, Boston).

Harles, John (1993), *Politics in the Lifeboat: Immigrants and the American Democratic Order* (Westview Press, Boulder, Colo.).

Hartney, Michael (1991), 'Some Confusions Concerning Collective Rights', *Canadian Journal of Law and Jurisprudence* 4/2: 293–314.

Hawkins, Freda (1989), *Critical Years in Immigration: Canada and Australia Compared* (McGill-Queen's University Press, Montreal).

He, Boagang (1998), 'Can Kymlicka's Liberal Theory of Minority Rights be Applied in East Asia?', in Paul van der Velde and Alex McKay (eds.), *New Developments in Asian Studies: An Introduction* (Kegan Paul, London).

Heater, Derek (1990), *Citizenship: The Civic Ideal in World History, Politics and Education* (Longman, London).

Held, David (1995), *Democracy and the Global Order—From the Modern State to Cosmopolitan Governance* (Polity Press, London).

——(1999), 'The Transformation of Political Community: Rethinking Democracy in the Context of Gloabalization' in Ian Shapiro and Casiano Hacker-Cordon (eds.), *Democracy's Edges* (Cambridge University Press, Cambridge), 84–111.

Hemming, John (1987), *Amazon Frontier: The Defeat of the Brazilian Indians* (Harvard University Press, Cambridge, Mass.).

Henderson, James Youngblood (1994), 'Empowering Treaty Federalism', *University of Saskatchewan Law Review* 58/2: 241–329.

Henry, Frances (1994), *The Caribbean Diaspora in Toronto: Learning to Live with Racism* (University of Toronto Press, Toronto).

Hobsbawm, E. J. (1990), *Nations and Nationalism since 1780: Programme, Myth and Reality* (Cambridge University Press, Cambridge).

Hoernlé, R. F. A. (1939), *South African Native Policy and the Liberal Spirit* (Lovedale Press, Cape Town).

Hollinger, David (1995), *Postethnic America: Beyond Multiculturalism* (Basic Books, New York).

——(1998), 'National Culture and Communities of Descent', *Reviews in American History*, 26: 312–28.

Horowitz, D. L. (1985), *Ethnic Groups in Conflict* (University of California Press, Berkeley).

——(1991), *A Democratic South Africa: Constitutional Engineering in a Divided Society* (University of California Press, Berkeley).

——(1997), 'Self-Determination: Politics, Philosophy and Law', in Shapiro and Kymlicka (1997: 421–63).

House of Commons Special Committee on Participation of Visible Minorities in Canadian Society (1984), *Equality Now!* (Ottawa).

Howse, Robert, and Karen Knop (1993), 'Federalism, Secession, and the Limits of Ethnic Accommodation: A Canadian Perspective', *New Europe Law Review* 1/2: 269–320.

Hughes, James (1999), 'Institutional Responses to Separatism: Federalism and Transition to Democracy in Russia' (paper prepared for presentation to ASN conference, New York, April 1999).

Hurrell, Andrew (1992), 'Brazil and the International Politics of Amazonian Deforestation', in Andrew Hurrell and Benedict Kingsbury (eds.), *International Politics of the Environment* (Oxford University Press, Oxford): 397–429.

Ignatieff, Michael (1993), *Blood and Belonging: Journeys into the New Nationalism* (Farrar, Straus, and Giroux, New York).

Ignatiev, Noel (1995), *How the Irish Became White* (Routledge, New York).

Ilishev, Ildus (1998), 'Russian Federalism: Political, Legal and Ethnolingual Aspects: A view from the Republic of Bashkortostan', *Nationalities Papers* 26/4: 723–39.

Jasanoff, Sheila (1996), 'Science and Norms in Global Environmental Regimes' in Hampson and Reppy (1996: 173–97).

Johnston, Darlene (1989), 'Native Rights as Collective Rights: A Question of Group Self-Preservation', *Canadian Journal of Law and Jurisprudence* 2/1: 19–34. Reprinted in Kymlicka 1995*b*.

Jupp, James (1995), 'The New Multicultural Agenda', *Crossings* 1/1: 38–71

Juteau, Danielle, Marie McAndrew, and Linda Pietrantonio (1998), 'Multiculturalism à la Canadian and Integration à la Québécoise: Transcending their Limits', in Rainer Baubock (ed.), *Blurred Boundaries: Migration, Ethnicity, Citizenship* (Ashgate Aldershot), 95–110.

Kaldor, Mary (1995), 'European Institutions, Nation-States and Nationalism', in Archibugi and Held (1995: 96–120).

Karklins, R. (1994), *Ethnopolitics and the Transition to Democracy: The Collapse of USSR and Latvia* (Woodrow Wilson Center Press, Washington).

Karmis, Dimitrios (1993), 'Cultures autochtones et libéralisme au Canada: les vertus mediatrices du communautarisme libéral de Charles Taylor', *Canadian Journal of Political Science* 26/1: 69–96.

Karst, Kenneth (1986), 'Paths to Belonging: The Constitution and Cultural Identity', *North Carolina Law Review* 64: 303–77.

Katz, Eric, and Lauren Oechsli (1993), 'Moving Beyond Anthropocentrism: Environmental Ethics, Development and the Amazon', *Environmental Ethics* 15: 49–59.

Khasanov, Mansur (1999), 'The Making of the Statehood of Tatarstan: Stages and Prospects', *PRISM: A Biweekly Journal on the Post-Soviet States* 5/5 (12 March 1999).

Kingsbury, Benedict (1995), '"Indigenous Peoples" as an International Legal Concept', in R. H. Barnes (ed.), *Indigenous Peoples of Asia* (Association of Asian Studies, Ann Arbor), 13–34.

——(1999), 'The Applicability of the International Legal Concept of "Indigenous Peoples" in Asia', in J. Bauer and D. Bell (eds.), *The East Asian Challenge for Human Rights*, (Cambridge University Press, Cambridge), 336–77.

Kloss, Heinz (1977), *The American Bilingual Tradition* (Newbury House, Rowley Mass).

Knopff, Rainer (1979), 'Language and Culture in the Canadian Debate: The Battle of the White Papers', *Canadian Review of Studies in Nationalism* 6/1: 66–82.

Kothari, Smithu (1996), 'Social Movements, Ecology and Justice', in Hampson and Reppy (1996: 154–72).

Krunowitz, R., Lichtman, J., McGloy, S., and Olsen, M. (1987), Toward Consent and Cooperation: Reconsidering The Political Status of Indian Nations', *Harvard Civil Rights-Civil Liberties Review*, 22: 507–622.

Kukathas, Chandran (1997), 'Cultural Toleration', in Shapiro and Kymlicka (1997: 69–104).

Kymlicka, Will (1989), *Liberalism, Community, and Culture* (Oxford University Press, Oxford).

——(1990*a*), *Contemporary Political Philosophy: An Introduction* (Oxford University Press, Oxford).

——(1990*b*), 'Two Theories of Justice', *Inquiry* 33 / 1: 99–119.

——(1995*a*), *Multicultural Citizenship: A Liberal Theory of Minority Rights* (Oxford University Press, Oxford).

——(1995*b*) (ed.), *The Rights of Minority Cultures* (Oxford University Press, Oxford).

——(1998*a*), *Finding Our Way: Rethinking Ethnocultural Relations in Canada* (Oxford University Press, Toronto).

——(1998*b*), 'Ethnic Relations in Eastern Europe and Western Political Theory', in Magda Opalski (ed.) *Managing Diversity in Plural Societies: Minorities, Migration and Nation-Building in Post-Communist Europe* (Forum Eastern Europe, Ottawa). A substantially expanded version will appear in Kymlicka and Opalski (2001).

——and Wayne Norman (1994), 'Return of the Citizen', *Ethics* 104 / 2: 352–81.

——(2000) (eds.), *Citizenship in Diverse Societies* (Oxford University Press, Oxford).

——and Magda Opalski (2001) (eds.), *Can Liberal Pluralism be Exported? Western Political Theory and Ethnic Relations in Eastern Europe* (Oxford University Press, forthcoming).

Lapidoth, Ruth (1996), *Autonomy: Flexible Solutions to Ethnic Conflict* (Institute for Peace Press, Washington, DC).

Laponce, J. A (1987), *Languages and their Territories* (University of Toronto Press, Toronto).

——(1993), 'The Case for Ethnic Federalism in Multilingual Societies: Canada's Regional Imperative', *Regional Politics and Policy* 3 / 1: 23–43.

Larmore, Charles (1987), *Patterns of Moral Complexity* (Cambridge University Press, Cambridge).

Lehning, Percy (1998) (ed.), *Theories of Secession* (Routledge, London).

Lejeune, Yves (1994), 'Le Fédéralisme en Belgique', in Seidle (1994: 171–86).

Lemco, Jonathan (1991), *Political Stability in Federal Governments* (Praeger, New York).

Lenoble, Jacques, and Nicole Dewandre (1992) (eds.), *L'Europe au Soir du Siècle: Identité et Démocratie* (Éditions Esprit, Paris).

Levy, Jacob (1997), 'Classifying Cultural Rights', in Shapiro and Kymlicka (1997: 22–66).

Lewis, Stephen (1992), *Report on Race Relations in Ontario* (Queen's Park, 1992).

Lewis-Anthony, Sian (1998), 'Autonomy and the Council of Europe—With Special Reference to the Application of Article 3 of the First Protocol of the European Convention on Human Rights', in Markku Suksi (ed.), *Autonomy: Applications and Implications* (Kluwer, The Hague), 317–42.

Light, Andrew, and Eric Katz (1996), 'Introduction: Environmental Pragmatism and Environmental Ethics as Contested Terrain', in A. Light and E. Katz (eds.) *Environmental Pragmatism* (Routledge, London).

Long, J. A. (1991), 'Federalism and Ethnic Self-Determination: Native Indians in Canada', *Journal of Commonwealth and Comparative Politics* 29 / 2: 192–211.

McCleary, Rachel (1991), 'The International Community's Claim to Rights in Brazilian Amazonia', *Political Studies* 39 / 4: 691–707.

McDonald, Michael (1991*a*), 'Questions about Collective Rights', in D. Schneiderman (ed.) *Language and the State: The Law and Politics of Identity* (Les Editions Yvon Blais, Cowansville).

McDonald, Michael (1991*b*), 'Should Communities Have Rights? Reflections on Liberal Individualism', *Canadian Journal of Law and Jurisprudence* 4/2: 217–37.

Macedo, Stephen (1990), *Liberal Virtues: citizenship, virtue and community* (Oxford University Press, Oxford).

——(1995), 'Liberal Civic Education and Religious Fundamentalism', *Ethics* 105/3: 468–96.

McGarry, John (1998), 'Demographic Engineering: The State-Directed Movements of Ethnic Groups as a Technique of Conflict Resolution', *Ethnic and Racial Studies* 21/4: 613–38.

Macklem, Patrick (1993), 'Distributing Sovereignty: Indian Nations and Equality of Peoples', *Stanford Law Review* 45/5: 1311–67.

McLaughlin, T.H. (1992*a*), 'Citizenship, Diversity and Education', *Journal of Moral Education* 21/3: 235–50.

——(1992*b*), 'The Ethics of Separate Schools', in Mal Leicester and Monica Taylor (eds.), *Ethics, Ethnicity and Education* (Kogan Page, London), 114–36.

McMahan, Jeff, and Robert McKim (1997) (eds.), *The Morality of Nationalism* (Oxford University Press, New York).

Magnusson, Warren (1996), *The Search for Political Space: Globalization, Social Movements and the Urban Political Experience* (University of Toronto Press, Toronto).

Mansour, Gerda (1993), *Multilingualism and Nation Building* (Multilingual Matters, Clevedon).

Margalit, Avishai, and Joseph Raz (1990), 'National Self-Determination', *Journal of Philosophy* 87/9: 439–61.

Margalit, Avishai, and Moshe Halbertal (1994), 'Liberalism and the Right to Culture', *Social Research*, 61/3: 491–510.

Martinez, Ruben Berros (1997), 'Puerto Rico's Decolonization', *Foreign Affairs*, Nov. 1997: 100–14.

Mead, Lawrence (1986), *Beyond Entitlement: the social obligations of citizenship* (Free Press, New York).

Medrano, Juan Díez (1995), *Divided Nations: Class, Politics and Nationalism in the Basque Country and Catalonia* (Cornell University Press, Ithaca, NY).

Mill, J. S. (1972), *Considerations on Representative Government*, in *Utilitarianism, Liberty, Representative Government*, ed. H. Acton (J. M. Dent, London).

Miller, David (1995), *On Nationality* (Oxford University Press, Oxford).

——(1998), 'Secession and the Principle of Nationality', in Couture *et al.* (1998: 261–82).

——*et al.* (1996), 'Symposium on David Miller's On *Nationality*', *Nations and Nationalism* 2/3: 407–51.

Milne, David (1991), 'Equality or Asymmetry: Why Choose?', in Ronald Watts and Douglas Brown (eds.) *Options for a New Canada* (University of Toronto Press, Toronto), 285–307.

Minow, Martha (1990*a*), *Making all the Difference: inclusion, exclusion and American Law* (Cornell University Press, Ithaca, NY).

——(1990*b*), 'Putting Up and Putting Down: Tolerance Reconsidered', in Mark Tushnet (ed.) *Comparative Constitutional Federalism: Europe and America* (Greenwood, New York), 77–113.

Modood, Tariq (1994), 'Establishment, Multiculturalism, and British Citizenship', *Political Quarterly* 65/1: 53–73.

Moore, Margaret (1998), (ed.), *National Self-Determination and Secession* (Oxford University Press, Oxford).

Moskos, Charles, and John Sibley Butler (1996), *All That We Can Be: Black Leadership and Racial Integration the Army Way* (Basic Books, New York).

Mouffe, Chantal (1992) (ed.), *Dimensions of Radical Democracy: Pluralism, Citizenship and Community* (Routledge, London).

Mulgan, Geoff (1991), 'Citizens and Responsibilities', in Andrews (1991: 37–49).

Myers, Norman (1992), 'The Anatomy of Environmental Action: The Case of Tropical Deforestation', in Andrew Hurrell and Benedict Kingsbury (eds.), *International Politics of the Environment* (Oxford University Press, Oxford).

Narveson, Jan (1991), 'Collective Rights?', *Canadian Journal of Law and Jurisprudence* 4/2: 329–45.

Nelson, Jack (1980), 'The Uncomfortable Relationship between Moral Education and Citizenship Instruction', in Richard Wilson and Gordon Schochet (eds.), *Moral Development and Politics* (Praeger), 256–85.

Neumann, Franz (1962), 'Federalism and Freedom: A Critique', in Arthur MacMahon (ed.), *Federalism: Mature and Emergent* (Russell and Russell, New York), 44–57.

Newman, S. (1996), *Ethnoregional Conflicts in Democracies: Mostly Ballots, Rarely Bullets* (Greenwood, London).

Nickel, James (1995), 'The Value of Cultural Belonging', *Dialogue* 33/4: 635–42.

Nietschmann, Bernard (1987), 'The Third World War', *Cultural Survival Quarterly* 11/3: 1–16.

Norman, W. J. (1994), 'Towards a Normative Theory of Federalism', in Judith Baker (ed.) *Group Rights* (University of Toronto Press, Toronto), 79–100.

——(1995), 'The Ideology of Shared Values', in Joseph Carens (ed.), *Is Quebec Nationalism Just?* (McGill-Queen's University Press, Montreal), 137–59.

——(1996), 'Prelude to a Liberal Morality of Nationalism', in S. Brennan, T. Isaacs, and M. Milde (eds)., *A Question of Values* (Rudopi Press, Amsterdam), 189–208.

——(1999), 'Theorizing Nationalism (Normatively): The First Steps', in Ronald Beiner (ed.), *Theorizing Nationalism* (State University of New York Press, Albany), 51–66.

Norris, Alexander (1998), 'Immigrant Students Back Bill 101', *The Gazette* (Montreal), 29 October.

O'Brien, Sharon (1987), 'Cultural Rights in the United States: A Conflict of Values', *Law and Inequality Journal* 5: 267–358.

O'Brien, Sharon (1989), *American Indian Tribal Governments* (University of Oklahoma Press).

Office of Multicultural Affairs (1995), *What is Multiculturalism?* (Office of Multicultural Affairs, Department of the Prime Minister, Canberra, April 1995).

Ogbu, John (1988), 'Diversity and Equity in Public Education: Community Forces and Minority School Adjustment and Performance', in R. Haskins and D. MacRae (eds.) *Policies for America's Public Schools: Teachers, Equity and Indicators* (Ablex Publishers, Norwood, NJ), 127–70.

Okin, Susan (1992), 'Women, Equality and Citizenship', *Queen's Quarterly* 99/1: 56–71.

——(1998), 'Mistresses of their own Destiny? Group Rights, Gender, and Realistic Rights of Exit' (presented at the American Political Science Association annual meeting, Sept. 1998).

Oldfield, Adrian (1990a), 'Citizenship: An Unnatural Practice?', *Political Quarterly* 61: 177–87.

——(1990b), *Citizenship and Community: civic republicanism and the modern world* (Routledge, London).

Parekh, Bhikhu (1994), 'Decolonizing Liberalism', in Alexsandras Shiromas (ed.) *The End of 'Isms'? Reflections on the Fate of Ideological Politics after Communism's Collapse* (Blackwell, Oxford), 85–103.

——(1997) 'Dilemmas of a Multicultural Theory of Citizenship', *Constellations* 4/1: 54–62.

Paris, David (1991), 'Moral Education and the "Tie that Binds" in Liberal Political Theory', *American Political Science Review* 85/3: 875–901.

Patil, S. H. (1998) 'State Formation in Federal India', in Abdulrahim Vijapur (ed.), *Dimensions of Federal Nation Building* (Manak, Delhi), 148–59.

Penz, Peter (1992), 'Development Refugees and Distributive Justice: Indigenous Peoples, Land and the Developmentalist State', *Public Affairs Quarterly* 6/1: 105–31.

——(1993), 'Colonization of Tribal Lands in Bangladesh and Indonesia: State Rationales, Rights to Land, and Environmental Justice', in Michael Howard (ed.) *Asia's Environmental Crisis* (Westview Press, Boulder, Colo.), 37–72.

Peterson, Nicolas, and Will Sanders (1998), *Citizenship and Indigenous Australians* (Cambridge University Press, Cambridge).

Pfaff, William (1993), *The Wrath of Nations: Civilization and the Furies of Nationalism* (Simon and Schuster, New York).

Phillips, Anne (1995), *The Politics of Presence: Issues in Democracy and Group Representation* (Oxford University Press, Oxford).

Philpott, Daniel (1995), 'In Defense of Self-Determination', *Ethics* 105/2: 352–85.

Pithard, Petr (1994), 'Czechoslovakia: The Loss of the Old Partnership', in Seidle (1994: 163–9).

Plamenatz, John (1960), *On Alien Rule and Self-Government* (Longman, London).

Pocock, J. G. A. (1992), 'The Ideal of Citizenship Since Classical Times', *Queen's Quarterly* 99/1: 33–55.

Pogge, Thomas (1995), 'How Should Human Rights Be Conceived?', in *Jahrbuch für Recht und Ethik* 3: 103–20.

Portillo, Mariano Negron (1997), 'Puerto Rico: Surviving Colonialism and Nationalism', in Frances Negron-Muntaner and Ramon Grossfoguel (eds.), *Puerto Rican Jam: Essays on Culture and Politics* (University of Minnesota Press, Minneapolis), 39–56.

Prucha, Francis Paul (1994), *American Indian Treaties: The History of a Political Anomaly* (University of California Press, Berkeley).

Putnam, Robert (1993), *Making Democracy Work: Civic Traditions in Modern Italy* (Princeton University Press, Princeton).

Raikka, Juha (1996) (ed.), *Do We Need Minority Rights?* (Kluwer, Dordrecht).

Rawls, John (1971), *A Theory of Justice* (Oxford University Press, London).

——(1980), 'Kantian Constructivism in Moral Theory', *Journal of Philosophy* 77/9: 515–72.

——(1982), 'Social Unity and Primary Goods', in A. Sen and B. Williams (eds.) *Utilitarianism and Beyond* (Cambridge University Press, Cambridge), 159–85.

——(1988), 'The Priority of Right and Ideas of the Good', *Philosophy and Public Affairs* 17/4: 251–76.

——(1993a), *Political Liberalism* (Columbia University Press, New York).

——(1993b), 'The Law of Peoples', in S. Shute and S. Hurley (eds.) *On Human Rights: The Oxford Amnesty Lectures 1993* (Oxford University Press, Oxford), 41–82.

Raz, Joseph (1986), *The Morality of Freedom* (Oxford University Press, Oxford).

——(1994), 'Multiculturalism: A Liberal Perspective', *Dissent*, Winter 1994: 67–79.

——(1998), 'Multiculturalism', *Ratio Juris* 11/3: 193–205.

RCAP (1996), *Report of the Royal Commission on Aboriginal Peoples*. ii: *Restructuring the Relationship* (Ottawa, 1996).

RCERPF—see Royal Commission on Electoral Reform and Party Financing.

Réaume, Denise (1991), 'The Constitutional Protection of Language: Security or Survival?', in D. Schneiderman (ed.) *Language and the State: the law and politics of identity* (Les Éditions Yvon Blais, Cowansville), 37–57.

——(1995), 'Justice between Cultures: Autonomy and the Protection of Cultural Affiliation', *UBC Law Review* 29/1: 121.

Rees, J. C. (1971), *Equality* (Macmillan, London).

——(1985), *John Stuart Mill's On Liberty* (Oxford University Press, Oxford).

Resnick, Philip (1994), 'Toward a Multination Federalism', in Seidle (1994: 71–90).

Resnik, Judith (1989), 'Dependent Sovereigns: Indian Tribes, States, and the Federal Courts', *University of Chicago Law Review* 56: 671–759.

Reus-Smith, Christian (1996), 'The Normative Structure of International Society', in Hampson and Reppy (1996: 96–121).

Rose, Peter (1989), 'Asian Americans: From Pariahs to Paragons', in James S. Frideres (ed.), *Multiculturalism and Intergroup Relations* (Greenwood Press, New York), 107–22.

Royal Commission on Electoral Reform and Party Financing (1991). *Reforming Electoral Democracy: Final Report*, vols. i and ii (Supply and Services, Ottawa).

Rubinstein, Alvin (1993), 'Is Statehood for Puerto Rico in the National Interest?', *In Depth: A Journal for Values and Public Policy* Spring 1993: 87–99.

Sagarin, Edward, and Robert Kelly (1985), 'Polylingualism in the United States of America: A Multitude of Tongues Amid a Monolingual Majority', in William Beer and James Jacob (eds.), *Language Policy and National Unity* (Rowman and Allenheld, Totowa).

Sakwa, Richard (1998), 'Liberalism and Postcommunism', presented at conference on 'Liberalism at the Millenijum', Gregynog, Wales, February 1998.

Sandel, Michael (1982), *Liberalism and the Limits of Justice* (Cambridge University Press, Cambridge).

——(1996), *Democracy's Discontent: America in Search of a Public Philosophy* (Harvard University Press, Cambridge, Mass.).

Schlereth, Thomas (1977), *The Cosmopolitan Ideal in Enlightenment Thought* (University of Notre Dame Press, Notre Dame).

Schlesinger, Arthur (1992), *The Disuniting of America* (Norton, New York).

Schmidt, Alvin (1997), *The Menace of Multiculturalism: Trojan Horse in America* (Praeger).

Schneiderman, David (1998), 'Human Rights, Fundamental Differences? Multiple Charters in a Partnership Frame', in Guy Laforest and Roger Gibbins (eds.), *Beyond the Impasse* (Institute for Research on Public Policy, Montreal) 147–85.

Schwartz, Warren (1995) (ed.), *Justice in Immigration* (Cambridge University Press, Cambridge).

Seekings, Jeremy, and Courtney Jung (1997), '"That Time was Apartheid: Now It's the New South Africa"', in Will Kymlicka and Ian Shapiro (eds.), *Ethnicity and Group Rights* (New York University Press, New York), 504–39

Seidle, Leslie (1994) (ed.), *Seeking a New Canadian Partnership: Asymmetrical and Confederal Options* (Institute for Research on Public Policy, Montreal).

Senelle, Robert (1989), 'Constitutional Reform in Belgium: From Unitarism towards Federalism', in Murray Forsyth (ed.), *Federalism and Nationalism* (Leicester University Press, Leicester), pp. 51–95.

Shachar, Ayelet (1998), 'Group Identity and Women's Rights in Family Law: The Perils of Multicultural Accommodation', *Journal of Political Philosophy* 6: 285–305.

——(1999), 'The Paradox of Multicultural Vulnerability', in Christian Joppke and Steven Lukes (eds.), *Multicultural Questions* (Oxford University Press, Oxford), 87–111.

Shadd, Adrienne (1994), 'Where are You Really From? Notes of an 'Immigrant' from North Buxton, Ontario', in Carl James and Adrienne Shadd (eds.), *Talking about Difference: Encounters in Culture, Language and Identity* (Between the Lines Press, Toronto).

Shafir, Gershon (1995), *Immigrants and Nationalists: Ethnic Conflict and Accommodation in Catalonia, the Basque Country, Latvia and Estonia* (State University of New York Press, Albany).

——(1998) *The Citizenship Debates: A Reader* (University of Minnesota Press, Minneapolis).

Shapiro, Ian, and Will Kymlicka (1997) (eds.), *Ethnicity and Group Rights* (New York University Press, New York).

Shue, Henry (1988), 'Mediating Duties', *Ethics* 98/4: 687–704.

——(1992), 'The Unavoidability of Justice' in *International Politics of the Environment*, eds. Andrew Hurrell and Benedict Kingsbury (Oxford University Press, Oxford).

——(1993), 'Subsistence Emissions and Luxury Emissions', *Law and Policy* 15/1: 39–59.

Simeon, Richard (1997), 'Citizens and Democracy in the Emerging Global Order', in Thomas Courchene (ed.) *The Nation State in a Global/Information Era* (John Deutsch Institute for Policy Studies, Queen's University, Kingston, Canada), 299–314.

Skinner, Quentin (1992), 'On Justice, the Common Good and the Priority of Liberty', in Mouffe (1992a: 211–24).

Smith, Graham (1996), 'Russia, Ethnoregionalism and the Politics of Federation', *Ethnic and Racial Studies* 19/2: 391–410.

Smith, Rogers (1997), *Civic Ideals: Conflicting Visions of Citizenship in American History* (Yale University Press, New Haven).

Solomon, Patrick (1994), 'Academic Disengagement: Black Youth and the Sports Subculture from a Cross-National Perspective', in Lorna Erwin and David MacLennan (eds.), *Sociology of Education in Canada* (Copp Clark Longman, Toronto), 188–99.

Spinner, Jeff (1994), *The Boundaries of Citizenship: Race, Ethnicity and Nationality in the Liberal State* (Johns Hopkins University Press, Baltimore).

Stanley, F. G. (1961), *The Birth of Western Canada: A History of the Riel Rebellions* (University of Toronto Press, Toronto).

Stark, Andrew (1992), 'English-Canadian Opposition to Quebec Nationalism', in R. Kent Weaver (ed.) *The Collapse of Canada?* (Brookings Institute, Washington, DC), 123–58.

Statham, Robert (1998), 'US Citizenship Policy in the Pacific Territory of Guam', *Citizenship Studies* 2/1: 89–104.

Strike, Kenneth (1994), 'On the Construction of Public Speech: Pluralism and Public Reason', *Educational Theory* 44/1: 1–26.

Svensson, Frances (1979), 'Liberal Democracy and Group Rights: The Legacy of Individualism and its Impact on American Indian Tribes', *Political Studies* 27/3: 421–39.

Swaney, James, and Paulette Olson (1992), 'The Economics of Diversity: Lives and Lifestyles', *Journal of Economic Issues* 26/2: 1–25.

Tamir, Yael (1993), *Liberal Nationalism* (Princeton University Press, Princeton).

Taylor, Charles (1991), 'Shared and Divergent Values', in Ronald Watts and D. Brown (eds.) *Options for a New Canada* (University of Toronto Press, Toronto), 53–76.

Taylor, Charles (1992*a*), 'The Politics of Recognition', in Amy Gutmann (ed.) *Multiculturalism and the 'Politics of Recognition'* (Princeton University Press, Princeton), 25–73.

——(1992*b*), 'Quel Principe d'Identité Collective', in Lenoble and Dewandre (1992: 59–66).

——(1997), 'Nationalism and Modernity', in McMahan and McKim (1997: 31–55).

Teague, Elizabeth (1994), 'Center-Periphery Relations in the Russian Federation', in Roman Szporluk (ed.), *National Identity and Ethnicity in Russia and the New States of Eurasia* (M. E. Sharpe, Armonk): 21–57.

Thomas-Woolley, Barbara, and Edmond Keller (1994), 'Majority Rule and Minority Rights: American Federalism and African Experience', *Journal of Modern African Studies* 32/3: 411–28.

Tilly, Charles (1975) 'Reflections on the History of European State-Making', in C. Tilly (ed.), *The Formation of National States in Western Europe* (Princeton University Press, Princeton), 3–83.

Todorov, Tzvetan (1993), *On Human Diversity: Nationalism, Racism and Exoticism in French Thought* (Harvard University Press, Cambridge, Mass.).

Tomasi, John (1995), 'Kymlicka, Liberalism, and Respect for Cultural Minorities', *Ethics*, 105/3: 580–603.

Toronto Board of Education (1988), *Education of Black Students in Toronto: Final Report of the Consultative Committee* (Board of Education, Toronto).

Tully, James (1995), *Strange Multiplicity: Constitutionalism in an Age of Diversity* (Cambridge University Press, Cambridge).

Turpel, M. E. (1989–90), 'Aboriginal Peoples and the Canadian Charter: Interpretive Monopolies, Cultural Differences', *Canadian Human Rights Yearbook* 6: 3–45.

——(1992), 'Does the Road to Quebec Sovereignty Run Through Aboriginal Territory?', in D. Drache and R. Perin (eds.), *Negotiating with a Sovereign Quebec* (Lorimer, Toronto), 93–106.

Valls, Andrew (1999), 'Reconsidering Black Nationalism' (paper presented at conference on 'Nationalism, Identity and Minority Rights', Bristol, September 1999).

Van Dyke, Vernon (1977), 'The Individual, the State, and Ethnic Communities in Political Theory', *World Politics* 29/3: 343–69.

——(1982), 'Collective Rights and Moral Rights: Problems in Liberal-Democratic Thought', *Journal of Politics* 44: 21–40.

——(1985), *Human Rights, Ethnicity and Discrimination* (Greenwood, Westport).

van Gunsteren, Herman (1978), 'Notes on a Theory of Citizenship', in Pierre Birnbaum, Jack Lively, and Geraint Parry (eds.), *Democracy, Consensus and Social Contract* (London, Sage), 9–35.

——(1998), *A Theory of Citizenship: Organizing Plurality in Contemporary Democracies* (Westview Press, Boulder, Colo.).

Varady, Tibor (1997), 'Majorities, Minorities, Law and Ethnicity: Reflections on the Yugoslav Case', *Human Rights Quarterly* 19: 9–54.

Verney, Douglas (1995), 'Federalism, Federative Systems and Federations: The United States, Canada, and India', *Publius: The Journal of Federalism* 25/2: 81–97.

Waldron, Jeremy (1992), 'Supeseding Historic Injustice', *Ethics* 103/1: 4–28.

——(1995), 'Minority Cultures and the Cosmopolitan Alternative', in Kymlicka (1995b: 93–121).

Waldron, Jeremy (1998), 'Whose Nuremberg Laws?', *London Review of Books* 20/6 (19 March 1998).

Walker, Graham (1997), 'The Idea of Non-Liberal Constitutionalism', in Shapiro and Kymlicka (1997: 154–84).

Wallace, Iain and David Knight (1996), 'Societies in Space and Time', in Hampson and Reppy (1996: 75–95).

Walzer, Michael (1983), *Spheres of Justice: A Defence of Pluralism and Equality* (Blackwell, Oxford).

——(1989), 'Citizenship', in T. Ball and J. Farr (eds.), *Political Innovation and Conceptual Change* (Cambridge University Press, Cambridge), 211–19.

——(1992a), 'The Civil Society Argument', in Mouffe (1992: 89–107).

——(1992b), *What it Means to be an American* (Marsilio, New York).

——(1992c), 'The New Tribalism', *Dissent* Spring 1992, 164–71.

——(1992d), 'Comment', in Amy Gutmann (ed.) *Multiculturalism and the 'Politics of Recognition'* (Princeton University Press, Princeton), 99–103.

——(1995), 'Pluralism in Political Perspective', in Kymlicka (1995b: 139–54).

——(1997), *On Toleration* (Yale University Press, New Haven).

Ward, Cynthia (1991), 'The Limits of "Liberal Republicanism": Why Group-Based Remedies and Republican Citizenship Don't Mix', *Columbia Law Review* 91/3: 581–607.

Webber, Jeremy (1994), *Reimagining Canada: Language, Culture Community and the Canadian Constitution* (McGill-Queen's University Press, Montreal).

Weber, E. (1976), *Peasants into Frenchmen: the modernization of rural France 1870–1914* (Chatto and Windus: London).

Weinstein, Brian (1983), *The Civic Tongue: Political Consequences of Language Choice* (Longman, New York).

Wheare, Kenneth (1962), 'Federalism and the Making of Nations', in Arthur MacMahon (ed.), *Federalism: Mature and Emergent* (Russell and Russell, New York), 28–43.

——(1964), *Federal Government*, 4th edn. (Oxford University Press, New York).

Wheatley, Steven (1997), 'Minority Rights and Political Accommodation in the "New" Europe', *European Law Review*, vol. 22 Supplement, pp. HRC63–HRC81.

White, Patricia (1992), 'Decency and Education for Citizenship', *Journal of Moral Education* 21/3: 207–16.

Williams, Dorothy (1989), *Blacks in Montreal 1628–1986: An Urban Demography* (Les Editions Yvon Blais, Cowansville).

Williams, Melissa (1998), *Voice, Trust and Memory: Marginalized Groups and the Failings of Liberal Representation* (Princeton University Press, Princeton).

Willigenburg, Theo van, Robert Heeger, and Wibren van den Burg (1995) (eds.), *Nation, State and the Coexistence of Different Communities* (Kok Pharos Publishing, Kampen).

Wilson, William Julius (1978), *The Declining Significance of Race* (University of Chicago Press, Chicago).

Young, Iris Marion (1990), *Justice and the Politics of Difference* (Princeton University Press, Princeton).

——(1993a), 'Justice and Communicative Democracy', in Roger Gottlieb (ed.), *Radical Philosophy: Tradition, Counter-Tradition, Politics* (Temple University Press, Philadelphia), 123–43.

——(1993b), 'Together in Difference: Transforming the Logic of Group Political Conflict', in Judith Squires (ed.), *Principled Positions: Postmodernism and the Rediscovery of Value* (Lawrence and Wishart, London), 121–50.

——(1996), 'Communication and the Other: Beyond Deliberative Democracy', in Seyla Benhabib (ed.), *Democracy and Difference: Contesting the Boundaries of the Political* (Princeton University Press, Princeton), 120–35.

——(1997), 'A Multicultural Continuum: A Critique of Will Kymlicka's Ethnic-Nation Dichotomy', *Constellations* 4/1: 48–53.

Index

Printed in the United Kingdom
by Lightning Source UK Ltd.
1032